CONTEMPORARY CATHOLIC APPROACHES TO THE PEOPLE, LAND, AND STATE OF ISRAEL

"The transformation in Catholic-Jewish relations in our times, was ushered in by Pope John XXII with the Second Vatican Ecumenical Council, despite the desire to address and even rehabilitate the Church's relationship with the Jewish People was resisted by many both on theological and political grounds.

According to the late Cardinal Loris Capovilla, who had served as the Pope's secretary, notwithstanding the opposition, it had been John XXIII's intention that after positively addressing the relationship between the Church and the Jewish People, diplomatic relations between the Vatican and the State of Israel would be established.

However, John XXIII did not even live to see the promulgation of the groundbreaking document Nostra Aetate, and apparently his successor Paul VI, was concerned with the adverse political and diplomatic consequences that might arise from taking such a step. The fact that the local church in the Land was Palestinian surely played a significant role in this regard.

Nevertheless, the intention in itself highlights John XXIII's understanding of the inextricable relationship between Jewry and the Land of Israel. This intention was only realized at the end of 1993 with the signing of the Fundamental Agreement between the Holy See and the State of Israel.

However, theological and political reservations regarding the latter continue within the Catholic Church as elsewhere, and inevitably impact upon Catholic-Jewish relations as a whole. This is well reflected in this impressive volume that spans a wide ideological spectrum. While these debates and differences may well persist, the ability to openly discuss them is also a sign of the transformation 'in our times' and surely offers the potential for much enrichment in the Catholic-Jewish conversation and relationship."

– **RABBI DAVID ROSEN,**
AJC Director, International Interreligious Affairs

"This book meets a powerful need. The Catholic Church now recognizes that God has not revoked his covenant or his promises with the Jewish people, and it is evident that these promises include the Land. At the same time, the Catholic Church holds that Jesus Christ has brought God's covenant and promises to fulfillment in himself. For more than one reason, then, it is long past time for Catholics to address theologically the current status of the Land and its relation to the State of Israel. With its wide range of perspectives, this book marks an extraordinary first step toward resolving the most important question for contemporary Jewish-Catholic dialogue. Highly recommended!"

– **MATTHEW LEVERING,** author of *Engaging the Doctrine of Israel: A Christian Israelology in Dialogue with Ongoing Judaism*

JUDAISM AND CATHOLIC THEOLOGY

SERIES EDITORS
Bruce D. Marshall, Southern Methodist University

Matthew Tapie, Saint Leo University

EDITORIAL BOARD
Alan Brill, Seton Hall University

Gavin D'Costa, University of Bristol

Jennifer Hart Weed, University of New Brunswick

David Novak, University of Toronto

CONTEMPORARY CATHOLIC APPROACHES TO THE PEOPLE, LAND, AND STATE OF ISRAEL

EDITED BY
Gavin D'Costa AND Faydra L. Shapiro

PREFACE BY
H. B. Pierbattista Pizzaballa, OFM
Latin Patriarch of Jerusalem

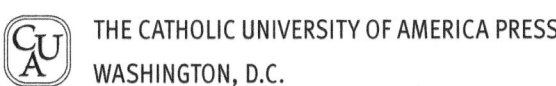

THE CATHOLIC UNIVERSITY OF AMERICA PRESS
WASHINGTON, D.C.

Copyright © 2022
The Catholic University of America Press

All rights reserved

Library of Congress Cataloging-in-Publication Data

NAMES
D'Costa, Gavin, 1958- editor. | Shapiro, Faydra, 1970- editor.
Pizzaballa, Pierbattista, 1965- writer of preface.

TITLE
Contemporary Catholic approaches to the people, land, and state of Israel
edited by Gavin D'Costa and Faydra L. Shapiro;
preface by H. B. Pierbattista Pizzaballa, OFM, Latin Patriarch of Jerusalem.

DESCRIPTION
Washington, D.C.: The Catholic University of America Press, 2022.
Series: Judaism and Catholic theology; 1
Includes bibliographical references and index.

IDENTIFIERS
LCCN 2021059477
ISBN 9780813234854 (paperback) | ISBN 9780813234861 (ebook)

SUBJECTS
LCSH: Palestine—In Christianity. | Israel (Christian theology)
Catholic Church—Relations--Judaism. | Judaism—Relations—Catholic Church.
Arab-Israeli conflict—Religious aspects—Christianity.

CLASSIFICATION
LCC BT93.8 .C66 2022 | DDC 956.9405—dc23/eng/20220105
LC record available at https://lccn.loc.gov/2021059477

Book design by Burt&Burt
Interior set with Meta Pro and Good Pro News Compressed

CONTENTS

Preface by H. B. Pierbattista Pizzaballa, OFM — ix

Introduction by Gavin D'Costa and Faydra L. Shapiro — xv

PART I: LISTENING AGAIN TO SCRIPTURE

1. The Return to the Land of Israel as an Eschatological Sign in the Light of Romans 11 — 3
   Lawrence Feingold

2. Land and Redemption: Why Does God Promise a Land? — 21
   Etienne Vetö, CCN

3. The Relationship of Israel to the Promised Land after Christ: Catholic Questionings — 42
   Jean-Miguel Garrigues, OP, and Eliana Kurylo, CB

4. The Resurrected Land of Israel — 58
   Isaac Vikram Chenchiah

PART II: MINING THE TRADITION

5. Land and State of Israel: Theological Reflections from a Roman Catholic Perspective — 81
   Christian M. Rutishauser, SJ

6. *Terra Viventium*: Biblical Promises, Fulfillment, and Thomas Aquinas's Christological Interpretation of the Land — 101
   Matthew A. Tapie

7. The Catholic Church and "Israel/Palestine": The Jewish People, the Land, Nation, and State — 122
   Gavin D'Costa

8. Does a Catholic Theology of Sacraments Help to Achieve an Affirmative Approach to the State of Israel? — 145
   Dirk Ansorge

PART III: SEEKING JUSTICE AND PEACE

9   A Catholic Perspective on the People,   169
Land, and State of Israel
David Mark Neuhaus, SJ

10   *Tractatio Theologico-Politica*: Palestinian Suffering   191
and the Official Catholic Teaching on the State of Israel
Antoine Lévy, OP

11   Christian Communities in Israel and Palestine   218
H. B. Michel Sabbah, Patriarch Emeritus

12   Christian-Jewish Relations from a Christian   234
Palestinian Perspective
Jamal Khader

PART IV: IN CONVERSATION: JEWISH RESPONSES

13   Jewish-Christian Relations and the Irrevocable   253
Problem of Political Theology
Karma Ben Johanan

14   Jews, Catholics, and Israel: 272
Can We Find a Shared Language?
Faydra L. Shapiro

Selected Bibliography   293
Contributor Biographies   297
Index   305

PREFACE

H. B. Pierbattista Pizzaballa, OFM
Patriarch, Latin Patriarchate of Jerusalem

Without doubt, the question of "the Land" is the main source of misunderstanding between Israelis and Palestinians. Experience shows that in many interfaith discussions, in those spaces that are consciously and carefully open to dialogue, this subject is simply felt to be too divisive. Palestinians and Israelis of course discuss this issue at great length among themselves. But in public meetings where Israelis and Palestinians are present, this topic is generally avoided in any direct way. "The Land" is an issue that gets talked around, rather than one that is intentionally engaged, head-on.

This volume, therefore, is a courageous one, because it openly raises this delicate and painful topic, a topic that is a source of deep tension and misunderstanding. But it is also a topic that is something very present and real, one that deeply impacts the daily lives of Israelis and Palestinians.

The authors who contribute to this volume are all aware of the wide spectrum of opinions and experiences in this area. They are also aware that these differences of opinion will probably remain.

But here is precisely why this volume, which tackles such a complex issue while grounded in a desire to engage each other respectfully and honestly, is so important. I can only congratulate the contributors. This is not an effort we can take for granted. I pray that over time we can create more examples of groups able to contribute to this difficult debate, while still belonging to different histories and perspectives. I hope for more groups like this, where, despite different ideas, there is still a common desire for mutual listening and recognition of each other's histories and hopes. That this volume is made up of contributions that both assert a position and at the same time recognize and invite the other's right to expression, is already significant.

There is often much confusion concerning this subject. In my view, it is first and foremost a political issue, linked to the two peoples who contend for the same land. But it is also a political issue with religious overtones, and as such one that is perceived to divide Jews, Muslims, and Christians. I am myself not convinced that this is the case. The position of a Palestinian Christian is not significantly different from that of a Palestinian Muslim. A Catholic of Jewish origin does not necessarily share the views of a Palestinian Catholic. This very volume also helps us to see that this is not necessarily a religious conflict, presenting as it does a range of views on this issue from scholars and theologians who are all Catholic.

Yet religion cannot be ignored. Obviously, from a scriptural and theological angle, there is much to say about this issue of "the Land." But at the same time, we ought not forget that theology must ultimately speak to the people and connect to their concrete needs and life experiences. Abstract academic theories and theologies are interesting, but they are not sufficient.

My job here is not to enter into the heart of this conversation. Rather, as a representative of the local Church, I limit myself to addressing readers and contributors, and to sharing in their desire for a peaceful and authentic encounter. This is also the desire of the Church: to be able to speak to everyone, with truth, regarding justice, rights, faith, and the role of religion in this conflict that often feels so painful and endless.

I am not myself an expert on this subject. And although I have been living here for thirty years, I am very aware that as an Italian I cannot presume to teach Israelis or Palestinians what it means to live with one another. Having said this, I can, however, present some of the needs and expectations that I have encountered and come to know directly from our local communities, pilgrims, and Catholic institutions, concerning the Land and State of Israel and Jewish-Christian relations.

First, between our two faiths, Catholicism and Judaism, there is a substantial difference in approach, from the religious point of view, to the issue of this land, the Holy Land. For us Catholics the revelation of the Old Testament and the New Testament is to be read through a theological, spiritual, and ethical lens. While biblical texts surely have even a political significance, they are not directly political. The biblical texts are the basis for defining criteria according to which concrete political choices must be made. They indicate the fundamental values of the civil, social, and religious life of a community that seeks to be inspired and guided by these texts.

In short, biblical texts are the basic reference point, without presenting concrete political directives. It is therefore necessary to undertake the effort of interpreting these texts, written out of historical and social contexts quite different from our own. The interpretation of the biblical texts is a discipline in itself, which must take into account the official teaching of the Church, which in its turn has a process of its own.

Hence we Catholics do not link the Bible to a political reading, or to a directive in a specific context. To claim, for example, that the Biblical texts require a blanket prohibition on blood transfusions strikes Catholics as absurd. To say simply that God has given the land to the Jewish people, and that it is therefore theirs because it is written in the Pentateuch, is an assertion at odds with a Catholic approach.

This is not to suggest that the Catholic Church is unconcerned with the temporal realm. The Church has had her own historical journey with political power, mobilizing scriptural interpretations that we can find uncomfortable in today's light. But this is not the place to analyze that past.

It is a fact today, established, definitive, and irreversible, that for the Catholic Church there is a clear distinction between the civil and political sphere and the religious sphere. The two spheres dialogue with each other, but they are clearly separate. We will no longer see cardinals as prime ministers, or Catholic nations, with all due respect to some nostalgic or nationalist parties that may hope otherwise.

We have noted that for the Catholic Church it is necessary to put a filter between the Holy Scriptures and life. The Bible must be interpreted and then accepted by the ecclesial community. We have also noted the importance of setting boundaries between religion and politics. Our history has taught us that it is vital to define very clearly the boundaries between politics and religion. So long as these borders remain fuzzy, the risk of manipulation is enormous.

This touches on one of the topics of Jewish-Catholic dialogue, about which there has never been much discussion, but which is nonetheless fundamental.

For a Jew, the relationship with the Land of Israel is a core component. It is not enough to have Jewish faith; it is not enough to belong to the Jewish people. The Jew has always prayed with an eye toward Jerusalem, and, as such, Jewishness comprises a political dimension.

As a believing Catholic, I think this is understandable. It is not a problem for me that a Jew has a spiritual, theological, and religious connection with this land. I, too, as a Christian, have a spiritual, theological, and religious bond with this land. That is why I am myself living here.

And I can appreciate that after two thousand years of exile, actually reaching the land to which one has always aspired is a tremendous change in the consciousness of a Jew. I can also understand that for Jews, there is enormous religious value in returning to the Land of Israel after two thousand years.

However, the religious bond with the political State of Israel is more challenging for Catholics to understand. Our commitment to a distinction between the religious and the political sphere makes it impossible to follow our Jewish friends in this direction. We do not question the Jewish religious and emotional connection with the Land of Israel. Nor are we discussing the political existence of the State of Israel. But asserting a direct link between the Jewish faith and the political life of a state, with its choices, policies, and institutions, becomes difficult to comprehend.

When Catholic pilgrims who visit the Holy Land are told that the State of Israel is a state that is both Jewish and democratic, they are confused. If it is a Jewish state, how can it be democratic? The question is not simply polemical but reflects an objective difficulty in understanding when our approaches are so profoundly different. We Catholics will need much more empathetic dialogue to help us to understand—without necessarily agreeing with—the Jewish approach here. And we need Jewish partners who understand enough about our commitments as Catholics to help us with this.

For the Catholic Church, dialogue with Judaism is constitutive of her own identity. She cannot be the Church if she is not in dialogue. And the dialogue with the people of the first Covenant, out of which Jesus and the early Church were born, is the first and the most important of these dialogues. But the Church intends to dialogue with Judaism on the religious level only, which can also be translated into common social and even religious initiatives. This approach to the political realm does not, I think, satisfy the concerns of most Jews.

The Palestinian-Israeli question and the issue of the land is, for the Catholic Church, an entirely political issue and not a religious one. Justifying land annexations in the name of a faith or biblical interpretation is incomprehensible to us. We can understand the political choice of the State of Israel, although we do not share it, but we do not understand the religious justification of that choice.

Perhaps we Catholics ought to simply strive to accept the Jewish people for what they are and as they are, with their own beliefs, traditions, and aspirations. Without projecting on them our idea of Judaism, but rather accepting theirs, including their approach to the issue of the Land, as constitutive part of their faith, even if we do not understand and agree. And I wonder if, on the Jewish side, there might be the same possibility of understanding, in disagreement with, our Catholic perspective.

Inextricably linked to the issue of the land is the matter of the peoples who inhabit it. Thus the second fundamental question we must consider, then, is how it is possible to respect a religious connection to the land, without considering the basic human rights of people who live on that same land. To annex land, in the name of a biblical-religious viewpoint, is not just a theoretical or abstract move. To do so means to deny a right to other peoples who live on that same land, to appropriate their living space.

There is a hierarchy of values, and as such not all values are equal and on the same level. What is the hierarchy of values in this case? Does the bond to the land prevail over the rights of a person who lives on that same land? If the State of Israel possesses some measure of messianic value, does its political decisions in the territories therefore have a religious value? I am not myself able to give an answer to these questions, nor is it my task to do so. But these questions are foundational ones for this conversation, and ones that inform many of the discussions to come.

At the same time, I understand that basic concepts such as *revelation, covenant, promises*, and *Jerusalem* can signify different things to our respective faith communities. These terms not only possess spiritual and theological significance, but also speak of an identity and the history of a concrete people. Maybe we Catholics could learn that the Bible speaks not only to our souls but also to our bodies, and with that accept that it is not correct to spiritualize everything in the Bible. And perhaps we should also accept the idea that there are issues on which we will continue to differ.

But I hope that, despite this, despite all our difference, we can continue to love and respect each other, Jews and Catholics, and keep discussing as friends with strong bonds this matter that is dear to both our lives and hearts, the Land of revelation, the Holy Land. And may this volume help to serve this purpose.

Introduction

ROMAN CATHOLIC THEOLOGY AND THE JEWISH PEOPLE IN THE LAND CALLED ISRAEL
WHY DOES THIS QUESTION ARISE FOR CATHOLIC THEOLOGIANS NOW?

Gavin D'Costa and Faydra L. Shapiro

For nearly two thousand years Roman Catholicism, along with most other Christian denominations, has had a consistently negative theology regarding the Jewish people. The plot line of this negative theology, called *adversus Judaeos* ("against the Jews"), was loosely this. The Jewish people had rejected the Jewish messiah, Jesus. They put him to death and cursed themselves for this sin. In Matthew 27:25 they say at the crucifixion: "Let his blood be upon us and on our children." The first sin was rejection of the messiah that their own Jewish scripture had foretold. The second sin was that of deicide, killing God, and the acceptance of its repercussions. They became a cursed people. The list of *adversus Judaeos* tropes expanded through different Christian periods and cultures. The Jewish people were cursed and doomed to wander the earth giving witness to the existence of the scripture—that pointed to the truth of Jesus Christ. They were dispelled from their land and the Temple destroyed as a punishment for their sins. Jesus Christ became the new Temple and Christians the new Israel. Judaism had no theological legitimacy.

There arose two traditions, admittedly difficult to disentangle: one was antisemitism, which can be understood as negative social and political treatment of Jews in society; the other was anti-Judaism, which can be understood as negative theological treatment of Jews in Christian theology. In principle, one might hold the latter and criticize the former. In practice, these traditions often fueled each other in complex ways. Both traditions took on new turns as they migrated from country to country. In England, for example, there arose an accusation that young children had been abducted to be used in macabre rituals that required the pure blood of a Christian child. William of Norwich and Little Saint Hugh of Lincoln were two such alleged victims. Walter Lacquer writes of this blood libel tradition: "Altogether, there have been about 150 recorded cases of blood libel (not to mention thousands of rumours) that resulted in the arrest and killing of Jews throughout history, most of them in the Middle Ages. In almost every case, Jews were murdered, sometimes by a mob, sometimes following torture and a trial."[1]

The dire elements of antisemitism within Christianity are well documented and should be mandatory reading for all Christians who are honest about their religion and its social and political outworkings.[2] But if there is some truth in the fueling of antisemitism through theological anti-Judaism, that question became particularly acute after the murder of some two thirds of world Jewry at the heart of Christian Europe in the *Shoah*, or Holocaust. While there is a considerable debate as to Christian theology's role in the causality of the Holocaust, and how much neo-paganism was the prime mover, there can be no question that many of these Christian traditions prepared and fed the soil of Nazi antisemitism.

It was only after the events of the *Shoah*/Holocaust that Christian churches in the West, rather than *ad hoc* individuals within them, began to reflect on this matter in a self-critical manner. Pope John XXIII, who granted an audience with the Jewish historian Jules Isaac,[3] was instrumental in moving the Catholic Church to address this issue formally. The Second Vatican Council (1963–65) taught that the deicide charge (that "Jews," at the time of Christ and all Jews subsequently, are and remain guilty for killing Jesus Christ) was

---

[1] Walter Laqueur, *The Changing Face of Antisemitism: From Ancient Times to the Present Day* (New York: Oxford University Press, 2006), 56.

[2] See, for example, Edward H. Flannery, *The Anguish of the Jews: Twenty-Three Centuries of Antisemitism*, Rev. (New York: Paulist Press, 1985); Jeremy Cohen, *The Friars and the Jews: The Evolution of Medieval Anti-Judaism*, 2nd ed. (London: Cornell University Press, 1984).

[3] Norman C. Tobias, *Jewish Conscience of the Church: Jules Isaac and the Second Vatican Council* (New York: Palgrave Macmillan, 2017).

not in keeping with the gospel.⁴ Isaac had argued that this one teaching was the generator of Christian antisemitism and anti-Judaism, and its removal would not clash with any doctrinal teaching of the Roman Catholic Church. Its removal, however, would allow for the churches to change their trajectory in terms of antisemitism. Isaac was aware that this had been achieved verbally in the Tridentine Catechism.⁵ It clearly needed restating and with authority behind it. The Council would provide that authority.

At the Second Vatican Council, two documents contained the "new" Catholic attitude: *Lumen Gentium*, 16 (The Dogmatic Constitution on the Church, 1964) and *Nostra Aetate*, 4 (The Declaration of the Church's Relation to Non-Christian Religions, 1965). The latter was central to deconstructing the "deicide" tradition (although never mentioning it by that name).⁶ Both documents contained references to Saint Paul's letter to the Romans 11:29 to underwrite the significance of the Jewish people to Christian identity. The verse read that "the gifts and the calling of God [to Israel] are irrevocable." Many scholars debated whether this verse also meant that post-biblical Judaism, what we might call "Rabbinic Judaism," was intended as part of the Pauline reference and thus was affirmed by the Council. Some argued that living Judaism was still a museum piece in Catholic theology. Only biblical Judaism had been affirmed. Others protested that the manner of the quotation signified living Judaism was the referent. In 2015, after fifty years, the matter was clarified by Rome when it made clear that the application of this verse to post-biblical Judaism (Rabbinic Judaism) only took place in 1980 by Pope Saint John Paul II in Mainz, Germany.⁷ Thus, 1980 marks the

---

4 See Gavin D'Costa, *Vatican II: Catholic Doctrines on Jews and Muslims* (Oxford: Oxford University Press, 2014), 113–60.

5 It argued that Christian sins "seem graver in our case than [they were] in that of the Jews; for the Jews, as the same Apostle says, 'would never have crucified the Lord of glory if they had known him' (1 Cor 2:8). We ourselves maintain that we do know him, and yet we lay, as it were, violent hands on him by disowning him in our actions." *The Tridentine Catechism of the Holy Catholic Church*, ed. John A. McHugh, OP, and Charles J. Callan, OP (1923), http://www.angelfire.com/art/cactussong/TridentineCatechism.htm.

6 See Augustin Bea, *The Church and the Jewish People: A Commentary on the Second Vatican Council's Declaration on the Relation of the Church to Non-Christian Religions*, ed. Philip Loretz (London: Geoffrey Chapman, 1966). Bea oversaw the document's passage within the Council. See also John M. Oesterreicher, "Declaration on the Relationship of the Church to Non-Christian Religions," in *Commentary on the Documents of Vatican II*, vol. 3, *Declaration on the Relationship of the Church to the Non-Christian Religions: Dogmatic Constitution on Divine Revelation: Decree on the Apostolate of the Laity*, ed. Herbert Vorgrimler (London: Burns and Oates, 1969), 1–136. Oesterreicher was involved in the drafting group.

7 Commission for Religious Relations with the Jews, *"The Gifts and the Calling of God Are Irrevocable" (Rom 11:29): A Reflection on Theological Questions Pertaining to Catholic-Jewish Relations on the Occasion of the Fiftieth Anniversary of "Nostra Aetate"* (2015), 39.

beginning of a new wave of Catholic theology that attended to this overturning of the *adversus Judaeos* tradition. If Rabbinic Judaism was in an irrevocable covenant with the true and living God, what did that mean about the Jewish religion and people? Writing about this 2015 document, Pope Emeritus Benedict XVI rightly said in 2018, there was no question about the validity of the Jewish religion, but what this meant in detail about a whole range of questions was unresolved in Catholic theology: "Both of these theses—that Israel is not replaced [*substituiert*] by the Church, and that the covenant was never revoked—are basically correct, but are in many ways imprecise and need to be given further critical consideration."[8] The range of questions that Benedict treats are just some of the most important, but they are not comprehensive. They include the status and meaning of the Temple cult, Jewish rituals, law and morality, the messiah, the promise of the land and the formal status of the *adversus Judaeos* tradition.[9] That Benedict included the promise of the land in his essay, regardless of his own conclusions on this matter, indicates this is definitely a part of the theological agenda of modern Roman Catholicism in its engagement with the Jewish people.

There are two sets of interlinking questions. First, what do Roman Catholics think about the land promise made to the Jewish people in terms of the Old Testament (where there can be no doubt that this is central to the Jewish covenant) and the New Testament? Does reading the Old Testament through the Christological lens of the New Testament permit the validity of the Old Testament claims regarding the Jewish people? What significance does the New Testament itself attribute to Jerusalem and the land for Christians? Furthermore, as Catholic theologians, we must also attend to the voices of the tradition and the magisterium on this matter. The second question relates these theological questions to the modern context of the Middle East. What do Roman Catholics think about the land promise in terms of the establishment of Israel in 1947/1948 and the *Nakba*, which happened concurrently, and which is the tragedy of displacement of hundreds of thousands of Palestinians that took place during this same period because of the declaration of a homeland for the Jews? Can the first event, the establishment of a

---

[8] Pope Benedict XVI, "Grace and Vocation without Remorse: Comments on the Treatise 'De Iudaeis,'" trans. Nicholas J. Healy, *Communio* 45 (Spring 2018): 163–84.

[9] See the excellent discussion of this document by Philip A. Cunningham and Adam Gregerman, "'Genuine Brotherhood' without Remorse: A Commentary on Joseph Ratzinger's 'Comments on "De Iudaeis,"'" *Studies in Christian-Jewish Relations* 14, no. 1 (2019). It is somewhat misleading about the operation of the ordinary magisterium (11) and thus the status of the *adversus Judaeo* tradition. It is not part of the ordinary magisterium.

Jewish nation which has drawn Jews from all the corners of the earth, relate to the biblical promises? Can the biblical promises entail such catastrophe for the Palestinian people, some of whom are Christians? Their voice in this debate is vital to ensure a balanced approach within the Catholic Church. Many European and American voices are often shaped by the history (and guilt) of the *Shoah*/Holocaust, which is emotionally a history that is not always embedded within Middle Eastern Christians. This volume is particularly powerful in bringing into conversation these often bitterly conflicting currents.

There are of course two other religious claims that are always co-present in this discussion, but not in the foreground of this volume. What of Jewish claims regarding the status of the land, and what of Muslim claims regarding the status of the land? These two vital voices are required for a full examination of the question from a Catholic viewpoint, but in planning the conference from which these essays are taken, we were acutely aware that such a complex interreligious conversation was premature. Catholics had hardly begun to discuss this issue between themselves.

In June 2019, the two editors of this volume, an Orthodox Jewish woman and a Roman Catholic layman, with the generous funding of the Philos Project and the involvement and hospitality of the Latin Patriarchate of Jerusalem, along with a lot of help from many friends, gathered together a range of Catholic scholars to address this difficult question about the theological status of the land—in the city of Jerusalem at Notre Dame Conference Center. The Catholic theologians came from Europe, the United States, and Israel/Palestine/Occupied Territories, and they included clergy and laity. It was a risky adventure. It involved building a platform of trust so that all parties could speak honestly and engage with each other. It was a humbling success, mainly due to the good faith of Catholics sharing a common starting point—a love of Christ, the Church, and each other—and recognizing this question to be so central to Catholic identity as well as to the future of conversations with Jews—and also of course, Muslims. This volume collects some of those essays (and one additional one) to present the findings of this meeting to a broader public. It is a landmark conference, and many participants and guests exclaimed that this kind of conversation seemed impossible before now—and that it needed to continue.

At the actual event, we ensured that there would be several Jewish Israeli and non-Catholic Christian Palestinian friends and formal responders to presentations. Their presence and interventions were a blessing in every way possible. It meant that a Catholic conversation about the land called Israel could take place with those who had deep vested interests in that land and its painful and tragic conflicts. It meant that many contributors revised their papers in the light of this diverse witness and questioning. Theology is profoundly political regardless of its own intentions, because embodied communities occupy space and time, land and homelessness, power and dispossession, and—in this instance—a willingness to speak and to listen to each other over such divides.

Having constructed the conference to attend to this disputed question at the heart of Catholic theology, we were deeply aware of the Jewish interlocutors that were generous enough to help Catholics think through these matters. For this reason we decided there should be two essays reflecting on the collection by Jewish thinkers. We were privileged with the presence of two such friends throughout the conference—one a co-organizer and co-editor of this volume—and they generously stepped into the fray, where angels might fear to tread. They delicately and incisively ask difficult questions to their Catholic friends while also opening up a vista to hear Jewish voices in the midst of this debate.

For the reader to get an overview of the rich diversity, we offer here a very brief and selective summary of each chapter.

Our papers begin, most fittingly, with attentive listening to God's word. Larry Feingold presents a theological reflection on scripture in "The Return to the Land of Israel as an Eschatological Sign in the Light of Romans 11," beginning with an assessment of how we might engage in typological readings without supersessionism. Rather than engaging the language of rights, Feingold argues that the return of a Jewish nation-state in the Land of Israel is replete with eschatological meaning, which he distinguishes from Protestant millenarianism. Feingold argues that this eschatological meaning should be read alongside the growth of various movements of Jewish-Christians, with the Jewish State offering the possibility of a space for a new kind of Jewish encounter with Jesus.

The overall question of the meaning and contours of the land promise is addressed by Vetö in "Land and Redemption: Why Does God Promise a Land?" Vetö recognizes that the land promise is an essential prism for rightly understanding both relationship with God and salvation. In asserting that God seeks a purified relationship to land, one based on sharing, Vetö sees a gift and a challenge for both the Jewish people and the nations of the world, allowing us to see both the ingathering of the Jewish people and the Palestinian presence in the land as providential.

Garrigues and Kurylo begin their contribution on "The Relationship of Israel to the Promised Land after Christ: Catholic Questionings" with an examination of the New Testament's apparent silence on the topic of the land promise. They ask if this situation implies that Catholics ought to perceive no religious significance in the Jewish return to the Land. With an investigation of the theme of the Land of Israel and eschatological hopes in a non-fundamentalist key, through the Church Fathers and into the nineteenth and twentieth centuries, the authors illustrate the theme of God's promise and its realization.

In "The Resurrected Land of Israel," Isaac Chenchiah uses Genesis to develop an analogy between land and body to show the intimate relationship between the nation of Israel and the Land of Israel. Out of this he argues that nations relate to one other through their land just as humans relate to each other through their bodies. Chenchiah re-reads the Exodus story together with a rabbi to show how Israel and Egypt become estranged from one another, and then proceeds to consider how a Christian belief in Christ as locus of reconciliation can shed light on the Land of Israel as locus of reconciliation between Israel and the Nations.

The volume then turns to contributions that examine the second essential authority Catholics locate in the deposit of faith: tradition.

In his contribution, "Land and State of Israel—Theological Reflections from a Roman Catholic Perspective" Christian Rutishauser asserts that the importance of the Land is not the Land itself, *per se*, but its role as the locus for God's "alternative" project of building a truly just society. Thus, making sense of both the Land and State of Israel requires attention to the nature and role of the Jewish people, both as an earthly reality and as a mystical entity. He argues that it is in the State of Israel that Judaism can live its vocation.

Matthew Tapie takes up exploring a different corner of Catholic tradition in "*Terra Viventium*: Biblical Promises, Fulfillment, and Thomas Aquinas's Christological Interpretation of the Land." Tapie notes certain weaknesses in the approach to land promise fulfillment in the Pontifical Biblical Commission's 2002 document, *The Jewish People and Their Sacred Scriptures in the Christian Bible* (JPSSCB). After examining Aquinas's Christological interpretation of the land promise in several key New Testament texts, Tapie suggests that some elements of this method could offer a hermeneutic that encourages a Christological reading of scripture within tradition, together with attention to post–*Nostra Aetate* teaching on the Jews and Judaism.

In his chapter, "The Catholic Church and 'Israel/Palestine': The Jewish People, the Land, Nation, and State," Gavin D'Costa recognizes that the Palestinian right to statehood is clearly embedded in diplomatic agreements of the Holy See. At the same time D'Costa shows that Catholic teaching increasingly ascribes a theological value to Jews living in the Land of Israel. With attention to the great delicacy involved in the question, D'Costa seeks to trace a way through Catholic documents that might allow for a "minimalist" theological affirmation of the State of Israel.

Dirk Ansorge takes up a unique question in "Does a Catholic Theology of Sacraments Help to Achieve an Affirmative Approach to the State of Israel?" Because in Catholic theology the sacraments serve to mediate God's intervention in the physical historical world, Ansorge seeks to explore the concept of sacramentality to yield helpful ways to understand the Jewish State. Based especially on the work of Austrian theologian Franz Schupp and the French theologian Louis-Marie Chauvet, Ansorge outlines some of the possibilities and limits in this approach.

Recognizing that issues of Catholic social teaching and the values of justice and peace are also central to this conversation, the collection then seeks to listen attentively to voices from this perspective.

In "A Catholic Perspective on the People, Land, and State of Israel," David Neuhaus offers a reflection arising from his own situatedness as a Catholic priest who is also a Jew and an Israeli. He notes the positive development that the Catholic Church now recognizes both the Jewish people and its connection to the Land of Israel, but he argues against the idea of Israel as a Jewish State. Neuhaus insists there cannot be Church support for a state that privileges the rights of any one group above those of others and that a truly Catholic approach is one that seeks justice for all those who live in the Holy Land, Jews and Palestinians.

Antoine Lévy takes up the question of the Church's theological disengagement from the issue of Israel in his piece, "*Tractatio Theologico-Politica*: Palestinian Suffering and the Official Catholic Teaching on the State of Israel." He considers and challenges several reasons that might explain the Church's tendency to avoid thinking about the State of Israel in religious terms. In contrast, Lévy maintains that the revolution in Catholic thinking about the Jewish people and God's ongoing faithfulness demands an engagement with the theological meaning of the Jewish people's return to the Land. He presents this historical development as a sign of God's ongoing providence to the Jewish people.

Patriarch Emeritus H. B. Michel Sabbah presents some essential context in his contribution, "Christian Communities in Israel and Palestine." Sabbah considers the lived experience of Palestinian Christians, particularly against the background of the Palestinian-Israeli conflict. Sabbah reminds us that in addition to the religious relationship between Jewish and Christian communities here, there is an additional lived relationship between two peoples at war. He argues that God can never be used to justify human acts of violence or to support one side in this conflict.

In "Christian-Jewish Relations from a Christian Palestinian Perspective," Jamal Khader invites readers into his Palestinian context to explore the effects of Western biblical readings and theologies on local Christians.

Vociferously rejecting religious arguments in favor of Zionism, he asserts that such claims "make the sufferings of the Palestinian people either irrelevant to God's plan or part of it." Instead, Khader explores a Palestinian theology of land, based on universalism, justice, and divine ownership, and offers a Christological reading of the Old Testament so that the Bible is not used to justify Palestinian suffering.

These contrasting perspectives are followed by two challenging responses from Jewish friends who are involved in the Jewish-Catholic conversation and were present throughout the conference, one from Karma Ben Johanan and a second by Faydra Shapiro.

We are profoundly grateful to the respondents at our Jerusalem conference at the Notre Dame Center: Hana Bendcowsky, Rev. Munther Isaac, Marci Lenk, Shadia Qubti, Rabbi David Rosen, and Khalil Sayegh. Their participation helped all our contributors to develop their thoughts in the face of the real people who live their daily lives in this midst of this conflict. The editors wish to extend special thanks to Anna Babcox, who assisted with the editing of the collection and was an invaluable assistant at the actual conference.

CONTEMPORARY CATHOLIC APPROACHES
TO THE PEOPLE, LAND, AND STATE OF ISRAEL

Part I

LISTENING AGAIN TO SCRIPTURE

1

THE RETURN TO THE LAND OF ISRAEL AS AN ESCHATOLOGICAL SIGN IN THE LIGHT OF ROMANS 11

Lawrence Feingold

The intention of this essay is *not* to give political guidelines or evaluations of current events in the Middle East, for which I have no expertise. On the contrary, my goal is to engage in a theological reflection upon current history in the light of Revelation, salvation history, and typology. This involves looking at current events as "signs of the times." In this case I will view these signs of the times as bearing significance beyond their own actuality, precisely as signs of future realities pointing to the fulfillment of history.

A NON-SUPERSESSIONIST TYPOLOGICAL UNDERSTANDING OF THE RELATION BETWEEN ISRAEL AND THE CHURCH

The theological significance of the Land of Israel and the Jewish presence there must be considered anew on the basis of the teaching of the Second Vatican Council on the continued election of the Jewish people. Many Catholics fail to see the theological significance of the Land of Israel and its relation to the Jewish people because of lingering supersessionist ideas, and/or because of the lack of a proper typological understanding of salvation history.[1] In order to read the return of the Jewish people to the Land of Israel correctly as a sign of the times, we need certain premises. A crucial premise

---

[1] Many evangelical Protestants, on the other hand, read the existence of the State of Israel as an eschatological sign, as I am advocating, but within the flawed perspective of millenarian views tied to dispensationalist interpretations.

is the fact, now taught by the Church in harmony with Romans 11:29, that the election and covenant of the Chosen People has not been revoked. If the Chosen People is still chosen, then their corporate return to the Holy Land, even if only incomplete and beset with human weakness, cannot be seen merely as an historical accident.

The right hermeneutic to understand Israel as an eschatological sign presupposes a view of the relation between Israel and the Church that involves typological fulfillment[2] without being supersessionist.[3] Supersessionism in its hard form[4] implies that the New Covenant has replaced the Old Covenant in such a way that the people of the Old Covenant no longer have any status as elect People of God with the corresponding obligations and promises of the covenant.[5] As such the promises given to Israel in the Old Covenant simply pass on to the Church as the new People of God.

Such a view is incompatible with the biblical principle of God's fidelity, which transcends and is not annulled by human infidelity.[6] It is also incompatible with Romans 11:28–29, which says of the Jewish people that

---

[2] See *Catechism of the Catholic Church*, 2nd ed. (Vatican City: Vatican Press, 1997), 117.

[3] There are three principal positions with regard to the relationship between Israel and the Church. The two extremes are hard supersessionism, on the one hand, and dual covenant theory (seeing each covenant as sufficient in itself), both of which should be rejected. The intermediate position can be referred to by the name of "fulfillment." It holds that Israel is fulfilled in Christ and the Church, but without holding that the Old Covenant was revoked by God or that Israel lost its status as elect People of God. For an outline of these three positions, see Gavin D'Costa, "The Mystery of Israel: Jews, Hebrew Catholics, Messianic Judaism, the Catholic Church, and the Mosaic Ceremonial Laws," *Nova et Vetera* 16, no. 3 (Summer 2018): 939–77, esp. 940–41.

[4] For this terminology and an explanation of this position, see Douglas Farrow, "Jew and Gentile in the Church Today," *Nova et Vetera* 16, no. 3 (Summer 2018), 979–93, at 985: "We may call 'hard' supersessionism the view that the Mosaic covenant has been abrogated in such a fashion that its beneficiaries, the Jews, are today without a covenant and are no longer God's people." Farrow speaks of "softer" forms of supersessionism that would not hold that the Mosaic covenant has been revoked. In this paper I refer to "supersessionism" only in its hard form, which seems incompatible with the recent Magisterium of the Church.

[5] Theologians have disagreed about when this occurred. St. Jerome saw the completion of the paschal mystery as marking this replacement. St. Augustine famously disagreed with him, putting the time at the promulgation of the Gospel which he thought coincided with the end of the apostolic age and the destruction of Jerusalem in AD 70. See Augustine, "Letter 82 to St. Jerome of AD 405," *Saint Augustine: Letters*, vol. 1 (1–82), trans. Wilfrid Parson (Washington, DC: The Catholic University of America Press, 1951), 390–420. From the same see also Jerome, "Letter 75 to St. Augustine of AD 404," *Saint Augustine: Letters*, vol. 1 (1–82), 342–67. St. Thomas Aquinas, in his treatise on the Old Law, *Summa Theologiae* I.II 103.4 ad 1, takes the position of St. Augustine in this controversy.

[6] See 2 Tm 2:13: "If we are faithless, he remains faithful—for he cannot deny himself"; Rom 3:3: "What if some were unfaithful? Does their faithlessness nullify the faithfulness of God?" See also Aquinas, *Commentary on the Letter of Saint Paul to the Romans*, lectio 1, no. 253–55, ed. Fabian Larcher (Lander, WY: Aquinas Institute for the Study of Sacred Doctrine, 2012), 87–88: "For if

"as regards election they are beloved for the sake of their forefathers. For the gifts and the call of God are irrevocable." This text was cited by the Second Vatican Council in *Nostra Aetate* 4: "Nevertheless, God holds the Jews most dear for the sake of their Fathers; He does not repent of the gifts He makes or of the calls He issues—such is the witness of the Apostle."[7]

This teaching of *Nostra Aetate* was made clearer by St. John Paul II in a discourse to representatives of the Jewish people in Mainz on November 17, 1980, in which the pope explicitly stated that the covenant of God with Israel had never been revoked:

> The first dimension of this dialogue, that is, the meeting between the people of God of the Old Covenant, *never revoked by God* [cf. Rom 11:29], and that of the New Covenant, is at the same time a dialogue within our Church, that is to say, between the first and the second part of her Bible.[8]

In the following paragraph John Paul II refers to the Jewish people as "present-day people of the Covenant concluded with Moses."[9] The *Catechism of the Catholic Church* 121 repeats the teaching that "the Old Covenant has

---

the Jews' prerogative were taken away on account of the unbelief of some, it would follow that man's unbelief would nullify God's faithfulness—which is an unacceptable conclusion. . . . This faithfulness would be nullified, if it happened that the Jews had no advantage, just because some have not believed. For God promised to multiply that people and make it great. . . . The reason is based on the fact that God in Himself is true."

[7] Romans 11:29 is also cited in the conclusion of the *Catechism of the Catholic Church* 839 on "The Relationship of the Church with the Jewish People."

[8] John Paul II, *Speech to the Representatives of the Jewish People in Mainz*, November 17, 1980. See the Commission for Religious Relations with the Jews, *Notes on the Correct Way to Present the Jews and Judaism in Preaching and Catechesis in the Roman Catholic Church* (June 24, 1985), 1.4: "The Holy Father has stated this permanent reality of the Jewish people in a remarkable theological formula, in his allocution to the Jewish community of West Germany at Mainz, on November 17th, 1980: 'the people of God of the Old Covenant, which has never been revoked.'" On the development this statement marks with respect to *Nostra Aetate*, see the Commission for Religious Relations with the Jews, "*The Gifts and the Calling of God Are Irrevocable*" (*Rom 11:29): A Reflection on Theological Questions Pertaining to Catholic-Jewish Relations on the Occasion of the 50th Anniversary of "Nostra Aetate"* (2015), 39.

[9] John Paul II repeated this teaching in his *Address to Representatives of the Jewish Organizations of the United States*, September 11, 1987; and in his *Address to Representatives of the Brazilian Jewish Community*, October 15, 1991: "This shared root also leads us to love this people, because, as the Bible says, 'the Lord loved Israel for ever' (1 Kgs 10:9), and made a covenant with her that has never been broken, depositing there the messianic hopes of the whole human race." Benedict XVI, *Visit to the Synagogue of Rome*, January 17, 2010, addressed the Jewish people as the "people of the Covenant," thus making clear that the Mosaic Covenant has not been revoked. For an analysis of the post-conciliar Magisterium on this subject see Gavin D'Costa, "The Mystery of Israel: Jews, Hebrew Catholics, Messianic Judaism, the Catholic Church, and the Mosaic Ceremonial Laws," *Nova et Vetera* 16, no. 3 (Summer 2018): 939–77, esp. 940–42.

never been revoked," and Pope Francis has also repeated it in *Evangelii Gaudium* 247: "We hold the Jewish people in special regard because their covenant with God has never been revoked, for 'the gifts and the call of God are irrevocable' (Rom 11:29)."[10]

This repeated teaching of the recent ordinary Magisterium of the Church, although not definitive, requires religious submission of mind and will (third grade of assent).[11] The Jewish people today cannot now be viewed by Catholics as having been dispossessed of the covenant and bereft of its promises and obligations, as theologians often assumed in the past.[12] They continue rather to be the people of the covenant made on Mount Sinai, which has never been revoked. This teaching cannot fail to affect the way one views the question of the Land of Israel today.

It can be seen from these magisterial texts that the right way to view the relationship between Israel and the Church cannot be that of replacement, as the term "supersessionism" implies. A reality is superseded when it is replaced by another. Rather than replacement, the relationship should be seen as properly typological.[13] A biblical type, as understood by the

---

10 See the Pontifical Biblical Commission, *The Jewish People and Their Sacred Scriptures in the Christian Bible* (2001), 161: "The New Testament takes for granted that the election of Israel, the people of the covenant, is irrevocable: it preserves intact its prerogatives (Rom 9:4) and its priority status in history, in the offer of salvation (Acts 13:23) and in the Word of God (13:46). But God has also offered to Israel a 'new covenant' (Jr 31:31); this is now established through the blood of Jesus. The Church is composed of Israelites who have accepted the new covenant, and of other believers who have joined them. As a people of the new covenant, the Church is conscious of existing only in virtue of belonging to Christ Jesus, the Messiah of Israel, and because of its link with the apostles, who were all Israelites. Far from being a substitution for Israel, the Church is in solidarity with it."

11 See Vatican Council II, *Lumen Gentium* (1964), 25: "This religious submission of mind and will must be shown in a special way to the authentic magisterium of the Roman Pontiff, even when he is not speaking *ex cathedra*; that is, it must be shown in such a way that his supreme magisterium is acknowledged with reverence, the judgments made by him are sincerely adhered to, according to his manifest mind and will. His mind and will in the matter may be known either from the character of the documents, [or] from his frequent repetition of the same doctrine."

12 See Bishops' Committee on the Liturgy, United States Conference of Catholic Bishops, *God's Mercy Endures Forever: Guidelines on the Presentation of Jews and Judaism in Catholic Preaching* (September, 1988): "Despite the Church's condemnation of Marcion's teachings, some Christians over the centuries continued to dichotomize the Bible into two mutually contradictory parts. They argued, for example, that the New Covenant 'abrogated' or 'superseded' the Old, and that the Sinai Covenant was discarded by God and replaced with another. The Second Vatican Council, in *Dei Verbum* and *Nostra Aetate*, rejected these theories of the relationship between the Scriptures."

13 Theologians who held a hard supersessionist position certainly also thought of the relationship as typological. Nevertheless, in holding that the antitype has *replaced* the type (rather than fulfilling it), there is a deviation from the logic of biblical typology, in which the type retains its own value while pointing beyond itself.

Catechism of the Catholic Church 117, is a reality described by the literal sense of the biblical words that itself analogically points to another reality in salvation history.[14] The reality that the type points to (the antitype) does not *replace* the type, although it often fulfills its meaning in a higher way. In other words, the existence of a spiritual sense of Scripture does not replace, annul, or stand in competition with the literal sense, on which it depends for its meaning.

The fact, therefore, that Israel is a type of the Church on earth and in heaven does not mean that she ceases to have her own historical reality as chosen by God, even now.[15] Similarly, the fact that the Old Covenant is a type of the New Covenant does not mean that the establishment of the New has made void the continuing implications of Israel's covenant with God. Biblical types have their own enduring historical reality, while also pointing beyond themselves. The type is not replaced by the reality it prefigures, for both can coexist together on two distinct planes,[16] as the Church militant now coexists with the Church triumphant, of which she is a type.

Israel's election is linked to her Messiah, and she bears witness to that hope.[17] Already in Genesis 12:2–3 we see the connection between Abraham's

---

[14] *Catechism of the Catholic Church* 117: "Thanks to the unity of God's plan, not only the text of Scripture but also the realities and events about which it speaks can be signs."

[15] See the Commission for Religious Relations with the Jews, *Notes on the Correct Way to Present the Jews*, 2.3–5: "From the unity of the divine plan derives the problem of the relation between the Old and New Testaments. The Church already from apostolic times (cf. 1 Cor 10:11; Heb 10:1) and then constantly in tradition resolved this problem by means of typology, which emphasizes the primordial value that the Old Testament must have in the Christian view. Typology however makes many people uneasy and is perhaps the sign of a problem unresolved. 4. Hence in using typology, the teaching and practice of which we have received from the Liturgy and from the Fathers of the Church, we should be careful to avoid any transition from the Old to the New Testament which might seem merely a rupture. The Church, in the spontaneity of the Spirit which animates her, has vigorously condemned the attitude of Marcion and always opposed his dualism. 5. It should also be emphasized that typological interpretation consists in reading the Old Testament as preparation and, in certain aspects, outline and foreshadowing of the New."

[16] See the Commission for Religious Relations with the Jews, "The Gifts and the Calling of God Are Irrevocable," 23: "The Church is called the new people of God (cf. *Nostra Aetate*, 4) but not in the sense that the people of God of Israel has ceased to exist. The Church 'was prepared in a remarkable way throughout the history of the people of Israel and by means of the Old Covenant' (*Lumen Gentium*, 2). The Church does not replace the people of God of Israel, since as the community founded on Christ it represents in him the fulfilment of the promises made to Israel. This does not mean that Israel, not having achieved such a fulfilment, can no longer be considered to be the people of God."

[17] See Feingold, "The Mission and Glories of the Chosen People," *The Hebrew Catholic* 88 (Winter 2010–2011): 14–20. See also the Commission for Religious Relations with the Jews, *"The Gifts and the Calling of God Are Irrevocable,"* 43: "The enduring role of the covenant people of Israel in God's plan of salvation is to relate dynamically to the 'people of God of Jews and Gentiles, united in Christ', he whom the Church confesses as the universal mediator of creation and salvation."

vocation to be the father of a great nation (together with the promise of the Land) with the promise of a blessing to all nations in his offspring. Indeed, Christ stands at the center of all God's plans, which certainly includes the election of Israel to be a people in which the Lord will come into his own in the fullness of time. Israel's identity and mission are inextricably linked to her Messiah, to whom her very existence and election point. This remains true even after his coming and in the time of the Church. Their witness has not terminated with his coming.[18] Their role is not finished until they corporately come to receive the fulfillment of God's promises to them by which "all Israel will be saved" (Rom 11:26). In the meantime Israel is a continual and impartial witness before the world of God's plan of salvation revealed in the Torah that culminates in the Messiah and his Church.[19] The existence and continued fidelity of the Jewish people to the covenant of Sinai, through so many centuries in the diaspora without a land, through so much persecution, tragedy, and trial, is a clear sign of a special providence and predilection of God in their behalf[20] and of the special role that they continue to play in His plans, until they shall finally come to recognize their Messiah.

TYPOLOGY OF THE RETURN TO THE LAND OF ISRAEL

The fact that the Old Covenant has not been revoked or abrogated has huge importance for understanding the relation today between the Jewish people and the Promised Land, for the Land of Israel is obviously a key promise of the Old Covenant. If the Old Covenant has not been revoked, then the relationship of the people of the Old Covenant with the Promised Land remains. This relationship with the Land obviously does not have the nature of a political right, or even of a religious right (for it is a covenantal gift and not a right), but of a profound typological *meaning*. The relationship of Israel with the Land is a type of the relationship of Israel with the Lord who indwelt

---

[18] See Abraham Joshua Heschel, *Israel: An Echo of Eternity* (New York: Farrar, Straus and Giroux, 1969), 221: "Our return to Zion is a major event within the mysterious history that began with a lonely man—Abraham—whose destiny was to be a blessing to all nations, and our irreducible commitment is to assert that promise and that destiny: to be a blessing to all nations."

[19] See Augustine, *The City of God*, trans. Henry Bettenson (NY: Penguin Books, 1984), 827; in which he says that the Jews "by the evidence of their own Scriptures . . . bear witness for us that we have not fabricated the prophecies about Christ."

[20] See the Commission for Religious Relations with the Jews, *Notes on the Correct Way to Present the Jews*, 6.1: "The history of Israel did not end in 70 CE. It continued, especially in a numerous Diaspora which allowed Israel to carry to the whole world a witness—often heroic—of its fidelity to the one God and to 'exalt him in the presence of all the living' (Tb 13:4), while preserving the memory of the land of their forefathers at the hearts of their hope (Passover Seder)."

in the Land, and it is a relationship expressed with nuptial imagery.[21] A non-supersessionist understanding of Israel means that Israel's exile and return to the Land must be understood within the logic of the covenant and salvation history, and thus is endowed with theological significance that merits reflection as a sign of the times.

ESCHATOLOGICAL SIGNS

Can we say anything more about the theological meaning of the reappearance of a Jewish State in Israel? I propose that the return of a Jewish nation-state in the Holy Land after nineteen centuries of continuous diaspora should be seen as an eschatological sign, taken in the broad sense of the term. Furthermore, I will argue that this fact should be reflected on in union with another phenomenon that is also a sign of the times: the recent rise in the number and organization of Jewish believers in Jesus.[22]

By the term "eschatological sign" I mean an *anagogical type*,[23] which is an historical event or reality that prefigures and typologically points to the culmination of history when seen in the light of faith. Eschatological signs have their own historical reality, but also serve as signs of a reality transcending history. Christ's Ascension is such a sign. Terminating the historical period of Christ's presence on earth, the Ascension reminds us that Christ "will come in the same way" as the Apostles "saw him go into heaven" (Acts 1:11). Another very different sign was the destruction of Jerusalem in AD 70, which figures prominently in Jesus' eschatological discourse.

It should be clear that the expression "eschatological sign" is not being used in the sense of a *proximate* marker of Christ's imminent return, but of an event that points to that return, even though the historical process leading there may still be very long in its unfolding. Eschatological signs are not meant to give us information or clues regarding the day and the hour that is hidden from the knowledge of the Church.[24] Rather, in their

---

21 See Isaiah 62:4–5.

22 These two signs are set against the backdrop of two other ongoing eschatological signs: the preaching of the Gospel to all nations, and a progressive apostasy among those who have already received the Gospel in the West.

23 See the *Catechism of the Catholic Church* 117: "The *anagogical sense* (Greek: *anagoge*, "leading"). We can view realities and events in terms of their eternal significance, leading us toward our true homeland: thus the Church on earth is a sign of the heavenly Jerusalem."

24 See Christ's answer to the Apostles in Acts 1:7 when they asked if he would then restore the kingdom to Israel: "It is not for you to know times or seasons which the Father has fixed by his own authority."

ambiguity and partial fulfillment in long development, they serve to nourish our yearning through the generations. Because of the excesses of some Protestant forms of millenarianism and false predictions of eschatological events, many theologians are understandably wary of proposing historical events as eschatological signs. In his eschatological discourse, however, Jesus does precisely this, especially with regard to the destruction of Jerusalem, but in such a way that they retain their ambiguity in that every generation can see some of these signs realized in their own time. This serves to foster hope and yearning while keeping hidden from the Church the knowledge of the day and the hour.

THE CORPORATE RETURN OF JEWS TO THE LAND OF ISRAEL AS AN ESCHATOLOGICAL SIGN

The Land of Israel, and Jerusalem in particular, have been seen as an eschatological type of the heavenly Kingdom for three millennia.[25] This is because of God's indwelling in the midst of Israel in the Temple in Jerusalem.[26] After the loss of the Temple and in long exile from the Land, Jerusalem continued to be the focus of eschatological yearning. The refrain "Next year in Jerusalem" has been an expression both of hope of Jewish return to the Land and of the greater hope for the fullness of intimacy with God in the heavenly Kingdom.[27] The Jewish exile from Israel for so many centuries is a profound type of humanity's and the Church's exile from the heavenly homeland. But if exile spurs yearning, return to the Land spurs hope for a more complete return to a "city with foundations": the heavenly Jerusalem.

Israel as a whole, and Jerusalem in particular,[28] cannot help being eschatological types; it is embedded by God into their identity. Israel cannot be

---

25 In the New Testament, see Galatians 4:26; Revelation 21:2–3, 9–11; and Hebrews 11:9–10 and 12:22. For a Jewish expression of this anagogic relation, see Heschel, *Israel: An Echo of Eternity*, 32–33: "God had a vision of restoring the image of man. So He created a city in heaven and called it Jerusalem, hoping and praying that Jerusalem on earth may resemble Jerusalem in heaven."

26 See Michael Wyschogrod, *Abraham's Promise: Judaism and Jewish-Christian Relations* (Grand Rapids, MI: Eerdmans, 2004), 101–3: "Above all, it is the land in which God takes his residence, in the Temple, in the Holy of Holies.... Because of this dual indwelling of God in the people and the land, when the people of Israel is missing from its land, the land is incomplete. There is thus a triadic relationship: the indwelling of God, Israel, and the land. We have thus reached the theological root of Israel's relationship to the land. The Land of Israel is the land chosen for God's indwelling and for the indwelling of the people of God."

27 See Heschel, *Israel: An Echo of Eternity*, 26.

28 See Heschel, *Israel: An Echo of Eternity*, 28–33.

seen as merely another land on the earth. It has a vocation to point beyond itself. Furthermore, it is not simply the land and the city that has served as an eschatological type. It is rather *the land wedded to its people*, populated with its faithful people, as portrayed in Isaiah 62:4–5.[29] The Land without its people during the Exile in Babylon is spoken of as "desolate" and "forsaken." The promised return to the Land will make her to be "married": "your land shall be married. For as a young man marries a virgin, so shall your sons marry you."

If that was true after the Babylonian exile, it is no less true after an exile of nineteen centuries. The fact that the Land of Israel is somehow "married" again, to use Isaiah's language, to the Jewish people cannot be regarded as theologically insignificant from the Christian perspective, as from the Jewish.[30] If Jerusalem is always an eschatological sign, how much more a Jerusalem in which the Land is "wedded" again in some sense to the People of the Promise. It makes sense, therefore, that the return of the Land and of Jerusalem to Jewish sovereignty after so many centuries of exile should be considered a sign of the times that should be read through the illumination of the Holy Spirit.

Since the People of Israel point by their very existence to the mystery of the Messiah, it follows that a return of the Chosen People to the Land after long exile can also be seen as a sign or type of the approach of the return of the Messiah.[31] This approach, of course, can involve a long stretch of time.[32] The principle for viewing Israel's return as an eschatological sign or type of

---

29 See Isaiah 62:4–5: "You shall no more be termed Forsaken, and your land shall no more be termed Desolate; but you shall be called My delight is in her, and your land Married; for the Lord delights in you, and your land shall be married. For as a young man marries a virgin, so shall your sons marry you, and as the bridegroom rejoices over the bride, so shall your God rejoice over you."

30 See Heschel, *Israel: An Echo of Eternity*, 14: "Jerusalem is not divine, her life depends on our presence. Alone she is desolate and silent, with Israel she is a witness, a proclamation. Alone she is a widow, with Israel she is a bride." See also 16–17: "Jerusalem, our hearts went out to you whenever we prayed, whenever we pondered the destiny of the world. For so many ages we have been love-sick. 'My beloved is mine, and I am his,' Jerusalem whispered. We waited through unbearably long frustration and derision. In our own days the miracle has occurred. Jerusalem has proclaimed loudly: 'My beloved is mine, and I am his!'. . . We, a people of orphans, have entered the walls to greet the widow, Jerusalem, and the widow is a bride again."

31 See Wyschogrod, who poses this question from the Jewish perspective, in *Abraham's Promise*, 102–3: "In our time, the people of Israel has returned to its land. Was it justified in doing so? Does this return signal the beginning of the redemption promised by God or is it a human act of will resulting from impatience and the secularization of Jewish consciousness? These are difficult questions to answer and will ultimately only be answered by history."

32 See Mark Kinzer, *Jerusalem Crucified, Jerusalem Risen: The Resurrected Messiah, the Jewish People, and the Land of Promise* (La Vergne: Wipf and Stock, 2018), 37.

Christ's return is the intimate connection between Israel and her Messiah,[33] for Christ recapitulates the history and destiny of Israel.[34] As Christ walked the way of the Cross, so Israel has tragically walked the way of the Cross through the centuries at the hands of the Gentiles. This tragic history of exile and persecution has all too often been interpreted in Christian apologetics as a divine punishment for Israel's failure to recognize Christ,[35] which has unfortunately fostered anti-Zionist thought in past centuries. For if the exile was a punishment of Israel's failure to recognize Christ, it was thought that the former should not end before the latter.[36] This perspective, however, is reminiscent of the prosperity gospel and is contrary to the salvific meaning of Christ's Cross. The tribulations of the Jewish people should be seen rather as an association in redemptive suffering, in the same way that martyrdom and multiple trials are not the sign of God's abandonment but rather of his granting us a share in his redemptive mission, even when we are not fully aware of it.[37] This intimate connection between Israel and her Messiah lead us to hope that the return to the Land bears an association with the unfolding process leading to the Lord's return.

---

[33] This principle is developed forcefully by Mark Kinzer in *Jerusalem Crucified, Jerusalem Risen*. See 15: "The Gospel of Luke depicts Jesus as a prophet who foresees the coming destruction of the holy city, and who superimposes the image of that judgment over the events of his own suffering and death. In this way, the atoning death of Jesus is linked to the future suffering of the Jewish people. I argue that the structure and content of Luke and Acts likewise points to a future redemption for the holy city. Since the destruction of the city is connected to the death of Jesus, we may infer that the redemption of the city is likewise connected to his resurrection. Thus, the first chapter lays out our basic thesis: the *euangelion* of the Messiah, crucified and risen, is also the *euangelion* of Jerusalem, crucified and risen."

[34] Christ's recapitulation of Israel, as of creation and history, is one of the key themes of the theology of St. Irenaeus, *Against Heresies*, 3.18.7; 5.14.1; and 5.21.1.

[35] See *Nostra Aetate* 4: "The Jews should not be presented as rejected or accursed by God, as if this followed from the Holy Scriptures"; *Notes on the Correct Way to Present the Jews*, 6.1: "We must in any case rid ourselves of the traditional idea of a people *punished*, preserved as a *living argument* for Christian apologetic."

[36] For a brief synopsis of the history of this anti-Zionist thought, see Edward H. Flannery, SJ, "Theological Aspects of the State of Israel," *The Bridge: A Yearbook of Judaeo-Christian Studies* 3, ed. John Oesterreicher (New York: Pantheon Books, 1958), 301–24, at 304–9. See, for example, Augustin Lémann, *L'avenir de Jérusalem: Espérance et chimères* (Paris: C. Poussielgue, 1901), 196, trans. Flannery, 304: "There is complete agreement between the Old and the New Testaments in treating any attempt to reconstitute a Jewish state in Jerusalem as a chimera. God's plan runs counter to the project of the Zionists."

[37] See Waltraud Herbstrith, *Edith Stein: A Biography/The Untold Story of the Philosopher and Mystic Who Lost Her Life in the Death Camps of Auschwitz* (San Francisco: Harper and Row, 1985), 162–69.

ACTS 1:6-11

It is significant that the account of Christ's Ascension in Acts 1:6–11 begins with the disciples asking him the Zionist question of whether he would "at this time restore the kingdom to Israel" (Acts 1:6). While many Christians today see this as a foolish question manifesting the very imperfect comprehension of the disciples, it is better to see it as the witness of Jewish eschatological hope common to Jews then and now.[38] The mission of the Messiah has to include, in the Jewish mind, the restoration and fulfillment of the Jewish relationship with the Land as the type and condition of their full intimacy with the Lord who dwelt in their midst in the Temple. Jesus answered not by rebuking the foolishness of the question. Instead, as on other occasions when asked about eschatological signs, he emphasized that knowledge of the day and hour of eschatological events is hidden from us: "It is not for you to know times or seasons which the Father has fixed by his own authority" (1:7). He then traces out once more the missionary mandate to give witness to the end of the earth, through the power of the Holy Spirit: "But you shall receive power when the Holy Spirit has come upon you; and you shall be my witnesses in Jerusalem and in all Judea and Samaria and to the end of the earth" (1:8). This implies that the restoration of a kingdom to Israel, unlike the witness that will build up the Church, will not be the work of the disciples empowered by the Spirit. But Jesus' response does not rule out a connection between the fulfillment of the mandate to be "witnesses . . . to the end of the earth" (Acts 1:8) and the restoration of a kingdom to Israel.

LUKE 21:23-24

A key New Testament text dealing with the subject of Israel's continuing relationship with the Land is Luke 21:23–24, in which Jesus foretells a long exile of the Chosen People: "For great distress shall be upon the earth and wrath upon this people; they will fall by the edge of the sword, and be led captive among all nations; and Jerusalem will be trodden down by the Gentiles, until the times of the Gentiles are fulfilled."[39] The captivity among all nations

---

[38] See Wyschogrod, *Abraham's Promise*, 99: "The Zionist question is addressed to the risen Jesus because to establish once again the sovereignty of Israel is the essential task of the Messiah as understood by Judaism."

[39] A related text is Matthew 23:37–39: "O Jerusalem, Jerusalem, killing the prophets and stoning those who are sent to you! How often would I have gathered your children together as a hen gathers her brood under her wings, and you would not! Behold, your house is forsaken and desolate. For I tell you, you will not see me again, until you say, 'Blessed is he who comes in the name of the Lord.'"

began to be fulfilled in 70 CE, but still more in 135 CE, continuing down the centuries. Jesus' words were prophetic beyond what could have been imagined even in the decades after 70 CE.

Jesus' words, however, seem to link this tragic reality with a time of repentance given to the Gentiles. In Matthew 24:14, Jesus says: "And this gospel of the kingdom will be preached throughout the whole world, as a testimony to all nations; and then the end will come." Indeed the preaching of the Gospel to all nations is another eschatological sign that we see more and more fulfilled. The return of Jews in a corporate way to the Land of promise thus seems tied to the progressive fulfillment of the missionary mandate. If Jerusalem is no longer "trodden down" by the Gentiles, this should be taken as a sign that the "time of the Gentiles" is becoming fulfilled through the spread of the witness of the Gospel. The phrase, "time of the Gentiles," could simply refer to a protracted period in which the Gentiles exercise political hegemony over the Holy Land. It seems more reasonable, however, to think that the phrase also has a broader theological significance, connected with the time of the missionary expansion of the Church to the ends of the earth. This supposition is strengthened by reading Luke 21:23–24 in the light of Romans 11:11–32.[40]

ROMANS 11 AND THE THEME OF ISRAEL'S RECOGNITION OF CHRIST

In Romans 11, St. Paul reflects on a different reality. The theme is not the loss of the Land (which had not yet occurred) but the failure of the leaders of Israel to recognize Christ. This prompts him to seek a providential meaning in this heart-wrenching reality through the permissive will of God that permits evils to make possible transcendent goods. He thus speaks of a blindness that has been permitted to come over much of Israel for the sake of the reconciliation of the Gentiles.[41] In Romans 11:11 he writes: "So I ask, have they stumbled so as to fall? By no means! But through their trespass salvation has come to the Gentiles, so as to make Israel jealous."

---

40 The two texts are put in conjunction in *Catechism of the Catholic Church* 674: "The 'full inclusion' of the Jews in the Messiah's salvation, in the wake of 'the full number of the Gentiles' (Rom 11:12, 25; cf. Lk 21:24)." The texts are also read in conjunction by Venerable Bede in a text quoted by Aquinas in the *Catena Aurea* on Luke 21:24: "Which indeed the Apostle makes mention of when he says, 'Blindness in part is happened to Israel, and so all Israel shall be saved' (Rom 11:25). Which when it shall have gained the promised salvation, hopes not rashly to return to the land of its fathers" Aquinas, *Catena Aurea*, ed. Newman (Oxford: John Henry Parker, 1847), 682–83.

41 A first answer to the question of whether God has rejected his people is that a remnant of Israel has been faithful through the mercy of God, including Mary, the Apostles, St. Paul, the disciples gathered into the Church at Pentecost, and the innumerable Jews evangelized by St. Paul and the other disciples throughout the Diaspora, such as Priscilla and Aquila (Jews from Rome with whom St. Paul stayed in Corinth), Timothy, Apollos, and many others. The Acts of the

St. Paul's reference to stumbling and trespass on the part of Jews that enabled salvation to come to the Gentiles can be taken in two senses. First, the blindness of Caiaphas and other members of the Sanhedrin made possible the redemption of the world through Christ's Passion. Second, the subsequent opposition of the majority of Israel to the preaching of the Apostles, as experienced by St. Paul, made possible the turn to evangelize the Gentiles, as we see repeatedly in the Acts of the Apostles. While benefitting from the disbelief of the leaders of Israel, the Gentiles received the Gospel from Israel in its faithful remnant: the Jewish Apostles and disciples of the Church of Pentecost. The mercy that came to the Gentiles came through Israel, directly through those who believed in Christ and indirectly through those who did not.

But after speaking of the providence of God in drawing good from a lack of sight and faith, St. Paul goes on to speak of the hope and benefit of the future lifting of that darkening and a coming to faith in Christ on the part of Israel: "Now if their trespass means riches for the world, and if their failure means riches for the Gentiles, how much more will their full inclusion mean! ... For if their rejection means the reconciliation of the world, what will their acceptance mean but life from the dead?" (Rom 11:12, 15).

In speaking of "acceptance" St. Paul seems to be referring to an eventual acceptance of the Gospel on the part of Israel. This full acceptance has been delayed for the sake of the Gentiles so that they might come in. This is stated more clearly in Romans 11:25–26: "I want you to understand this mystery, brethren: a hardening has come upon part of Israel, until the full number of the Gentiles come in, and so all Israel will be saved; as it is written, 'The Deliverer will come from Zion, he will banish ungodliness from Jacob.'"[42]

The Father will draw Israel to faith in Christ, but a hardening has been permitted for a time—the time of the Gentiles—so that their full number

---

Apostles tells us that many of the Pharisees and priests came to believe. In Acts 21:20, James tells Paul: "You see, brother, how many thousands there are among the Jews of those who have believed." Furthermore, some sociologists argue that large numbers of Hellenistic Jews converted to Christianity in the first centuries of the Church. See Rodney Stark, *The Rise of Christianity: A Sociologist Reconsiders History* (Princeton, NJ: Princeton University Press, 1996).

42 See Matthew 23:39, in which Jesus says to Jerusalem: "Your house will be deserted, for, I promise, you shall not see me any more until you say: Blessed is he who comes in the name of the Lord!'" This should be taken to mean that the acceptance by his people is a condition for his being seen again at his return in the Second Coming. See Dale Allison, "Matt. 23:39 = Luke 13:35b as a Conditional Prophecy," *Journal for the Study of the New Testament* 5, no. 18 (1983): 75–84. Allison argues (p. 77) that Matthew 23:39 should be read as a condition for Christ's return: "When his people bless him, the Messiah will come." Another significant New Testament text in this regard is Acts 19:21: "Repent therefore, and turn again, that your sins may be blotted out, that times of refreshing may come from the presence of the Lord, and that he may send the Christ appointed for you, Jesus, whom heaven must receive until the time for establishing all that God spoke by the mouth of his holy prophets from of old." See Mark Kinzer, *Jerusalem Crucified, Jerusalem Risen*, 30.

may come in. We can connect this with Jesus' prophecy about the Gospel being preached to all nations (Mt 24:14). The *Catechism of the Catholic Church* 674 takes up St. Paul's prophecy in Romans 11, connecting it with other texts:

> The glorious Messiah's coming is suspended at every moment of history until his recognition by "all Israel," for "a hardening has come upon part of Israel" in their "unbelief" toward Jesus (Rom 11:20–26; cf. Mt 23:39). St. Peter says to the Jews of Jerusalem after Pentecost: "Repent therefore, and turn again, that your sins may be blotted out, that times of refreshing may come from the presence of the Lord, and that he may send the Christ appointed for you, Jesus, whom heaven must receive until the time for establishing all that God spoke by the mouth of his holy prophets from of old" (Acts 3:19–21). St. Paul echoes him: "For if their rejection means the reconciliation of the world, what will their acceptance mean but life from the dead?" (Rom 11:15). The "full inclusion" of the Jews in the Messiah's salvation, in the wake of "the full number of the Gentiles" (Rom 11:12, 25; cf. Lk 21:24), will enable the People of God to achieve "the measure of the stature of the fullness of Christ," in which "God may be all in all" (Eph 4:13; 1 Cor 15:28).

"LIFE FROM THE DEAD"

What does St. Paul mean in speaking of "life from the dead" in Romans 11:15?[43] His point is that if a lack of faith in Christ in many in Israel did not fail to have beneficial consequences for the Gentiles, their acceptance in its time will have still more beneficial consequences, bringing about "life from the dead." But what is the specific meaning of "life from the dead"?

St. Thomas gives three possible interpretations, all mutually compatible. Their acceptance will mean "life from the dead" literally, in that it will mark the approach of the general resurrection. In the spiritual sense it seems that there is a double meaning. On the one hand, "life from the dead" indicates the spiritual resurrection of Israel through faith in Christ. On the other hand, it may also refer to the spiritual resurrection of many Gentile Christians who will fall away from the faith in the time of the great apostasy spoken of by St. Paul in 2 Thessalonians 2:3, and who will be brought back by the witness

---

[43] See Feingold, "The Conversion of Israel and the Second Coming: 'What will their acceptance mean but life from the dead?' (Rom 11:15)," AHC Conference 2010, in *The Hebrew Catholic* 88 (Winter 2010–2011): 14–20, from which this section is drawn.

of the faith in Christ of the people of Israel. In his commentary on Romans 11:15, St. Thomas writes:

> If the loss of the Jews provided the occasion for the reconciliation of the world, in that through the death of Christ we are reconciled with God, what will their acceptance be but life from the dead? That is, that the Jews are received again by God.... *What will that reception accomplish, if not that the Gentiles be made to rise unto life?* For the Gentile faithful will grow cold, according to Mt 24:12: "And because wickedness is multiplied, most men's love will grow cold." Or also those who completely fall—deceived by the Antichrist—will be *restored to their pristine fervor by the converted Jews*. And thus as through the fall of the Jews the Gentiles were reconciled after being enemies, so after the conversion of the Jews, the end of the world being imminent, there will be the general resurrection, through which men will go from death to immortal life.[44]

This interpretation implies that when Jews come in significant numbers to faith in Christ, as we see increasingly in recent decades, they will have an historic ecclesial mission to accomplish, which is to confirm their Gentile brethren—fallen-away Catholics—in the faith.[45] They obviously also have a mission with regard to their own people, both in terms of faith and in being living witnesses of reconciliation and Catholic social doctrine.

In light of the events of the last seventy years, I would propose that there could be a fourth significance of the phrase "life from the dead," although it is not a principal sense. The rebirth of the State of Israel after nineteen centuries has often been compared to a resurrection, a fulfillment of the imagery of Ezekiel's dead bones that have life blown into them by the Spirit (Ez 37).[46] This fourth meaning can be seen to have a typological relation to the other three.

---

44 St. Thomas Aquinas, *Super epistolas S. Pauli lectura*, ed. Raphael Cai (Turin: Marietti, 1953), 1:166, no. 890 (my translation and italics). See also Steven C. Boguslawski, *Thomas Aquinas on the Jews: Insights into His Commentary on Romans 9–11* (New York: Paulist Press, 2008), 98.

45 See Charles Cardinal Journet, "The Mysterious Destinies of Israel," *The Bridge: A Yearbook of Judaeo-Christian Studies* 2, ed. John Oesterreicher (New York: Pantheon Books, 1956), 84–85: "Now, must one assume that Israel's reintegration will mark the end of history, giving the signal for the Last Judgment and for the final restoration of the universe? Or may one assume that Israel's return will take place within the very web of historic time, that indeed it is meant to influence the course of the centuries to come after it?" Journet responds that "both opinions are found within the Church," but nevertheless he prefers the second interpretation as being more in harmony with St. Paul's texts in Romans 11:12 and 15: "Impossible, he [St. Paul] declares in the first, that Israel's restoration should not be of inestimable benefit to the other peoples, since even its stumbling marvelously profited them."

46 See Heschel, *Israel: An Echo of Eternity*, 109–22, 220–21: "The wonder of the risen Israel and the gratitude to Him who has raised martyred Israel from the dead belong together. We are

THE LAND OF ISRAEL AND THE ENCOUNTER WITH JESUS

We have examined two signs of the times that have eschatological significance—the return of Jewish sovereignty to Israel and the emergence of large numbers of Jewish believers in Jesus. It is reasonable to see these two realities as not entirely unrelated. On the one hand, both speak to a fulfilment of the time of the Gentiles. Secondly, it seems legitimate to connect the return to *Eretz Yisrael* with renewed possibility for a corporate encounter of the Jewish people with Jesus in a way different than in the diaspora.[47]

In Israel Jesus is more easily seen for what he is, a Jew of the Land, a *sabra* born and nourished in Second Temple Judaism. This encounter can serve first of all to improve Jewish perceptions of Christianity as something more normal, since so many Christian sites are located in their land, and Israeli tour guides very often explain Christian sites to Christian pilgrims and tourists.

Secondly, the Land of Israel makes it possible (admittedly on a very small scale) for Israelis to encounter Christian liturgy in Hebrew, so that they can see it as something not totally alien to their culture, but very deeply rooted in it, with regard to both sacrifice and the indwelling divine presence (*Shekinah*).[48]

SOCIAL JUSTICE AND HOLINESS IN THE LAND

By speaking of the State of Israel as a theologically significant sign of the times that must be understood within the logic of the Old Covenant, I am not advocating any particular political position, but reflecting on how political realities can transcend their own focus on temporal advantage in the here and now by pointing to what lasts, "to the city which has foundations, whose

---

witnesses of the resurrection. And being a witness is a transformation. The return to the land is a profound indication of the possibility of redemption for all men. Our return to Zion is a major event within the mysterious history that began with a lonely man—Abraham—whose destiny was to be a blessing to all nations, and our irreducible commitment is to assert that promise and that destiny: to be a blessing to all nations."

47 See Edward H. Flannery, SJ, "Theological Aspects of the State of Israel," in *The Bridge: A Yearbook of Judaeo-Christian Studies* 3, ed. John Oesterreicher (New York: Pantheon Books, 1958), 324: "With Father Congar, we may then think that God wished to bring a representative cross section of the Jewish people to the Holy Land in order to bring it there face to face with the great question of the Messiah. Israel's restoration to the land of promise, even though under secular auspices, may thus be a distant preparation for her final encounter with grace."

48 See Feingold, *The Eucharist: Mystery of Presence, Sacrifice, and Communion* (Steubenville, OH: Emmaus Academic, 2018), 39–69.

builder and maker is God" (Heb 11:10). Eschatological signs cannot be taken as blueprints or justifications for particular political options, and their sign value adds a greater responsibility and mission to more fully embody human justice so as to point better to the divine. Scripture speaks of the unique holiness required of Jerusalem as the city of God: "O Lord, who shall sojourn in thy tent? Who shall dwell on thy holy hill? He who walks blamelessly, and does what is right, and speaks truth from his heart; who does not slander with his tongue, and does no evil to his friend."[49]

This holiness should be understood according to the biblical teaching on social justice, further developed by Catholic social doctrine. This, I take it, is the meaning of a problematic phrase from the Commission for Religious Relations with the Jews, *Notes on the Correct Way to Present the Jews* 6.1: "The existence of the State of Israel and its political options should be envisaged not in a perspective which is in itself religious, but in their reference to the common principles of international law." As I have argued, the Catholic faith has to view the existence of the State of Israel in a religious perspective that recognizes the continuing reality of the Old Covenant, never revoked. But in evaluating political options, one must look for guidance to Catholic social teaching, which is in deep continuity with God's Word to Israel. Whatever her shortcomings, the fact that the State of Israel is seen to have theological significance as an eschatological sign of the times means that the Church

---

[49] Ps 15:1–3; see also Ps 24:3–4. Heschel cites these and other texts in speaking of the ethical challenge of Jerusalem in *Israel: An Echo of Eternity*, 33–37. See also Michael Wyschogrod, *Abraham's Promise: Judaism and Jewish-Christian Relations* (Grand Rapids, MI: Eerdmans, 2004), 102: "When Israel sins the divine indwelling in the people and in the land is diminished." From the Christian perspective, see, for example, Benedict XVI, *Homily in Josafat Valley*, Jerusalem, May 12, 2009: "This is the hope, this the vision, which inspires all who love this earthly Jerusalem to see her as a prophecy and promise of that universal reconciliation and peace which God desires for the whole human family. Sadly, beneath the walls of this same City, we are also led to consider how far our world is from the complete fulfilment of that prophecy and promise. . . . Gathered beneath the walls of this city, sacred to the followers of three great religions, how can we not turn our thoughts to Jerusalem's universal vocation? . . . How much needs to be done to make it truly a 'city of peace' for all peoples, where all can come in pilgrimage in search of God, and hear his voice, 'a voice which speaks of peace' (cf. Ps 85:8)! Jerusalem, in fact, has always been a city whose streets echo with different languages, whose stones are trod by people of every race and tongue, whose walls are a symbol of God's provident care for the whole human family. As a microcosm of our globalized world, this City, if it is to live up to its universal vocation, must be a place which teaches universality, respect for others, dialogue and mutual understanding; a place where prejudice, ignorance and the fear which fuels them, are overcome by honesty, integrity and the pursuit of peace. There should be no place within these walls for narrowness, discrimination, violence and injustice. Believers in a God of mercy—whether they identify themselves as Jews, Christians or Muslims—must be the first to promote this culture of reconciliation and peace, however painstakingly slow the process may be, and however burdensome the weight of past memories."

should care greatly about and pray both for her continued existence and her flourishing in social justice and solidarity.

CONCLUSION

I would like to close by reflecting on the conclusion of Romans 11. After tracing his anguish over the division between Israel according to the flesh and the Church, St. Paul ends the section by reflecting on the mutual dependence of Jew and Gentile on each other, so that God may bestow his mercy on each through the other. After speaking about how God does not repent of his promises to Israel (11:29), he says to the Gentile Christians: "Just as you were once disobedient to God but now have received mercy because of their disobedience, so they have now been disobedient in order that by the mercy shown to you they also may receive mercy. For God has consigned all men to disobedience, that he may have mercy upon all" (11:30–32).

Recognition of mutual dependence and complementarity in God's salvific plan is the necessary condition for achieving unity and communion among individuals and peoples who are diverse and possess complementary gifts. Let us pray that this recognition of mutual dependence may point out paths of peace for those complementary groups—Jews and Palestinians, Jews and Christians, and Jews and Gentiles within the Church—who live together in the Holy Land and the world.

2

LAND AND REDEMPTION
WHY DOES GOD PROMISE A LAND?
Etienne Vetö, CCN

Questions come in a cluster when one addresses the relationship between *Am Yisrael* and *Eretz Yisrael* from a Catholic point of view. The first step in handling a complex problem is to distinguish the questions it contains and to determine to what fields these questions pertain. One question, or set of questions concerns the legal and political legitimacy of the presence of the Jewish people on this land and of the constitution of the modern State of Israel. These are questions of international law and international political order, and I will not examine them in this paper.

The other questions pertain to the field of theology. I will distinguish three aspects. The first theological question is whether, in God's design, *Eretz Yisrael* is promised and given to *Am Yisrael*, under what conditions, and in what time frame. This means studying the teaching of the Old Testament and analyzing whether the New Testament has brought any change.[1] We are in the field of biblical scholarship and biblical and historical theology.

The second question is whether the ingathering of the Jewish people on the land of their forefathers in the twentieth century and the relative safety and self-determination that has come with it can be understood as part of God's providential design and action; and also whether this ingathering can be considered a fulfillment of the (messianic) promises contained in the Scriptures. The former is not the same question as the latter: one may

---

1 Ideally this question should also be studied from the viewpoint of Tradition, but this will not be possible within the limits of this paper.

answer positively to the first and negatively, or by refraining to judge, to the second. According to a "Chalcedonian principle" of theology, one cannot separate them, but one should not confuse them. They are also different from a methodologic point of view: biblical scholarship has a scientific dimension, while interpreting history and discerning God's hand in it, if at all possible, is an art rather than a science. The degree of certainty of the first will always be superior to that of the latter.

The third theological question is how to reconcile the scriptural teaching and the interpretation of the events of the twentieth century with the presence of the Palestinian people on the land. Though not only a theological question, it truly is theological, because it may seem to challenge positions that support an ongoing validity of the land-promises to *Am Yisrael*. And it is clearly part of the second theological question, because it is not possible to fully discern the meaning of the ingathering of the twentieth century without taking into account the presence of another people on the land. Most approaches will either consider this question as contingent, because a-theological, or as the only valid one, either by refusing to consider that theology applies to the relation to the land, or by invoking the priority of ethical, political, or existential theologies. Conversely, I will argue that it is a central problem which needs to be introduced into the discussion of the other two, and I will ground its theological status on the notion of the "signs of the times" exposed by the Second Vatican Council, which sets it at the crossroads of different dimensions of theology—true theology can neither be disconnected from historical, sociopolitical, and existential situations, nor can it be a-biblical or a-systematic.

These are the three main questions Catholic theology can confront and that will constitute the horizon of this paper. Some would add a fourth one, closely related to the second, about the theological status and legitimacy not only of the ingathering of the people, but also of the modern State of Israel. However, Catholic tradition is very wary of conferring a theological meaning to any concrete state as such—and of course even more to the policy of any given government. The maximum that can be said is that, if one considers the ingathering as providential, the state is a "necessary historically contingent arrangement" which serves as a means toward that theologically grounded end.[2] For the rest, I believe that the precise question of the State of Israel is to be considered as part of the legal-political field, and I will not address it.

However, the three theological questions are much too wide to be addressed in just a few pages. I will treat them indirectly by focusing on

---

[2] See Gavin D'Costa, *Catholic Doctrines on the Jewish People after Vatican II* (Oxford: Oxford University Press, 2019), 64–143.

another, rarely examined, one, which I believe to be a key to all investigations regarding the relation between *Am Yisrael* and *Eretz Yisrael*: why does God promise and give the land? Understanding God's design and the true significance of the gift of the land will offer the foundation and the finality of the promise, of its conditions and of its validity in time. It will also give the necessary theological tools and criteria to confront the questions of the presence of two peoples on the land and of the meaning of the events of the twentieth century.

I will argue that the land is a key facet in a conception of the relationship to God and of salvation that takes into consideration both the corporal and corporate dimensions (1). However, the specific and unique traits of the relation that God establishes between *Am Yisrael* and *Eretz Yisrael* also oblige us to redefine the people's link to the land. I will thus also argue that what is at stake is a purified or transfigured conception of the land and of possessing the land (2), which includes the call to share the land (3). Now, even though *Am Yisrael* has a unique calling, it is a calling for the nations: both the corporal-corporate and the purified-transfigured aspects of this theology of the land are a teaching for all nations in relation to land (4). These four parts will give the opportunity to shed some light on the first and third theological questions of the promise of the land and of the Palestinian people. At the end of the paper I will then evoke how this reflection may help confront the second question, by offering some criteria for discerning the meaning of the ingathering of the Jewish people on *Eretz Yisrael* during the past century.

THE LAND AS PART OF THE CORPORAL AND CORPORATE DIMENSIONS OF THE PEOPLE'S RELATIONSHIP TO GOD AND TO SALVATION

The land is part of the first calling of Abraham by God: he needs to leave his land and family to become a great nation: the "land [that God] will show [Abraham]" (Gn 12:1) is part of the establishment of the new people.[3] One of the reasons for the gift of this land is simply the subsistence of the people: it is a good land, full of fruit and mines, "a land where you may eat bread without scarcity, where you will lack nothing" (Dt 8:9). It is also the land "flowing with milk and honey" (Ex 3:8) where the people, after their time in Egypt, will be free from the material and social hardships of captivity and slavery. It is a land where the descendants of Abraham will be able to live (Gn 12:7;

---

[3] The book of Genesis presents promises of the land to the Patriarchs and their descendants; to Abraham: Genesis 12:1, 7; 13:17; 15:18–21; 17:8; to Isaac: Genesis 26:4; to Jacob-Israel: Genesis 28:13; 35:12.

15:18; 17:8) and thus become a family, a stock, and a people. The whole process described by the Torah between the exodus from Egypt and the entrance into the land is a progression through which the people become a people, with a structure (see Ex 18:13–26) and commandments, which regulate its daily life. Taking possession of the land is part of the development that leads to full peoplehood.

However, it is not just any structure and law: their aim is to establish and structure the relationship between God and his people. The land is given not only for subsistence, security, and freedom, nor even so as to become a people, but also as the concrete framework for this relationship: it is the place where God is worshipped. On this land Shabbat is observed by each and by all—one can note that the land itself participates in Shabbat, through its rest every seven years. The land allows for the Torah to be observed in all its commandments.[4] It is the place where God lives among God's people: "I will give to you and to your offspring after you the land.... And I will be their God" (Gn 17:8). The culmination of the inhabitation of God among the people is the Temple: "A cloud filled the house of the Lord so that the priests could not stand to minister because of the cloud; for the glory of the Lord filled the house of the Lord. Then Solomon said, 'The Lord has said that he would dwell in thick darkness. I have built you an exalted house, a place for you to dwell in forever'" (1 Kgs 8:10–12).

Moreover, the land is not only related to the people's worship of God, but also from the very start it is closely associated to Israel's mission to be the blessing of all the nations: "Go ... to the land I will show you. I will make of you a great nation.... In you all the families of the earth will be blessed" (Gn 12:1–3; see also 28:14). In a sense, mysteriously, Abraham and his descendants are established on the land not only for themselves but for others, for all. Their life on the land is a testimony to the nations of the one and saving God, the God of Israel. We will see more clearly in the fourth section of this paper in what way this blessing for the nations can be related to the land.

The very conception of relationship to God and, by extension, of salvation, is here at stake. Relationship to God is not only spiritual and individual: it is corporal and corporate. Let us note that both of these terms have the same root: *corpus*, body. Relationship to God touches both the individual and the collective bodies. The dietary laws of *kashrut*, for instance, underline that the body is part of the order of one's partnership with God, and

---

4 See Alain Marchadour and David Neuhaus, *The Land, the Bible, and History: Toward the Land That I Will Show You* (New York: Fordham University Press, 2007), 23–24; see also Walter Brueggemann, *The Land: Place as Gift, Promise, and Challenge in Biblical Faith* (Minneapolis: Fortress Press, 2002), 56–62.

purification, as expressed mainly in Leviticus 12–15, witnesses to the fact that salvation includes the body. An ever better understanding of the discussions on food and the Law in the New Testament indicates that it most probably does not abolish *kashrut*.[5] Likewise, the central importance of healings in Jesus' and the apostles' ministry confirm that the corporal dimension of salvation touches the body: these healings are the sign of the fullness of redemption. They open the way for, accompany, and confirm the forgiveness of sins and liberation from the powers of evil.[6]

Moreover, the individual body cannot experience these aspects in isolation from the collective body. Of course, relationship to God depends on and is expressed through ethical behavior, which has a strong social dimension: the Torah insists on the attention to the poor, the widow, the orphan, the stranger—which naturally includes concrete attention to their corporal needs. It depends on and is expressed through common worship and observance of the *mitzvot*. However, relationship to God includes many other dimensions of corporate life: the continuous existence and history of a people, civil society, culture, economy, and politics. These are all part of what makes a human existence, and without them there is no full relationship to God. Obviously, all these dimensions are themselves in dire need of healing and purification. This is precisely the way in which they become the framework for salvation, both as saved and as part of salvation. Salvation which does not touch these aspects is incomplete. This shows that relationship to God and salvation are much fuller and more comprehensive than what we often imagine. Now, all these aspects of corporal and corporate life are related to living on the land, which provides food and commodity, shelter, space for coexistence, and all the long-term socio-economic-political and cultural dimensions of the human being.

A confirmation of this corporal and corporate dimension of salvation is that all these aspects made possible by a land are called to be entirely accomplished in the eschatological times. Redemption is not only the salvation of individuals but the establishment of the "kingdom of God" (see Dn 3:33). This kingdom has a strong interior dimension in the New Testament (see Lk 17:20–21; Rom 14:17), but it is also related to the concrete restored "Kingdom for Israel" (Acts 1:6). And it definitely has a corporate dimension. The New

---

5 See Daniel Boyarin, *The Jewish Gospel: The Story of the Jewish Christ* (New York: The New Press, 2013), 102–28. See also Gary Gilbert, "Notes on the Acts of the Apostles," *The Jewish Annotated New Testament*, vol. 2, ed. Amy-Jill Levine and Marc Zvi Butler (Oxford: Oxford University Press, 2017), 244.

6 Walter Kasper, *Jesus the Christ* (London: Burns and Oates, 1976), 95–99; Denis Biju-Duval, *Le psychique et le spirituel* (Paris: l'Emmanuel, 2001), 277.

Jerusalem is neither a synagogue nor a church: it is a city (Rv 21:9–27), the concentrated *locus* of a people. This stresses that eschatology does not point to another existence. The eschaton is the accomplishment of this present existence. It does not occur by escaping from this world and from history, but it is a transfiguration of this world. The New Jerusalem is set in a "new heaven and a new earth" (Rv 21:1), where "new" is better understood as "renewed," rather than as "other." For *Am Yisrael*, *Eretz Yisrael* is thus the *locus* for a life in full relationship with God and for receiving and living out the fullness of salvation and of redemption.[7]

THE CALLING TO A PURIFIED AND TRANSFIGURED RELATION TO THE LAND (1)

Of course, including the land—and all the dimensions of peoplehood—into relationship with God and salvation is fraught with danger. Does this not open the door to theologically founded nationalisms and conquests? We risk "idolatry of the land." We risk justifying crimes and horrors by claiming them to be the will of God. I will argue that God's design in giving a land is precisely to "convert" and "purify" our comprehension of the relationship between a people and their land. The land is the *locus* of salvation for the people of Israel but only when the people's relation to the land itself is "saved." The notion of a "God-given land" may be understood on a theological level, but if it truly is a theological expression, it certainly has a unique meaning that can only be received through revelation. This renewed comprehension is not an easy task: indeed, one of the main temptations for the people of Israel, at all times, is to be "like the other nations" (1 Sm 8:20).[8] That, however, is not their role, nor does it correspond to their identity, and this aspect concerns quite radically their bond to the land.

One classical way of proceeding is to underline that the relationship to the land is gradually spiritualized and universalized throughout the Old Testament and in an even more radical way in the New Testament. This would mean that the relationship of *Am Yisrael* to *Eretz Yisrael* is strongly

---

[7] While I do not share the whole of Rabbi Abraham Kook's thoughts on the relation between *Am Yisrael* and *Eretz Yisrael*, it is interesting to note that this complete vision of salvation is what motivates for him the aspiration of the Jewish people to live there: "Knesset Israel aspires for the amendment of the world in all its fullness, for original, purifying forgiveness, that comes not only from the salvation of the human soul and the betterment of human will in itself . . . but rather [offers] an overarching restoration that will remove the very roots of sin." Abraham Isaac Kook, *Shmonah Kvatzim*, 5:51, Sefaria, accessed November 4, 2019, https://www.sefaria.org/Shmonah_Kvatzim.5.51.1.

[8] See Jean-Louis Ska, "Israël et ses problèmes d'identité." *Vous serez mon peuple et je serai votre Dieu (Ez 36,28): réalisations et promesses*, ed. François Lestang (Bruxelles: Lessius, 2016), 21–51.

relativized and to a major extent replaced by the relationship of all peoples to the whole earth. Though there is no space here to enter a detailed justification of my position, I wish to offer a less linear reading. There truly is a reordering of the relation to the land and an opening to a universal dimension, already in the *Tanakh* and then in the New Testament,⁹ but this does not replace the Torah's teaching; it interprets it and deepens it. For instance, many readings of the third beatitude in Matthew, "Happy are the meek, for they shall inherit the land (*tèn gèn*)" (Mt 5:4), understand *gè* to mean the whole earth and not *Eretz Yisrael*. However, here Matthew clearly echoes Psalm 37, "the meek shall inherit the land" (37:11), where the expression "inherit the land" occurs five times and almost certainly means *Eretz Yisrael*. One may legitimately consider that the words of Jesus concern the nations and their land, but this is a second stage; the first meaning of the beatitude relates to *Am Yisrael* and their land. There is no supersessionism of the land in the New Testament, no revocation of the promises made to the people of Israel as regards the land.

How then should we understand the conversion of the people's relation to their land? A Christian can take the model of the Risen Christ to understand what this means: Christ is fully corporal, he retains his own body, but it is a transfigured body. Aquinas explains, for instance, that the risen body is substantially and numerically identical to the earthly one, but that they are in a different "disposition (*dispositio*)."¹⁰ There truly is God-given relation of the people of God to the land, to that specific land, but this relation is called to be profoundly transfigured.

For instance, there is an intimate bond between the people and the land, but one cannot put people and land at the same level. The people can be people of God outside of the land. The people of Israel are born outside of the land; they are formed through God's election and the giving of the Torah before they inhabit the land. One tribe, the Levites, does not receive any part of the land at all. The people experience exile during the biblical period and a prolonged exile and diaspora after that, during which it develops other ways of worshipping God and of observing the commandments.¹¹ This does not mean that the bond to the land is broken: Jerusalem and the land that

---

9 See Marchadour and Neuhaus, *The Land, the Bible, and History*, 47–48; 60–62.

10 See Thomas Aquinas, *Summa contra gentiles*, IV, q. 84–85.

11 Michael Wyschogrod, renowned Orthodox Jewish thinker, stresses the "ambivalence of the land in Jewish consciousness": it is "an integral part of election," but because Israel becomes a full-fledged people before its entry in the land and survives as a people after it is severed from the land, "there is a curious dispensability to the tie between Israel and the land"; "[Israel] is apparently less dependent on the land than any other people." Michael Wyschogrod, *Abraham's Promise: Judaism and Jewish-Christian Relations* (Grand Rapids, MI: Eerdmans, 2004), 92.

surrounds it continue to be the center of Jewish prayer, concern, and eschatological hope. However, in the diaspora an extraordinary wealth of cultural and religious achievements that are part of Jewish identity has been developed. The Jewish people have most often had two poles: Jerusalem and Alexandria, or Babylon, or Vilna, or New York. Without putting these at the same level, one can still assume that the balance between diaspora and living in *Eretz Yisrael* is essential and that all Jews are not called to live in the land.

More fundamentally, not setting the people and the land at the same level implies that the people are more important than the land. God inhabits the Temple and the land, but God does so to live among the people.[12] Inhabiting the land is at the service of the people and not vice versa. This means that if ever a situation comes in which one needs to choose between the land and the soul of the people, it is better to lose the people's land than to lose the people's soul, because that would mean losing the people. If living on the land puts the people's soul at risk because it leads to nationalism, oppression, or segregation, if this one day becomes clearly the case, then it means losing Judaism—and in this event, it is better to lose the land. Even more radically, this also signifies that all peoples, Jews, Palestinians, and all nations, as such, are more important than the bond of one people to their land. Never should the relationship to one's land be set at the same level, be given the same value, as the existence and dignity of a people, of any people.[13] Concretely speaking, the God-given relation of the *Am Yisrael* to *Eretz Yisrael* cannot be taken as an absolute if it is at the cost of the integrity and dignity of the Palestinian people—and reciprocally, the relation of the Palestinian people to their land is not an absolute if it puts to risk the existence and dignity of the Jewish people.

Another aspect of this renewed or transfigured relation to the land is that there are conditions for possessing the land: "If your hearts turn away

---

12 See Wyschogrod, *Abraham's Promise*, 169.

13 Interpreting God's command to annihilate the peoples that inhabited Canaan when the people of Israel conquered it is a difficult task. Interestingly, this order does not refer to all peoples. This may indicate that the main reason for destroying or banishing peoples is not to make space but to combat idolatry and child-sacrifices (see Marchadour and Neuhaus, *The Land, the Bible, and History*, 25–27). This then brings up the question of whether Christians and Muslims living today in Israel are to be considered as idolatrous. Some currents of Judaism believe so, but authoritative trends which have roots in great thinkers, such as Maimonides regarding Islam and Meiri or Rivkes regarding Christianity, distinguish between these religions and the idolatrous practices of the peoples living in Canaan in the ancient times. See Jacob Katz, *Exclusiveness and Tolerance: Studies in Jewish-Gentile Relations in Medieval and Modern Times* (New York: Schocken Books, 1961), 156–81; *Orthodox Rabbinic Statement on Christianity: To Do the Will of Our Father in Heaven: Toward a Partnership between Jews and Christians*, 2015, sec. 5, accessed November 4, 2019, http://cjcuc.org/2015/12/03/orthodox-rabbinic-statement-on-christianity/.

and you do not hear ... you shall not live long in the land" (Dt 30:18). This must be immediately nuanced because in some cases God's mercy is first and the land is given precisely for the people to purify their ways (see Dt 9:4-5). However, we have already seen that, essentially, the land is given to allow for a certain type of life, made up of worship of God, justice (*mishpat*), and righteousness (*tsedaka*). This is a constitutive part of God's design in giving the land. The Torah insists on this, and the gospels drive the point home, so to speak, precisely in the beatitude we have already evoked: "Happy are the meek, for they shall inherit the land" (Mt 5:5). The Torah comes before the land, chronologically and axiologically. In the same way as the people come before the land and are the end of the possession of the land, so do righteousness and justice. Living outside of the land according to the Torah (or, more widely speaking, ethically) is superior to living on the land in disagreement with it (or unethically). Likewise, the calling to be a blessing and a "light unto the nations" (Is 42:6; 49:6) is part of the calling of the people of Israel on the land. In the end, even though living ethically or according to the Torah and as a light to the nations is not an absolute condition for *inheriting* the land, it may well be a condition for *remaining* on the land. This means that even if the land is given by God, establishing the people on this land, or reestablishing it, is not to be considered a definitive accomplishment. The people have lost the land before, and, biblically, this is understood as a consequence of unfaithfulness. The promise is that the people will inherit the land and that even if they lose it, they will be able to come back one day; however, the promise is not that they cannot lose the land. On the contrary, it is still possible for the *Am Yisrael* to lose *Eretz Yisrael*.

The question of the borders of the land falls into the same category of notions that need to be purified or transfigured. The promises of the land which include a description of the territory given by God each entail different borders. In Genesis 15:18-21 and Joshua 1:7-8 the territory is vast and encompasses central parts of Mesopotamia and Egypt; but the territory actually taken by the Israelites in the book of Joshua is much smaller, as is the territory promised in Genesis 17:8, Deuteronomy 34:1-4, and Numbers 34:1-12. This may well mean that precise borders are not part of God's promise; they are for humans to decide, according to human rules. Perhaps this is why Abraham insists on buying a part of the land that God promises him (Gn 23:1-24): it is given by God but this does not abolish legal rights and social agreements.[14] Likewise, when the tribe of Dan does not manage to conquer and maintain the part of the land promised to them by God, they choose

---

[14] See Marchadour and Neuhaus, *The Land, the Bible, and History*, 19-20.

another, which becomes their promised land (see Jgs 18). The ultimate foundation for this is that no one possesses the land in an exclusive way; no one but God. Even those who receive the land remain "aliens": "The land shall not be sold in perpetuity, for the land is mine, with me you are but aliens and tenants" (Lv 25:23); "The Patriarchs confessed that they were strangers and foreigners on the earth" (Heb 11:13).

The fact that the borders are imprecise will also allow the New Testament to open the way for an extension of the land, represented by the passage between the witness given by the Twelve during the life of Jesus only to the house of Israel (Mt 10:6) and their witness to all the nations after Christ's resurrection (Mt 28:19–20). Interestingly an analogous theme can be found in rabbinic literature. Abraham Bar Hiyya (eleventh–twelfth century CE), for instance, explains that one possible interpretation of "When the Lord shall enlarge [the] borders [of Israel]" (Dt 12:20) is that all the earth becomes *Eretz Yisrael*.[15] The borders become, so to speak, "porous." Through *the* Holy Land, each land and the whole earth can become *a* Holy Land. Once again, this does not mean that the borders are dissolved: the whole earth is transformed through the Land of Israel, not without it, not by replacing it. If Israel is a light unto the nations, this light can and should spread outside of Israel, without ever losing Israel as its source.

THE CALLING TO A PURIFIED AND TRANSFIGURED RELATION TO THE LAND (2): SHARING THE LAND

The most burning issue today is the presence on the land of another people, the Palestinian people. In this case, especially, the notion of purification or conversion of the relation of the people to the land can be illuminating. I will argue that there is an ethical and, even more precisely, a theological meaning to the presence of the Palestinian people on a land that is also theirs. Theologically speaking, it seems to me that this presence is what the Second Vatican Council calls a "sign of the times"[16]: not simply a reality on the ground to be taken into consideration through the light of the

---

15 "The Eternal Blessed be He, dispersed Israel among the nations in all the habitations of the world so that in the time to come, as they rise from their tombs, they will sit in their places and settle all the habitations of the world; and all the lands of the world will be called *Eretz Yisrael*. Or, *Eretz Yisrael* will enlarge itself so much until it fills all the world." Abraham Bar Hiyya, *Megillat Ha-Megalleh* [The Scroll of the Revealer], ed. Z. Paznansky and Y. Guttman (Berlin: Mekitzi Nirdamim, 1924), 109–10.

16 See Vatican Council II, *Gaudium et Spes*, no. 4 (December 7, 1965).

Revelation—even though doing so is already sound theological practice—but more precisely a God-given reality through which God chooses to speak to mankind. In this case, I believe, this sign of the times can be interpreted as a divine mandate to *share* the land.

How can I say this? A sign of the times needs to be founded on Scripture and, in turn, needs to illuminate Scripture. There are biblical precedents for sharing the land. This sharing can be part of God's design as a temporary test, as is the case with the continuing presence of Jebusites who lived in Jerusalem: "In order to test Israel, whether or not they would take care to walk in the way of the Lord as their ancestors did, the Lord had left those nations [in Jerusalem], not driving them out at once, and had not handed them over to Joshua" (Jgs 2:22–23; see also Jo 15:63). More radically, it is impressive to see that this cohabitation exists from the beginning and in a peaceful way. One of the first things that Abraham does upon reentering Canaan is to share it with Lot, letting the latter choose the part he wants, which is the most fruitful one (see Gn 13:5–12). Let us note that Lot is Abraham's nephew, not part of the descendants to whom the land is promised. Conversely the presence of the Palestinian people illuminates this first Abrahamic sharing, confirming that it was not only the fruit of historical contingency but that it may well be one of the conditions according to which God gives the land, or one of the ends for which God gives it. If one considers that *Eretz Yisrael* is promised by God to God's chosen people, can one truly imagine that the presence of another people on the land is purely contingent? We will come back to the question of discerning God's action in the ingathering of the Jewish people on the land in the twentieth century, but if one asserts that God's hand is at work there, then the presence of the Palestinian people cannot be exterior to God's design.

For this reason, it seems coherent to interpret both the scriptural foundation and the historical situation as a form of divine calling to a transfigured relation to the land that makes it a "land-to-be-shared." God really does give the land, but God gives it to two peoples, precisely to be shared. God gives it for the full protection, subsistence, and development of the people of Israel, but also for their coexistence with another people. This means that there is a similar call for the Palestinian people: their presence is legitimate, they also have a God-given right to full protection, subsistence, and development—and they are likewise called to share. The legitimate presence of two peoples on one land is a test for the people of God, as it is for the Palestinian people. No other people takes the place of Israel as people of God; no other people receive the land as their promised land, according to a divine word revealed in the Bible. However, there is a mysteriously unique place for the Palestinian people in the history of salvation: to be the people with whom Israel shares the land of the promise; to be the people who share the land with Israel; to be associated in a special way with the chosen people. This does not define any precise political solution: there are different ways to share a land and, as was already the case for the determination of borders, this pertains to the realm of human decisions, agreements, and, hopefully, creative thinking. However, the fullness of God's design, the eschatologically transfigured relation of *Am Yisrael* to *Eretz Yisrael*, implies giving access to the land to others. As Ezekiel underlines in a prophetic vision, resident strangers will not only be welcome but will even be given land in the same way as the tribes of Israel: "The [resident aliens] shall be to you as citizens of Israel; with you they shall be allotted an inheritance among the tribes of Israel" (Ez 47:22). The idea here is not that Palestinians are "resident aliens"—the land is also theirs—but just to underline that the biblical promises comprise the full acceptance of others receiving the land in inheritance.

Obviously, this renewed relation to the land, especially if it includes sharing it, is hugely demanding. It may be perceived as requiring the unacceptable—both by Jews and Palestinians. It is not something either could wish for naturally and spontaneously. Even more, in the light of the present situation, it will seem quite unrealistic. Divine calling often asks for a step into the unplanned, the unknown, the seemingly undesirable and impossible in human terms. It requires purification, conversion and a deep transformation of human mind and heart. In Christian terms, it requires the God-given gift of grace and can only be fully realized eschatologically.

However, another difficulty of my proposal is that a theological reflection of this kind written by a Catholic theologian can understandably be seen as an illegitimate exterior intervention. Indeed, my intention is to contribute to a Catholic theological understanding of *Eretz Yisrael*—as the central paradigm of the transfigured body of the Risen Christ well shows. Even if most of my reasoning is based on an attentive reading of the Old Testament, many Jewish thinkers would strongly object to a "theologized" notion of sharing the land, even more than a political or ethical one. A poignant text by Zvi Yehuda Kook, son of the first chief rabbi of Palestine, Rav Abraham Isaak Kook, and leading thinker in the field of Zionism, expresses the pain caused to him by the division of the land. In 1967, he recalls his conflicting emotions in 1948 as people celebrate the news of the UN resolution in favor of the establishment of the modern State of Israel:

> When the People streamed into the streets to celebrate and rejoice, I could not go out and join in the jubilation. I sat alone and silent; a burden lay upon me. During those first hours I could not resign myself to what had been done. I could not accept the fact that indeed 'they have ... divided My

land' (Joel 4:2)! Yes [and now after nineteen years] where is our Hebron—have we forgotten her?! Where is our Shechem, our Jericho,—where?!—Have we forgotten them?! And all that lies beyond the Jordan—each and every clod of earth, every region, hill, valley, every plot of land, that is part of *Eretz Yisrael*—have we the right to give up even one grain of the land of God?! On that night, nineteen years ago, during those hours, as I sat trembling in every limb of my body, wounded, cut, torn to pieces—I could not then rejoice.[17]

However, there also are serious scholars in the Jewish world who offer reflections that confirm the centrality of the Palestinian question and the necessity to interpret it not only on a strictly political-social level, but also as a religious question. The French Jewish philosopher and sociologist Shmuel Trigano, a Zionist, underlines this: "How can one address the Palestinian question as a question which is at the heart of the answer offered by political Zionism (*Comment penser la question palestinienne au cœur de la réponse sioniste politique*)? . . . The [Palestinian] question needs to be heard as bearing claims as important and as pressing as the hope offered by the idea of returning to Zion."[18] For Trigano it is not only a practical problem posed to the institutions of the State of Israel, but it questions the "Jewish identity" itself.[19] Although it is basically a new situation in Jewish history, it brings to light a fundamental Levitical aspect of Jewish identity, its radical mobility, which prevents it from ever being weighed down by being too strongly rooted in and glued onto a *humus*.[20] Concretely, the Palestinian presence

---

17 Zvi Yehuda Kook, "On the 19th Anniversary of Israel's Independence Weeks Before the Unification of Yerushalaim," accessed October 26th, 2019, http://www.israel613.com/books/ERETZ_ANNIVERSARY_KOOK.pdf.

18 Shmuel Trigano, "Lettre 48 sur la paix et les Palestiniens," *Un exil sans retour? Lettres à un Juif égaré* (Paris: Stock, 1996), 329.

19 See Trigano, *Un exil sans retour?*, 334.

20 "This part of [Jewish identity] is precisely that which is borne by the tribe of the Levites in the midst of the people of Israel: it is the mobile element that sets a limit to the people being rooted in the humus of the land (*l'enracinement dans la glèbe*), that maintains the memory of the origin and orients towards the future times." Trigano, *Un exil sans retour?*, 332. This is similar to the thesis expounded by Amnon Raz-Krakotzkin, according to which exile is the cornerstone of Jewish identity. See Amnon Raz-Krakotzkin, *The Scaffolding of Sovereignty: Global and Aesthetic Perspectives on the History of a Concept* (New York: Columbia University Press, 2017), 393–419. "Exile" here is defined as being a minority stance in a dominant order; inside the order but at a critical distance. It is a concept with a theological dimension because it stresses that the present order is in need of redemption and that one should never become fully rooted in it and consider it whole and accomplished. From this point of view, one can and should be "in exile" also on *Eretz Yisrael*. Raz-Krakotzkin's thesis is too one-sided—reducing Judaism to exile is dangerous—but it does bring to light an essential characteristic of Jewish identity.

is a call to accomplish the vocation of Israel to *shalom* and reveals what is true peace, which cannot happen against or without the "other," the former enemy, but only by giving space to this other: "Peace, *shalom*, is not the reign of absence of trouble, serenity and silence. Peace is full of noise and debates because to make peace is precisely to make space for the 'other'. Peace, the unity given by peace, is not total but rather it is dual."[21] Obviously, making space for others implies a form of self-sacrifice, and Trigano is clear about this as well: "If the 'other' is to survive as such in the situation of peace, there needs to be a certain degree of gift, of gratuity, of loss (which infringe on the integrity of the subject and opens the subject to the 'other')."[22] This loss, however, leads to growth and true fecundity.

Another author who can help give some traction to the idea of sharing the land from a Jewish perspective is Franco-Israeli Rabbi David Meyer. He expounds the notion of "partial voluntary exile of sovereignty," through which the people can choose to give up a measure of the sovereignty on the land that has been rightfully given to them, with the aim of "inventing a new modality of relation to the land."[23] As a scholar of rabbinic literature, Meyer grounds the legitimacy of giving up sovereignty on the halachic notions of *hefker*, according to which the property of an object can be abandoned to another, and *hekdesh*, according to which an object or property can be given up so as to be dedicated to a sacred (Temple) usage.[24] Declaring an object *hekdesh* can be done by an individual but also, collectively, by a rabbinic tribunal. Meyer's proposal is more radical than mine, because he applies these expressions to Jerusalem to stress that all parties could so to speak "give up" their claim to sovereignty over the city so as to restore its potential of holiness. This is not what I intend. However, the idea that *halakha* regulates the voluntary giving up of property and that this can have religious reasons shows that the Abrahamic sharing of the land promised to him with Lot need not be an exception. Meyer stresses that some realities should be considered as outside of the framework of possession, as an expression of the existence

---

21 Trigano, *Un exil sans retour?*, 335.

22 Trigano, *Un exil sans retour?*, 335.

23 See David Meyer, Michel Remaud, and Tareq Oubrou, *La Vocation de la Terre sainte: un juif, un chrétien, un musulman s'interrogent* (Bruxelles: Lessius, 2014), 80. Meyer grounds the voluntary dimension of sharing the Holy Land on Irving Greenberg's idea that after Auschwitz, Judaism has entered into a third phase of its history, in which Jews are invited to assume more responsibility in the Covenant, which becomes a "voluntary Covenant." See Irving Greenberg, *The Third Great Cycle of Jewish History: Voluntary Covenant: The Third Era of Jewish History, Power and Politics* (New York: CLAL, National Jewish Center for Learning and Leadership, 1988), 8–9.

24 See Meyer, Remaud, and Oubrou, *La Vocation de la Terre sainte*, 83.

of a common good, the essence of which is to be sharable and shared. This is similarly expounded by Gershom Scholem:

> Every object confined to the dimensions of time and space carries with it the characteristic of ownership, which reflects its temporality. Possession, however, caught as it is in the same finiteness, is always unjust. It is for this reason that no system based on possession, regardless of how it is built, can lead to justice. *Justice, rather, lies in the nature of an object that cannot be possessed.* This alone is the object through which other objects become freed of ownership.[25]

The idea here is not to recuse possession or private property but to stress the priority of the common good and the fact that some significant realities transcend possession. This could well be the case of *Eretz Yisrael*.

A CALLING FOR ALL NATIONS

Once again, this call to a renewed relation to the land is challenging for *Am Yisrael*, as it is for the Palestinian people. It sets them in a unique situation. However, this uniqueness is not a call to exceptionalism: what is at stake concerns the whole of humanity. If truly the people of Israel are called to be a "light unto the nations," this means that both the intimate bond between the people and the land and the conversion of this relation are a calling for all peoples. *Am Yisrael* is unique but its role is to show the way to all.

God's promise of a land to God's people testifies that each people is related to a land. Living on a land in peace and self-determination is part of full peoplehood and offers the possibility of welcoming salvation in a full manner, i.e., salvation that touches and heals and eventually transfigures all dimensions of the human being, including the most corporal and corporate, such as history, culture, society, economy, and politics. Of course, this implies that all peoples should have a land—it is a call for justice in this regard for the different peoples who today are denied this fundamental heritage. It is also the foundation, at a more individual level, for love of one's homeland or land of adoption, which is not to be immediately equated to and rejected as a form of nationalism. Nationalism is the perversion of a legitimate deep-set desire of living with others on a land to build a society, and of the corporal relation to one's environment. Land is thus part of the

---

[25] Gershom Scholem, *Lamentations of Youth: The Diaries of Gershom Scholem*, ed. A. D. Skinner (Cambridge, MA: Belknap Press of Harvard University Press, 2007), 142. Quoted by D. Meyer during a private conversation.

promise of God for each people—whether we consider the Jewish people, the Palestinian people, or any other.

However, God's gift is also a calling, and a saving act, which in itself purifies (or should purify, if received in the right way) the relationship to the land. Like *Am Yisrael*, each and every people is called to a transfigured relation to its land, precisely as the other side of the coin of this full salvation. In this renewed relation to the land, the people, and all other peoples, are more important than the land. Justice, welcoming the poor and the alien, are always a priority over possessing the land. Likewise, the land is a place of subsistence and protection, but it is in a deeper way a place given to live ethically and religiously. Boundaries are not to be dissolved; nevertheless, they are called to be open. They offer security, but they can and should also be points of contact, of exchange, and passageways between peoples and cultures. In the end, land is given both for self-determination and for sharing, both as a refuge for a people and to enable this people to offer refuge to others. God's gifts are also tests, invitations to conversion. Relation to their land represents for each people a constant challenge, because it is a constant call for coexistence and sharing: sharing with those who have nothing, sharing with those who are alien, sharing with other people(s).

In the end, the present situation in the Holy Land is not only a local issue but a sign and challenge for all peoples: "Such a complex situation should provoke us into inventing novel political solutions.... Is a new way of coexisting between peoples fermenting here? Such is the virtual backdrop of the crisis in the Middle-East. Judea-Samaria or the West Bank may well be this *locus* of transition for the international political order where new relations between nations will be invented."[26] The specific way in which *Eretz Yisrael* is given to *Am Yisrael* illuminates the true meaning of a people's relation to the land. It helps understand what truly is a homeland. It is thus part of the "blessing for all the families of the earth" promised to Abraham and his descendants.

CRITERIA FOR DISCERNMENT OF THE MEANING OF THE INGATHERING OF THE JEWISH PEOPLE IN *ERETZ YISRAEL* IN THE TWENTIETH CENTURY

From a theological point of view, probably the most difficult question related to *Eretz Yisrael* is how to understand the ingathering of the Jewish people on the land of their forefathers during the twentieth century. Is it simply a human endeavor? Or is God's hand to be seen at work? Could it even be

---

26 Trigano, *Un exil sans retour?*, 334–35.

the messianic realization of God's promises? These are not exactly the same questions, but they are related, and I will consider them together. I cannot develop a full answer within the limits of the present paper, because it is not a direct part of the question "Why does God give a land?" However, I will simply explore whether the reflections expounded so far offer some criteria to approach these issues. Indeed, the main difficulty here is that we are not dealing with the biblical text or with theological-ethical-political notions related to peoplehood and land, but with history. That God can and does act in history, i.e., that there is a Salvation History, is foundational to Jewish and Christian teaching. However, history is messy and determining what is from God or not is in no way an exact science. It asks for an art, the art of discernment. This is why the first step is to uncover some criteria for discernment.

If the relation to *Eretz Yisrael* is part of the identity of *Am Yisrael* as a people; if subsistence and self-determination on the land is the framework of their relation to God, of the full practice of the Torah, and of the fullness of salvation; then the ingathering of the Jewish people on the land may possibly be the result of providence and even the fulfillment of the promises. Moreover, one key notion in our reflection has been that of the signs of the times—events through which God speaks to mankind. Now if the presence of the Palestinian people can be a sign of this kind, so can the ingathering of the Jewish people. To a certain extent one cannot separate these two realities: both are to be referred to providence, or neither is. A sign of the times needs scriptural bases, and indeed, in many ways the ingathering of the twentieth century echoes the promises of the *Tanakh*. From a Christian point of view, the fact that the New Testament does not invalidate the promises of the land confirms this.

Naturally, Christian theology often has a difficulty in principle with the idea of an earthly messianic accomplishment of the promises regarding a specific land. Does it not infringe on the unicity and fullness of Jesus Christ's messiahship? Does it not reduce the completeness and universality of salvation to an earthly and singular dimension? I believe the contrary is true: precisely because Jesus has inaugurated the messianic ages, other realizations of these ages can come to be. The Catholic Church teaches, following Paul, that the gifts and promises of God are irrevocable (see Rom 11:29) and that "the Old Covenant [was] never revoked by God."[27] The accomplishment of

---

[27] John Paul II, *Speech to the Representatives of the Jewish People in Mainz*, November 17, 1980. See also *Catechism of the Catholic Church* 121; Commission for Religious Relations with the Jews, *"The Gifts and the Calling of God Are Irrevocable" (Rom 11:29): A Reflection on Theological Questions Pertaining to Catholic–Jewish Relations on the Occasion of the 50th Anniversary of "Nostra Aetate,"* (2015).

the promises to those who remain God's chosen people is coherent with the messiahship of Christ. Moreover, the reflections expounded above underline to what extent the fullness of salvation includes the corporal and corporate. To resist salvation that truly touches and transforms this world may well be a form of unconscious Gnosticism. And what is realized for *Am Yisrael* as the chosen people of God, as we have also insisted, is to the benefit of all nations. For these reasons, a full Christian eschatology needs to include these promises and the final ingathering of the chosen people in the Holy Land. From all these points of view, Catholic theology can discern that God's hand is possibly at work in the ingathering of the twentieth century and that it may be an accomplishment of the promises.

However, two difficulties arise. The first one is that, although the ingathering is part of the messianic promises, these promises clearly have not been entirely fulfilled. All suffering, injustice, and war have not disappeared. The majority of Jewish inhabitants in *Eretz Yisrael*, to name only these, do not live according to the Torah. Israel, as a country, is not perceived, not massively at least, as a light for the nations. One clearly cannot say that the full and effective realization of the messianic promises has been brought by or is encapsulated in the ingathering of the Jewish people on the land of their forefathers. The situation is strangely similar to that of Christianity when confronted with the same promises of the Old Testament: they are not all effectively realized by Jesus Christ and will only be so at the Second Coming. There is an "already" but also a "not yet" of redemption. Likewise, can we say, as many disciples of Rav Kook now do,[28] that it is just the beginning of the redemption? This is more acceptable than considering it a fully effective accomplishment, but it calls for one important reservation: as said above when examining the ethical conditions for remaining on the land, *Am Yisreal* can lose *Eretz Yisrael*. This possibility is still real today. Because of this, one cannot consider the ingathering as the irreversibly definitive realization of this messianic dimension. It is thus difficult to conceive that the fullness of messianic existence on *Eretz Yisrael* will evolve smoothly and naturally, in pure continuity from the present situation, without some degree of rupture and without further special eschatological divine intervention. In the end, the ingathering may possibly be the first step of the messianic accomplishment of the promises, but certainly not their full, effective and definitive realization.

The second difficulty is a more obvious and a more burning one. If the ingathering of *Am Yisrael* on *Eretz Yisrael* is a realization of the messianic

---

[28] Thinkers such as Ben-Zion Bokser or Bezalel Naor, for instance.

promise of the land, or at least an act of divine providence, how can it imply so much suffering for the Palestinian people? How can something related to God in favor of one people provoke so much evil for another? We are confronted with a true mystery, or at least a major problem. In front of this it is comprehensible that many consider that God cannot have anything to do with these events. At the very least, it is clear that there can be no satisfying response to the question of a possible theological meaning of the ingathering of the Jewish people on the Holy Land without finding an adequate response to the suffering of the Palestinian people.

One way of understanding the difficulty posed by Palestinian suffering is that God's hand has truly been at work in the ingathering, but that the human response and involvement have fully or partially contradicted God's design. Providence entails both divine and human involvement, and human incomprehension and sin can impede God's action and render it unsuccessful. This latter view is quite coherent with all I have argued above. The gift of the land is not simply a gift, but also a calling and a challenge. It is a test—for both the Jewish and the Palestinian peoples. For something that is initially inspired or originated by God to be fully considered an act of providence or a realization of the promises, it also needs to correspond to God's design in its human development. Discernment is not only to be held about the past but also about the present and the future: "each tree is known by its own fruit" (Mt 7:44).[29] The questions about the events of the twentieth century become questions about the whole process and concern to a certain extent the twenty-first century more than the twentieth.

In this discernment the different dimensions of the renewed relation to the land expounded above can offer precious criteria. Will *Am Yisrael* resist idolatry of the land and set the people's soul and the people(s) above possession of the land? Will *Am Yisrael* live ethically on the land—and possibly according to the Torah? Will it be possible for the borders to be an open place of exchange? Will it be possible to share the land with the poor and the stranger—and more specifically and in an institutional way, with the Palestinian people? Naturally, all this is not possible to achieve without the active constructive involvement of the Palestinian people, and the last question in particular needs to be posed to them as well. My position is not

---

29 Ignatius of Loyola is one of the main thinkers on discernment in Catholic spiritual tradition, and he stresses that it is not possible to pose a full discernment about a decision or an act without evaluating it according to its consequences and concrete fruitfulness. See Ignatius of Loyola, "Spiritual Exercises," *Spiritual Exercises and Selected Works*, ed. G. E. Ganss (New York: Paulist Press, 1991), 205–7; Letter 169, "To the Fathers and Scholastics at Coimbra," May 7, 1547, *Letters and Instructions*, ed. M. Palmer, J. W. Padberg, and J. L. McCarthy (Saint Louis, MO: Institute of Jesuit Sources, 2006), 165–75.

particularly original, since thinkers like M. Wyschogrod also point in this direction: "Does this return [of the people of Israel on their land] signal the beginning of the redemption promised by God or is it an act of will resulting from impatience and the secularization of Jewish consciousness? These are difficult questions to answer and will ultimately be answered by history."[30] However, the idea of a converted and renewed relation to the land offers some precise criteria for this answer "by history." Moreover, it helps us understand that the timeframe is not only history, but also eschatology, since the full accomplishment of the promises, including the manner of inhabiting the land which corresponds to God's design, will only be fully realized eschatologically.

After this short exposition it is not possible to conclude in a fully satisfactory manner about what theological reading to give of the ingathering of *Am Yisrael* on *Eretz Yisrael* during the twentieth century. It would ask for a more in-depth theological reflection on the history of salvation and divine providence, for instance. However, I believe we have come to some clarity and that it is possible to make three statements. Two extremes should be ruled out. On the one hand, one cannot say that it is the full, effective, and definitive fulfillment of the messianic promises of the *Tanakh*. On the other hand, neither can one say that considering it as a first step of this fulfillment, or at least as divine providence, is impossible in the light of Catholic faith. It may well be from God; it may well be a messianic reality. A third aspect completes the latter: one cannot make a full and final judgment without considering the long-term fruit of the ingathering, on an historical and on an eschatological level. Have I eluded the difficulty of taking a position by delaying a possible answer until later times and until the *eschaton*? To avoid doing this I will propose a fourth affirmation: attaining a solution to the Palestinian question that would offer a just solution for both the Jewish and the Palestinian peoples could be considered a major sign (though never an apodictic one) that the ingathering is providential and perhaps messianic. Although the Palestinian question does not encapsulate the whole calling of *Am Yisrael* on *Eretz Yisrael*, it is central, and it is a major obstacle to seeing God's hand in the events of the twentieth century. In a way, one could say that the question is no longer: "*Was* or *is* the ingathering divine providence?", but: "*Will we be able to make* the ingathering *correspond to* divine providence?"

* * * * *

---

30 Wyschogrod, *Abraham's Promise*, 102–3.

Why does God promise a land? God does so to offer to *Am Yisrael* and to all nations the fullness of salvation, which is corporate and corporal and includes an intrinsic relation to a land and all that a land allows for. However, God gives a land also to impart to God's people and to all nations a purified and "saved" relation to the land, which is an equally central dimension of the fullness of salvation. The model, effective source, and accomplishment of this is the risen body of the Lord: a true body, Jesus' body, which retains the traces of its history, but exists according to a renewed, transfigured, mode of being.

The question "why?" was a detour, similar to the detour Moses chose to take to reach the burning bush (see Ex 3:3). Has this detour helped obtain some clarity concerning the three theological questions posed at the start of this paper? I believe so, even if they are but modest steps. Understanding the reason for the gift of the land to *Am Yisrael* helps to discern that this truly is the teaching of the Scriptures, but also that it is more than a simple gift: it is a calling and a challenge. This reorients the first question: it does not suffice to ask whether the land is promised, but one also needs to ask how the promise should be received. Likewise, understanding how important the land is for the chosen people to fulfill their calling, but understanding it precisely as a calling and a test, allows us to determine criteria to discern the meaning of the ingathering of the Jewish people on *Eretz Yisrael* in the twentieth century. The hand of God may well be at work, and it may be the (non-definitive) beginning of the fulfillment of the messianic promises, but this will only be confirmed by history (and in the *eschaton*), through the extent to which the renewed relation to the land will become effective. Finally, in this perspective, the Palestinian people take on a central dimension in a theological approach to the relation of *Am Yisrael* to *Eretz Yisrael*, because they can be understood as a sign of the times indicating God's calling to the transfigured relation to land, and because a just solution for both peoples to the Israeli-Palestinian conflict is one of the surest signs that the ingathering is indeed providential.

The threefold task of a Catholic theology of *Eretz Yisrael* is to take into consideration the biblical promises made to *Am Yisrael*, to apply serious discernment to the ingathering of the Jewish people in the twentieth century, and to perceive the full theological significance of the presence of the Palestinian people on the land—without confusing these questions, but without ever separating them either.

3

THE RELATIONSHIP OF ISRAEL TO THE PROMISED LAND AFTER CHRIST
CATHOLIC QUESTIONINGS

Jean-Miguel Garrigues, OP
Eliana Kurylo, CB

At first sight at least, the silence of the New Testament on the subject of what happens to the Land of Israel in the fulfillment of the promises is very striking. When in a key passage Paul specifies, in a long list that could be considered exhaustive, the privileges that still belong to that part of the people of Israel who have not believed in Christ, he mentions "the sonship, the glory, the covenants, the giving of the law, the worship, and the promises; to them belong the patriarchs" (Rom 9:4), but not the land, as one might have expected. At least explicitly, for from a Jewish point of view the land is normally included under the heading of "the promises." It is furthermore difficult to understand as applying to the Land of Israel expressions of Christ so universal in scope as "All authority in heaven and on earth[1] has been given to me. Go therefore and make disciples of all nations..." (Mt 28:18–19), "The Son of man has authority on earth to forgive sins" (Mk 2:10), or "When the Son of man comes, will he find faith on earth" (Lk 18:8). One finds the same universal meaning in numerous other references to the earth and land in the rest of the New Testament (cf. Rom 9:17, 9:28; 10:18; 1 Cor 10:26; Eph 4:9; Col 3:2; Js 5:5 and many passages in the book of Revelation). Certainly, the

---

[1] In the French original, *terre* (earth), as γῆ in New Testament Greek, means indistinctly "earth" and "land."

New Testament uses the term "Land of Israel" (Mt 2:20–21) as well as similar expressions (cf. Mt 2:6; 4:15). But, when one examines the context, these passages are concerned to designate geographical territories by the name which was theirs (cf. Jn 3:22) or they are references to the promise of the Land of Israel in the Old Testament (cf. Acts 7:3–4, 13:19; Heb 11:9), without anything being said to us about its fulfillment in the New Covenant.

The firm silence of the New Testament on what happens after Christ to God's promise of the Land of Israel is one of the reasons that leads the Catholic Church to a great reserve with regard to any "divine right" of Israel to the Promised Land. Ze'ev Safrai, in his historical-literary research *Seeking out the Land*, emphasizes that:

> The religious and literary symbols of the sanctity attributed to the Land draw upon the sanctity of Jerusalem. . . . The Land is hallowed not only because of the presence of the holy city in its midst; rather the sanctity of the latter apparently infuses the entire Land. The sanctity of Jerusalem in the Second Temple period constituted the model of thought and the nucleus of beliefs concerning the sanctity of the Land.[2] . . . The centrality of Jerusalem is in fact emphasized in the basic tradition contained in all the Gospels and is one of its central tenets. As in the majority of Second Temple writings, the Gospels stress the sanctity of Jerusalem, but they are silent about the sanctity of the Land of Israel.[3]

The clearest reference to the Land of Israel in the New Testament, even if it is indirectly expressed, is found in the eschatological discourse of Jesus in St. Luke. Christ announces the capture of Jerusalem and a new exile of the people in relation to the land: "For great distress shall be upon *the land*[4] and wrath upon this people; they will fall by the edge of the sword and be led captive among all nations . . ." (Lk 21:23–24). It is clear that here "the earth" can only be the land of "this people" whose members will be "led captive among all nations." It therefore concerns a prophecy of the second

---

[2] Ze'ev Safrai, *Seeking out the Land: Land of Israel Traditions in Ancient Jewish Christian and Samaritan Literature 200 BCE–400 CE* (Boston: Leiden and Brill, 2018), 224. This is also one of the main arguments in the excellent book of Mark Kinzer, *Jerusalem Crucified, Jerusalem Risen: The Resurrected Messiah, the Jewish People and the Land of Promise* (Eugene: Cascade Books, 2018).

[3] Safrai, *Seeking out the Land*, 232. For further reading on this subject, see William David Davies, *The Gospel and the Land: Early Christianity and Jewish Territorial Doctrine* (Berkley: University California Press, 1974); and David Flusser, *Jerusalem in the Literature of the Second Temple* (Grand Rapids, MI: Eerdmans, 1984).

[4] We have here replaced the word "earth" by the word "land" in the English translation we are using (NSV).

and more complete diaspora of the people of Israel, which took place after the Second Jewish War of 135 CE. But it is the next part of the prophecy of Jesus which is the most significant and astonishing in this New Testament passage: "... and Jerusalem will be trodden down by the Gentiles, until the times of the Gentiles are fulfilled" (Lk 21:24). Let us first note that the mention of Jerusalem confirms that the earth here in question is truly the Land of Israel, of which Jerusalem is the head and the center. We are going to see later what is meant first by "Jerusalem trodden down by the Gentiles," and then by "until the times of the Gentiles are fulfilled."

At the time of the entry of the people of Israel into the Promised Land, God fulfills his promise in giving them every place on which their feet had trod. This significant expression recurs several times in Deuteronomy and in the book of Joshua. "Every place on which the sole of your foot treads shall be yours" (Dt 11:24; cf. 1:36). "Every place that the sole of your foot will tread upon I have given to you" (Jo 1:3). "Surely the land on which your foot has trodden shall be an inheritance for you" (Jo 14:9). The expression "trodden under foot" is thus well in line with the gift of the Promised Land to Israel in the Hebrew Bible.

In this same Hebrew Bible or Old Testament, God is going to use this same expression to signify that to punish his people he will cause his land to be "trodden under foot" by the pagan nations. In relation no doubt to the Assyrian invasion of Sennacherib in 701 BCE, Isaiah said: "When the oppressor is no more, and destruction has ceased, and he who tramples under foot has vanished from the land" (Is 16:4). It is a reminder that the same God who has given the Promised Land to his people can, to punish them, cause them to be trodden under foot by the pagan nations. That is why at the time of the profanation of Jerusalem and of the Temple by Antiochus Epiphanes in 167 BCE the First Book of Maccabees uses the same expression. "The sanctuary [of Jerusalem] was trampled down" (1 Mc 3:45). "Thy sanctuary is trampled down and profaned" (1 Mc 3:51). When the Maccabees had the walls of Jerusalem rebuilt, they did it "to keep the Gentiles from coming and trampling them down as they had done before" (1 Mc 4:60). The word of Jesus in St. Luke depends directly on this existing biblical tradition. The members of the people, punished by God "because you did not know the time of your visitation" (Lk 19:44), are going to be "led captive in among all nations and Jerusalem will be trodden down by the Gentiles" (Lk 21:24; see Daniel 8:13, which is the basis for the language of "trampling" in 1 Maccabees).[5]

---

5 Some of the Jewish apocryphal writings also use the imagery of punishment and God's impartial justice even toward his beloved people but also in the spirit of optimism and hope of Jerusalem being rebuilt in the future. See Michael E. Stone, "Reactions to Destructions of the Second Temple," *Journal for the Study of Judaism* 12, no. 2 (1981): 195–204; and Kenneth R. Jones, *Jewish*

But this situation of deportation outside the Promised Land is not definitive, for it has a limit that God has fixed in his providential design: "until the times of the Gentiles are fulfilled." The times in question here (καιροί in Greek) are the moments of grace that God destines for the pagans for their conversion (cf. Mt 24:14). St. Luke mentions here the word of Jesus that Paul would announce and that is the basis for what he himself reveals in the letter to the Romans: "A hardening has come upon part of Israel, until the full number of the Gentiles come in, and so all Israel will be saved" (Rom 11:25–26). The end of the "times of the pagans" corresponds to the salvation of all Israel and to the "deliverance of Jerusalem" (Lk 2:38), which can no longer be "trodden down by the pagans." The same expression of a domination of Jerusalem by the pagans during a time limited by God is found in the book of Revelation: "the nations . . . will trample over the holy city for forty-two months" (Rv 11:2).

Does this mean that for Catholics the return of the people of Israel to the land promised by God to Abraham and "to his posterity . . . forever" (Gn 13:15) and the words "I have given this land to your descendants . . ." (Gn 15:8) can be perceived only as a secular event, without any religious meaning in the providential design of God? The Jewish commentaries on these well-known verses explain the ownership of the Promised Land and the time of the Gentiles in the following way:

> The permanent acquisition of the Land of Israel by the Jewish people is God's will. From the moment He created the world He already intended that the Jewish people inherit the Land. . . . Temporarily, however, He allowed non-Jewish nations to occupy it. . . . The Land of Israel acquired its sanctity when it was conquered by Joshua. This sanctity did not persist because it was the result of a war. Consequently, when the Land was taken from them (the 1st destruction of Jerusalem and the conquest of Judah by Babylon), the initial effects of the conquest were annulled. When, upon the return of the exiles, Ezra consecrated the Land, he did not do so with war, but with legal acquisition . . . and thus it remains sanctified to this day. . . . A later military conquest by non-Jewish nations would not interfere with the sanctity of the Land, because the mechanism by which the sanctity was conferred was by forging a bond with the Land though settling in it. . . . The Land of Israel will be occupied in its entirety in the Messianic Era.[6]

Reactions to the Destruction of Jerusalem in A.D. 70: Apocalypses and Related Pseudepigrapha, Supplements to the Journal for the Study of Judaism 151 (Leiden: Brill, 2011).

6 *The Five Books of the Torah with Commentary from Classic Rabbinic Texts* (New York: Kol Menachem and Gutnick, 2006), 83–85.

The authority of the Catholic Church does not say anything in advance about the near future of the divine plan, which only reveals itself as it is accomplished in history. A great majority of Christians—a minority among the Catholics and the Orthodox in Europe—think that the return of Israel to the Promised Land belongs in a certain way to God's governance, in a much more indirect and even paradoxical way nevertheless than the sacred history of the Bible, such as we find it for example in the book of Joshua or Ezra. Hence their reticence in regard to any fundamentalist interpretation of the Zionist project and its realization in Israel since 1947, such as they see to be very widespread in Evangelical Protestantism often trying to help to hasten the above-mentioned Messianic Era by concrete material actions and encouraging the Diaspora Jews' return to the Land of Israel.

This, however, has not prevented the recognition of the State of Israel, for that has been done on the secular grounds of the legitimacy that international law guarantees to a state whose existence was determined by the international community through the United Nations and whose borders came to be peacefully accepted in law or de facto by her neighbors. That should not in any way prevent the Catholic Church from recognizing the religious obligation that the Law of Moses imposes on the practicing Jew to live and to worship first of all in the Land of Israel. Such recognition implies that the Law of Moses legitimately entails religious obligations on Jews, even Jewish believers, after the death and resurrection of Jesus, and that the Land of Israel retains a special sacred status in the post-Ascension era. Biblical Israel had also been able to do this for six centuries, in the epoch of the Second Temple, from 538 BCE to 135 CE.

In other respects, European Catholics are tormented by a bad conscience that awakens in them the reproach regularly addressed to them by the Arabs whom they had formerly colonized: after the Second World War, the Westerners would have allowed the State of Israel to be established at the cost of the Palestinians because they wanted to be freed from the fault of having made life impossible for the Jews in Christian Europe by a rejection that had led to the *Shoah*. Had not Theodor Herzl had the idea of a national Jewish state while he was in Paris, the capital of the nation of the rights of man, where he witnessed the degradation of Captain Dreyfus? This all helps to explain the attitude of "wait and see" of a majority of Catholics (perhaps with the exception of the USA) with regard to the present-day development of the people of Israel in the Promised Land, while two small minorities among them oppose one another sharply in the name respectively of a fundamentalist Zionism and of a pro-Palestinian "liberation theology."

What are those two opposing trends whose ideas have influenced some of the Catholic and Protestant theologians and writers? Faydra Shapiro, one of the co-editors and contributors to this volume, gives the following explanation of Christian Zionism in her book under the same title:

> Christian Zionism is a general label for a specific orientation and emphasis within evangelicalism that ascribes vital theological, and often eschatological, importance to the Jews living in Israel.... Christian Zionists see their own solidarity with the Jews and the modern nation-state of Israel to be a matter of paying homage to the God of Israel and honoring his priorities and promises.... [The movement, however,] is highly controversial and vilified from many corners at a time when Israel faces severe criticism around the world for its treatment of Palestinians and its approach to the issue of Palestinian statehood.[7]

On the other side of the Israeli society, the difficult socio-political context, the wars, the regular outbursts of violence, and the general feeling of discrimination by the Arab population in the newly created State of Israel contributed to a new theological reflection. According to pro-Palestinian theologians:

> The Jews are a people chosen by God, a consecrated people, a nation of priests, whose vocation is to live out in their own history, the history of the whole of humanity. In this way, the Jewish people is prophetic, a witness of God among the nations, chosen to serve the "Salvation of Humanity" rather than to establish itself in any particular national way.... What is the solution for the Palestinian people? First of all, it lies in the Christian uncovering of the true vocation of the Jews, that is, spirit rather than nation building and in the integration of Jewish citizens by all nations.... Jews also need to accept all the inhabitants of Palestine as citizens with full and equal rights. In doing this, the Jewish community will promote active participation in the political life of Palestine, without any discrimination, [and] will use all available resources for the development of all the citizens.[8]

The local Catholic parishes and Protestant denominations in Israel can be and in fact often are marked by the colors of those two opposing currents nevertheless striving for social justice and peace using the means available to them, such as volunteer work, cross-cultural, educational and cultural programs, round tables, and conferences, etc.

7 Faydra L. Shapiro, *Christian Zionism: Navigating the Jewish-Christian Border* (Eugene, OR: Cascade Books, 2015), 6.

8 Jean Corbon et al., "What Is Required of the Christian Faith Concerning the Palestine Problem," *Biblical and Theological Concerns* in *Towards a Jewish Theology of Liberation*, ed. Mark H. Ellis (Waco, TX: Baylor University Press, 2004), 154.

Two authors contributing to this volume, David Neuhaus and Jamal Khader, raise their concerns about the social and theological issues in connection with the modern State of Israel in their articles. They show that some of the demands and the ideas of the pro-Palestinian theology are indeed justified and important for preserving human rights in the Land of Israel today. At the time when the Christian Zionists lend their hand in order to help with the resurrection of the Jewish nation, who for many centuries experienced statelessness and exile, the Palestinian 21 percent of the state's population is faced with discrimination and experiences, sometimes on a daily basis, the mystery of suffering and the cross. The Catholic Church, who in her social teaching recognizes the dignity of every human being, is called upon for help also, and especially in the Land of Israel. The actions of her pastors and lay members try to bring remedy to the ones experiencing difficulties. However, as the two authors point out, even if the Church is successful in bringing some relief and consolation to the local population, her voice is often muffled by other concerns of the political leaders of the country.

The political ideas of Zionism are also found to be controversial by a minority of the ultra-orthodox Jewish population. For them the creation of the State of Israel denied the election of the Jews as the beloved people of God. Even though the settling in the land was allowed by the rabbinic authorities, it was supposed to be based on the principles of Torah. The article entitled "Judaism and Zionism," written by Yerahmiel Domb,[9] is a good example of a fundamentalist Jewish approach to the issue of the land. The author demonstrates that the Zionist movement contributed to uprooting of the values of Judaism in general. By creating a country governed by political rules apparently giving everyone freedom, safety, and independence, the Zionist pioneers and founders have reduced the holy nation to the level of all the other nations of the world, whose states are not governed by God's precepts but simply by lay principles:

> Will organizing a fighting force [of the sort] that has provided security to other nations of the world provide for us, too, security and strength in the land, national honor and respect in the world, retention of power and a secure future? Or are we something different from all other nations of the world, a chosen people whom God has elected from amongst all peoples, to be governed by manifest divine providence, under the divine order of the Torah's commandments and warnings of reward and punishment, exile and redemption?"[10]

---

[9] Yerahmiel Domb, "Judaism and Zionism," in *The Jewish Political Tradition*, ed. Michael Walzer et al., vol. 1, *Authority* (New Haven and London: Yale University Press, 2000), 481–483.

[10] Domb, "Judaism and Zionism," 483.

Those Catholics who seek in a non-fundamentalist way to find a providential meaning in the return of Israel to the Promised Land do so in the perspective of the eschatological fulfillment of the promises of the Old Testament linked to the glorious coming of Christ, which the *Catechism of the Catholic Church*[11] (cf. 673–74), following Paul, makes dependent on the eschatological conversion to Christ of "all Israel" (Rom 11:26; see 11:12–15). It is in this way that Catholics can search the New Testament in a new way on the subject of the Promised Land, beyond its apparent silence on this matter.

Eschatology in many Christian movements has been too often reduced to an empowering symbol or a utopian vision of justice and peace in this world. "Central to [Catholic] eschatology is the concept of hope: Hope is orientated toward the kingdom of God, not as heaven alone but as the renewal and re-creation of the whole world."[12] God is actively present in the human history. He is not just a mere or a distant spectator.

> The Kingdom of God cannot be reduced to the reign of God within the individual soul or modernized in terms of personal existential confrontation or dissipated to an extra worldly dream of blessed immortality. The Kingdom of God means that God is King and acts in history to bring history to a divinely directed goal.[13]

The Catholic Church teaches that eschatological fulfillment of his promises by the Lord must take place though the particular spatio-temporal concretization of the Land of Israel and of Jerusalem. It is an affirmation that could surprise the majority of Catholics today. In effect their faith reflects a teaching in the Church that, though not magisterial (official), is at least common, according to which since St. Augustine all forms of millennialism[14] are excluded, and in consequence those passages of the New Testament about Jerusalem and the Land of Israel are interpreted in a metaphorical manner. And yet what the Catholic Church condemns in millennialism is "the claim ... to realize within history that messianic hope which can only be realized

---

11 The *Catechism of the Catholic Church* is a compendium of Catholic doctrine that serves as a reference text for teaching. It presents Catholic faith within the context of the Church's history and tradition. It was promulgated by Pope John Paul II on December 8, 1992.

12 Richard P. McBrien, *Catholicism: New Study Edition* (New York: Harper-Collins, 1994), 935.

13 George Eldon Ladd, *The Presence of the Future: The Eschatology of Biblical Realism* (Grand Rapids, MI: Eerdmans, 1974), 331.

14 "Millennialism—This term is often applied loosely to any religious outlook that envisages a transformation of earthly life and the ushering in of a golden age, in which, commonly, a faithful group are rewarded." See the full article in *A Dictionary of Jewish-Christian Relations* (Cambridge: Cambridge University Press, 2005), 294.

beyond history through the eschatological judgment."¹⁵ But that doesn't seem to exclude that God himself brings his holy history regarding humanity to fulfillment through an ultimate mediation of the people of Israel, linked to Jerusalem and to the Promised Land.

It was this type of millennialism that the Fathers of the Church professed with some variations during more than four centuries up to St. Augustine, who on this point followed the Platonist allegorizing of Origen through the Donatist bishop Tyconius, which taught that the millennium represented symbolically the time of the Church. Following Papias, bishop of Hierapolis in Asia Minor (cf. Col 4:13) toward 130–140, " the hearer of John, and a companion of Polycarp [of Smyrna],"¹⁶ of Jewish-Christian tradition, that pillar of orthodox faith, St. Irenaeus of Lyon taught this kind of eschatological millennialism. It was the same with Melito of Sardis, and with Justin Martyr in the second century, and with Hippolytus of Rome, Tertullian, Cyprian of Carthage, Methodius of Olympus, Lactantius, and Victorinus of Pettau in the third century. In the fourth century Jerome and Augustine themselves hesitated before abandoning a form of millennialism.

For this eschatological millennialism, Jerusalem didn't mean simply a geographical site, for as early a Father as Irenaeus of Lyon thought that the Antichrist would rebuild the Temple in Jerusalem.¹⁷ But the supersessionism¹⁸ of these millenialist Fathers did not allow them to see any positive connection between this place and the Jewish people. More largely for them it is only the Christians who inherit the holy city and the land without any connection with the genealogical Israel, not even on the basis of Romans 11:25–27. This is an important difference between the intention of the New Testament and what these early Fathers taught.

Irenaeus of Lyon believed that the final act of human history and its culmination would take place in Jerusalem.

> After the Antichrist has reduced the whole world to the state of a desert, has reigned for three years and six months [cf. Rv 11:2] and ... has sat down in the Temple of Jerusalem [cf. Mt 24:15; Mk 13:14; 2 Thes 2:3–10],

---

15 *Catechism of the Catholic Church*, 676.

16 St. Irenaeus, *Adversus Haereses*, V, 33, 4, https://www.newadvent.org/fathers/0103.htm.

17 Irenaeus, *Adversus Haereses*, V, 25, 2.

18 "In recent decades the term 'supersessionism' has gained currency among theologians and biblical scholars to refer to the traditional Christian belief that since Christ's coming the Church has taken the place of the Jewish people as God's chosen community, and that God's covenant with the Jews is now over and done. By extension, the term can be used to refer to any interpretation of Christian faith generally or the status of the Church in particular that claims or implies the abrogation or obsolescence of God's covenant with the Jewish people."
See the full article in *A Dictionary of Jewish-Christian Relations*, 413.

the Lord will come from the heights of heaven, on the clouds, in the glory of his Father [cf. Mt 16:27; Mk 13:26], and he will cast into the lake of fire the Antichrist and his followers [cf. Rv 19:20]."[19]

Let us not forget that Irenaeus, who heard Bishop Polycarp of Smyrna speak to him about John,[20] was so close personally with regard to the book of Revelation that he could say: "For that was seen no very long time since Revelation, but almost in our day, towards the end of Domitian's reign."[21] He was convinced that the millennialism that he was teaching was founded on the apostolic tradition of Asia Minor that went back to John himself (see Rv 20): "the elders who saw John, the disciple of the Lord, related that they had heard from him how the Lord used to teach in regard to these times."[22]

Underlying the millennialism of Irenaeus, there is the fact that he was confronted by the hyper-spiritual allegorizing of the Gnostics. "Some ... endeavor to allegorize [prophecies]."[23] Irenaeus, however, is convinced that the realism of the apostolic faith requires a very definite refusal of this allegorizing which led to Gnostic contradictions:

> If, however, any shall endeavor to allegorize [prophecies] of this kind, they shall not be found consistent with themselves in all points, and shall be confuted by the teaching of the very expressions [in question].... For all these and other words were unquestionably spoken in reference to the resurrection of the just, which takes place after the coming of Antichrist, and the destruction of all nations under his rule.[24]

For Irenaeus the final resurrection announced by the prophets of Israel and by Christ is an eschatological event which will have its first impact on the earth, and quite specifically on the Promised Land:

> These events cannot be located in super-celestial places—for "God will show forth the splendor [of Jerusalem] to all the earth that is under the heavens" (Bar 5:3): But in the times of the kingdom, the earth has been called again by Christ [to its pristine condition], and Jerusalem rebuilt after the pattern of the Jerusalem above.[25]

---

19 See Irenaeus, *Adversus Haereses*, V, 33, 4. Cf. *Adversus Haereses*, V, 25, 2.
20 Irenaeus, *Adversus Haereses*, III, 3, 4. *Adversus Haereses*, V, 25, 2.
21 Irenaeus, *Adversus Haereses*, V, 30, 3.
22 Irenaeus, *Adversus Haereses*, V, 33, 3. Cf. *Adversus Haereses*, V, 33, 4.
23 Irenaeus, *Adversus Haereses*, V, 35, 1.
24 Irenaeus, *Adversus Haereses*, V, 35, 1.
25 Irenaeus, *Adversus Haereses*, V, 35, 2. Cf. *Adversus Haereses*, V, 35, 1.

The *Catechism of the Catholic Church* points to this kind of eschatological realism when it teaches: "Though already present in his Church, Christ's reign is nevertheless yet to be fulfilled 'with power and great glory' by the king's return to earth" (671). And further on: "Before his Ascension Christ affirmed that the hour had not yet come for the glorious establishment of the messianic kingdom awaited by Israel [cf. Acts 1:6–7] which, according to the prophets, was to bring all men the definitive order of justice, love and peace [cf. Is 11:1–9]" (672). In effect, to the apostles who had asked him before the Ascension: "Lord, will you at this time restore the kingdom to Israel?" (Acts 1:6), Jesus did not reply that there was no messianic restoration to await but that it was not yet the hour: "It is not for you to know times or seasons which the Father has fixed by his own authority" (Acts 1:7).[26]

For Irenaeus the divine promise of the gift of the Land of Israel "forever" to Abraham and to "his posterity" (Gn 13:15) must have its fulfillment in an eschatological realism quite other than an allegorical spiritualism: "Now God made promise of the earth to Abraham and his seed; yet neither Abraham nor his seed, that is, those who are justified by faith, do now receive any inheritance in it; but they shall receive it at the resurrection of the just. For God is true and faithful; and on this account He said, 'Blessed are the meek, for they shall inherit the earth'[27] [Mt 5:5]."[28]

In the nineteenth century, a Russian philosopher, theologian, and poet Vladimir Solovyov upheld an eschatological theocratic ideal in connection with the Jewish people. He was often attacked by the press for his critique of antisemitism, but his bold and sometimes controversial ideas inspired other thinkers who emerged after him, including in the Catholic Church. He believed that Jews and Christians needed to humbly cooperate in order to accomplish their national and religious ideals and collectively inherit God's blessings on earth. He was convinced that "Different nations may have different privileges, according to their special historical position and national vocation, so long as this does not conflict with mutual love and general solidarity."[29] For Solovyov there was no necessary contradiction between

---

26 If it is not for the apostles to know the time and the moment of the glorious fulfillment of the messianic kingdom, it is because it does not belong to Christ to reveal it to them. As the *Catechism of the Catholic Church* says: "What he admitted to not knowing in this area [cf. Mk 13:32], he elsewhere declared himself not sent to reveal [cf. Acts 1:7]," 474.

27 Here we have followed the English RSV, which has "the earth," where the French has "la terre," which can also mean "the land."

28 Irenaeus, *Adversus Haereses*, V, 32, 2.

29 Vladimir S. Solovyov, *A Solovyov Anthology*, (London: SCM Press, 1950), 122.

the theocratic[30] ideas of Judaism and Christianity. He was convinced that the same God was truly present in the Christian churches as well as the synagogues, and that despite being despised by many in his as well as in the neighboring countries, the Jews had yet an important political and eschatological role to play: "Once upon a time the flower of the Jewish race served as a receptive ground for the divine incarnation and in the same way Israel of the future will serve as an active medium for humanizing material life and nature and for creating the new earth wherein righteousness dwells."[31] Solovyov expressed his ideas most clearly in his work commonly known as *Three Conversations*[32] and particularly in "The Tale of the Antichrist."

For Vladimir Solovyov "familial otherness, such as that of Christians (Catholics and Orthodox) and Jews, is intended by God as a historical necessary good as a schooling for love."[33] The Land of Israel is this kind of school of love par excellence where Jews and non-Jews need to die to their prejudices in order to rise together in mutual respect and as witnesses of hope. In his chapter in this volume, Etienne Vetö, in a similar spirit, proposes a statement that the land belongs to everyone. It belongs to the Jews as it is the land of their promise, it belongs to the Arabs as they have dwelled there and watched over it during the centuries of various occupations, and it also belongs to the nations as it is the cradle of the Christian faith and the birthplace of Jesus Christ. This land that has received so much of God's attention is today a common spiritual heritage, and so it is everyone's responsibility to sustain it and make it possible for the message of salvation to continue to be spread from there and in there.

In our day Jacques Maritain did not hesitate to write extensively on the role of the Jewish people. In several of his works[34] he tried to examine the meaning of the Diaspora, their persecution, their mission, and their land. Maritain was certain that God entrusted the land of Canaan to the people of

---

30 The idea of theocracy supposes that "from the everlasting creation by God . . . there follows the conclusion that the world, after the completion of creation, continues to be guided by God, and is hence a theocracy. As universal as is the creation of God, so universal is His political rule over the nations of mankind, and over the creation which has been entrusted to them. God is not merely 'Father' of His creation, but also 'King' of his nations." Isaac Breuer, "Judaism and National Home," in *The Jewish Political Tradition, Vol. 1: Authority*, ed. Michael Walzer et al. (New Haven and London: Yale University Press, 2000), 484.

31 Solovyov, *A Solovyov Anthology*, 123.

32 The full title and the modern edition: *War, Progress, and the End of History: Three Conversations* (New York: Lindisfarne Press, 1990).

33 Vladimir Solovyov, *The Burning Bush: Writings on Jews and Judaism* (Notre Dame, IN: University of Notre Dame Press, 2018), 178.

34 *Le Mystère d'Israël*; *On the Philosophy of History*; and *On the Church of Christ*, among others.

Israel and that it was given to them forever. The land given to them wasn't of divine right, but the return of the Jews and the creation of a secular state was a sign that divine promises are without repentance (Rom 11:29): "It appears to me, consequently, that once the Jewish people has put its feet again upon the land which God gave to it, no one will be able anymore to wrest it from it; and that to wish the disappearance of the State of Israel is to wish to reject into nothingness this return which finally was accorded to the Jewish people."[35]

Maritain was of the opinion that we touch two realities in the Land of Israel: the struggle for survival and the resurrection of the Jewish nation, but also the mystery of redemption carried by the Church, who started her ministry precisely there. Maritain was aware that fully joining the reality of the State of Israel and that of the Church was (and still is) far from possible at this point in history.[36] He hoped, however, that there would be a moment in time when the olive tree of Israel would flower again in its entirety and the cross of redemption symbolizing the Christ and his Body the Church would finally recognize themselves and would constitute but a single tree/cross, in order to offer salvation to the people of all the world.[37] This mutual reconciliation would be "like a prelude to the resurrection ... so that, before the end of time, the earth itself would pass through a moment when it would be granted the peace that is the gift of the Lamb of God."[38]

Elias Friedman, a South African Jew who became a Catholic Carmelite priest and went on to become the spiritual founder of the Association of Hebrew Catholics[39] summarizes Maritain's stance about the Land of Israel, in his book *Jewish Identity,* in the following way: "God has willed a representative body of Jews to return to their ancient homeland for purposes of his own. To these ends he has made use of many instruments, including Modern Zionism, however imperfect it might have been."[40] Friedman as well

---

[35] Jacques Maritain, *On the Church of Christ: The Person of the Church and Her Personnel* (London: Notre Dame University Press, 1973), 153.

[36] French Bishops' Conference, *Statement by the Bishops' Committee for Relations with Jews*, 1973: "Israel and the Church are not complementary institutions; their permanent vis à vis is a sign that the divine plan is not yet complete. Christians and Jews are thus in a situation of mutual contest, or according to Saint Paul, of 'jealousy' with regard to unity (Rom 11:14; cf. Deut 32:23)." In Elias Friedman, *Jewish Identity* (New York: The Myriam Press, 1987), 111.

[37] See Jacques Maritain, *On the Church of Christ*, 155–58.

[38] Jacques Maritain, *De l'Eglise du Christ: la personne de l'Eglise et son personnel*, dans *Oeuvres complètes*, tome XIII, 298; my translation.

[39] Association of Hebrew Catholics—a voluntary association of Catholics of both Jewish and non-Jewish origins. It was launched in 1979 by Elias Friedman, OCD, a Hebrew Catholic friar, and Andrew Sholl, a holocaust survivor. The AHC seeks to help preserve the corporate identity and heritage of the people of Israel within the Catholic Church. For more information go to https://www.hebrewcatholic.net.

[40] Friedman, *Jewish Identity*, 86.

as many other Jews who entered the Catholic Church would find consolation in Maritain's approach to the Land and the State of Israel. They and their families, like many other survivors of the Second World War, experienced the consequences of *Shoah* and the antisemitism; they too were exposed to the alienation and solitude of the Jewish identity in the world. The Land remains an important place for them since their spiritual heritage allows them to pray and deeply appreciate both Jewish and Catholic heritage and places of worship. The fact that God's providence has allowed the Jewish people to find a safe haven, even if through the imperfect means of political Zionism, sustains their hope that the Jewish right to exist as a nation will continue to be recognized on the international level and that God's purposes, however mysterious at times, will be realized precisely in the Land for the wellbeing of his beloved people and that of all the nations.

In 1973 the French Bishops' Conference addressed Christians in the name of the Catholic Church, asking them to approach the reality of the Jewish State with respect:

> Jewish existence has been constantly divided between life in dispersion among the nations and aspiration to nationhood in its own Land. It is a striving that creates many problems for the Jewish conscience itself. To understand the striving and the controversy which it provokes in all it dimensions, Christians must not allow themselves to be led away by interpretations that misconceive the communal and religious ways of life of Judaism, or by well-meant but hurriedly adopted political standpoints. They should take account of the interpretation which the Jews themselves set upon their regathering about Jerusalem—in the name of their faith, they consider it as a blessing.[41]

The message of the Bishops' Conference is still valid for our times. Just as the Catholic Church defends the social rights of the Palestinian population in the State of Israel, she also defends the rights of the Jewish people to be treated with respect and to have the freedom to live in their country. In the same document the French bishops express their hopes that the social and political differences will be overcome in the future, at the same time challenging Christians to be interested in the peace process in the Land and perhaps to perceive it not only as human but also as Divine work:

> Let us turn attentive eyes to this Land visited by God and cherish the eager hope that it become a place where all its inhabitants, Jews and non-Jews, may live in peace. It is a cardinal question that faces Christian and Jew

---

[41] *Statement by the Bishops' Committee for Relations with Jews*, in Friedman, *Jewish Identity*, 110.

alike, to know whether the regathering of the scattered congregations of the Jewish people, end-product of the interplay of persecution and political forces, will, in the end, prove, or fail to prove, to be one of the paths of Divine justice for the Jewish people, and, at the same time, for all the peoples on earth. How can Christians remain uninterested in what is being decided in that Land today?[42]

The Catholic Church, especially since the Second Vatican Council, has continued to encourage the attitude of humility in common dialogue with regards to the Land and the Jewish and the Christian traditions present there. The gestures (the visit of John Paul II at the Western Wall) and teachings particularly of the recent popes and their openness to Jewish-Christian dialogue have brought about a great advancement in Jewish-Catholic reconciliation and mutual understanding. It is true that the relationship of the Church and the State of Israel is still far from perfect, and mutual criticisms spring up now and again. Yet, those tensions do not prevent the development and the multiplication of the Jewish-Christian dialogue institutions, conferences, and informal meetings in and outside of Israel. This is also a sign that the eschatological hopes discussed in this article are starting to be fulfilled.

In conclusion, even if there is a great multiplication of religious and political views about the Land of Israel, let us not forget that it all began with God's promises. Moved by his faith Abraham set out for a faraway country, relying on nothing but hope; and by the same hope Moses was led to leave Egypt and lead the Hebrews to the land of Canaan. After the centuries of wars and conflicts, God, for his own purposes, has allowed the return of his people to the place designated today by the political boundaries and laws. The Catholic Church, recognizing the political status of the land, perceives the role of this place also on the eschatological level. Even if there are difficulties there caused by man, this "must not be held to be the final word of the One who poses glory against futility and freedom against servitude (Rom 8:19–22) because creation will reach its hoped-for end in liberation from futility and corruptibility, verified in the glorification of the children of God."[43] This land, precisely because it is riddled with tensions and so continuously called to be the school of humility, mutual love, and understanding, is already a prototype and so paradoxically a premise of God realizing his promises and his victory over sin and suffering in the world.

---

[42] *Statement by the Bishops' Committee for Relations with Jews*, in Friedman, *Jewish Identity*, 110.

[43] Horst Balz, "Early Christian Faith as Hope against Hope," in *Eschatology in the Bible and in Jewish and Christian Tradition*, ed. Henning Graf Reventlow (Sheffield: Sheffield Academic Press, 1997), 35.

And as the land is promised by Jesus to "the meek," this also gives us a precious indication of the way in which God brings to a successful conclusion the realization of his plan in the New Covenant. The first piece of promised land, that of the cave at Machpelah, was not originally conquered, but purchased by Abraham as a "funeral concession" (Gn 23:9) and the burial place for Sarah, for himself (cf. Gn 25:9), and for their descendants (cf. Gn 49:29–32; 50:13). The land is given by God first of all as a place of burial, of a paschal journey through death, as a place of waiting and of welcome for the Resurrection. Is it not this that is shown by the sole passage in the synoptic gospels where there is mention of the Land of Israel in a way that is both immediate and explicit? It is the moment when Jesus is going to die on the cross: "Now from the sixth hour there was *darkness over all the land*" (Mt 27:45; Mk 15:33; Lk 23:44; emphasis added). The Land of Israel is linked with the Passover of Jesus in the obscurity of death, and then of the tomb, that will on the third day give up his body to the life of the Resurrection. It is only in going through death and resurrection that "the meek will receive the land as an inheritance" (Mt 5:5). This doesn't sever the promise of the land from the genealogical Israel, but it gives the only paschal way of the realization of this promise, which is a "gift without repentance" (Rom 11:29).

4

THE RESURRECTED LAND OF ISRAEL
Isaac Vikram Chenchiah

This essay originates from a desire to contribute to a Catholic theology of *Eretz Yisrael*, which, born out of a deep engagement with Judaism, would aid in the resolution of current deadlocks, not by ignoring or diluting what is most dear to Judaism but by entering into its depths.[1] Indeed, a Catholic theology of *Eretz Yisrael* that is not intelligible in Jewish terms would neither lead to fruitful Jewish-Catholic dialogue nor influence Jewish thought. Motivated thus, this essay focuses on the foundational narrative of the Jewish people, the exodus. Reading this narrative under the combined tutelage of a Jewish rabbi, Rabbi David Fohrman; a Jewish-Christian evangelist, Matthew; and the Christian fathers John Chrysostom and Chromatius, we propose that though the historical exodus liberated the people of Israel at the expense of the Egyptians, this was a concession to Pharoah's "hardness of heart" (Mt 19:8) and "from the beginning it was not so" (Mt 19:8). In parallel with this, we develop an analogy beginning with Adam and Eve, and proceeding to Abraham, between land and the human body.

These two strands interact in two ways. First, we develop an understanding of land as a medium of international relationality, which in turn leads to the idea of a space that relates nations to God; such a sacred space is a temple. *Eretz Yisrael* is the land of the Jewish Temple. Christian piety too holds that

---

1 This essay was initially inspired by an Aristotelian reading of Michael Wyschogrod's theology of the land and people of Israel in which the land is to people as body to soul. I thank members of the Post-Graduate Theology Reading Group at the Department of Theology and Religious Studies, University of Bristol, especially Gavin D'Costa and Lindsey Askin, for valuable comments on earlier drafts of this essay. I thank Marcie Lenk for alerting me to the danger that the gendered analogies presented here might be misinterpreted as an instrumentalization of the female body.

Eretz Yisrael is the land of the Temple, that is the land of Christ, whose own body is the true Temple (Jn 2:21). Thus, Jews and Christians agree that *Eretz Yisrael* is temple-land, though they understand this differently. Second, nevertheless, because we have developed an analogy between land and body, agreement between Jews and Christians that *Eretz Yisrael* is temple-land is no mere notional agreement. Rather, Jews and Christians share an analogous understanding of *Eretz Yisrael*. This allows us also to share a hope that the prophetic vision of *Eretz Yisrael* as a land of justice will be actualized.

In the second section, we begin with Genesis with the observation that the human person is intimately related to land. It is part of his origin, and part of his telos bearing "witness of his sin,"[2] as does his—and *her*—body. Likewise, *Am Yisrael*, i.e., the people Israel, and *Eretz Yisrael*, i.e., the Land of Israel, form an organic unity. By uniting with a land, a people becomes a nation, and the biblical text hints that precisely qua nation will Israel fulfill the purpose of its election. To discern how this might be, we turn to the Exodus narrative and discover that, analogously, Egypt is Israel's mother.[3] While, from the Israelite perspective, their time in Egypt was a gestation during which they developed from a family into a people, from the Egyptian perspective this was a pregnancy-gone-wrong, resulting in a painful birth and estrangement between mother and child. Rabbi David Fohrman deduces from his reading of Exodus that this estrangement was a deviation from the intended relationship between Israel and Egypt and offers hope for reconciliation. Combining this with the typology of Matthew's infancy narrative, we claim that Christ has initiated this reconciliation. Developing the analogy between body and land, we argue that nations relate to each other through

---

[2] This phrase is from Augustine's *Confessions* bk. 1, ch. 1, trans. Edward Bouverie Pusey.

[3] The analogy between body and land developed here is a gendered analogy with a focus on the female body. Thus Egypt is not just parent but specifically mother to Israel, and the exodus is not just generation but specifically parturition. So that this is not misperceived as an instrumentalization of the female body, the underlying biblical and theological motivations for this are outlined here.

In the biblical text God is *Father* to Israel; and Israel is in turn a first-born *son*. Since in Christian thought Christ is *the Son* of the divine *Father* and a human *mother*, it is natural to expand father-son/God-Israel dyad into a father-mother-son/God-Egypt-Israel triad. This then sets up an analogy between Egypt and the Theotokos. Now, Catholic thought sees the Theotokos as the new Eve, and such a new Eve was made possible by the incarnation. Combining these, analogously the incarnation makes possible a new Egypt. The old and new Egypts are then analogous to Eve and the Theotokos.

If Egypt is seen as mother to Israel, then the exodus is not just a generation but a parturition. This allows me to relate the old and new exodus to the "In pain shall you bear children" of Genesis 3:16 and the traditional Christian belief that the Theotokos gave birth to Christ with no pain or injury to herself, respectively. Thus the analogy is gendered since the biblical texts and Catholic doctrines that underpin it are themselves gendered.

their land just as humans through their bodies. Thus *Am Yisrael* relates to the nations through *Eretz Yisrael*.

As the body of Christ is itself the locus of the reconciliation of all things (Col 1:19–21; Eph 2:14–16), so also *Eretz Yisrael*, the body of *Am Yisrael*, will be the locus of reconciliation between Jew and Gentile. We are confident of this because Christ is risen.

BODY AND LAND IN THE TORAH

> Our land is our body.
> —Caesarius of Arles (AD 470–542)[4]

"In the Beginning" of Humanity

> The Lord God formed man from *the dust of the earth*. He blew into his nostrils the breath of life, and man became a living being. The Lord God planted a *garden* in Eden ... and placed there the man whom He had formed.... The Lord God took the man and placed him in the *garden* of Eden, to till it and tend it. (Gn 2:7–8, 15, emphasis mine)[5]

In the second creation account in Genesis, man is intimately related to the earth: it is both his material cause, i.e., that of which he is made, and, at this point in the narrative, his final cause, i.e., that for which he is made. Land is the common denominator uniting man's materiality—his bodiliness—and his teleology. Consequently the eating of the forbidden fruit affects man both bodily and terrestrially (Latin: *terra*, earth). Bodily, "I will make most severe your pangs in childbearing; in pain shall you bear children" (Gn 3:16), and "You [shall] return to the ground—For from it you were taken. For dust you are, and to dust you shall return" (Gn 3:19). Terrestrially, "Cursed be the ground because of you.... Thorns and thistles shall it sprout for you" (Gn 3:17–18), and "The Lord God banished him from the garden of Eden" (Gn 3:23).

The close connection between body and land is reinforced when Cain, who has inflicted *bodily* harm on his brother, finds himself like Adam

---

[4] Commentary on Genesis 12:1 in *Old Testament II: Genesis 12–50*, Ancient Christian Commentary on Scripture, ed. M. Sheridan (Downers Grove, Illinois: Intervarsity Press, 2002).

[5] Unless otherwise stated all quotations from the *Tanakh*, i.e., the Hebrew Bible, are taken from the Jewish Publication Society's translation (1985); New Testament quotations are from the Revised Standard Version, Catholic Edition.

alienated from the *land*, which will henceforth provide neither food nor home for him. "If you till the soil, it shall no longer yield its strength to you. You shall become a ceaseless wanderer on earth" (Gn 4:12). Thus the opening chapters of Genesis reveal that man's alienation from God—succinctly expressed in Adam's "I was afraid ... so I hid" (Gn 3:10) and Cain's "I must avoid your presence" (Gn 4:14)—is manifested both in his body through painful procreation and death, and in his land (i.e., the earth) through its infertility and his exile. Having considered the progenitors of our race, our fathers in flesh, we shall next move to Abraham, our father in faith (see Rom 4:11), in whose life the motifs of body and land are interwoven in the concept of nation.

At the Beginning of the Jews
THE BIBLICAL TEXT

> Go forth from your native land ... to the land that I will show you. And from your father's house ... I will make of you a great nation (Gn 12:1-2).

This intertwining of body and land continues into the beginning of Jewish history with the development that both terms are now understood communally rather than individually. Abraham is called to leave his *father's house*, that is, his people, and his *native land*, that is, the land of his people—for one's native land is not merely the place of one's birth or upbringing but rather the land of one's people.

In exchange he is promised, "I will make of you a great nation." Ephraim Speiser sees in the use of the word "nation" rather than "people" an implicit reference to *both* people and land: "It is significant that God promised to make of Abraham a great 'nation' (*goy*), not 'people' (*am*), for a 'nation' requires a territorial base, since the concept is a political one, while a 'people' (*am*) does not."[6] He elaborates:

> The term in question is *goy*, not *am*; and rightly so. ... There is nothing casual or accidental about this phraseology. It is consistent, invariable, and exclusive. It is applied again to Abraham in Gn 18:18, to Jacob in Gn 46:3 and Dt 26:5, and to Moses in Ex 32:10, Nm 14:12 and Dt 9:13.[7] The reason, then, behind the patriarch's departure from Mesopotamia and the

---

6 Ephraim Speiser, *Genesis: Introduction, Translation, and Notes*, vol. 1 (New York: Anchor Bible, 1964), 86.
7 Similarly to Ishmael, Gn 17:20; 21:13,18. (Footnote in original.)

Israelites' liberation from Egypt was that Israel might be a nation. The *am* had been in Egypt for centuries anyway, where its numbers are stated to have become very large (Ex 1:9).[8]

Speiser also explores the differences in connotations between the Hebrew terms *am* and *goy* and the English terms "people" and "nation":

> The modern concept of 'people' is at best only a rough approximation to the biblical concept of *am*. The main difference lies in the suggestion of blood ties and the emphasis on the individual, both of which features are peculiar to the Hebrew term. On the other hand, *goy* comes rather close to the modern definition of 'nation'. In any case, the gap between Hebrew *am* and *goy* is greater than that between our 'people' and 'nation'.[9]

Aelred Cody agrees with this, writing:

> From what we have seen we can conclude that while *am* throughout the Old Testament refers to a people or nation in its aspect of centripetal unity and cohesiveness, *goy* is linked inseparably with territory and government and what we would today call *foreign relations*. ... The strong connexion of the term *goy* with land tenure made it a fitting word to use in contexts having to do with the Israelite possession of the promised land, without which the Chosen people could not become an authentic *goy*.[10]

Commenting on Exodus 19:6, "you shall be to Me a kingdom of priests and a holy nation," which is the only place in the *Tanakh* where Israel is called a "holy nation" rather than "holy people,"[11] he says: "*Goy* and *mamlaka*[12] belong together naturally as two complements constituting a unity which possesses a land and which, established on that land, enters as a sovereign nation into relations with the world at large.[13]

---

8 Ephraim Speiser, "'People' and 'Nation' of Israel," *Journal of Biblical Literature* 79, no. 2 (1960): 163.

9 Speiser, "'People' and 'Nation' of Israel," 160.

10 Aelred Cody, "When Is the Chosen People Called a Goy?" *Vetus Testamentum* 14, no. 1 (1964): 5; emphasis mine.

11 Cody offers the explanation that "*goy* is required in this text by the complementary parallel *mamlaka*" (see footnote 10) but this does not explain the use of the phrase "kingdom of priests" in the first place.

12 That is, "rule," "sovereignty," or "kingdom." Cody, "When Is the Chosen People Called a Goy?," 3.

13 Cody, "When Is the Chosen People Called a Goy?," 3–4.

Notice that Speiser relates the land presupposed in "nation" to the divine purpose for which Israel was elected, and Cody to Israel's relations to the world at large. Indeed, in Exodus 19:6, Israel is a "holy nation" precisely in the context of "all peoples" and "all the earth": "If you will obey Me faithfully and keep My covenant, you shall be My treasured possession among all the peoples. Indeed, all the earth is Mine, but you shall be to Me a kingdom of priests and a holy nation" (Ex 19:5–6).

"OUR LAND IS OUR BODY"

Philo interpreted Abraham's migration allegorically,[14] and his influence is evident[15] on Ambrose, for whom: "Abraham represents the mind. . . . This mind then was in Haran, that is, in caverns, subject to the different passions. For this reason it is told, 'Go from your country,' that is, from your body."[16] Caesarius of Arles continues this interpretation but subsumed it into a typological[17] reading by saying:

> As the apostle says, "Now all these things happened to them as a type, and they were written for our correction, upon whom the final age of the world has come" (1 Cor 10:11). Therefore, if what happened corporally in Abraham was written for us, we will see it fulfilled spiritually in us if we live piously and justly. "Leave your country", the Lord said, "your kinsfolk and your father's house." We believe and perceive all these things fulfilled in us, brothers, through the sacrament of baptism. *Our land is our body*; we go forth properly from our land if we abandon our carnal habits to follow the footsteps of Christ.[18]

At first glance this does not seem very different from Ambrose's interpretation except for the reference to baptism. However, whereas for Ambrose "body" was a synonym for the passions (see quote above), Caesarius here uses "body" literally. This can be seen from the continuation of his commentary:

---

[14] Philo, "On the Migration of Abraham," *Philo: Vol. IV (Loeb Classical Library)*, trans. F. H. Colson and G. H. Whitaker (London: William Heinemann, 1985), 132–267.

[15] Commentary on Genesis 12:1 in Sheridan, *Old Testament II: Genesis 12–50*.

[16] Commentary on Genesis 12:1 in Sheridan, *Old Testament II: Genesis 12–50*.

[17] That is, pertaining to the way, in Christian reading, in which an event in the Old Testament foreshadowed one in the New Testament. Readings are of actual, historical events that closely resemble one another while remaining distinct. Typological reading leaves intact the plain narrative meaning of the biblical text.
   Condensed from Jason D. Byassee, "Typology," in *The Cambridge Dictionary of Christian Theology*, ed. Ian A. McFarland et al. (Cambridge: Cambridge University Press, 2011), 523.

[18] Commentary on Genesis 12:1 in Sheridan, *Old Testament II: Genesis 12–50*. Emphasis mine.

"Leave your country," says the Lord. Our country, that is, our body, was the land of the dying before baptism, but through baptism it has become the land of the living. It is the very land of which the psalmist relates: "I believe that I shall see the bounty of the Lord in the land of the living" (Ps 27:13, Septuagint). Through baptism, as I said, we have become the land of the living and not of the dying, that is, of the virtues and not of the vices.

Body and land continue to be interwoven, though more subtly, in the next decisive moment in salvation history, the exodus. To this we now turn.

OUT OF EGYPT I CALLED *MY SON*: "THE TRUE AND IDEAL ISRAEL"

"When Israel was a child, I loved him," says the prophet Hosea, speaking on behalf of God, "and out of Egypt I called my son" (Hos 11:1, RSV). The evangelist Matthew sees this as a prophecy, fulfilled in Christ's sojourn to Egypt. Since we will be reading this text closely, for the reader's convenience the text Mathew 2:13–21 is reproduced here:

> Now when they [the wise men] had departed, behold, an angel of the Lord appeared to Joseph in a dream and said, "Rise, take the child and his mother, and flee to Egypt, and remain there till I tell you; for Herod is about to search for the child, to destroy him." And he rose and took the child and his mother by night, and departed to Egypt, and remained there until the death of Herod. This was to fulfil what the Lord had spoken by the prophet, "Out of Egypt have I called my son." Then Herod, when he saw that he had been tricked by the wise men, was in a furious rage, and he sent and killed all the male children in Bethlehem and in all that region who were two years old or under, according to the time which he had ascertained from the wise men. Then was fulfilled what was spoken by the prophet Jeremiah:
> "A voice was heard in Ramah, wailing and loud lamentation, Rachel weeping for her children; she refused to be consoled, because they were no more."
> But when Herod died, behold, an angel of the Lord appeared in a dream to Joseph in Egypt, saying, "Rise, take the child and his mother, and go to the Land of Israel, for those who sought the child's life are dead." And he rose and took the child and his mother, and went to the Land of Israel.

Typology, Prophecy, or Recapitulation?

Typology: At first glance Matthew appears to be engaging in a straightforward typological reading of the *Tanakh*: Israel is a type of Christ, and it being called out of Egypt is a type of Christ's own journey from Egypt back to Israel.

However, on closer investigation the typology appears forced at best, and inverted at worst: There is evidence neither for Christ being enslaved in Egypt; nor for his exit ("exodus") being opposed by the Egyptians. No "signs and wonders" (Ex 7:3, RSV) accompanied the Holy Family's return to Israel; nor did the Egyptians suffer any injuries on his departure. On the contrary, in the context of Matthew's narrative (Mt 2:13–21), this is a positive reference to Egypt. Indeed, Matthew appears to deliberately highlight this through the sandwich structure of the narrative, in which the escape to Egypt (Mt 2:13–15) and the return from Egypt (Mt 2:19–23) bookend the massacre of the infants (Mt 2:16–18). Moreover, especially in the context of Egypt, that Herod "killed all the male children in Bethlehem" (Mt 2:16) cannot but remind the attentive reader of the Pharaoh who commanded that Hebrew sons should be killed (Ex 1:16, 22)—except that here it is Herod who commands infanticide and Egypt that affords Christ refuge![19]

Prophecy: Additionally, Matthew's claim that Christ's escape to and return from Egypt occurred "to fulfil what the Lord had spoken by the prophet" (Mt 2:15) is puzzling, since Hosea is clearly talking about past events.

Jerome's commentary on Hosea might help resolve this puzzle. Jerome draws on both the Hebrew and Greek texts and notices that while the Masoretic text of Hosea 11:1 has "son" (*ben*) in the singular, the Septuagint has the plural "children":

> It remains that we should say that what precedes typologically in other respects applies in truth and in its fulfilment to Christ.... Therefore, what is thus written, "Israel was a very little one, and I loved him," and "out of Egypt I called my son," is said indeed about the people of Israel, who are called out of Egypt, who are loved, who were called in the time after the error of their idolatry something like an "infant" and a "very little one"; but in its completion [this] is referred to Christ.[20]

---

[19] R. T. France raises similar difficulties with the (purported) typology. R. T. France, *The Gospel of Matthew*, The New International Commentary on the New Testament (Grand Rapids, MI: Eerdmans, 2007).

[20] Jerome, commentary on Hosea in *Commentaries on the Twelve Prophets*, ed. Thomas P. Schick (Downers Grove, IL: Intervarsity Press, 2017).

In other words the Septuagint text is historical, but the Masoretic text is prophetic; since Matthew quotes the Masoretic text, he is, rightly, quoting the text as prophecy. However, the Masoretic text offers no sign of being prophetic:[21]

> I fell in love with Israel
> When he was still a child;
> And I have called [him] My son
> Ever since Egypt. (Hos 11:1)

Recapitulation: Daniel Carroll suggests that the text is prophetic in that Christ recapitulates[22] the history of Israel.

> Mt 2:15 cites Hos 11:1 as "fulfilled" in Jesus. How can this be, if the allusion in Hosea to the exodus is retrospective and not a prediction? The answer is that in the gospel of Matthew the life of Jesus recapitulates the history of Israel in many ways. For example, paralleling the movement from bondage to Sinai, Jesus comes out of Egypt (Mt 2), goes through the waters (of baptism; Mt 3), is tempted in the desert (forty days and nights; Mt 4), and then goes to a mountain to speak of the law (Mt 5–7). He is the true and ideal Israel.[23]

Turner agrees with this with the additional observation that the theological motif that Matthew shares with Hosea is that of divine sonship:

> In its original context, Hos 11:1 is not a prediction of Jesus but a reminiscence of the exodus. This was at least as clear to Matthew as it is to modern interpreters. But Hos 11:1 alludes to a theological motif that was dear to Matthew: divine sonship. The exodus demonstrated Israel's unique status as God's firstborn son. What was true of Israel on a metaphorical level is more profoundly true of Jesus the Messiah.... In Hos 11:1 the exodus provides a historical pattern of God's loving preservation of his son Israel from

---

[21] See David L. Turner, *Matthew*, Baker Exegetical Commentary on the New Testament (Grand Rapids, MI: Baker Academic, 2008), 180–81, and references therein for a critique of the view that Matthew reads Hosea 11:1 as a *prediction* of Jesus.

[22] "Recapitulation" describes an understanding of the work of Christ characteristic of the thought of Irenaeus of Lyon. The Greek word *anakephalaiosis*, which it translates, means a summing up or drawing together. The term enters Christian theology from Ephesians 1:10, which speaks of "summing up all things in Christ." For Irenaeus, Christ retraces in some way the whole of human history. Condensed from Paul Parvis, "Recapitulation," in *The Cambridge Dictionary of Christian Theology*, 434.

[23] Commentary on Hosea 11:1 in Tremper Longman III and Daniel E. Garland, *Daniel–Malachi*, The Expositor's Bible Commentary (Grand Rapids, MI: Zondervan, 2009).

Pharaoh's wrath. From a Christian perspective, this past event is recapitulated by God's loving preservation of his Son, Jesus, from Herod's wrath.[24]

Nevertheless this is not entirely satisfactory: The Egypt that offers refuge from Herod's wrath can hardly be said to form a "historical pattern" with the Egypt from whose wrath Israel had to be preserved. If Matthew wanted to make a case that "Jesus the Messiah ... typologically repeats crucial events of Biblical redemptive history,"[25] he appears not to have paid attention to the most significant feature of that redemptive history!

In fact Turner[26] notices something unusual with this reading of Matthew: "It is unusual that Matthew places this fulfilment quotation before the departure of Jesus from Egypt, to which it refers. Generally, fulfilment formulas are inserted after the narration of the events to which they refer."

Recapitulation–of What Could Have Been–and Thus a Fulfilled Prophecy

But what if Matthew located the "fulfilment quotation" at exactly the usual location, namely after the narration of the fulfillment? This is undeniably the case for Matthew 2:16–18 and Matthew 2:19–23, so it is natural to read Matthew 2:13–15 with the same hermeneutic. As R. H. Gundry points out,

> The quotation [in Mt 2:15] comes before the return from Egypt to Palestine. Matthew's fulfilment-quotations regularly refer backward to what has already happened in the narrative. The clause immediately preceding the present stresses residence in Egypt till Herod's death, not departure from Egypt after Herod's death.[27]

Read this way, what event, according to Matthew, fulfills the prophecy of Hosea? Not Christ's departure from Egypt, but rather his entry into and sojourn in Egypt! Thus, we submit that Matthew is referring, not to the Egypt that enslaved Israel, not to the "house of bondage" (Ex 20:2), but to the Egypt that offered the nascent Israel refuge from famine—to Abraham (Gn 12:10), Jacob, his sons, and their families (Gn 45:17–20)—and then, for a while, nurtured Israel.

---

24 Commentary on Matthew 2:15b in Turner, *Matthew*.
25 Commentary on Matthew 2:15b in Turner, *Matthew*.
26 And also R. T. France, commentary on Matthew 2:13-15 in *The Gospel of Matthew*.
27 Robert H. Gundry, *Matthew: A Commentary on His Handbook for a Mixed Church under Persecution* (Grand Rapids, MI: Eerdmans, 1995), 34.

Thus, contra R. T. French, for example, who reads Matthew as setting up "the typological model for the new-born Messiah to play the role of the new Moses, who will also deliver his people (cf. Mt 1:21),"[28] our claim is that in Matthew 2:13–15 Christ is a type of the patriarchs Abraham and Jacob, and the twelve sons of Jacob, who found refuge and nurture in Egypt. Note that this is a more extensive recapitulation of Israel's history, for it begins with the very beginning of Israel's story—in the Genesis narrative, Abraham's sojourn in Egypt occurs almost immediately after his call, in Genesis 12:10—and not midway with its bondage in Egypt as, for example, in Daniel Carroll's reading (see quote above).

The text is indeed typological but not in that Christ, like Israel, was liberated from Egypt, but in that Christ, like Israel, was nurtured in Egypt. Indeed, French admits that

> If it is supposed that typology must depend on exact correspondences, Matthew's typology here is decidedly loose, not only in that Jesus is seen both as the deliverer and the delivered, but also in that whereas Moses escaped from Egypt and returned to it, Jesus (like Israel) does the opposite.

But, in our reading, Matthew's typology is quite tight and does correspond quite exactly—not to Moses but to the Patriarchs. French attempts, quite carefully, but not entirely satisfactorily, to clarify Matthew's typology, but is ultimately unable to overcome the awkwardness of having to see as "new Moses" the one who was protected *by* Egypt *from* an ostensibly Jewish tyrant. Incidentally, we agree with these commentators that Herod is a type of Pharaoh and the massacre of the innocents a type of his infanticide. But notice how Matthew deliberately sets this at a geographical distance from Christ, or rather, inverts the roles of the lands of Israel and Egypt. Indeed, John Chrysostom both notices this role inversion and identifies the type correctly: "Isn't this remarkable: While Palestine plots, it is Egypt that receives and preserves the One for whom the plots are designed! This is reminiscent of the patriarch Jacob, who also sought succor in Egypt, anticipating the coming of our Lord."[29]

What, then, of the view, expressed by Carroll above but of ancient Christian provenance, that Jesus recapitulates history?[30] Here we query

---

[28] Commentary on Matthew 2:1–12 in R. T. France, *The Gospel of Matthew*.

[29] See commentary on Matthew 2:14 in Manlio Simonetti, ed., *New Testament 1a: Matthew 1–13*, Ancient Christian Commentary on Scripture (Downers Grove, Illinois: Intervarsity Press, 2001).

[30] For Christ's recapitulation of the history of Israel, see J. Kennedy, *The Recapitulation of Israel: Use of Israel's History in Matthew 1:1–4:11*, Wissenschaftliche Untersuchungen Zum Neuen Testament, 2. Reihe (Tubingen, Germany: Mohr Siebeck, 2008).

whether recapitulation should be understood as a repeat of history—"history repeats itself: the first time as Israel, the second time as Christ."[31] Clearly no, since there is no suggestion that Christ recapitulates the worship of the golden calf or the apostasy of Solomon. On the contrary, as Carroll says above, "He is the true and ideal Israel." Rather, Christ recapitulates history by completing what was lacking and in doing so he *full*-fills prophecy.

But could we have a true and ideal Israel without a "true and ideal Egypt"? Chromatius offers a commentary that hints that Christ recapitulates—in the sense above—also the history of Egypt:

> God the omnipotent Father, moved by devotion, sent His Son into Egypt. He did so that Egypt . . . might now receive Christ, the hope for salvation. How great was God's compassion as shown in the advent of his Son! Egypt, which of old under Pharaoh stood stubborn against God, now became a witness to and home for Christ.[32]

But if Christ's recapitulation of the history of Israel's relationship with Egypt involves this history being reconfigured, what might a reconfigured exodus look like? Rabbi David Fohrman has proposed an answer to this question, and to this we now turn.

OUT OF EGYPT I CALLED MY SON: "THE TRUE AND IDEAL EXODUS"

> Time past and time future
> What might have been and what has been
> Point to one end, which is always present.
> —T S Eliot, "Burnt Norton" (*Four Quartets*)

David Fohrman's Reading of Exodus

Rabbi David Fohrman[33] presents a close reading of the Exodus narrative from which he concludes that the primary goal of the exodus, so far as Egypt was concerned, was to make the true God manifest to Egypt. Had Pharaoh responded well, Israel would have left Egypt, *escorted* by Egyptians. Fohrman

---

31 This is a play on Karl Marx's famous statement that history repeats itself, "the first as tragedy, then as farce." Karl Marx, "Der 18te Brumaire des Louis Napoleon," *Die Revolution* (1852).

32 Commentary on Matthew 2:15 in Simonetti, *New Testament 1a*.

33 David Fohrman, *The Exodus You Almost Passed Over* (New York: Aleph Beta Press, 2016). This section is my summary of his thought.

reaches this conclusion on the basis of textual parallels between the narrative in Genesis 50:1–14 of Jacob's burial in Canaan and the narrative of the Exodus. First, Fohrman notes that Jacob was mourned for by *Egypt*,[34] the funeral procession appears to have taken a route to Canaan similar to that later taken by the Israelites,[35] was accompanied by "all the officials of Pharaoh, the senior members of his court, and all of Egypt's dignitaries" (Gn 50:7) and "chariots too, and horsemen ... it was a very large troop" (Gn 50:11).

Next, Fohrman observes that these same (or similar) elements appear in the narrative of the actual exodus. Consider, for example, the "chariots, horsemen, troops" in Genesis 50:11. As the Israelites are leaving Egypt, God tells Moses, "Then I will stiffen Pharaoh's heart and he will pursue them, that I may gain glory through Pharaoh and all his host" (Ex 14:4). This phrase, of God "gaining glory" through "Pharaoh, his chariots and his horsemen" is repeated twice more (Ex 14:17, 14:18). And sure enough, "all the chariot horses of Pharaoh, his horsemen and his warriors (Ex 14:9; cf. Gn 50:11 above) pursue Israel, and in due course "the waters turned back and covered the chariots and the horsemen" (Gn 14:28).

A casual reader might conclude that in the destruction of Pharaoh's chariots and the death of his horsemen God has "gained glory." But Fohrman points out that a well-known Talmudic commentary rejects this reading:

> The Holy One, Blessed is He, does not rejoice in the downfall of the wicked. For R. Shmuel bar Nachman said in the name of R. Yonatan: In the moment [when Egypt was destroyed at the Sea], the ministering angels wished to sing in joy in the presence of the Holy One. But the Holy One said to them: My own creations [the Egyptians] are drowning in the Sea, and you want to sing before Me?[36]

Fohrman concludes that what glorified God was that the Pharaoh, his chariots, and his horsemen *accompanied* the Israelites; it was not from their deaths that God gained glory but from their presence. But that the accompaniment took the form of pursuit and not escort—this was contrary to the divine intent. The exodus has diverged—began to diverge when Pharaoh said, "Who is the Lord that I should heed Him?" (Ex 5:2)—from the blueprint established in the "proto-exodus" of the burial of Jacob.

---

[34] "The Egyptians bewailed him seventy days" (Gn 50:3).

[35] "When they came to Goren ha-Atad, beyond the Jordan" (Gn 50:10). Goren ha-Atad is to the west of the Jordan, so "beyond" implies approaching Canaan from the east.

[36] *Megillah* 10b, quoted in Fohrman, *The Exodus You Almost Passed Over*, ch. 20.

"The True and Ideal Exodus"

Though he does not say this himself, Fohrman also presents enough textual evidence to motivate the conjecture that being thus accompanied by Egypt, which was then the great power of that region, would have obviated any need for a conquest of Canaan.[37] Rather, the Israelites would have reached a negotiated settlement, perhaps a three-way settlement also involving Egypt, that would have allowed them to claim the promised land without bloodshed.

This claim rests on a detail in the account of Jacob's burial:

> And when the Canaanite inhabitants of the land saw the mourning at Goren ha-Atad, they said, "This is solemn mourning *on the part of the Egyptians.*" That is why it was named Abel-mizraim [Interpreted as "the mourning of the Egyptians"]. (Gn 50:11, emphasis mine)

Rashi[38] (whom Fohrman quotes) comments,

> Goren ha-Atad, i.e., the threshing floor of Atad. It was so called because it was surrounded by a hedge of thorns (not because thorns were threshed there). Our Rabbis[39] explained that it was so called in consequence of an incident that occurred there—that all the kings of Canaan and the princes of Ishmael came to wage war against them, but as soon as they saw Joseph's crown hanging over Jacob's coffin they all rose and hung their crowns on it and thus wreathed it with crowns like a threshing floor that is surrounded with a hedge of thorns.

In other words when the kings of Canaan and the princes of Ishmael saw that the funeral party was under Egyptian protection ("Joseph's crown") not only did they abandon their war plans, but they actually joined the funeral.[40] In the exodus, the Israelites, however, lacking Egyptian backing, could neither persuade the Canaanites to negotiate with them nor offer them anything in exchange for the land.

Finally, perhaps along the way the Egyptians too would have received the Torah at Sinai. A well-known midrash[41] holds that God offered the Torah

---

[37] The views expressed in this section are mine, not Fohrman's.
[38] Shlomo Yitzchaki (1040–1105), medieval French rabbi and biblical commentator.
[39] Talmud, *Sotah* 13a.
[40] My reading here diverges from Fohrman's. He points out that Canaan, the grandson of Noah (Gn 9:20–27), and Ishmael were both alienated from their families, just as Joseph had been. In Fohrman's reading, their descendants see, in Joseph's reconciliation with his family, a sign of hope for their own longed-for reconciliation with Israel.
[41] Midrash Sifri.

to all nations, but Israel alone accepted it. This aligns with my proposal here: precisely by rejecting the word of God, spoken through Moses and Aaron, and through "signs and wonders" (Ex 7:3, RSV), Egypt, through its pharaoh, rejected the Torah.[42]

Fohrman ends his book on a hopeful note:

> The Exodus, as it actually happened in history, did not accomplish everything it might have. There is work yet to do to complete its unrealized vision. The procession that departed Egypt was a shadow of what it might have been. It will be the destiny of Jew and Gentile to one day realize the promise of that journey as it should have taken place.[43]

To see what the realization of this vision might mean for Egypt, let us return to the theme of "body and land," now in the context of Egypt.

OUT OF *EGYPT* I CALLED MY SON: "THE TRUE AND IDEAL EGYPT"

> We emerged from the crucible of Egypt, head first against the banks of the sea. The waters broke. We emerged through a narrow canal to become the children of Israel, no longer Hebrews. The taskmasters who had held us in the womb of Egypt came after and, like afterbirth, perished in the process.
> —Mitchell Chefitz, *White Fire: Angels Flying from Holy Letters*[44]

Egypt Is the Mother of Israel

God is the father of Israel (Jer 31:7), but Egypt is its mother. She received into herself the patriarchs Abraham and Jacob, adopted as her own their sons Joseph[45] and Moses (Ex 2:1–10),[46] and in the fullness of time brought forth Israel. But because she disobeyed the commandment "Let my people go" (Ex 5:1),[47] most severe were her pangs in childbearing and in pain she bore her child (cf. Gn 3:16); this is the actual exodus. Yet her urge is for her

---

42 However, the Septuagint originated in Egypt; cf. quote by Chromatius above.

43 Fohrman, *The Exodus You Almost Passed Over*, ch. 30.

44 Mitchell Chefitz, "The Reed Sea," *White Fire: Angels Flying from Holy Letters* (Wordclay, 2010).

45 Fohrman argues that by giving Joseph a new name and a wife (Gn 41:45) the pharaoh is, in effect, adopting him as his son; Fohrman, *The Exodus You Almost Passed Over*, Chapter 22, "The Triangle."

46 Note the parallel between Joseph and Moses, who are, narratively, the first and last Israelite in Egypt.

47 These are the first words spoken by Moses and Aaron to Pharaoh.

husband, that is God, and He shall rule over her (cf. Gn 3:16). Thus, at the second exodus (Mt 2:19–21), "without corruption[48] she brought forth God the Word."[49] By his sojourn in Egypt, Christ elevated—"recapitulated"—her from Eve to Theotokos. In other words, bringing Matthew into dialogue with Fohrman: Matthew agrees with Fohrman's exegetical claim that the historical exodus fell short of its vision—but adds that Christ has began the realization of "the promise of that journey as it should have taken place."[50]

Moreover, because Egypt is the paradigmatic Gentile nation, not only in Exodus but in the whole Torah, the reconciliation we are speaking of is not just between Israel and Egypt but between Israel and all Gentile nations.[51] To broaden our theology of international relations from Egypt in particular to nations in general, we shall next develop the thought that Egypt is the mother of Israel into a more general notion of land as relational.

Land Is a Medium of Relationality

What is a body? Although contemporary western culture emphasizes the (purported) autonomy of human bodies, in fact, as a moment's reflection reveals, bodies are intrinsically relational. It is through our bodies that we relate to the material world and to other persons. Indeed, we may say that humans are embodied relations. But if, as we have argued, land is related to body, then a people's land also embodies their relationality to other peoples. We can now appreciate more fully why God chose not merely a people (*am*) but rather a nation (*goy*), the difference, as Ephraim Speiser points out, being a "territorial base."[52] In his words:

> Yet we are told also on many occasions—and have the independent evidence of grammar and phraseology to the same effect—that, in terms of God's own connection with the people, Israel was his *am*. It was chosen and treated as such. But *to carry out God's purpose*, as that purpose is expressed

---

[48] That is, with neither pain nor injury to herself.
[49] From the "Axion Estin," a hymn to the Theotokos in eastern Christianity.
[50] Fohrman, *The Exodus You Almost Passed Over*, ch. 30.
[51] A possible contemporary exemplar might be India and Israel, where the immigration (*aliyah*) of Indian Jews to Israel, some from communities whose presence in India predates Christianity, and in the absence of any persecution or antisemitism, has coincided with the increasingly close ties between the two countries. However, the growing closeness of ties can also be explained by geopolitical factors. Moreover, the modern pre-1984 immigration of Jews to Palestine placed the native Arab population in position analogous to that of the Egyptians of the Egypt into which Joseph's family immigrated. Thus, perhaps Palestinians too could be seen by Israelis to be in a maternal relationship to them.
[52] Speiser, *Genesis*, 86n2.

by the Bible as a whole, the *am* was not enough; what was needed was the added status and stability of nationhood in a land specifically designated for that purpose.[53]

We conclude that the divine purpose includes the Chosen People relating, through their land, qua people, to other peoples.[54] Thus the gift of land, far from isolating *Am Yisrael* from other peoples, is a gift of a medium of relationality to other peoples—and thus it is a gift to all nations.[55]

Land as Divinely Relational Is Temple-Land

The Hebrew Bible too sees land as a medium of relationality, but not so much relationality between humans as relationality between humanity and God. This idea is introduced early with God "moving about in the garden [of Eden]" (Gn 3:8); returns when Jacob recognizes Bethel[56] as "abode of God" and "gateway to heaven" (Gn 28:10–19); and results at last in Solomon's Temple, which was filled with the glory of God (2 Chr 7:1–2). Thus the *land on which the Temple stood* is an elevation of land-as-relational from the plane of intra-human relations to the plane of human-divine relations.

For Maimonides, this temple-land (and, more broadly, the land of Jerusalem) retains its holiness in spite of the destruction of the Temple "because the sanctity of the Temple and Jerusalem stems from the *Shechinah*,[57] and the *Shechinah* can never be nullified."[58] Since the Temple as building was destroyed long before Maimonides, his reasoning seems to be that it was not so much the building that was sanctified by the *Shechinah* but rather the land on which it stood. This is supported by his mention of Jerusalem in this context since the built environment of the city had vastly changed since the time of David/Solomon. If nevertheless, for Maimonides, it still retains

---

53 Speiser, "'People' and 'Nation' of Israel"; emphasis mine.

54 Qua persons they would relate to other persons by being embodied.

55 Note that it is not being claimed that *Ertez Yisrael* is a gift to all peoples *in the same manner*. Rather, that, in having been gifted in one way to *Am Yisrael*, it has also been gifted, in another way, to all peoples. This is formally similar to Wyschogrod's claim that God is Father to all, but not in the same way to Jew and Gentile. Michael Wyschogrod, "A Chosen Nation," *The Body of Faith: God in the People Israel* (Lanham, MD: Rowman and Littlefield, 2000).

56 Literally, "house of God."

57 That is, the divine presence. See, for example, Sharon Koren, "Shechinah" in *The Cambridge Dictionary of Judaism and Jewish Culture*, ed. Judith R. Baskin (Cambridge: Cambridge University Press, 2011), 546.

58 Maimonides, *Mishneh Torah* (New York: Moznaim Publishers, 1998), Book 8, Sefer Avodah [The Book of Service], Chapter 7, Beit Habechirah [Laws of the Temple], 6:16. Note that since *Shechinah* in rabbinic literature functions like *kavod* in the Hebrew Bible (cf., e.g., Sharon Koren, op. cit.), Mainmonides is alluding to 2 Chronicles 7:1–2, cited above.

it sanctity, then the sanctity cannot stem from what is transient—the buildings, but what is permanent—the land.

God's opening words to Pharaoh, "Let my people go that they may celebrate a festival for me" (Ex 5:1) link the exodus to the worship of God. Tragically Pharaoh rejects the implicit invitation to *enquire*, "Who is the Lord that I should heed him?" Instead, he uses these very words to *reject* the divine command, thus settling for a demonstration of divine power rather than a revelation of the divine name—which is revealed to Moses immediately thereafter (Ex 5:22ff. especially 6:3). Jerusalem and Zion[59] feature prominently in the prophetic promise that Pharaoh's rejection is not the last word, that knowledge of God and his commandments will be offered again to all nations. For example:

> The many peoples/nations shall go and shall say:
> "Come, let us go up to the Mount of the Lord,
> To the House of the God of Jacob;
> That he may instruct us in his ways,
> And that we may walk in his paths."
> For instruction shall come forth from Zion,
> The word of the Lord from Jerusalem. (Is 2:3; Mi 4:2)

Thus, while all peoples, including *Am Yisrael*, relate to other peoples through their land, *Eretz Yisrael* is in addition, uniquely, the land through which God relates to all peoples. Precisely in this way is *Eretz Yisrael* a gift to all nations.

THE TEMPLE AND *ERETZ YISRAEL*
The Temple

> The love of Israel requires the love of all mankind.
> —Avraham Yitzhak Kook, *Orot Yisrael*, 4:5[60]

The biblical account of the origin of the Temple follows a similar pattern to the one we have described for the exodus. The first to desire the building of a temple, David, was forbidden to do so, for he had "shed much blood" (1 Chr 22:8, 28:3). It appears implicit in this that, although David's efforts to establish

---

[59] The site of the Temple is one of the meanings of "Zion." Cf., e.g., Baskin, *The Cambridge Dictionary of Judaism and Jewish Culture*.

[60] Cited in David Dishon, "'The Beauty of Yefet in the Tents of Shem': Gentiles and Jews in the Thought of Rav Kook," *Havrruta* (Fall 2008): 83.

the nascent Israelite nation were not per se sinful (any more than the exodus under Moses was sinful), nevertheless, insofar as they involved violence against Gentiles,[61] they, like the exodus, fell short of the divine blueprint.

We conclude, then, that for *Eretz Yisrael* to be a land through which God and humanity are related—which we have argued above occurs through temple-land—*Eretz Yisrael* needs first to become a land that is rightly related to Gentile lands. In other words, to be a land of justice, not only *within* its borders but also *at* it borders.[62]

"Divine wisdom to execute justice" (1 Kgs 3:28) characterized the builder of the (first) Temple, Solomon. The building of the Temple was entrusted to one who, when invited by God, "Ask, what shall I grant you?" (1 Kgs 3:5), requested, not long life, not riches, *nor the death of his enemies*, but rather "discernment in dispensing justice" (1 Kgs 3:11).

The subsequent history of Israel confirms that justice is a prerequisite for the continued existence of the Temple.[63] The prophets locate the reason for the destruction of the (first) Temple, not in regional geopolitics, but in the failure to "do justice and to love goodness" (Mi 6:8).

That God might abide among them is the very reason that the Israelites were brought out from the land of Egypt.[64] Because the dwelling of God presupposes justice, insofar as *Eretz Yisrael* is not a land of justice it is still an extension of *Eretz Mitzraim*, "the house of bondage" (Ex 20:2).[65]

Eretz Yisrael

One last facet remains to be developed in the analogy between body and land that this essay has explored: temple-land, we have argued, is the supernatural raison d'etre of *Eretz Yisrael*. But surely in Christian thought it is the body of Christ that is the true temple? Was it not in Christ's own body that "the fulness of God was pleased to dwell" (Col 1:19)?

---

61 For example, Jerusalem was captured from the Jebusites (2 Sm 6–9; 1 Chr 11:4–7).

62 The *am* dimension of this principle is the well-known teaching that God desires "goodness, not sacrifice" (Hos 6:6).

63 Thus among religious Zionists the view may be found that "social reform in the spirit of the Prophets" is needed before Jews can even visit the Temple Mount. Motti Inbari, "Religious Zionism and the Temple Mount Dilemma—Key Trends," *Israel Studies* 12, no. 2 (2007): 46, footnote 42. This ethical demand is not limited to Jews or even Israelis but extends to all humanity: "The love of Israel requires the love of all mankind."

64 "I the Lord am their God, who brought them out from the land of Egypt that I might abide among them" (Ex 29:46).

65 See also Michael Wyschogrod, "Reflections on the Six-Day War after a Quarter Century," in *Abraham's Promise: Judaism and Jewish-Christian Relations*, ed. R. Kendall Soulen (Grand Rapids, MI: Eerdmans, 2004).

Indeed, but this human temple is, qua human, related to land precisely because, as we have already argued, humans are related to land not only collectively but also in the singular. In other words, while Jews and Christians might disagree on the identity of the true temple, they can both agree on the identity of "temple-land": it is *Eretz Yisrael* in general and Jerusalem in particular.[66] For Jews the relation between Temple and temple-land is the relation between a building and the land on which it stands; for Christians it is the relation between a person and his homeland. In other words, for Christians, *Eretz Yisrael* is temple-land because Jesus was an Israelite.[67]

The Resurrection of *Eretz Yisrael*

While both the Jewish Temple and the Christian temple (i.e., the body of Christ) were destroyed,[68] Christians hold, in addition, that their temple has been resurrected. The resurrection of Christ gives Christians grounds to hope[69] that *Eretz Yisrael* will attain its true telos by becoming a land of justice. Then would *Am Yisrael* have truly returned from exile. This is the resurrected Land of Israel.

Where does this leave the current State of Israel? How is it related to the nation of Israel of this paper? On the one hand the citizenship and land of the State of Israel draws from *Am Yisrael* and *Eretz Yisrael*, respectively; on the other hand it can hardly be contested that it is not yet wholly a land of justice.[70] The logic of this essay suggests, then, that the State of Israel is potentially, but not yet actually, the nation of Israel of this essay. It may be compared to biblical Israel under Saul, still awaiting the establishment of the Davidic dynasty and Solomon's reign of justice.[71]

---

66 Cf. Maimonides, quoted above.

67 The Gospels use the more specific term "Nazarene" (Mt 2:23, Mk 14:67). The argument here is consistent with traditional Christian piety that sees *Eretz Yisrael* as "Holy Land" precisely because it is the land on which Jesus walked. Note that this rationale for such piety is identical to that of Maimonides.

68 For a survey of how various New Testament texts relate the death of Jesus to the destruction of the Temple see P. W. L. Walker, *Jesus and the Holy City: New Testament Perspectives on Jerusalem* (Grand Rapids, MI: Eerdmans, 1996).

69 "Hope," not in the sense of "wish" but as a theological virtue. See M. Douglas Meeks, "Hope" in *The Cambridge Dictionary of Christian Theology*, 225–26.

70 See footnote 61.

71 See also Michael Wyschogrod, "A King in Israel," *First Things* no. 203 (2010); where Wyschogrod proposes that Israel "be declared a Davidic monarchy without a reigning king." Wyschogrod's objective is to make "the messianic hope of the Jewish people" a part of "the self-understanding of the state of Israel" while "excluding a messianic interpretation of the present state of Israel." The view expressed in this essay is consonant with this.

PART II

MINING THE TRADITION

5

LAND AND STATE OF ISRAEL
THEOLOGICAL REFLECTIONS FROM A ROMAN CATHOLIC PERSPECTIVE

Christian M. Rutishauser, SJ

The conflict around Israel/Palestine greatly arouses both secular and religious feelings. Personal faith, collective religious identity, European history, as well as sociocultural and political developments combine in an inextricable mixture. Objective argument and fundamental reflection are necessary in order to give the two ethnicities and the three faith traditions living between the Jordan and the Mediterranean their appropriate respective space and to take into account the universal significance of the Land. In order to enable disentanglement, political, social, cultural and religious aspects must be distinguished. It is necessary to perceive the various theologies and world views that people connect with Israel today.[1] At the same time, the ability is required to then relate these to one another. The goal is to do justice to all who are affected so that they might have a future in this Land, which belongs to the "House of Islam," which is holy to Christians, and which for Jews is a home before God.

The following reflections are a contribution to the question regarding the significance today of the Land promise in the Hebrew Bible. The return

---

This paper has been translated and modified from its original publication as "Eretz Israel—Ein Land das Christen heilig ist," *Zeitschrift für christlich-jüdische Begegnung im Kontext*, no. 1 (2019), 14–25.

[1] One attempt at this: Peter Bingel and Winfried Belz, *Israel kontrovers: Eine theologisch-politische Standortbestimmung* (Zürich: Rotpunktverlag, 2013).

of so many Jews to *Eretz Yisrael* since the end of the nineteenth century and the establishment of the State of Israel also call upon Christians to think anew about the question of the Land in the Bible. I am writing as a Roman Catholic theologian from Europe who is committed to Jewish-Christian dialogue. In this context, the Church first of all rejects the theology of substitution which claims that the Church as *verus Israel* has replaced Judaism as the people of God in salvation history. In its documents, the Church speaks of God's "covenant" with the Jewish people "that has never been revoked."[2] Thus, the Church must also pay attention to Judaism's close connection with *Eretz Yisrael*, since the promise of the Land is a firm part of God's covenant with Israel, a fact that is often disregarded.[3] At the same time, the Roman Catholic Church knows of its connection through baptism with the Palestinian Christians of all denominations. The covenant of the New Testament in Christ is no less firm than that of Sinai; these must be understood in reference to one another.[4] Even though so far a theology of the Holy Land has hardly been developed among Roman-Catholic theologians, there is nevertheless a rich tradition of political theology, as for example the theology of liberation.[5] Above all, since the nineteenth century, a Catholic social teaching has developed that is alive to this day and which the popes continue to develop. In forming a secular society, everywhere on earth should consider its principles, because the Church is concerned with peace and justice among all human beings. In Israel/Palestine this must be combined with unique biblical and dogmatic specifications, something that until now has hardly happened. In addition, the Church also looks with esteem to the spiritual-theological tradition of Islam, as is testified by *Nostra Aetate* and

---

[2] Commission for Religious Relations with the Jews, *"The Gifts and the Calling of God Are Irrevocable" (Rom 11:29): A Reflection on Theological Questions Pertaining to Catholic–Jewish Relations on the Occasion of the 50th Anniversary of "Nostra Aetate,"* (2015). The fact that Pope Emeritus Benedict questioned this consensus in 2018 had an immediate effect, as we shall see further on.

[3] Adam Gregerman, "Is the Biblical Land Promise Irrevocable?: Post-*Nostra Aetate* Catholic Theologies of the Jewish Covenant and the Land of Israel," *Modern Theology* 34, no. 2 (2018): 142.

[4] From the wealth of literature on determining the relationship: *Reinterpreting Revelation and Tradition: Jews and Christians in Conversation*, ed. John T. Pawlikowski and Hayim Goren Perelmuter (Franklin, WI: Sheed and Ward, 2000); "Judentum und Christentum," *Theologische Realenzyklopädie (TRE)* (Berlin: Walter de Gruyter, 1987), 391–403; Johannes Oesterreicher, "Unter dem Bogen des Einen Bundes: Das Volk Gottes: seine Zweigestalt und Einheit," *Judentum und Kirche: Volk Gottes*, ed. Josef Pfammatter and Franz Furger (Zürich: Benziger, 1974), 7–69.

[5] Although there are hardly any Palestinian Roman Catholic liberation theologians, there are representatives among the Lutherans and Anglicans. See Raheb Mitri, *Ich bin Christ und Palästinenser: Israel, seine Nachbarn und die Bibel*, (Gütersloh: Gütersloher Verlagshaus, 1994); *Faith in the Face of Empire: The Bible through Palestinian Eyes*, (Maryknoll N.Y.: Orbis Books, 2014); also see Naim Stifan Ateek, *Recht, nichts als Recht: Entwurf einer palästinensisch-christlichen Theologie*, (Fribourg Brig: Edition Exodus, 1990).

the Vatican documents on Catholic-Muslim dialogue. Without developing Muslim positions in this article, let it be stated here that the Qur'an speaks of the "blessed Land" for the children of Israel and itself develops a close relationship with Jerusalem as a holy place and city, but it does not know of a divine promise of Land in relationship to Israel/Palestine. Rather, this Land belongs to the traditional "house of Islam," and the idea of Palestine as a "holy area" only developed during the twentieth century in the context of national-religious thinking.[6]

Against the background of this rich theological tradition since the Second Vatican Council, the reflections in this article aim beyond the present-day politics in the Middle East conflict. However, they were written with the awareness of this conflict in the Land and of the injustice that people are suffering every day. First of all, a sketch will be given of how the Land is presented in the Hebrew Bible (I). Then some Jewish-theological reflection will be taken up that in view of the Middle East conflict considers the Land and the State of Israel in such a way that they are compatible with non-Jewish positions (II). There will follow a presentation of the Christian reinterpretation of the Old Testament promise of the Land and Christianity's understanding of the Land as Holy Land (III). In the fourth section, Christian-theological voices that interpret Zionism and the establishment of the State of Israel are to be heard (IV). Finally, I shall suggest an understanding of the Land and State of Israel in the context of a theology of Judaism that is based on Roman Catholic ecclesiology and social teaching (V). The chapter will end with a brief word on a theology of history (VI).

THE PROMISE OF A LAND IN THE HEBREW BIBLE[7]

Whatever the situation might have been at the time of the nomadic patriarchs and matriarchs, and however the Exodus is reconstructed historically, the Torah text that is normative for faith speaks of a land promise to Abraham and Jacob (Gn 12:1; 15:18; 17:8; 28:13ff.). They go to the Land that God shows them, although the fact that the Land is already populated is not disregarded. However, both Abraham and Jacob and his sons must again leave the Land. The entire Joseph narrative speaks of the departure from the Land to a foreign country because of famine and strife between brothers (Gn 12:10–20;

---

[6] Friedmann Eissler, "Islamische Ansprüche auf das 'Land'—Jerusalem und das heilige Land in Koran und Islam," *Wem gehört das 'Heilige Land?': Christlich-theologische Überlegungen zur biblischen Landverheissung*, ed. Berthold Schwarz (Frankfurt: Peter Lang, 2014), 91–131.

[7] In greater detail, Ludger Schwienhorst-Schönberger, "Land," *Wörterbuch alttestamentlicher Motive*, ed. Michael Fieger, Jutta Krispenz, and Jörg Lankau (Darmstadt: Wissenschaftliche Buchgesellschaft, 2013).

Gn 37–50). With his first purchase of land, Abraham acquires only a piece of ground for Sarah's grave (Gn 23). Prior to this, a permanent living in the Land is not given. The Israelite people, on the other hand, is established as such in Egypt (Ex 1:1–7). The promise of land begins to be fulfilled with the departure of the Israelites from slavery in Egypt: Abraham's journey into the Land corresponds with the Exodus through the desert to the promised Land, which lasted more than forty years. Four of the five books of the Torah describe this journey, during which the Israelites learn to be a people that does not build its culture on exploitation and injustice like the Egyptians, but according to God's teaching. The Israelites are to become God's people. This is the Hebrew Bible's alternative project. But here as well: Because of its unteachability, the people together with its leader Moses is buried before it enters the Land (Dt 1:34ff.; 34:1–8). The entry into the Land is not described until the book of Joshua, so in a book that according to Jewish reading belongs to the early prophets. The written Torah, which is at the center of the covenant between God and God's people, only describes the journey to the Land.

In the book of Joshua, the settling in the Land is described as a conquest full of violence, which at times also legitimizes the destruction of the indigenous population (Jo 6) with the same radicalness with which deviants among the Israelites themselves are eliminated (Nm 16). The political organization of society in the Land varies considerably in the course of history: Upon the loose covenant between tribes in the time of the so-called judges, follows the introduction of the monarchy, which is presented critically in the books of Samuel insofar as on the one hand, the monarchy might endanger and be in competition with the sovereignty of God and of God's commandments. On the other hand, the monarchy represents an alignment with other nations, as for example with Egypt, which biblical tradition itself criticizes (1 Sm 8). But the Exodus was supposed to overcome precisely a society based on injustice and hierarchies of power. The alternative, to be a particular, holy people of priests belonging to the God of the Exodus (cf. Ex 19:5) was what was at stake. However, David and Solomon became the type of ideal kings. Upon the destruction of the two kingdoms of Israel and Judea in the years 722 and 586 BCE followed the time of expulsion from the Land. After the Babylonian exile, the people were not at first politically independent, until the Hasmonean State (167–63 BCE) achieved a priestly-theocratic government. Afterward, the Jewish people were under Roman authority until, in 70 CE, Jerusalem was destroyed, and in 137 CE, the people were expelled from Judea.

This brief survey shows that the people's political sovereignty in the Land was often only for a brief time. In addition, the movement away from the Land and back to the Land constantly continued. Both movements mark biblical tradition. But above all, this tradition also takes up texts promising the Land and conquering the Land, which are meant to digest the experience of exile in Babylon and to make a new future in the Land also possible.[8] On the one hand, the Land is thereby given as an unconditional gift (Gn 12; 15); on the other hand, conditions are also formulated to which life in the Land is bound. These can be summarized in the following points: (1) Upon entering the Land, it becomes clear that there is already an indigenous population (Dt 4; 7). The people of Israel are not an indigenous population. The God of the Bible is so crazy that he leads a people into a Land that is already populated. The biblical Land theology is not a theology of *Blut und Boden* (blood and soil). It is not arguing a natural rights claim. (2) The Israelites receive the Land as a loan from the real owner, namely God himself (Dt 9:4–5). (3) The gift of the Land is a basis for an alternative society that lives the Torah in justice also for the foreigner (Dt 7:8). The Land is given for an ethical project, not for an ethnic one. (4) The Israelites do not have a right to remain in the Land; if they do not fulfill the job given them, they are expelled (Lv 18:24–30). God not only promises the Land, but also expels from the Land. There is no theology of the Land without a theology of the diaspora. The movement between the two places, not only living in them, is significant. (5) Life in the diaspora is interpreted as God's punishment, the return as reconciliation. Already with the prophets, the return to the Land is connected with messianic hope: God himself will lead the people back from their dispersal (Ez 37:21–22; Jer 23:7–8; etc.). The destruction of Jerusalem and its reconstruction, the expulsion from Jerusalem and the return to the city are always understood as punishment, forgiveness and God's renewed fidelity to God's people. In any case, the return to the Land is connected ever more with a renewal of the covenant (Jer 29–32), with a perspective for the future (Gn 12:1–3), and even with an eschatological time (Mi 4:1–5; Is 66:22). (6) The promise of the Land is independent of a particular political form in which the people of God organizes itself in the Land. God wants to remain the ultimate sovereign in every political form of organization.

---

[8] On the historico-critical reconstruction of texts promising the Land: Ulrike Bechmann, "Die Auslegung biblischer Landverheissungen: Ein Beispiel für die Ambivalenz kontextueller Theologien," *Der Nahostkonflikt: Politische, religiöse und theologische Dimensionen*, ed. Dirk Ansorge (Stuttgart: Kohlhammer, 2010), 55–69.

JEWISH-THEOLOGICAL INTERPRETERS OF THE LAND

Judaism is rightly counted among the great world religions, since it claims to bear universal truth. It has spread over the whole world, and during every period of time it makes possible a religious way of life that is holistic. The Land of Israel has thereby always remained a spiritual point of reference. The longing, but also the commandment to live in *Eretz Yisrael* over and over again brought Jews to return to the Land, to make a so-called *aliyah*. The diaspora and the Land form two poles in Jewish thought and faith that stand in reference to one another. However, an evaluation of the Land that is only positive and a negative one of the diaspora would be too simple, for Jewish existence is based on a life of the Torah, while the return to the Land was left in traditional-rabbinic thinking to the messianic end of time. Thus it is no coincidence that the great Jewish cultural achievements were produced in the diaspora. Let us mention only Jewish philosophy and mysticism, the great legal collections as well as the Babylonian Talmud. Even the Hebrew Bible itself came about in connection with the Babylonian exile and may be called in the words of Heinrich Heine the "portative homeland" of the Jews.[9] As well, life outside of *Eretz Yisrael* is considered to be positive because of the prophetic assignment to be a light for the nations, to be for them a model of righteousness and justice, as well as to bring the faith in the God of Israel. From Isaiah (Is 42:6; 49:6) to the present, the universal significance of Judaism is described in this way.[10]

Different reasons are given for making *aliyah*, so for returning to the Land and living in the Land: As we have seen, the gathering of the people in the Land has been interpreted since biblical times as a messianic or eschatological sign. Even if modern Zionism was first of all a secular movement to create a national home for the Jews, it is also understood in a religious sense at least since the Six-Day War in 1967. The father of Zionism who is interpreted messianically is the Chief Rabbi of the pre-State Jewish community in *Eretz Yisrael*, Rabbi Abraham Isaac Kook, who died in 1935. Today, the settler movement in the West Bank is based on an eschatological-messianic theology.[11] This states that the State of Israel, which is recognized by international law, was established at the edge of the biblically promised Land, so to speak *ante portas*. But key areas of *Eretz Yisrael* are unambiguously Samaria,

---

9 Heinrich Heine, *Sämtliche Werke*, vol. 13 (Munich: Winkkler, 1964), 128.

10 The detailed preamble to one of the most recent documents of Jewish Orthodoxy: European Rabbinical Conference and the Rabbinical Council of America, *Between Jerusalem and Rome: Reflections on 50 Years of Nostra Aetate* (2017).

11 Hagemann Steffen, *Die Siedlerbewegung: Fundamentalismus in Israel* (Schwalbach: Wochenschau-Verlag, 2010).

Judea, and Jerusalem, so these areas have been occupied since 1967. Another theological reason for life in the State of Israel consists in being able to live, as far as is possible, all of the commandments of the Torah in the Land and also to form a Jewish society. Thus the thinking of Yeshayahu Leibowitz, who lived in Jerusalem until his death in 1994, but who often sharply criticized Israeli politics. In a similar way Rabbi Joseph B. Soloveitchik saw it; he lived in the USA and was formerly the honorary president of the religious-Zionist movement *Mizrachi*; he refused to be made Chief Rabbi in the State of Israel. He believed that after the sufferings of the *Shoah* and through Zionism, God was inviting his people to live in Israel in order there to build a fully orthodox Jewish life; in this, Soloveitchik is very far from messianic thinking.[12] Abraham J. Heschel as well does not see in the newly established State of Israel a sign of the end of time but rather a divine consolation and a help following the *Shoah*: "Israel helps us to bear the torment of Auschwitz without despairing entirely, helps us to feel a ray of God's shining in the jungle of history."[13]

In this connection, cultural Zionism, which wanted to unfold the Hebrew language and culture in the Land of the Bible, should also be mentioned. Along with Simon Dubnov and Ahad Ha'am, Martin Buber was one of its great representatives. Buber was marked by religious socialism and aimed at a Hebrew humanitarianism which was to give the Jewish people a renewed identity in *Eretz Yisrael*.[14] Buber spoke over and over again of the fact that this ideal had to be implemented in the Land in the face of the political difficulty of living together with the Arabs. His writings on Jewish-Arab coexistence are today unfortunately hardly relevant. However, this humanitarian cultural Zionism would be an alternative to the national-religious Zionism, which ever more wants Jewish identity to dominate at the cost of both the Christian and the Muslim Palestinian population. Today, other theological thinkers such as David Meyer, who lives in Toronto, are seeking ways of access to the Land that are compatible with Palestinian coexistence. He says that a new access to *Eretz Yisrael* must be found.[15] He speaks of a "rabbinization" of the Land and means by this that it must be understood like the holy text of the Torah: The ambiguity of the Land, its positive relationship to the diaspora,

---

12 Joseph B. Soloveitchik, *Kol dodi dofek: Listen—My Beloved Knocks* (New York: KTAV, 2006), 43–89.

13 Abraham J. Heschel, *Israel: Echo der Ewigkeit* (Neukirchen-Vluyn: Neukirchener Verlag, 1988), 73.

14 Buber Martin, *Israel und Palästina: Zur Geschichte einer Idee* (Zürich: Artemis, 1950).

15 David Meyer and Bernard Philippe, *Europe et Israël, deux destins inaccomplis: Regards croisés entre un diplomate et un rabbin* (Paris: Lessius, 2017), 91–112.

its holiness that is removed from political power calculations, etc., must be made conscious. Without being able to introduce here further Jewish-theological positions regarding the Land, Christian theology must deepen its understanding of the many Jewish ways of access to the Land.[16] Otherwise there is a great danger of understanding Land and State of Israel either only in a secular or only in a religious fundamentalist way.

THE HOLY LAND OF THE CHRISTIANS

Calling it the "Old Testament," Christians made the Hebrew Bible their own scripture of Revelation, and they thereby interpreted the promise of the Land as fulfilled through Joshua's conquest of the Land. For Joshua's namesake, Jesus of Nazareth, the Land also has significance, since in his movement he gathers the people from the edges, that is to say from Galilee. He leads the people to the center, to Jerusalem. However, for this new Joshua the trademark for access to *Eretz Yisrael* is precisely nonviolence: "Blessed are the meek [those who do not use violence], for they will inherit the Land" (Mt 5:5). In addition, according to the childhood narrative in the Gospel according to Matthew, Jesus, as before him the Israelites, is led from Egypt into the Land (Mt 2:13–23). Thus the connection between the people and the Land of Israel is not done away with in the New Testament, something which can be seen especially in the first two chapters of the Gospel according to Luke: Jesus, the newborn, is to be the ruler over the house of Jacob (1:32–33) and to free Israel from the hand of the enemies (1:68–75).[17] However, in its basic dictum the New Testament does not present a movement into the Land. On the contrary, it goes out from the Land: "Go, and make disciples of all nations" is the mission given by the risen Jesus (Mt 28:19). In the Acts of the Apostles and in the letters of Paul, the spreading of early Christianity outside the Land is described. But a connection with the Land and with Jerusalem remains thereby, when Paul's communities in Asia Minor collect money (Act 11:27–30; 2 Cor 8–9). In gratitude, the connection to Jerusalem is upheld, whence God's teaching is brought to all nations, as is described in the pilgrimage of nations in Isaiah 2 and Micah 4: "Salvation comes from the Jews" (Jn 4:22). The Land where people live as disciples of Christ according

---

16 Eugene Korn, *The Jewish Connection to Israel, the Promised Land: A Brief Introduction for Christians* (Woodstock: Jewish Lights, 2008).

17 Extensively on this: Klaus Wengst, "Zum Glanz für Dein Volk Israel," *Mache Dich auf und werde Licht!: Ökumenische Visionen in Zeiten des Umbruchs*, ed. Dagmar Heller (Frankfurt: Lembeck, 2008), 234–39.

to divine teaching is now the whole earth. Paul testifies to this and over and over again refers to Abraham as the guarantor of the covenant that has been opened for all through Christ (Rom 4). What is noticeable in this is that the promise of the Land is missing. This is also the case in Paul's listing of the privileges of the Israelites' election (2 Cor 11:21ff.). The goal of the Christian way is now no longer the earthly but the heavenly Jerusalem. Its description is the New Testament's vanishing point in Revelation 21–22. Paul writes: "Our home is in heaven" (Phlm 3:20). Thus two things can be said of early Christianity: On the one hand, the poles in the Land and in the diaspora are dissolved. The promise of the Land is seen as fulfilled in Christ and becomes universalized. God can be adored everywhere in the world. God wants to be adored in "spirit and in truth" (Jn 4:19–24). Justin Martyr, for example, formulated this explicitly.[18] On the other hand, the Land is spiritualized in view of heaven and the human soul. Origen writes: "I do not seek a holy place on earth but in the heart. . . . The holy place is the pure soul."[19]

When in the fourth century Christianity became the Roman Empire's state religion and the expectation of a historical end of time was definitively dropped, a new interest in the Land of the Bible developed. But for the Christians it is no longer a matter of a promised Land. Nor do they want to live in the Land; this is no longer a commandment for them. Rather, in looking back historically, the Land becomes a place of remembering the salvific deeds of God. For Christians it becomes the Holy Land because God, the Holy One, worked there, and because God's Son, Jesus Christ, once lived there. In the thinking of salvation history, the Land becomes a sacramental reference to God's deeds. Now, individual holy sites and places of pilgrimage are identified in the Land based on biblical texts. Already Egeria, on her pilgrimage between 381 and 384 CE, lets the local population show her where the biblical events took place. In the field, she reads the biblical text about it, prays, and marks the place. The great councils of Nicea, Constantinople, Chalcedon, and Ephesus in the fourth and fifth centuries on the other hand lead to the building of memorial churches in the Land so that the newly formulated faith can be celebrated.[20] The sites, and over and beyond them the whole Land, acquire ever more of a liturgical-sacred function.

The new understanding of the Holy Land and of its spiritualization brings forth three corresponding realities that mark Christianity everywhere

---

18 Quoted in Pierre Maraval, "Die Anfänge der Pilgerfahrten," *Welt und Umwelt der Bibel: Archäologie, Kunst, Geschichte* 2, no. 2 (2000): 27.

19 Maraval, "Die Anfänge der Pilgerfahrten," 27.

20 Biberstein, "Das Evangelium wird begehbar: Ein Netz der Erinnerungen," *Welt und Umwelt der Bibel: Archäologie, Kunst, Geschichte* 4, no. 16 (2015): 33–37.

on earth: (1) Where martyrs died following Jesus, everywhere in the world memorial churches are built over their graves. These correspond with the magnificent church of the tomb and resurrection in the place of the death and resurrection of Jesus in Jerusalem. (2) The pilgrims now bring souvenirs from the Holy Land home with them, first and foremost relics from the surroundings of Jesus' execution and the bones of the apostles. And relics are mobile memorials and make it possible to erect altars and churches for them everywhere in the world. They correspond with the holy sites in the Holy Land. From the Middle Ages on, after their return home, pilgrims to Jerusalem have a copy of the tomb of Jesus built in various places in Europe. Thus the Holy Land with its sacred sites spreads everywhere by means of church and memorial buildings. (3) The heavenly Jerusalem also receives corresponding space in the Gothic cathedrals with their colored glass windows and their candelabras, which represent the heavenly city with the twelve gates. The Gothic church buildings were inspired by Revelation 21–22. Medieval Christianity's longing for the heavenly home and for the Holy Land is also a motivation for the Crusades. In this war, the holy sites are to be made accessible again to the pilgrims. Along with this goes a basic re-sacralization of the Land, which picks up the theology of the Land of the priestly schools in the Temple in Jerusalem.[21]

CHRISTIAN VOICES ON THE LAND AND STATE OF ISRAEL TODAY

When Theodor Herzl turned to Pope Pius X in 1904 and asked for support for political Zionism, the latter answered: "We cannot prevent Jews from going to Jerusalem, but we shall never approve of this."[22] A rethinking only happened after the *Shoah*. With *Nostra Aetate*, the Second Vatican Council takes a fundamentally positive position as regards Judaism. Fifty years later, the Church even speaks explicitly of a unique Jewish-Christian relationship. However, the Land issue and the position as it regards the State of Israel is hardly a topic within this frame. Pope Pius XII in his 1948 encyclical *In Multiplicibus Curis* speaks of the Palestine issue and demands—at the moment of the foundation of the Israeli state—an internationalization of Jerusalem and Bethlehem. At the same time, he created the "Papal Mission

---

[21] Dirk Ansorge, "Das christliche Konzept der 'terra sancta' und der Staat Israel: Theologische und politische Aspekte," *Der Nahostkonflikt: Politische, religiöse und theologische Dimensionen*, ed. Dirk Ansorge (Stuttgart: Kohlhammer, 2010), 146–50.

[22] Michael J. Pragai, *Sie sollen wieder wohnen in ihrem Land: Die Rolle von Christen bei der Heimkehr der Juden ins Land Israel* (Gerlingen: Bleicher, 1984), 183.

for Palestine," which is concerned with the Palestinian war refugees. The Holy See only takes up diplomatic relations with the State of Israel in 1993, whereby the relations are on the political level and that of international law. Even though the preamble of the fundamental contract speaks of the unique nature and the universal significance of the Land, the Vatican to this day maintains silence as regards a theological reflection on the Land and State of Israel.[23] Like all Christian theologians of the large Church in Europe, the Vatican demands justice and peace for Israelis and Palestinians, protection for the holy sites, the development of the local Church and its institutions, as well as the freedom of religious practice for Christians, Jews, and Muslims in the Land. In the year 2000, the Holy See officially took up contact with the office of the Palestinian Autonomy, and to this day it speaks in favor of a two-state solution. Since John Paul II, every pope has visited both Israel and the Palestinian areas.[24]

If one searches for a theological reflection on the return of so many Jews to *Eretz Yisrael* and on the existence of the State of Israel, a declaration of the French Bishops Conference in 1973 and of that of Brazil in 1984 cannot be overlooked. They call the return a "blessing" and connect Zionism with God's paths of justice.[25] The US bishops wrote in 1975, with somewhat greater distance, of the particularly close connection of the Jews to their Land, which should be respected. In 1984, Pope John Paul II wrote in his apostolic letter *Redemptionis Anno* regarding Jerusalem and the Land, that Muslim, Christian, and Jewish interpretations of the Land must be taken into consideration, so that Jerusalem may indeed be "a symbol of peace and harmony," a "symbol of coming together, of union, and of universal peace for the human family."[26]

He does not speak of Zionism. In official documents of the Catholic Church after 1985, every theological assessment of the Land and State of Israel is missing, which can be led back to the Vatican document *Notes on the Correct Way to Present the Jews and Judaism in the Preaching and Catechesis of the Catholic Church*. These *Notes* contain the following decisive passage:

---

23 Ralph Rotte, *Die Aussen- und Friedenspolitik des Heiligen Stuhls: Eine Einführung* (Wiesbaden: Springer, 2007), 143–49.

24 Matthias Kopp, *Franziskus im Heiligen Land: Päpste als Botschafter des Friedens: Paul VI.—Johannes Paul II.—Benedikt XVI.—Franzi* (Kevelaer: Butzon und Bercker, 2014).

25 All Church and Jewish documents on the Christian-Jewish relationship are collected in *Die Kirchen und das Judentum*, vol. 1–2, ed. Rolf Rendtorff and Hans Hermann Henrix (Paderborn: Bonifazius, 2001).

26 Marchadour and Neuhaus, *The Land, the Bible, and History* (New York: Fordham University Press, 2007), 204.

> The history of Israel did not end in 70 A.D. . . . It continued especially in a numerous Diaspora which allowed Israel to carry to the whole world a witness—often heroic—of its fidelity to the one God and to "exalt him in the presence of all the living" (Tb13:4), while preserving the memory of the land of their forefathers at the hearts of their hope. Christians are invited to understand this religious attachment which finds its roots in Biblical tradition, without however making their own any particular religious interpretation of this relationship. . . . The existence of the State of Israel and its political options should be envisaged not in a perspective which is in itself religious, but in their reference to the common principles of international law. The permanence of Israel . . . is a historic fact and a sign to be interpreted within God's design.[27]

The text says that the religious interpretations of the Land in Judaism should be understood but not taken on by Catholics. These latter should see the relations with the State of Israel only according to international law, so in a secular way, even if God's plan is mirrored therein. Judaism in the diaspora on the other hand is interpreted theologically, namely to glorify God among the nations. Joseph Ratzinger–Benedict XVI in his most recent article also interprets theologically the dispersion of the Jews from the Land in connection with their rejection of Jesus Christ and gives the diaspora a spiritual meaning as well. At the same time, he refuses to interpret the return to the Land and the state theologically, even if a side sentence says that in this one can recognize God's fidelity.[28] Both texts lack logic. Even if the State of Israel is a secular reality, not only the Jewish diaspora but also the Jewish presence in *Eretz Yisrael* must be interpreted theologically, also because the author writes as well that the existence of Judaism *as such* demands an interpretation of faith.

In a further reflection it will be important, on the one hand to distinguish between living in the Land and the state, and on the other hand to develop a Catholic theological perspective of our own, which understands more deeply both the return of the Jewish people to the Land and also the presence of non-Jews there, and which thereby sees the Jewish diaspora as well. For this, the Pontifical Biblical Commission's 2001 document, *The Jewish People and their Sacred Scriptures in the Christian Bible*, is not sufficient. For it remains exegetical. It sketches the biblical theology of the Land. At the same time, it also refers to the conquering of the Land as presented

---

[27] Commission For Religious Relations with the Jews, *Notes on the Correct Way to Present the Jews and Judaism in the Preaching and Catechesis of the Catholic Church* (June 24, 1985).

[28] "Gnade und Berufung ohne Reue. Anmerkungen zum Traktat 'De Iudaeis,'" *IKaZ Communio* 47 (2018): 328–31.

in the book of Joshua, saying that this may not be imitated. This refers in particular to the so-called ban, according to which Joshua had to destroy everything that was not Israelite in the Land.[29] Of course these are important exegetical statements in view of the present situation in the Middle East.

Individual theologians in the Roman Catholic Church only rarely say anything concerning the Land and State of Israel, even those who participate with intensity in Jewish-Christian dialogue. For Franz Mussner, the establishment of the State of Israel was a "sign of hope."[30] Jacques Maritain wrote that this was a state like every other, but at the same time also a "sign of God's irrevocable promise to his people Israel."[31] Johannes Österreicher, who participated in the writing of *Nostra Aetate* in 1963, saw the State of Israel as a "beacon of God's fidelity to the covenant."[32] And in 1962, Daniel Rufeisen fought as a baptized Jew and a Carmelite for Israeli citizenship based on the Zionist Law of Return. He interpreted the existence of the Hebrew-Catholic communities in Israel as a resurgence of Judeo-Christianity.[33]

In Europe's Protestant theology, Zionism became an important topic, particularly because in Germany, theology's aberrations under the influence of National Socialism had to be reappraised. If for Karl Barth Judaism was first a "mirror of judgment,"[34] he later called the young State of Israel a "sign of the election and of God's providential grace and fidelity to Abraham's seed."[35] Berthold Kappert, Jürgen Moltmann, Peter von der Osten-Sacken, and Friedrich Wilhelm Marquart should also be mentioned as examples of those theologians who all speak along the lines of Karl Barth of God's fidelity toward politically organized Judaism in *Eretz Yisrael*. In addition, Helmut Gollwitzer, in conversation with Rolf Rendtorff, sees the biblical promise of the Land as effective behind the establishment of the State of Israel.[36] But he

---

[29] The Pontifical Biblical Commission, *The Jewish People and their Sacred Scriptures in the Christian Bible*, no. 56–57 (2001).

[30] Franz Mussner, *Traktat über die Juden*, 2nd ed. (München: Kösel, 1988), 35.

[31] Quoted in Walter Kickel, *Das gelobte Land: Die religiöse Bedeutung des Staates Israel in jüdischer und christlicher Sicht* (München: Kösel, 1984), 135.

[32] Johannes Österreicher, *Der Baum und die Wurzel: Israels Erbe—Anspruch an die Christen* (Freiburg Basel Wien: Herder, 1968), 58.

[33] Christian M. Rutishauser, "Daniel Rufeisen und die Frage nach jüdisch-christlicher Identität," in *Religion zwischen Mystik und Politik "Ich lege mein Gesetz in sie hinein und schreibe es auf ihr Herz (Jer 31, 33),"* Jerusalemer Theologisches Forum 35, ed. Winkler Ulrich (Münster: Aschendorff Verlag, 2020), 295–316.

[34] Karl Barth, *Kirchliche Dogmatik*, vol. 2, 2, 224; 231.

[35] Quoted in: Kickel Walter, *Das gelobte Land. Die religiöse Bedeutung des Staates Israel in jüdischer und christlicher Sicht* (München: Kösel, 1984), 186.

[36] Helmut Gollwitzer and Rolf Rendtorff, *Thema: Juden—Christen—Israel: Ein Gespräch mit einer Entgegnung von Nathan Peter Levinson* (Stuttgart: Radius, 1978), 56–77.

does not accept a messianic interpretation of the Jews' *aliyah*; he calls the colonial national State of Israel a deformity and refers to the injustice done to the Palestinians through its establishment. The fact that Palestinians and Jewish Israelis now live side by side in the Land is for him due to God's providence and a mission from God. Arnold A. van Ruler on the other hand sees Christ and the Church, as well as the people of Israel and the Land promise, as means on the path toward salvation history's goal, the Kingdom of God. As regards the newly established State of Israel, he carefully says that he is not permitted to say with certainty whether this is a fulfillment of the Land promise.[37]

On the Protestant side, these balanced positions that see not only the entire Middle Eastern conflict, but also connect historico-theological and ethical considerations with one another, are confronted with two extremes: On the one hand, the Palestinian theology of liberation which rejects every theological significance of the return of large parts of the Jewish people. It perceives Zionism solely as a historical phenomenon in the context of European colonialism and nationalism. With theological arguments, it insists solely on social and political justice in the Land, just as for every other conflict on earth. Mitri Raheb, Naim Stifan Ateek, and Isaac Munther are among its representatives, as well as the so-called Kairos Document.[38] They concentrate solely on the issue of social justice and peace in the face of the suffering of the Palestinians. As to the Land theology that is presented there, the biblical promise of Land is universalized. Jesus Christ brought a "new teaching" and Mark 1:27 is quoted. The texts no longer have particular significance for the Jewish people, and such an interpretation is only a "dead letter."[39] The Palestinian Kairos movement for justice and peace represents a substitution theology, since Christianity alone is the heir to the biblical tradition and interprets the Land promise correctly. The movement tends toward anti-Judaism, as Israel's right to exist is also contested.

On the other hand, there is Evangelical-Christian Zionism, which started in Europe in the nineteenth century and today is widely spread above

---

[37] Andreas Hahn, "Ein Zeichen von Gottes Treue: Erwägungen zur theologischen Einordnung des Landbesitzes für Israel anhand der Ansätze von Arnold A. van Ruler und Jürgen Moltmann," *Wem gehört das "Heilige Land?": Christlich-theologische Überlegungen zur biblischen Landverheissung*, ed. Berthold Schwarz (Frankfurt: Peter Lang, 2014), 289–91.

[38] One example is Isaac Munther's argument in *From Land to Lands, from Eden to the Renewed Earth: A Christ-Centred Biblical Theology of the Promised Land* (Langham Cumbria: Langham, 2015), 347–73. See also the anthology *Theologies of Liberation in Palestine-Israel: Indigenous, Contextual, and Postcolonial Perspectives*, ed. Nur Masalha and Lisa Isherwood (Cambridge, UK: Pickwick, 2014).

[39] World Council of Churches, *A moment of truth: A word of faith, hope and love from the heart of Palestinian suffering* (December 11, 2009), 2.2.2. and 2.3.

all in the USA.⁴⁰ The Jews' return to their Land and the establishment of the State of Israel is read here based on the Land promise in the Old Testament. The biblical Israel is equated with the State of Israel. Zionism and the foundation of the state are signs of the messianic end of time in which a competition must come about and Jesus will return. The conversion of the Jews to Christ is expected to come at this time in a wonderful way. Thus the periodical *Israelkatuell.de* says in its masthead: "This periodical proclaims the message that Israel is a sign of God for the fulfillment of biblical prophecy and an indication of the speedy return of Jesus Christ."⁴¹ Zionist land theology is taken up uncritically and connected both with faith in Christ's return at the end of time and with the idea of mission to the Jews. Paul's eschatological vision developed in Romans 9–11, that all of Israel will be saved in Christ, is connected with the Jews' historical *aliyah*. From a biblical point of view, this is problematic since on the one hand no one, not even Christ himself, can know when a certain time is the historical end of time (Mt 24:36). On the other hand, it completely disregards ethical issues concerning the oppression of the Palestinians, and international law is not recognized. Palestinians are seen only as Muslim enemies of the Jewish State. As regards a theology of history, such a position is also not acceptable, since it believes it can decipher God's plan of salvation in history in too one-sided a way.

JUDAISM AS PEOPLE OF GOD ALONGSIDE THE CHURCH

In view of the described accesses to *Eretz Yisrael* and to the establishment of the State of Israel, it seems to me appropriate from a Roman Catholic perspective to approach the issue of the Land by way of Judaism as a faith community and as "people of God." Not the Land as such is in the center, but God's initiative to build an alternative culture that is not marked by injustice, as in Egypt. As we have seen, the point is to create a priestly-royal nation, and for this a Land is also necessary. The significance of the Jews living in the Land, as well as in the diaspora, must also be seen by Christian theology, since the Land promise is given with the "covenant that has never been revoked" and concerns the existence of the Jewish people. Just as fundamental as the

---

40 Donald M. Lewis, *The Origins of Christian Zionism: Lord Shaftesbury and Evangelical Support for a Jewish Homeland* (Cambridge, UK: Cambridge University Press, 2010); Ulrich Kadelbach, *Zionismus: Christlich-jüdischer Wettlauf nach Jerusalem* (Bad Schussenried: Hess, 2015); Stephen Spector, *Evangelicals and Israel: The Story of American Christian Zionism* (Oxford: Oxford University Press, 2009).

41 *Israel Aktuell*, Christians alongside Israel's Austria, 2008, https://www.israelaktuell.at/publikationen/israelaktuell/.

Sabbath, which qualifies Jewish time, is the relationship of *Eretz Yisrael* and diaspora, which structures Judaism's space. If for Christians the commandments of the Torah are fulfilled in Christ and "canceled" in the sense of Hegel, and if the Land of the Bible is for them Holy Land that makes sacramentally present the history of salvation, then the assessment of the Jewish presence in the Land and the State of Israel can only go by way of a reflection on the relationship between the Church and the Jewish people. This spatial relationship of the Church and the Jewish people is mirrored in the Christian binomial "Holy Land" and the rest of the world, as it is in the Jewish binomial of the promised Land and the diaspora. Both are ultimately founded on the structure of the Christian Bible, which presents a unity in time of the Old and the New Testament.[42]

This access to the return of many Jews to the Land of Israel places in a subordinate position the dimension of time, which always resonates in every theology of history regarding *Eretz Yisrael*. It relativizes the question whether the establishment of the State of Israel must be understood messianically or in terms of the end of time. Rather, it looks at the question of how the Jewish people must be understood as a faith community, and which constitutive elements belong to it. Just as in ecclesiology a differentiated theological understanding of the Church has grown over the course of time, an "Israelology" must be developed. The question concerning the Church's constitution calls for the question regarding the constitution of the Jewish people. After a juridical and institutional understanding of the Church reigned for centuries in Roman Catholic theology, this was broadened again in the twentieth century and made whole in the conciliar text *Lumen Gentium*:[43] Along with the hierarchical leadership structure, all the baptized were seen. Together they form the members of the one body of Christ. The Church no longer defines itself so much as *societas perfecta*, but rather as the people of God on pilgrimage. Above all, the concept of mystery or of sacrament became important; it connects and forms a bridge between the visible, worldly side of the Church and the invisible, spiritual dimension of all Christians. Thus the Church is always a really existing, historically active society. It takes on social forms that are historically conditioned, just as a constitutive hierarchical structure of ministries has also come to the fore. It exists in history and

---

[42] Cf. Christoph Dohmen and Thomas Söding, *Eine Bibel—Zwei Testamente: Positionen biblischer Theologie* (Paderborn Zürich: Schöningh, 1995).

[43] The first five chapters of *Lumen Gentium* formulate the worldly-spiritual nature of the Church. On the development of this ecclesiology: Peter Hünermann, "Theologischer Kommentar zur dogmatischen Konstitution der Kirche," *Herders Theologischer Kommentar zum Zweiten Vatikanischen Konzil*, vol. 2 (Freiburg Basel Wien: Herder, 2009), 171–288.

can also become guilty, at least its members. It can and must therefore also be assessed ethically. However, at the same time the Church is also a spiritual reality, a people of God on pilgrimage and a mystical body of Christ, established by God. Those who are baptized as well as those who are consecrated are marked by a spiritual distinction that cannot be destroyed. The Church is a metaphysical community incarnated in concrete society.

Judaism, which has grown in multiple ways in history, is to be seen in the same double structure. On the one hand, it is a Jewish people that really exists with its institutions of the rabbinate and the courts, its *Lehrhäuser* (houses of learning) and synagogues, etc. At various times and in various cultures, various social structures are added to the constitutive structural elements. And Judaism is also related constitutively to *Eretz Yisrael*, where a state has now been established. This earthly side is to be assessed ethically in just as various ways and is also subjected to historical change. Although Jews are spiritually called forth out of the nations as a kingdom of priests and kings and are obliged to be holy, they become guilty in the course of history and have to bear responsibility. However, on the other hand, the Jewish people is also a spiritual-metaphysical reality that connects all who were born of a Jewish mother or who through conversion profess Judaism. God goes with his people through all historical adversity, both in the *Shoah* and in the political act of establishing a state. God is faithful to his people in the covenant and in the promise of the Land in which they are to live according to the Torah.

This perception of Judaism makes it possible to distinguish between a fundamental affirmation and criticism of ethical behavior, also as regards the Land—and even the State of Israel. In addition, the worldly side of Judaism, as that of the Church, is seen as something that is subjected to historical change. But just as priestly ministries and parish structures belong to the Church, the rabbinate and synagogues as well as the Land belong to Judaism. Does a state belong to Judaism, constitutively or as an expression of plenitude? In any case, in the state a frame is created in which Judaism can live its vocation. The really existing constitution is always a "sign" that in a sacramental way points to God, especially when the human person thereby becomes open to God's Spirit and acts accordingly. Thus the establishment of the State of Israel can be seen as a kind of resurrection after the *Shoah* or as fulfillment of the Land promise. On the other hand, the return of the Jews to the Land in great numbers is not yet what is religiously decisive. Demography alone does not have a spiritual quality. It comes to be when an alternative culture is lived according to God's justice. The worldly-material is a necessary precondition, but it is not sufficient in order to be truly God's people. This is true for the Jewish people as also for the Church as sacrament of God in the world.

In order to do justice to the desire for social justice, the rabbis developed a rich halakhic tradition. In view of a sovereign State of Israel, the *halakha* must today be developed further as a social and political teaching. The issue is not a halakhic state but a *halakha* which strives for justice and dignity for all in the Land. A theologico-political theory is needed of the kind that is for example developed by Michael Walzer[44] or the Shalom Hartman Institute in Jerusalem. In the secular State of Israel, dealings with minorities, with foreigners, with other religious traditions in one's own state, employment laws, etc. should also reflect Jewish sources. The fact that Israel is today a secular constitutional state is not a blemish or a disadvantage. On the contrary. Judaism is not in the Land for itself but for the non-Jews there as well. Also in *Eretz Yisrael* it is supposed to be a "light for the nations." Not only Jews and secular people live in the Land, but also two other faith communities, Christians as well as Muslims. The "people of God among the Arabs," which is to say the Church, as well as the Palestinians, must also be taken into account. It can only be willed by God that various ethnicities and faith communities live together in *Eretz Yisrael* as at every time in history. Therefore the Vatican also maintains diplomatic relations with Israel and with Palestine. Pope Francis has spoken repeatedly for the two-state solution, not as a compromise but because God made a covenant not only with Judaism.[45] Above all, social justice in the Holy Land is his desire more than the question of political sovereignty. The implementation of values such as those presented by Catholic social teaching are thus also to be joined with every theology of the Land: the connection of the religious and the social dimension of life; the dignity of the human person; basic political rights for all; the option for the poor; the connection of love and justice; the advancement of the common good; the principle of structural subsidiarity; structures of political participation; economic justice for all; the social obligation of property; worldwide and global solidarity; the active advancement of peace; etc.[46] Whichever political solutions will be found in Israel/Palestine, the Catholic bishops in the Holy Land note in their most recent document, "Righteousness and Peace will embrace one another" of May 20, 2019, that the dignity and justice for all who live in the Land are to be respected: "Only

---

44 Michael Walzer, *The Jewish Political Tradition*, vol. 3 (New Haven: Yale University Press, 2018).
45 Pope Francis, *Homily in Manger Square* (Bethlehem, May 25, 2014).
46 On Catholic social teaching and its values: Theodor Herr, *Katholische Soziallehre: Eine Einführung* (Paderborn: Bonifatius, 1987); Bernhard Sutor, *Katholische Soziallehre als politische Ethik: Leistungen und Defizite* (Paderborn München Wien: Schöningh, 2013).

a peace based on dignity, mutual respect and equality as human beings will save us, allow us to survive and even thrive in this land made holy by the witness of our ancestors, patriarchs and prophets, which we continue to make holy by our striving for justice, our thirst for peace and the mutual love we have for one another."[47] The life and the society in the Land of the Bible only have special value in correspondence with the Bible if their aim is justice and peace, humaneness and the humanity of all who live there.

IS A THEOLOGY OF GOD'S HISTORY WITH "GOD'S PEOPLE" POSSIBLE?

The Jewish people as also the Church are faith communities, called by God into this history and placed there in order to bring justice and an alternative culture, reconciliation and salvation. It is necessary to consider their respective different natures and historical forms, which implicate the social and the political in different ways. Only in this way can they live their vocation. Moreover, faith in the God of the Bible has always meant for Jews and for Christians that God works not only in the life of individual people but also in history among the nations, whether this be through and in the history of Judaism and the Church or in the secular history of the nations. In this sense, the return of the Jews to *Eretz Yisrael* in the twentieth century can and must be understood as part of secular history. At the same time, theological reflection should speak to this in order to recognize how God's doing shows itself therein. However, one must consider the perspective in which this is done.

The path of the classical theology of history, in which the human person so to speak looks over God's shoulder to see how God leads the nations, no longer seems possible, since the failure of all such theories in earlier centuries. The human person cannot give a total interpretation of history. He and she only have a worm's-eye view of this world, not a bird's-eye view that would be like God's. Nevertheless, we can discover traces of God in history where societies develop toward greater justice, freedom, and humaneness. The concept of salvation history is thereby not passé, but it must be understood appropriately: On the one hand, it signifies all historical processes that lead to more salvation. The human being's ethical activity under God's leadership plays a decisive part in this. On the other hand, the concept of salvation history can be used regarding the activity of the Church and of the Jewish people, insofar as both collectives came into being through

---

47 The Latin Patriarchate of Jerusalem, "Assembly of Catholic Ordinaries calls on people of Holy Land to build bridges of respect and love," May 20, 2019, https://www.lpj.org/assembly-catholic-ordinaries-invites-people-of-the-holy-land-to-build-bridges-of-respect-and-love/.

God's covenant initiative. Here we are dealing with God's choice, but not in the sense of predestination. Rather, the Church and the Jewish people *per definitionem* gather together those people who with social commitment have let themselves become involved in God's working. The Sinai "covenant that was never revoked," which Christians call the "Old Covenant," and the "New Covenant," which was sealed in Christ on Golgotha, present a spiritual foundation on which Christian faith builds. Of course, this does not mean that everything that is done in the name of the Church and of Judaism fosters justice and humaneness, freedom and peace. The collective's deeds are also fallible, as was already said. But in the Church that really exists, as also in the Jewish people, the people of God "subsists" in different ways, to take up the theological concept in *Lumen Gentium* 8. How God leads in history remains mysterious and in need of being further reflected upon: After the attempt to annihilate it in the *Shoah*, the Jewish people in modern times has arrived at a political entity in *Eretz Yisrael*. Today it acts in history with a State of Israel. The Roman Catholic Church, however, which has had a Church-State for centuries, today only has a political arm through the Vatican City State and the Holy See as a subject of international law. The way in which a spiritual community and a political reality interact is more complex than what the secular separation of religion and politics wants to make believe. In Israel/Palestine God is surely working, and this in a way that no human being is able to imagine.

6

TERRA VIVENTIUM
BIBLICAL PROMISES, FULFILLMENT, AND THOMAS AQUINAS'S CHRISTOLOGICAL INTERPRETATION OF THE LAND
Matthew A. Tapie

A key principle of contemporary Catholic teaching is that Christians must strive to understand how Jews define themselves, and among the elements of the Jewish experience is a religious attachment to the land.[1] However, some have argued that understanding Jewish attachment to the land is not enough. Since Jewish views of the land have biblical roots, and the Church claims Israel's scriptures as her own, the Orthodox Jewish theologian Michael Wyschogrod argued decades ago that Catholics "must also take these [biblical] ties seriously, not only as something that Jews have but as something the Church must struggle with."[2] In Wyschogrod's view, if evangelical Christians find too little difficulty validating a Jewish right to the Land of Israel on the basis of biblical promises, the Vatican errs in the other direction. For Wyschogrod, spiritualizing the promises of the land is "an ancient strategy not easy to defend in the new theological climate of Jewish-Christian dialogue."[3]

I would like to thank Alan Brill, Robert Wilken, Ellen Charry, Reinhard Hütter, Matthew Levering, Bruce Marshall, Thomas Humphries, and David Maayan, for reading drafts of this chapter.

[1] Pontifical Commission for Religious Relations with the Jews (PCRRJ), *Guidelines and Suggestions for Implementing the Conciliar Declaration "Nostra Aetate" (n. 4)*, December 1, 1974. In 1987, St. Pope John Paul II said, "Catholics recognize among the elements of the Jewish experience that Jews have a religious attachment to the Land, which finds its roots in biblical tradition." *Meeting with the Representatives of the Jewish Organizations* (September 11, 1987).

[2] Michael Wyschogrod, "The Bishops and the Middle East," *First Things* (April 1990): 16.

[3] Wyschogrod, "The Bishops and the Middle East," 16.

In addition to understanding Jewish views of the land, a Catholic approach to theological questions on biblical promises regarding the land in scripture should attend to the Church's teaching on the principles of correct biblical interpretation, including the principle that the interpreter read scripture within the living tradition of the Church.[4] According to the Catechism, the fathers' approach to scripture, which includes typological reading, is a guide and model for modern exegetes.[5] Based on these principles it seems contemporary Catholic reflection on the land should take seriously traditional interpretations of the land in scripture, including allegorical readings.

However, as some scholars have observed, the Pontifical Biblical Commission's (PBC's) 2002 document, *The Jewish People and Their Sacred Scriptures in the Christian Bible* (*JPSSCB*) sets allegorical reading aside when it discusses fundamental Old Testament themes, including the land.[6] Although *JPSSCB* discusses the land promise at length, it does not do so with attention to the tradition. I seek to remedy this problem by putting the document in dialogue with aspects of St. Thomas Aquinas's interpretation of the land. I argue that Aquinas's anagogical interpretation of the land as *terra viventium* (the land of the living), in Psalm 27:13, deepens the connection between the Pontifical Biblical Commission's symbolic reading of land in the New Testament, and their interpretation of land in the Old Testament.

---

4 Vatican Council II, *Dei Verbum* no. 12 (November 18, 1965); *Catechism of the Catholic Church*, 112–13. According to the Catechism, the other two principles state that readers be attentive to the unity of the whole scripture, of which Christ is the center, and be attentive to the coherence of the truths of faith among themselves and within the whole plan of Revelation. See also no. 109–10; no.114–27.

5 In the Catechism, patristic principles and methods, including typological reading, are discussed and encouraged in no. 128: "The Church, as early as apostolic times, and then constantly in her Tradition, has illuminated the unity of the divine plan in the two Testaments through typology, which discerns in God's works of the Old Covenant prefigurations of what he accomplished in the fullness of time in the person of his incarnate Son"; no.129: "Christians therefore read the Old Testament in the light of Christ crucified and risen. Such typological reading discloses the inexhaustible content of the Old Testament; but it must not make us forget that the Old Testament retains its own intrinsic value as Revelation reaffirmed by our Lord himself"; *Dei Verbum*, no. 23; Benedict XVI, *Verbum Domini*, no. 37; Pontifical Biblical Commission, *The Jewish People and Their Sacred Scriptures in the Christian Bible*; Pontifical Biblical Commission, *The Interpretation of the Bible in the Church*, no. 99; see also the encyclical of Pius XII, *Divino Afflante Spiritu*, no. 28–30; Pope Leo XIII, *Providentissimus*: EB 110–111.

6 Denis Farkasfalvy, "The Pontifical Biblical Commission's Document on Jews and Christians and Their Scriptures: Attempt at an Evaluation," *Communio: International Catholic Review* 29 (Winter 2002): 715–37; Roch Kereszty, "The Jewish-Christian Dialogue and the Pontifical Biblical Commission's Document on 'The Jewish People and Their Sacred Scriptures in the Christian Bible,'" *Communio: International Catholic Review* 29, no 4 (2002): 738–45; Matthew Levering, "The Pontifical Biblical Commission and Aquinas's Exegesis," *Pro Ecclesia* 13, no. 1 (2004): 25–38; Reinhard Hütter, "'In.' Some Incipient Reflections on the Jewish People and Their Sacred Scriptures in the Christian Bible," *Pro Ecclesia* 13, no. 1 (2004): 13–24.

This essay is organized in three parts. In the first section, I examine the Christological interpretation of the land promise in Aquinas, which has yet to be considered in Christian theological reflection on the land. In particular, I examine Aquinas's interpretation of some of the most influential New Testament texts on the land in the tradition: Matthew 5:5, Hebrews 12:22, and Galatians 4:26. In the second section, I present the *JPSSCB*'s teaching on the fulfillment of the land promise. I hope to show that although the *JPSSCB* advances a symbolic interpretation of the land based on New Testament texts, it does so without attention to a rather sophisticated tradition of Christological interpretation of the Old Testament that strives to maintain continuity between the two testaments. In the third section, I offer a reflection on how elements of Aquinas's approach to scripture might provide a hermeneutic for Christological reading of scripture within tradition, and with attention to post-Conciliar affirmation of the permanent theological significance of Jews and Judaism.

AQUINAS ON THE FULFILLMENT OF THE LAND PROMISE

Christian theologians reflected upon the meaning of the biblical land promises in scripture long before the Pontifical Biblical Council and Thomas Aquinas. Jews and Christians in antiquity interpreted the promise of land in scripture through their respective views of the character of the messianic age.[7] In exchanges with Jewish interlocutors, Origen (ca. 184–253) discussed the meaning of biblical promises concerning the land, and of Jerusalem.[8] Origen's study of Hebrew, his visits to synagogues, and his disputes with Jewish teachers allowed him to articulate a Christian view of the Holy Land that would strongly influence Christian reflection on the topic for centuries.[9] For Origen's Jewish interlocutors, the oracles of the prophets speak of the Land of Israel and the future of the Jewish people in the land. Origen wrote, "When the Scriptures speak of . . . building a city of God [Jewish interpreters] mean that these things will happen in space and time . . . a real building of a city."[10] Origen based part of his reply in Galatians 4:26 ("The

---

[7] "Appeal to the original historical setting is only one side of Jewish exegesis of the prophets, and that the least important." Robert L. Wilken, *The Land Called Holy* (New Haven, CT: Yale University Press, 2009), 109. See also Harry M. Orlinsky, "The Biblical Concept of the Land of Israel: Cornerstone of the Covenant between God and Israel," in *The Land of Israel: Jewish Perspectives*, ed. Lawrence A. Hoffman (Notre Dame, IN: University of Notre Dame Press, 1986), 46–55.

[8] Wilken, *The Land Called Holy*, 67.

[9] Wilken, *The Land Called Holy*, 67.

[10] Wilken, *The Land Called Holy*, 76.

Jerusalem above is free and she is our mother..."), and Hebrews 12:22 ("You have come to Mount Zion and to the city of the living God, the heavenly Jerusalem.").[11] In addition to these texts, Origen says Matthew 5:5 ("Blessed are the meek for they will possess the land") refers to a "sublime region," located in the presence of Christ at the right hand of God.[12] He understands the land inheritance in Matthew 5:5 as the same land mentioned in Psalm 37:34 ("He shall exalt you to inherit the land"). For Origen, this Psalm concerns a land "located above the earth" which is a "good land, holy land, great land, land of the living."[13] For Origen, these texts mean that when the scriptures speak of Jerusalem they do not refer to a city in Judea. In Origen's view, Jerusalem, "does not designate a future political center but a spiritual vision of heavenly bliss."[14] For Origen, the prophets were speaking of a heavenly country. Origen's views reflect what would become the central Christian interpretative tradition.[15]

Like Origen, Aquinas was deeply shaped by scripture as evidenced in his upbringing in liturgical and biblical-patristic culture;[16] his training in the

---

11 Wilken, *The Land Called Holy*, 70. Origen was responding to Jewish and Christian interlocutors who understood the promise to refer to the establishment of a future political center in Judea. He directs his interpretation against the alternative exegetical tradition. Wilken, *The Land Called Holy*, 69. Some Christians sided with Jewish interpreters not in denying Jesus was the Messiah, but by adopting chiliast (from the Greek for "thousand") interpretations that held Christ would one day return to rule on earth for a thousand years. According to Wilken, chiliasm (millennialism, also called millenarianism) is the belief that God would establish a future kingdom on earth centered in Jerusalem. Wilken, *The Land Called Holy*, 56–62. According to Wilken, the distinctive mark of the chiliastic tradition is not the idea of a thousand-year reign, but the belief that Christian hope is centered on an earthly city of Jerusalem that will be rebuilt. Wilken, *The Land Called Holy*, 56–57. In Origen's view, chiliast interpretation compromised Christianity because it failed to read the oracles through the lens of the New Testament, and specifically the claim that the scriptures have been fulfilled in Jesus Christ. "It is clear that what disturbs [Origen] is that if the chiliasts are correct, the promises of the prophets cannot have been fulfilled in the coming of Christ and hence the messianic age has not yet begun." Wilken, *The Land Called Holy*, 77. Origen rejected the idea of a holy land located on earth "not because he preferred allegory to history but because he was attentive to a new set of historical events. If Jesus of Nazareth was the Messiah, the prophecies about the messianic age had already been fulfilled, and it was the task of biblical interpreters to discover what the scriptural promises meant in light of this new 'fact.'" Wilken, *The Land Called Holy*, 77. Christian spiritual reading of the oracles was not a strategy but a messianic interpretation of the text based in the historical event of Christ's advent. For Origen, the advent of Christ in the land of Bethlehem is the most important literal sense. "Paradoxically," Wilken explains, "in the language of early Christian exegesis, the spiritual sense *was* the historical sense." Wilken, "*In novissimis diebus*: Biblical Promises, Jewish Hopes, and Early Christian Exegesis," in *Remembering the Christian Past* (Grand Rapids, MI: Eerdmans, 1995), 119.

12 Wilken, *The Land Called Holy*, 75.

13 Wilken, *The Land Called Holy*, 75.

14 Wilken, *The Land Called Holy*, 70.

15 Wilken, "*In novissimis diebus*," 105.

16 Fergus Kerr, "Thomas Aquinas," *The Medieval Theologians: An Introduction to Theology in the Medieval Period*, ed. G. R. Evans, 1st ed. (Malden, MA: Wiley-Blackwell, 2001), 201–20.

monastic tradition of *lectio divina*; his attraction to the Order of Preachers; and his discussion of scripture in the inaugural sermons at the university of Paris, not to mention the requirements of the office of *magister in sacra pagina* itself.[17] Perhaps the clearest indications that Aquinas was a theologian of scripture is the frequent use of the Word of God in the *Summa theologiae*[18] as highest authority, which was a commonplace practice in the scholastic hierarchy of sources;[19] the fact that Aquinas wrote commentaries on five Old Testament books (Psalms, Job, Isaiah, Jeremiah, and Lamentations); two commentaries on the Gospels (Matthew and John); and all of the Pauline letters.[20]

Aquinas valued both literal, and spiritual senses of scripture.[21] For Aquinas, the literal sense refers to that which the human author intends. However, because the Holy Spirit can intend more than humans can comprehend, "there may be many literal senses of a text."[22] This "multifaceted literal sense" is the first important level of signification since it is the basis

[17] Jean-Pierre Torrell, *Saint Thomas Aquinas*, vol. 1, *The Person and His Work*, rev. ed. (Washington, DC: The Catholic University of America Press, 2005), 54. The inaugural sermons can be found in *Thomas Aquinas: Selected Writings*, ed. and trans. Ralph McInerny (London: Penguin Classics, 1999), 3–17.

[18] Pim Valkenberg, *Words of the Living God: Place and Function of Holy Scripture in the Theology of St. Thomas Aquinas* (Leuven: Peeters, 2000), 207.

[19] Servais-Théodore Pinckaers, "The Sources of the Ethics of St. Thomas Aquinas," in *The Ethics of Aquinas*, ed. Stephen J. Pope (Washington, DC: Georgetown University Press, 2002), 19.

[20] Eleonore Stump, "Biblical Commentary and Philosophy," in *The Cambridge Companion to Aquinas*, ed. Norman Kretzmann and Eleonore Stump (Cambridge: Cambridge University Press, 1993), 252–68. This section relies upon the following English translations of Aquinas's commentaries published by the Aquinas Institute for the Study of Sacred Doctrine: Aquinas, *Commentary on the Gospel of Matthew Chapters 1–12*, vol. 33 of *Works* (Lander, WY: Aquinas Institute for the Study of Sacred Doctrine, 2013); *Commentaries on the Letters of Saint Paul to the Galatians and Ephesians*, vol. 39 of *Works* (Lander, WY: Aquinas Institute for the Study of Sacred Doctrine, 2012); *Commentary on the Letter of Saint Paul to the Hebrews*, vol. 41 of *Works* (Lander, WY: Aquinas Institute for the Study of Sacred Doctrine, 2012); *Expositio super Isaiam ad litteram*, Aquinas Institute for the Study of Sacred Doctrine, available online at https://aquinas.cc/la/en/~Isaiah. Citations consist of the abbreviated Latin titles for the commentaries (*In Ioannem* and *Ad Ephesios*), followed by chapter, lecture, and paragraph numbers. For example, *Super Matthaeum* is abbreviated to *Super Matt.*; *Ad Hebraeos* is abbreviated to *Ad Heb.*; *Ad Galatas* is *Ad Galat.*; according to the Aquinas Institute for the Study of Sacred Doctrine, the closest available version of Aquinas's text of scripture appears to be the Clementine Vulgate of 1598; the closest English translation of this version of the Vulgate is the Douay-Rheims version.

[21] For Aquinas's comments on hermeneutics see *Summa theologiae*, I 1.10 ad. 2; *Quaestiones de quodlibet*, 7.6.1–3, 145–48; *ad Galatas*, 4.7; *Quaestiones disputatae de potentia*, 4.1. Robert Busa, *Sancti Thomae Aquinatis opera omnia* (Stuttgart: Fromman-Holzboog, 1980). English translation from St. Thomas Aquinas, *Summa theologica*, trans. Fathers of the English Dominican Province, 5 vols. (New York: Benzinger Bros., 1948).

[22] Stephen E. Fowl, "The Importance of a Multivoiced Literal Sense of Scripture: The Example of Thomas Aquinas," in *Reading Scripture with the Church: Toward a Hermeneutic for Theological Interpretation*, ed. A. K. M. Adam (Grand Rapids, MI: Baker Academic, 2006), 35–50.

for any spiritual interpretation of the text. The spiritual sense refers to the words in the Old Testament that designate or point to realities in the New Testament. The spiritual sense is often organized into three levels of meaning that correspond to three periods of salvation history: Old Testament *figurae* of things in the New Testament (allegorical meaning); moral action of Christians (tropological meaning); and words that foreshadow future glory (anagogical).[23]

Aquinas employs a substantive anagogical interpretation of *terra* in his commentary on Matthew 5:5 ("Blessed are the meek: for they will possess the land").[24] After clarifying what meekness means in the context of this beatitude (i.e., when one is not provoked to anger even when one has a just cause), Aquinas says that land in this verse can be taken literally, and cites Chrysostom's view that Matthew 5:5 refers to a promise of possessions to those who are gentle. However, Aquinas then says that the beatitude is "better explained" as referring to the future, and that Hilary "speaks this way." The rewards in the beatitudes are essentially "one in reality, eternal happiness, which the human intellect does not grasp. Hence it was fitting to describe it by means of various goods known to us...."[25] For this reason, Aquinas says "land" in 5:5 is best explained as referring to "the future," and that, in this sense, the term can be explained in many ways. First, he says the meek will "possesses the land" in the sense that they will possess "the glorified body of Christ, because they will be conformed to that brilliance in their own body." He then cites Isaiah 33:17: "his eyes will see the king in his beauty, they will see the land far off," along with Philippians 3:21, "who will reform the body of our lowness made like to the body of his glory." Second, the land can be understood to refer to creation itself, in bondage to decay: "This land is the land of the dead for a while, because it is subjected to corruption, but it will be freed from corruption, according to the Apostle (Rom 8:21). Therefore this land, when it is glorified and freed from the servitude of corruption will be called the land of the living." Here, Aquinas uses the phrase *terra viventium* or "land of the living" (from Psalm 27:13: "I believe I shall see the good things of the Lord in the land of the living."), but he does not cite the psalm until his fourth reason. Third, land can refer to where the blessed are, which he says is the heaven of the Holy Trinity. His fourth reason echoes part of the first reason: the meek will possess the land in the sense that

---

[23] Thomas Prügl, "Thomas Aquinas as Interpreter of Scripture," *The Theology of Thomas Aquinas*, ed. Rik Van Nieuwenhove and Joseph Wawrykow (Notre Dame, IN: University of Notre Dame Press, 2005), 393–94.

[24] Aquinas, *Super Matt.*, 5.2.420.

[25] Aquinas, *Summa theologiae*, I.II 69.4 ad. 1.

they will possess their own glorified body. And he cites Psalm 27:13, using the phrase "land of the living" for a second time.

In his commentary on Hebrews 12:22 ("You have come to Mount Zion and to the city of the living God, the heavenly Jerusalem . . ."), Aquinas says that this text indicates three things are promised in the New Testament: (1) the hope of future glory; (2) participation in the Church; (3) and familiarity with God.[26] He then explains that in future glory (the first promise), two things will particularly gladden the just: (a) the enjoyment of the Godhead and (b) companionship with the saints. Enjoyment of the Godhead consists in two things: the intellect's vision of God, and the will's attainment of the perfect good, i.e., God, who "lulls the appetite altogether."[27] As in his Matthew 5:5 comment, Aquinas cites Isaiah 33. "Zion" signifies the loftiness of divine contemplation, and he cites Isaiah 33:20: "Look upon Zion, the city of our solemnity." His use of Isaiah 33 in the context of Hebrews 12:22 seems to indicate that he understands parts of this chapter of Isaiah to refer to the beatific vision. Isaiah 33:17 reads, "His eyes shall see the king in his beauty. . . ." Aquinas then explains that this vision referenced in Hebrews 12:22 includes the joy that comes from sharing this perfect good in the company of "those to be saved" (second promise), and the familiarity they will have with the Father, the Son, and the Spirit (third promise).[28] Aquinas says that in this city of the living God, the heavenly Jerusalem, "there will be in this land the vision of experiential peace, because there will be nothing disturbing, either interior or exterior."[29] He then strings together several other Psalms on Jerusalem as a symbol of perfect peace that is free from corruption, and he then cites Galatians 4:26.[30]

That this heavenly Jerusalem is a mystery in Aquinas's view, becomes clear in his commentary on Galatians 4:26 ("But that Jerusalem which is above is free, which is our mother"), which shares elements of his Hebrews 12:22 comment. Aquinas says that the Apostle's words, "that Jerusalem which is above is free," disclose a mystery. The heavenly Jerusalem is "above" in that it consists of sublime face-to-face vision of God. Aquinas then says that the name "Jerusalem" itself indicates that she is a "peacemaker," i.e., "a vision of peace," since perfect peace will be experienced there. In this world, the land of the dead for a while, there is truly good peace, but it is imperfect because

---

26 Aquinas, *Ad Heb.*, 12.4.705.
27 Aquinas, *Ad Heb.*, 12.4.706; cf. *Summa theologiae*, I.II 2.8.
28 Aquinas, *Ad Heb.*, 12.4.707–710.
29 Aquinas, *Ad Heb.*, 12.4.706.
30 Aquinas, *Ad Galat.*, 4.4.261–4.

it is subject to disturbance.³¹ Perfect peace is had only in the vision of God, in the heavenly Jerusalem, or what Aquinas calls in another place, "our native land."³² This peace is then linked once more to the idea of creation's freedom from corruption (and Romans 8:21 is cited again), and Aquinas then cites Revelation 21:2 ("I saw the holy city, the new Jerusalem, coming down out of heaven from God.").

Since Isaiah 33 is cited by Aquinas in his comments on both Matthew 5:5 and Hebrews 12:22, it is worth taking a closer look at his interpretation of land in this chapter of his commentary on Isaiah.³³ In a number of places, Aquinas interprets Isaiah's prophecy to literally refer to return from Babylonian exile, which demonstrates that he reads for both literal and spiritual meanings. However, chapter 33 in particular is central for his view of the beatific vision as it relates to the promise of the land. While discussing the presence of God "as dwelling," he explains that Isaiah 33:17 ("his eyes shall see the king in his beauty") refers to the vision of God.³⁴ As he did in his Matthew 5:5 comment, Aquinas then identifies the "location" of this vision of God as the "land of the living" (borrowing once again, the phrase from Psalm 27:13): "The land, namely, of the living: I believe to see the good things of the Lord in the land of the living."³⁵ *Terra viventium* is at the heart of Aquinas's interpretation of Isaiah 33:20, "Look upon Zion the city of our solemnity: thy eyes shall see Jerusalem."

> And first he sets down the hope that he himself has. Secondly, he exhorts others to the same.... His petition was that he might see God; and hence he says, "I believe," that is, I have a firm trust, "To see the good things of the Lord," that is, to see him face to face; Job 19:25: "I know that my Redeemer liveth ... and in my flesh, I shall see my God;" ... that is, those things that are in the Lord ... [those things] are the same as himself: Wisdom 7:11: "All

---

31 Aquinas discusses what I have referred to as the Christological peace of the Church in his commentary on Ephesians. See *Ad Ephesios* 2.5.111; 2.6.131. This peace consists of Christ drawing together Jews and Gentiles in one body. Commenting upon Paul's metaphor for the convergence of Jews and Gentiles as a structure being built into a holy temple (Ephesians 2:21), with Christ as the cornerstone, Aquinas says Christ is called a cornerstone on account of the convergence of both Jews and Gentiles, whom he refers to as "two walls" joined to a corner. "As two walls are joined at the corner," he writes, "so in Christ the Jewish and pagan peoples are united." Matthew Tapie, "'For He is Our Peace': Thomas Aquinas on Christ as Cause of Peace in the City of the Saints," *Journal of Moral Theology* 5, no. 1 (January 2016): 111–28.
32 Aquinas, *In Ioan*, 14.7.1962–3.
33 An English translation of the Commentary on Isaiah is available online from the Aquinas Institute.
34 Aquinas, *Super Isaiam*, 33.
35 Aquinas, *Super Isaiam*, 33. He actually cites Psalm 26, but it refers to 27.

good things came to me together with her etc." And where? "In the land of the living." The vision of God is eternal life, as it is said in John 17. This land belongs to those who die. For just as the land is receptive in respect to the heaven that fertilizes it, so is the way of the blessed immediately perfected by God.[36]

Some biblical scholars understand the phrase "land of the living," in Psalm 27:13, as an epithet of the Jerusalem Temple where there was access to the life-giving presence of God.[37] Aquinas is keen to recognize its importance as a way of communicating the presence of God in the land, but he obviously interprets this Christologically, and on an anagogical level of meaning. Psalm 27:13 is key for how Aquinas interprets the biblical land promise as the promise of a land of perfect peace where glorified bodies behold the face of God. Ironically, the land of the living, in Aquinas's view, belongs to those who die, and at the resurrection of the dead, are perfected through the removal of corruption from their bodies, and from the earth itself.

I now turn to an examination of the fulfillment of the land promise in the *JPSSCB* to show how Aquinas's Christological reading of Psalm 27:13 and Isaiah 33:17 deepens the connection of the *JPSSCB*'s symbolic interpretation of the land in the New Testament to the promises of land in the Old Testament.

THE PONTIFICAL BIBLICAL COMMISSION ON FULFILLMENT OF THE LAND PROMISE

JPSSCB was composed in the spirit of *Nostra Aetate*'s call for biblical and theological studies, and with attention to Christian-Jewish dialogue.[38] The document is rather comprehensive in scope, and merits deep study by Catholics. It contains three sections: 1) the role of the Old Testament in the New; 2) fundamental Old Testament themes taken up in the New; and 3) the Jews in the New Testament. Here, I focus on how the authors of the document understand the concept of fulfillment as it relates to the land.

---

36 Aquinas's commentary on the Psalms is unfinished, and includes only the first fifty-four Psalms. Some English translations by F. F. Reilly are available at Saint Thomas Aquinas's Works in English, the Dominican House of Studies, https://web.archive.org/web/20171109041703/https://dhspriory.org/thomas/PsalmsAquinas/index.htm.

37 Note on Psalm 27:13 in *The Catholic Study Bible*, ed. Donald Senior (Oxford: Oxford University Press, 2016); see also the note on Psalm 27:13 in *The Jewish Study Bible*, ed. Adele Berlin and Marc Zvi Brettler (Oxford: Oxford University Press, 2004).

38 *JPSSCB*, 86.

The preface of *JPSSCB* develops themes in *Nostra Aetate*, as do the Pontifical Commission for Religious Relations with the Jews and the PBC. In *Nostra Aetate*, Christ is presented as the fullness of religious life. In *Notes on the Correct Way to Present the Jews and Judaism in Preaching and Catechesis in the Roman Catholic Church*, the Old Testament is described as preparation for the New, and Christ is presented as the "key" to the Christian reading of the Jewish scriptures.[39] *JPSSCB* echoes these themes when its authors affirm that Christ is presented by gospel writers as the fulfillment of the scriptures of the Old Testament, and that the Christological interpretation of biblical promises finds its basis in the New Testament itself.[40] The preface of *JPSSCB* extends previous teaching of the PBC that the fathers' approach to scripture is the basis of Catholic theology, and that the teachings of the Old and New Testaments are unified.[41] The fathers "created nothing new" in their Christological interpretations of the Old Testament.[42] Christological fulfillment safeguards the unity of the Christian Bible against the Marcionite tendency to divide the two testaments.[43] The preface of *JPSSCB* presents the Christological reading of the Old Testament as the exegetical solution to what might be referred to as the lingering "Marcionism of the West" (a phrase not used by the Commission but coined by Abraham Joshua Heschel), which the Commission thinks is exhibited in the work of Adolf von Harnack and Rudolph Bultmann. These scholars insisted that Christianity reject the Old Testament.[44] Contrary to this position, *JPSSCB* declares that "Without the Old Testament, the New Testament would be an unintelligible book, a plant deprived of its roots and destined to dry up and wither."[45] According

---

[39] *Dei Verbum* 4, 7; Commission For Religious Relations with the Jews, *Notes on the Correct Way to Present the Jews and Judaism in the Preaching and Catechesis of the Catholic Church* 2.3–8 (June 24, 1985); *The Interpretation of the Bible in the Church*, 99.

[40] *JPSSCB*, Preface.

[41] "The Fathers of the Church, who had a particular role in the process of the formation of the canon, likewise have a foundational role in relation to the living tradition which unceasingly accompanies and guides the Church's reading and interpretation of Scripture." *The Interpretation of the Bible in the Church*, 99. For *Dei Verbum*'s orientation to this line of thinking, see Brian Daley, "Knowing God in History and in the Church: *Dei Verbum* and 'Nouvelle Theologie,'" in *Ressourcement*, ed. Flynn, Murray, and Kelly (New York: Oxford University Press, 2011), 350–51.

[42] *JPSSCB*, Preface.

[43] An example of this sensibility to guard the unity of the testaments can be found in de Lubac's study of Origen's exegesis. De Lubac thought the defense of the unity of the Christian Bible against the Marcionite threat required a recovery of patristic and medieval scriptural hermeneutics. See Kevin Hughes, "Deep Reasonings: *Sources Chretiennes, Ressourcement*, and the Logic of Scripture in the Years before—and after—Vatican II," *Modern Theology* 29, no. 4 (October 2013): 38.

[44] *JPSSCB*, Preface.

[45] *JPSSCB*, 84.

to *JPSSCB*, the most direct avenue into this way of reading is St. Augustine's interpretation of the Bible. As is well known, the interpretation of the Old Testament was an obstacle for Augustine, and he attempts to overcome the difficulty by relying upon Ambrose, who had adopted Origen's principles. These principles are as follows: the internal unity of the Bible is a rule of interpretation, and Christ is the meeting point of all the Old Testament pathways. The Christological reading of the fathers is presented as the solution to negative Gentile views of the Old Testament.

In the beginning of the body of document, *JPSSCB* expresses the concern that this fundamental orientation is crucial for Catholic interpretation of scripture, and that it is an approach in danger of being jettisoned: "Today, there is the danger of denying outright all Patristic exegesis and the very idea of a Christian and Christological reading of Old Testament texts."[46] However, the document then abruptly sets aside patristic exegesis after associating it with arbitrary interpretations that did not respect the original meanings of the text. Aquinas is then incorrectly presented as representative of a return to the literal sense in the history of biblical exegesis.[47]

JPSSCB then moves on to examine how fundamental themes in Jewish scripture, such as divine revelation, Jerusalem, Temple, and promises, have changed over time, and how the literal sense of these terms is "re-read in the light of Jesus Christ in the New Testament."[48] The authors express sensitivity to the idea of Christological interpretation: "This poses real and delicate questions ... [concerning] the legitimacy of an interpretation of the promises over and above their original, obvious meaning."[49]

The promise of land, among other promises, is then presented as a question: "Is the Promised Land first and foremost a geographic location?" The various ways the land was interpreted in the Hebrew Bible is discussed, including the settling of the land under Joshua, the condition of moral purity in the land, the notion of God as owner of the land, the loss of land in exile, the hope of return with emphasis on Jerusalem, and the Temple as the eschatological future attraction for the nations.[50] The relation of the land and covenant is also examined.[51]

---

46 *JPSSCB*, 20.

47 *JPSSCB*, 20. Beryl Smalley, "William of Auvergne, John of La Rochelle and St. Thomas Aquinas on the Old Law," in *St. Thomas Aquinas, 1274–1974: Commemorative Studies* (Toronto: Pontifical Institute of Mediaeval Studies, 1974), 11–71.

48 *JPSSCB*, 54.

49 *JPSSCB*, 54.

50 *JPSSCB*, 56.

51 *JPSSCB*, 37.

After this analysis of land in the Old Testament, the interpretation of the land in the New Testament is presented:

> The New Testament does not develop much further the theme of the promised land. The flight of Jesus and his parents to Egypt and their return to the "land of promise" (Mt 2:20–21) clearly retraces the journey of the ancestors; a theological typology undergirds this narrative. In Stephen's discourse which recalls their history, the word "promise" or "promised" is found side by side with "land" and "heritage" (Acts 7:2–7). Although not found in the Old Testament, the expression "land of promise" is found in the New (Heb 11:9), in a passage which, undoubtedly, recalls the historical experience of Abraham to better underline its provisional and incomplete character, and its orientation towards the absolute future of the world and history. For the author, the "land" of Israel is only a symbolic pointer towards a very different land, a "heavenly homeland". One of the beatitudes transforms the geographical and historical meaning into a more open-ended one, "the meek shall possess the land" (Mt 5:5); "the land" is equivalent here to "the kingdom of heaven" (5:3,10) in an eschatological horizon that is both present and future.[52]

The section then moves toward the importance of Christ's fulfillment of all the Old Testament promises. The answer to the question posed above regarding the land is that although a literal land was promised in the Old Testament, "all the promises of salvation associated with the coming of the Messiah are fulfilled."[53] This notion of fulfillment assumes the detailed treatment of the concept discussed earlier in the document. We turn now to this complex idea in *JPSSCB*.

According to the *JPSSCB*, Christ's fulfillment takes place in a way that transcends the literal sense of Old Testament promises. The authors explain how promises are to be interpreted in light of a fulfillment dynamic that includes "continuity, discontinuity, progression."[54] It is worth quoting their

---

[52] *JPSSCB*, 57. Immediately after this explanation of how the geographical concept of the land is transformed in the New Testament, the document states: "It should not be forgotten, however, that a specific land was promised by God to Israel and received as a heritage; this gift of the land was on condition of fidelity to the covenant (Lv 26; Dt 28)." When the document recalls that a specific land was promised by God to Israel and received as a heritage, it is restating what has already been said above with regard to land in the Old Testament: that this land was promised; that this land was received. The statement, and language regarding the covenant in other places in the document, should not be read out of context of the document's emphasis on progressive continuity (40). The document stresses that Christian interpretation of biblical promises requires attention to the fulfillment dynamic emphasized throughout the document.

[53] *JPSSCB*, 63.

[54] *JPSSCB*, 64.

statement on how the transcendent nature of Christ's fulfillment excludes literal "photographic anticipations of future events":

> Christian faith recognizes the fulfilment, in Christ, of the Scriptures and the hopes of Israel, but it does not understand this fulfilment as a literal one. Such a conception would be reductionist. In reality, in the mystery of Christ crucified and risen, fulfilment is brought about in a manner unforeseen. It includes transcendence. Jesus is not confined to playing an already fixed role—that of Messiah—but he confers, on the notions of Messiah and salvation, a fullness which could not have been imagined in advance; he fills them with a new reality; one can even speak in this connection of a "new creation". It would be wrong to consider the prophecies of the Old Testament as some kind of photographic anticipations of future events. All the texts, including those which later were read as messianic prophecies, already had an immediate import and meaning for their contemporaries before attaining a fuller meaning for future hearers. The messiahship of Jesus has a meaning that is new and original.[55]

In other words, Christ's fulfillment in the New Testament is in continuity with God's promises in the Jewish scriptures, and yet this continuity also assumes a new reality that could not have been imagined; fulfillment is based on the literal sense yet transcends it. In Christ, salvation takes on a new dimension where his person and work become central: "Jesus ... fulfils in his person, above all in his paschal mystery, all the promises of salvation associated with the coming of the Messiah. He is Son of David of course, but also Suffering Servant, Son of Man and eternal Son of God. In him, salvation takes on a new dimension."[56] The fullness that could not have been imagined is that "Christ's covenant is founded on the blood of a human being who transforms his death as a condemned man into a generous gift."[57] In the Christian interpretation, fulfillment of promises is already realized in this mystery of Christ.[58]

The authors of *JPSSCB* understand fulfillment to include both continuity and transcendence, or what they refer to as "progressive continuity," which involves "breaks" at certain points.[59] "Continuity concerns above all the covenant relationship, while the breaks concern the Old Testament institutions

---

[55] *JPSSCB*, 21.
[56] *JPSSCB*, 63.
[57] *JPSSCB*, 40.
[58] *JPSSCB*, 21.
[59] *JPSSCB*, 40.

that were supposed to establish and maintain that relationship." It becomes clear at this point that the *JPSSCB* does not understand Christ's fulfillment to include the future rebuilding of a political center in Jerusalem.

> The ancient promise [for the reign of God] is now fulfilled, in a fruitful tension between the already and the not-yet. Certainly at the time of Jesus, the Old Testament concept of a "reign of God" that was imminent, terrestrial, political, and centered on "Israel" and in "Jerusalem", was still strongly entrenched (Lk 19:11), even among the disciples (Mt 20:21; Acts 1:6). But the New Testament as a whole brings about a radical change, which was already evident in intertestamental Judaism where the idea of a heavenly, eternal kingdom makes its appearance (Jubilees XV:32; XVI:18).[60]

In addition to land, therefore, fulfillment as progressive continuity also affects Jerusalem, and the Temple: "None of the great Old Testament themes escapes the new radiation of Christological light."[61]

For the *JPSSCB*, the book of Revelation presents one such break in its eschatological vision of the new Jerusalem.[62] Indeed, the Lamb of God is presented as the new Temple; heaven is the new Jerusalem. The authors of *JPSSCB* even say that a temple will no longer be needed: "In history, the victory over the forces of evil will go hand in hand with a new creation that will have God himself as light, and a temple will no longer be needed, for the Almighty God and the Lamb will be the Temple of the heavenly city, the new Jerusalem (Rev. 21:2, 22)."[63]

Other New Testament texts are understood to present this break. The authors understand Jesus to announce replacement of the Temple by a new sanctuary, Christ's body. After his resurrection, the disciples "understand that the new Temple was his risen body (Jn 2:22)."[64] Paul tells believers that they are members of this body (1 Col 12:27) and the "temple of God" (3:16-17) or "of the Spirit" (6:19). Far from being silent on the land, in the New Testament, land, Temple, and Jerusalem are fulfilled by Christ in a way that is present (Heb 12:22) and future (Rv 21:2-3, 9-11).[65] The mother of Christians is "the Jerusalem above" (Gal 4:26).

---

60 *JPSSCB*, 61

61 *JPSSCB*, 65.

62 *JPSSCB*, 40; 83.

63 *JPSSCB*, 26.

64 *JPSSCB*, 51.

65 *JPSSCB*, 51.

JPSSCB also describes these breaks as ruptures that are at the same time a "progression," rooted not only in the New Testament, but in intertestamental Judaism.[66] "Nevertheless, it cannot be denied that the passage from one Testament to the other also involves ruptures. These do not submerge continuity.... Yet these ruptures impinge upon institutions like the Levitical priesthood of the Jerusalem Temple. But it is also clear that the radical replacement in the New Testament was already adumbrated in the Old Testament and so constitute a potentially legitimate reading."[67] According to *JPSSCB*, a tradition of symbolic interpretation in the Old Testament is the basis for extending figural interpretation of the holy city, and its Temple, in the light of the inauguration of Christ's kingdom.[68] In the concluding paragraph to its reflection on shared themes, the authors of the *JPSSCB* state that the advent of Christ extends this Old Testament process of symbolic reinterpretation of land, Temple, and Jerusalem:

> The hope placed in the royal house of David, although defunct for six centuries, becomes the essential key for the reading of history: it is concentrated from now on in Jesus Christ, a humble and distant descendant. Finally, as regards the Land of Israel (including the Temple and the holy city), the New Testament extends the process of symbolisation already begun in the Old Testament and in intertestamental Judaism.[69]

Additionally, under section 4, in the document's final general conclusion, the PBC states that Christ's fulfillment relativizes the material edifice of an earthly Temple: "As regards the earthly Temple, the New Testament, borrowing terms prepared by the Old Testament, relativises the adequacy of a material edifice as a dwelling place of God (Acts 7:48)...."

As David Neuhaus and Alain Marchadour have observed, land in the New Testament "takes on a different meaning, and undergoes an important evolution and transformation; it is molded and reworked by the person of

---

66 *JPSSCB*, 64.

67 *JPSSCB*, 64

68 *JPSSCB*, 65. Jean Daniélou explains that the origin of typological reading of promises in the New Testament is actually the Old Testament: "the prophets announced to the people of Israel that in the future God would perform for their benefit deeds analogous to, and even greater than those He had performed in the past.... These prophecies constitute a primary typology that might be called eschatological, for the prophets saw these future events as happening at the end of time. The New Testament, therefore, did not invent typology, but simply showed that it was fulfilled in the person of Jesus of Nazareth." Jean Daniélou, *The Bible and the Liturgy* (Notre Dame, IN: University of Notre Dame Press, 1966), 4–5.

69 *JPSSCB*, 65.

Jesus in his life, death, and resurrection."[70] In *JPSSCB*, the authors likewise claim that in the New Testament there is a transformation of the land in light of Jesus of Nazareth. The *JPSSCB* advances the claim that Christ's risen body is the fulfillment of the land promise in a twofold sense that is both present and future. For the PBC, a Catholic reading of biblical promises should be interpreted through a Christological lens shaped by the New Testament, and the land promise in particular is fulfilled by Christ in a way that redefines land and the material of the Temple. As *JPSSCB* states, the Jewish reading of the Bible, which includes interpretation of the land promise, is a possible interpretation that deserves respect. Catholics can affirm the multifaceted literal sense of this promise yet interpret its fulfillment differently, in the light of the resurrection of Christ.

In the light of Aquinas's interpretations, the contours of what the *JPSSCB* calls the reshaping of the land promise become clearer—especially the connections between the Old Testament concepts of land, Temple, and Jerusalem, and those same concepts in the New Testament. Indeed, for Aquinas, Psalm 27:13–14, and Isaiah 33:17, contain a hidden meaning: the references to land, seeing the king, and seeing the Lord refer to the resurrection of the dead, and perfect experiential peace in the beatific vision. Aquinas's Christological reading of these Old Testament texts establishes a unity between what the *JPSSCB* calls the tradition of symbolic interpretation in the Old Testament, and land in the New Testament. His anagogical interpretations allow him to connect the ideas of trust in God's promise for life in the land in the Old Testament with life in the land in the New. For this reason, Aquinas would not understand New Testament texts on these themes (land, Temple, Jerusalem) to present breaks with Israel's scriptures. For Aquinas, the promise to inherit the land is a biblical promise to see God face-to-face in the *terra viventium*, or land of the living. The biblical promise of land refers to a state of perfect peace not plagued by violence and death. Aquinas's interpretation of land therefore adds eschatological depth to the symbolization of the land described by the PBC, and upholds the unity of the testaments, which the preface of the *JPSSCB* states is crucial for Catholic reading of scripture.

---

[70] Alain Marchadour and David Neuhaus, *The Land, the Bible, and History: Toward the Land That I Will Show You* (New York: Fordham University Press, 2007), 64–86.

CHRISTOLOGICAL INTERPRETATION OF SCRIPTURE WITHIN TRADITION AND AFTER *NOSTRA AETATE*

The authors of *JPSSCB* acknowledge that the claim that Christ is the fulfillment of God's promises to Israel is "in serious disagreement with the vast majority of the Jewish people who do not accept this fulfilment."[71] This disagreement has had deadly consequences for Jews. A Catholic approach to reading scripture within tradition, and informed by *Nostra Aetate* no. 4, seems to face a difficulty.

The Church teaches that the fathers' interpretation of the Bible is a guide and model, and that Catholics should interpret scripture within the tradition. However, some texts in patristic and medieval biblical commentaries contain anti-Jewish teachings. These ideas were repudiated by *Nostra Aetate* no. 4: "the Jews should not be presented as rejected or accursed by God, as if this followed from the Holy Scriptures." This means Catholics must reject interpretations of scripture within the tradition that portray diaspora Judaism as divine punishment.[72]

After *Nostra Aetate*, the Church recognized that the flesh of this people, in whom the witness to the Holy One of Israel exists perpetually unto the end of time, are the friends of God, not enemies.[73] In post-Conciliar Catholic teaching, Christ's fulfillment of God's promises to Israel is affirmed alongside affirmation of the permanent theological significance of Jews and Judaism. In section 6, "Judaism and Christianity in History," of the 1985 document *Notes on the Correct Way to Present the Jews and Judaism* immediately after stating that Christians are invited to understand Jewish ties to the land, the authors affirm the permanence of Israel as a people: "The permanence of Israel (while so many ancient peoples have disappeared without trace) is a historic fact and a sign to be interpreted within God's design." The authors of *Notes* seem to embrace a theology of signification when they state the people is a sign is to be interpreted. And they then immediately turn to the olive tree metaphor of Romans 11, and quote a statement of St. John Paul II that the election of Israel is expressed well by St. Paul's olive tree metaphor: "It remains a chosen people, 'the pure olive on which were grafted the branches

---

71 "The New Testament then expresses at one and the same time its attachment to Old Testament revelation and its disagreement with the Synagogue." *JPSSCB*, 88.

72 Marchadour and Neuhaus, *The Land, the Bible, and History*, 118.

73 Aquinas applies Christ's words to the disciples, "I have called you friends," to the Jews, on account of their receiving the knowledge of God: "the words of God were committed to them, as to his friends: I have called you friends (John 15:15)." *Ad Romanos*, 3.1.250.

of the wild olive which are the gentiles.'"[74] They also state the implications of this positive affirmation of the Jewish people as sign: "We must in any case rid ourselves of the traditional idea of a people punished, preserved as a living argument for Christian apologetic."[75] Section 6 not only implies God wills the existence of the Jewish people as a sign. The section can also be seen to reject the anti-Jewish elements of Augustine's typological reading of the story of Cain and Abel.[76]

Aquinas's approach to scripture may assist the Church in rereading scripture within tradition, and with these post-Conciliar concerns in mind. Critical evaluation of a father's interpretation of scripture has precedent in Aquinas's biblical commentaries. Throughout the commentaries he regularly engages with prior interpreters of scripture, such as Augustine, Jerome, Ambrose, Hilary, Origen, Basil, Gregory of Nyssa, and Chrysostom (among others). If he understands an interpreter to be mistaken, he will say so.[77] In some cases, Aquinas insists that one father's interpretation is better than another's (as he did when he preferred Hilary's reading of Matthew 5:5 over Chrysostom's). Aquinas sometimes says a father comes close to a solution on a difficult text but a clearer answer is needed.[78] In some cases he affirms several possible literal meanings advanced by different fathers.[79] In other cases he puts forward his own answer after only quoting others. As Stephen Fowl has pointed out, Aquinas's approach to reading scripture within the tradition allows for flexibility.[80]

With this flexible approach in mind, perhaps we can return to *Notes* and its statement that the permanence of the Jewish people is a historic fact and sign to be interpreted in God's design. Perhaps one way to consider Jews and Judaism as an ongoing sign in God's design is through a reflection on the "root" in St. Paul's statement in Romans 11:18, "remember that it is not you that support the root; but the root that supports you." This root could

---

[74] John Paul II, *To the Delegates of the Episcopal Conferences for Relations with Judaism*, March 6, 1982.

[75] *Notes*, sec. 6 (emphasis added).

[76] Augustine, *Reply to Faustus*, in *Nicene and Post-Nicene Fathers*, First Series, vol. 4 (Peabody, MA: Hendrickson Publishers, 1994) 12.11–12, 16.21. See also Aquinas's approving description of this reading of Genesis 4 in his commentary on Matthew 27:25. *Super Matt.*, 27.1.2343.

[77] Fowl, "Multivoiced Literal Sense," 37.

[78] Leo J. Elders, "The Presence of the Church Fathers in Aquinas' Commentaries on the Gospel of Matthew and the Gospel of John," in *Reading Sacred Scripture with Thomas Aquinas: Hermeneutical Tools, Theological Questions, and New Perspectives*, ed. Piotr Roszak and Jörgen Vijgen (Turnhout: Brepols, 2015), 261.

[79] Fowl, "Multivoiced Literal Sense," 37.

[80] Fowl, "Multivoiced Literal Sense," 37.

be interpreted to refer to the distinctiveness of Jewish flesh, the flesh from which Christ came. The idea that the Church draws present sustenance from the Jewish people today implies the ongoing fleshly existence of this people in perpetuity is vital for Christian faith.

The nature of the "support" which the root that is Israel continues to provide the Church can be clarified through reflection on the relationship of the Jewish people to Christ's circumcised body.[81] This relation between Israel and Christ can be expressed by what Aquinas understood as the three "appearances of the Son of God": Incarnation, resurrection, and second coming.[82]

First, consider that Christ was circumcised on the eighth day. In this event in the early life of Christ, a direct link between the permanent election of Israel, Torah, and the Church's faith in the Incarnation becomes manifest. The circumcision of Christ is a permanent reminder of his umbilical link to the Virgin Mary, his Jewish Mother. According to Aquinas, the first reason Christ was circumcised was "in order to prove the reality of his human nature, in contradiction to the Manicheans, who said that he had an imaginary body."[83] The ongoing flesh of Israel therefore is sustenance for the Church in that it witnesses, throughout the era of grace, to the Incarnation; to the reality of Christ's human nature (that he was really born).

---

81 Some scholars will find my reading of Israel as a sign of Christ as supersessionist. It seems to me that the term, "progressive continuity," described by the PBC, is possibly more helpful since the notion of a progressive continuity can account for the complexity of a Christological fulfillment that simultaneously includes multiple discontinuities and continuities. Christ fulfills land, Torah, and Temple, in various and complex ways. For example, Jon Levenson has demonstrated that belief in resurrection of the dead is crucial for rabbinic tradition, and that the resurrection of the dead is based in the Jewish scriptures. The Christian idea of the land promise as referring to the land of the resurrection of the dead is in progressive continuity with aspects of this Jewish biblical eschatology, which means it is continuous with Israel's scriptures in some ways, and deeply discontinuous in others. This sort of fulfillment simultaneously expresses continuity and discontinuity on both literal and spiritual levels of interpretation. Jon D. Levenson, *Resurrection and the Restoration of Israel: The Ultimate Victory of the God of Life* (New Haven: Yale University Press, 2006).

82 According to Aquinas there is a threefold appearing of the Son of God. Aquinas, *Super Isaiam*, Prologue. However, it should be noted that I am departing from Aquinas here. For the most part, Aquinas thinks these rites *were* figures, and are no longer figures of Christ. However, in II.II 10.11 Aquinas says that when the Jews observe their rites after the passion of Christ, the Christian faith is represented in a figure "so to speak." It seems he implies the rites figure Christian faith or Christian mode of life, and not only the passion: "All these things happened to them in figures. Consequently the reasons for these observances may be taken in two ways, first according to their fittingness to the worship of God; secondly according as they foreshadow something touching the Christian mode of life." I.II 102.6. In my view, the Old Law continues to figure the three appearances of Christ, Christ's faith, and the Christian mode of life. It also seems to me that any anagogical understandings of the Old Law would continue to figure, after the passion.

83 Aquinas, III 37.1.

A second sense in which the people is a sign corresponds to the second appearance of the Son of God, the resurrection. Since Christ's resurrected body retains its wounds, Jewish circumcision could also be said to figure the circumcised Jewish flesh of Christ's resurrected body. Far from destroying the law, Christ built an eternal fence around the Torah in his circumcised and glorified body. Therefore, the ongoing distinctiveness of Jewish flesh maintained in observation of circumcision remains a figure or sign not only of the Incarnation, but also of Christ's resurrection (that his body died; and that his body was raised).

The third way in which the people is a sign corresponds to the third appearance of the Son of God, the second coming. The permanent distinctiveness of this faithful people, as well as their prayer for the throne of David and Zion, are a sign that figures the perfect state of peace at the second coming. The faith of the Church includes belief in the second coming of Christ, when he will appear in what Aquinas calls the land of the living. Circumcision today might figure the reality of the resurrected body of Christ at the second coming in a twofold sense that corresponds to Christ's resurrected body, and the bodies of those resurrected from the dead. First, the rite of circumcision today figures the flesh of the Deliverer who will come to judge the living and the dead, when all Israel will be saved (see Rom 11:26). Second, circumcision could be said to continue to figure what the fathers and Aquinas called the "eighth era." In their reflections on why circumcision took place on the eighth day, the fathers said the eighth day was a symbol that referred to the eighth era, which they understood as the resurrection of the dead.[84] In line with this patristic tradition, Aquinas says in I.II 102.5 ad. 1 that circumcision was a figure of the resurrection of the dead, namely the removal of corruption from our bodies: "The figurative reason for circumcision was that it foreshadowed the removal of corruption, which was to be brought about by Christ, and will be perfectly fulfilled in the eighth age, which is the age of those who rise from the dead." In his commentary on Romans, Aquinas adds that circumcision prefigures the resurrection of the dead, "when all possibility of suffering and death is removed from the bodies of the elect."[85] Circumcision can therefore be said to signify both the circumcised body of Christ as well as his removal of corruption from our bodies, and the earth, in the land of the living.

In so far as election of God's people includes both Jews and Christians, the resurrection of the dead will include a removal of all suffering and death

---

[84] Jean Danielou, *The Bible and the Liturgy* (Notre Dame, IN: University of Notre Dame Press, 1966), 262–86.

[85] Aquinas, *Ad Romanos*, 4.2.348.

from our bodies, especially persecuted bodies, thus fulfilling the reward in Matthew 5:10, "blessed are the persecuted." Perhaps on this Day, when the Deliverer comes to judge the living and the dead, he will also address Christian neglect of Paul's warning in Romans 11:18 not to boast against the Jewish people, especially Christians who sought to uproot and burn that well-cultivated olive tree from the diaspora soil of Christian Europe in the burning of the Talmud in 1242; in forced baptism of Jews (and separations of forcibly baptized Jewish children from their parents); or in assisting Nazi persecution and destruction of Jews from 1933–1945.

7

THE CATHOLIC CHURCH AND "ISRAEL/PALESTINE"
THE JEWISH PEOPLE, THE LAND, NATION, AND STATE
Gavin D'Costa

The Catholic Church has a clear diplomatic stance (legal and juridical) in relation to the "Jewish people living in the land that is called Israel." In this chapter I want to argue that there is also a tentative theological position discernible on this issue. Its delicacy is due to the question's theological complexity and the fraught circumstances within which it is asked. To many, the State of Israel is predicated upon the destruction of the Palestinian people, and its nationhood is an extension of European colonialism.[1] For others, it is an instrument of political messianism—sometimes secular (as with earlier socialist Zionism) and increasingly religious, and often both.[2] The historical reality on the ground is deeply contested. It raises a theological question: Is there a Roman Catholic biblical view regarding Jewish people living in the land called Israel?

In this chapter I shall be arguing that there is a theological position emerging within official Catholic documents, not with magisterial force, that attends to the complex issues. Discerning what this position is, is important for Catholics grappling with these issues.

---

[1] Edward W. Said, "Zionism from the Standpoint of Its Victims," in *The Edward Said Reader*, ed. Moustafa Bayoumi and Andrew Rubin (London: Granta Books, 2000), 114–68.

[2] See, for example, Aviezer Ravitzky, *Messianism, Zionism, and Jewish Religious Radicalism*, trans. Michael Swirsky and Jonathan Chipman (Chicago: University of Chicago Press, 1996).

THE QUESTIONS

Let me first specify the questions I will address:

1. Does the Jewish *people* settling in the *land* designated within the United Nations 1947 Agreement have any positive theological significance for Catholics? If "no," I should stop now. If a possible "yes," however tentative, there immediately follows another question.

2. What of the non-Jewish peoples, especially the *Palestinians*, many of whom lived there prior to 1948; and what of their displacement, subsequent refugee status, loss of nationhood—and present treatment within Israel/Palestine? If this second question is answered that the Palestinians have equal international rights to the land and a right to a state, there follows another question.

3. Does theologically affirming the Jewish people settling the land (as in question 1), necessarily lead to a theological affirmation of the *State of Israel*? Would saying yes to question 1, lead to theologically affirming the state? Does saying no to question 3, undercut an affirmation regarding the people and the land?

The answers developed here are the beginnings of a much longer conversation amongst Catholic theologians inside and outside of Israel/Palestine. The trajectories possible permit plurality within the Catholic Church, as is seen in this volume. In this paper, I argue for one particular trajectory and give reasons for questioning the alternatives.

A POSSIBLE CATHOLIC ANSWER IN THREE STEPS
Palestine and the Palestinians—the Right to a State (Question 2)

Methodologically, I begin with question 2 for a heuristic reason: the answers to the other two questions will be clearer because of the answer given to this question.

The Holy See has developed a clear perspective on the Palestinian question. This has emerged since 1993, become formal in 2000, and developed in 2015. It has been implicit in all actions of the Holy See since 1948 that the active care of Palestinian refugees has been central to its approach to the region.[3] The year 1993 marks the peace agreement signed in the Rose

---

3 See George Emile Irani, *The Papacy and the Middle East: The Role of the Holy See in the Arab-Israeli Conflict, 1962–1984* (Notre Dame, IN: University of Notre Dame Press, 1986). For a treatment

Garden of the White House between Rabin and Arafat. Given that both sides had reached an agreement, the Holy See felt permitted to advance in securing agreements with both parties related to its own communities and Holy Places, thereby keeping its neutrality intact as per Article 24 of the Lateran Treaty of 1929.[4]

The Fundamental Agreement of 1993 between the Holy See and Israel led to full diplomatic relations in 1994. Likewise with Jordan in 1994. Due to shifts within the Palestinian leadership, the parallel Basic Agreement with the Palestinian Liberation Organization (on behalf of the Palestinian Authority) had to wait until 2000. That was followed by a Comprehensive Agreement between the State of Palestine and the Holy See in 2015, whereby the Holy See recognized the pre-1967 borders in accordance with the United Nations 1947 Mandate and affirmed a two-state solution as part of the Agreement.[5] Resurrected was the Holy See's earlier concern for a *corpus separatum*, an international status for Jerusalem and the Holy Places.

In return, the Holy See secured freedom of religion for its own communities within the Palestinian state, juridical freedoms for its religious personnel, and legal standing for its properties, with an agreement that taxation required clear principles based on the Holy See's special status. These are similar to goals established in the 1993 agreement with Israel. Not addressed in the 2015 agreement under matters of religious freedom were issues of mission or conversion. Given that the Palestinian leadership could involve significant elements from Hamas in the future, these Agreements are hopeful signposts, while still requiring clarification and elaboration.

---

of the period prior to that covered by Irani, see Sergio I. Minerbi, *The Vatican and Zionism: Conflict in the Holy Land, 1895–1925*, trans. Arnold Schwarz (Oxford: Oxford University Press, 1990). Less balanced but also helpful is Andrej Kreutz, *Vatican Policy on the Palestinian-Israeli Conflict: The Struggle for the Holy Land* (New York: Greenwood, 1990).

4 "In regard to the sovereignty appertaining to it also in international matters, the Holy See declares that it desires to take, and shall take, no part in any temporal rivalries between other States, nor in any international congresses called to settle such matters, save and except in the event of such parties making a mutual appeal to the pacific mission of the Holy See, the latter reserving in any event the right of exercising its moral and spiritual power. The Vatican City shall, therefore, be invariably and in every event considered as neutral and inviolable territory." (see Treaty of Conciliation, 1929, http://www.aloha.net/~mikesch/treaty.htm)

5 Opening preamble: "Expressing full support for a just, comprehensive and peaceful settlement of the question of Palestine, in all its aspects, in accordance with international law and all relevant United Nations resolutions, as well as for an independent, sovereign, democratic and viable State of Palestine on the basis of the pre-1967 borders, on the West Bank, including East Jerusalem, and the Gaza Strip, living side by side in peace and security with all its neighbours." See "Comprehensive Agreement Between the Holy See and the Palestinian Authority," Bibliotecanonica (2015). See also: Leonard Hammer, "2015 Comprehensive Agreement Between the Holy See and the Palestinian Authority: Discerning the Holy See's Approach to International Relations in the Holy Land," *Oxford Journal of Law and Religion* 6, no. 1 (2017): 162–79.

These agreements establish that no answer to questions 1 and 3 above can preclude the Holy See's firm commitments to social justice and international law regarding the rights and freedoms of the Palestinian people and a Palestinian state living in peace with its neighbors. The agreement follows international law protocols arising from the UN mandate. However, on the ground today there are many models for achieving Palestinian state autonomy—a single state with federations, a two-state solution, and so on.[6] The principles of the agreement are important. The precise details of how this should happen are for future free negotiations involving all parties. It is worth noting that the foundations for this position taken by the Holy See arise both from its high esteem of international law and principles of social justice, the latter deriving from revelation, thus gaining serious traction upon all Catholics, not just those living in Palestine, Israel, and the Middle East.[7]

I am not denying the diplomatic and pragmatic concerns underlying the Holy See's agreements with the Palestinians. These agreements in themselves do not provide theological arguments. However, the Church's own diplomacy is, according to its own norms, guided by revelation. Hence, a Catholic would be encouraged to develop the theological rationale for this position in far more detail. Furthermore, it would be important to examine Palestinian theological reflections on our three questions, and especially Catholic Palestinian reflections, to properly think through these matters.[8]

With this tentative conclusion, let us turn to the first question regarding the Jewish people and their settling in the land called Israel.

Does the Jewish Settling in the Land Designated within the United Nations 1947 Agreement Have Any Theological Significance for Catholics? (Question 1)

We first need to take a brief step back to see why the Catholic Church must address this issue. It requires us to note the affirmation of the validity of the Jewish covenant with God arising from the Second Vatican Council and being subsequently developed by the magisterium.

---

6 See, for example, Hasan Afif El-Hasan, *Is the Two-State Solution Already Dead?: A Political and Military History of the Palestinian-Israeli Conflict* (New York: Algora Publishing, 2010); Yehouda Shenhav, *Beyond the Two-State Solution: A Jewish Political Essay*, trans. Dimi Reider (Cambridge: Polity Press, 2012).

7 The relationship between social justice and revelation is made clear in Pontifical Council for Justice and Peace, *Compendium of the Social Doctrine of the Church* (Dublin: Veritas, 2005), 74; see Levi's essay in this collection.

8 I am particularly indebted to Jamal Khader, David Neuhaus, and Michel Sabbah for the persistent and graceful questioning they provided. None of them would agree with my manner of answering questions 1 and 3.

Between the Second Vatican Council's *Nostra Aetate* (1965) and the document celebrating its fiftieth anniversary, *"The Gifts and the Calling of God Are Irrevocable" (Rom 11:29): A Reflection on Theological Questions Pertaining to Catholic-Jewish Relations on the Occasion of the Fiftieth Anniversary of "Nostra Aetate,"* number four (2015; called *Gifts* from here on),[9] we witness a series of moves within Catholic theology regarding the Jewish people. These developments are still in progress. *Gifts* outlines three important milestones in Catholic teaching that relate to my first question: is there theological significance of Jewish people in the land?

First, "supersessionist" theology, sometimes called "replacement" theology, is rejected. Supersessionism is the view that the covenant that God made with the Jewish people has become invalid and inoperative.[10] This does not call into question the Catholic view that the Church is the fulfillment of Jewish biblical faith, but rather that fulfillment does not entail supersessionism. Disentangling the distinction between fulfillment and supersessionism is far from resolved. *Gifts* criticizes some Church fathers and doctors of the Middle Ages for holding supersessionist views that should now be rejected.[11] This is a bold step and quite rare in official Church documents. It is also honest. The *Catechism* allows for the abandonment of some traditions, which is quite different from the authority of Tradition which is to be honored and the source of the critique of traditions.[12]

The rejection of supersessionism arose from the rereading of Romans 9–11, mentioned in both *Lumen Gentium* and *Nostra Aetate*, combined with the rejection of the deicide charge against all Jews secured in *Nostra Aetate*.[13] The logic of the position meant that those Jews who are invincibly ignorant of the truth of the gospel are in a valid covenant with the true and living God, who is faithful to his promises and gifts. One of these promises and gifts to

---

9 Commission for Religious Relations with the Jews, *"The Gifts and the Calling of God Are Irrevocable" (Rom 11:29): A Reflection on Theological Questions Pertaining to Catholic–Jewish Relations on the Occasion of the 50th Anniversary of "Nostra Aetate,"* (2015).

10 For a good discussion of supersessionism, see R. Kendall Soulen, *The God of Israel and Christian Theology* (Minneapolis, MN: Fortress Press, 1996).

11 Commission for Religious Relations with the Jews, *Gifts*, 17.

12 *Catechism of the Catholic Church*, 83: "Tradition is to be distinguished from the various theological, disciplinary, liturgical or devotional traditions, born in the local churches over time. These are the particular forms, adapted to different places and times, in which the great Tradition is expressed. In the light of Tradition, these traditions can be retained, modified or even abandoned under the guidance of the Church's Magisterium." This is a far more fraught process than the quote indicates, but the principle is clear.

13 For good background, see John Connelly, *From Enemy to Brother: The Revolution in Catholic Teaching on the Jews, 1933–1965* (Cambridge, MA: Harvard University Press, 2012).

the Jewish people in the Old Testament regards the land—and that is why our question is being asked today more poignantly.

The second milestone is that postbiblical Judaism, what I call Rabbinic Judaism, is the inheritor of these promises and gifts of the covenant, as are Christians. There was a lively debate after the Council as to whether Vatican II affirmed only biblical Judaism or also Rabbinic Judaism. *Gifts* 39 states that the Council documents did not affirm Rabbinic Judaism, which was only positively affirmed by Saint Pope John Paul II in 1980. He reiterated this teaching after 1980, as have Pope Benedict and Pope Francis.[14]

However, this affirmation of Rabbinic Judaism leaves many questions unresolved: Which form of Judaism is being identified as authentic postbiblical Rabbinic Judaism by Catholics? How does that relate to secular Judaism, let alone minority religious groups within Judaism that deem others to have strayed from the path? This question is germane as the Jewish people who came from Europe were, like most Zionist leaders, secular Jews. Many social historians argue that the distinction between secular and religious Jews is difficult to maintain as many secular Jews keep religious practices and employ religious terminology.[15] Nevertheless, this clarification regarding Rabbinic Judaism once again focuses on the question of whether the Jewish "return" to/"occupation" of the land has theological significance given the biblical promises.

The third milestone, which in this instance is more like a series of pebbles in the dust than a milestone, is noting small, significant clues that give a tentative affirmative answer that the Jewish people in the land called Israel has theological significance for Catholics. None of these clues can be termed formal magisterial teaching. None of these clues can undo the just cause of Palestinian statehood supported by the Holy See. But together, these clues point to a significant sea change in Catholic attitudes to the Jewish people in the land called Israel.

The first surprisingly occurs in May 1917. Nahum Sokolow presented the "Zionist" cause to Pope Benedict XV purely as a movement to help Jews escape persecution, not as the foundation of a Jewish state. The pope is reported to have responded: "It is providential; God has willed it."[16] Here is a vestige of biblical theology related to the land. Cardinal Pietro Gasparri,

---

14 See Gavin D'Costa, *Catholic Doctrines on the Jewish People after Vatican II* (Oxford: Oxford University Press, 2019), 1–26.

15 See Yosef Gorny, "Judaism and Zionism," in *The Blackwell Companion to Judaism*, ed. Jacob Neusner and Alan J. Avery-Peck (Oxford: Blackwell, 2000), 477–94.

16 See Kreutz, *Vatican Policy on the Palestinian-Israeli Conflict*, 34; drawing on Sergio Minerbi, *L'Italie et le Palestine 1914–1920* (Paris: Presses Universitaires de France, 1970), 63–64.

then secretary of state, had already told Sokolow regarding his attenuated non-state Zionism: "from the Church you will have no opposition. On the contrary, you may count on our sympathy. We shall be glad to see the land (sic [in original]) of Israel."[17] This theological response by Pope Benedict XV and Secretary of State Gasparri was made on the assumption that Zionism was not about endorsing a political messianic nation-state, but about saving Jewish lives. Neither of them addressed the issue of the local inhabitants of Palestine. Neither of them perhaps envisaged the scenario that would unfold forty years later.

The second clue is found in the Commission for Religious Relations with Jews, *Notes on the Correct Way to Present the Jews and Judaism in Preaching and Catechesis in the Roman Catholic Church* (1985).[18] Recall, this is before the Fundamental Agreement of 1993 with Israel and after John Paul II's 1980 Mainz address. This document has been read in very different ways.[19] The entire text is important:

> The history of Israel did not end in 70 CE (cf. *Guidelines* II). It continued, especially in a numerous Diaspora which allowed Israel to carry to the whole world a witness—often heroic—of its fidelity to the one God and to "exalt him in the presence of all the living" (Tobit 13:4), while preserving the memory of the land of their forefathers at the hearts of their hope (Passover Seder).
>
> Christians are invited to understand this religious attachment which finds its roots in Biblical tradition, without however making their own any particular religious interpretation of this relationship (cf. Declaration of the US Conference of Catholic Bishops, November 20, 1975).

---

[17] Leonard Jacques Stein, *The Balfour Declaration* (London: Vallentine Mitchell, 1961), 407. It is not clear if this is Stein or Sokolow's "sic," or the English translation of Sokolow's Russian by Mr. Florian Sokolow (see 406n48).

[18] There are important national bishops' conference documents, especially the French 1973 (see below), the Brazilian [see National Conference of Brazilian Bishops, *Orientations for Catholic-Jewish Dialogue*, Council of Centers of Jewish-Christian Relations (October 1, 1983) https://www.ccjr.us/dialogika-resources/documents-and-statements/interreligious/ncbb1983] and the American (1975), that form a backdrop to this statement. It cites the US Bishops' Conference statement (see below).

[19] Adam Gregerman, "Is the Biblical Land Promise Irrevocable?: Post-*Nostra Aetate* Catholic Theologies of the Jewish Covenant and the Land of Israel," *Modern Theology* 34, no. 2 (2017): 137–58. Gregerman reads it as a *general* statement against giving the land promise to the Jews any Christian religious significance. Marchadour and Neuhaus concur, but based on biblical exegesis. Alain Marchadour and David Neuhaus, *The Land, the Bible, and History: Toward the Land That I Will Show You*, 1st ed. (New York: Fordham University Press, 2007), 63–88. Eugene Fisher, in contrast, suggests that this text is simply against fundamentalist readings, both Jewish and Protestant, in "Reflections on 'the Common Bond,'" *Christian Jewish Relations* 18 (1985): 54–57.

The existence of the State of Israel and its political options should be envisaged not in a perspective which is in itself religious, but in their reference to the common principles of international law.

The permanence of Israel (while so many ancient peoples have disappeared without trace) is a historic fact and a sign to be interpreted within God's design. We must in any case rid ourselves of the traditional idea of a people punished, preserved as a living argument for Christian apologetic. It remains a chosen people.[20]

The first paragraph moves away from Vatican II's biblical Israel and clearly indicates Rabbinic Judaism. It acknowledges the biblically and liturgically based hope for the promised land. There is an identifying of the Jewish witness of faith in the one true God to the world, sometimes heroically witnessed—and the longing for the land of their forefathers, found embedded in Jewish liturgy. The connection between these two apparently disparate religious values is found in the citation of Tobit 13:4. The use of Tobit, from the intertestamental period, is not recognized as part of the *Tanakh*, but related to the early Jewish community. The choice of Tobit helps establish the validity of the claim on Catholic grounds. Further, Tobit tells of the people witnessing to God in their dispersion, but also their hope of being reunited, singing God's praises in Jerusalem. The juxtaposition between Jewish witness and "heroic" witness clearly indicates Jewish fidelity to their faith amidst terrible persecutions after biblical times. The use of "heroic" echoes the Catholic term used for saints in their heroic virtue when witnessing to the faith. It is rare to find the term used by the Vatican of a non-Catholic, let alone a non-Christian.[21] The longing for the land and persecution of the Jewish people implicitly connect the *Shoah* and the refuge taken in Palestine by Jews fleeing this terror.[22] The prayer of the Passover Seder cited in the document ends: "Next year in Jerusalem." This contains earlier prayers for the city's restoration and the return of the people. This paragraph therefore takes very seriously many articulations of Jewish self-understanding, with some Catholic endorsement by virtue of citing it.

20 See John Paul II, "Address to Representatives of the West German Jewish Community," Mainz, West Germany, November 17, 1980.

21 For a treatment of the concept of heroic witness, see Kenneth L. Woodward, *Making Saints: How the Catholic Church Determines Who Becomes a Saint, Who Doesn't, and Why* (New York: Simon and Schuster, 1994), 221–51. It is a term related to the Roman Catholic tradition of saints. However, for an argument to extend it beyond Catholicism, related to Eastern Church martyrs and using Pope Francis to justify this analogical extension, see Hugh Somerville Knapman, *Ecumenism of Blood: Heavenly Hope for Earthly Communion* (New York: Paulist Press, 2018).

22 While Jewish martyrs are greatly honored, it is not usual within Judaism to seek martyrdom. Martyrdom is considered *kiddush Hashem* (the sanctification of God's name).

Rabbi Irving Greenberg expresses the force of the connection of these two events graphically:

> In this generation . . . have occurred . . . [two] major normative events in Jewish history. . . . They are the event of the Holocaust—unparalleled tragedy and destruction, towering over the other great tragic watershed of 1,900 years ago, the destruction of the Second Temple—and the event of the rebirth of Israel—the experience of redemption as has not been experienced by Jews on this scale since the Exodus.[23]

If paragraph one deals with Jewish self-understanding, the next paragraph establishes two further points. First, the Jewish attachment to the land "finds its roots in Biblical tradition." Jewish self-understanding is biblically justified. This refers to the Old Testament teachings that have authority as revelation for Catholics. We must wait until the Pontifical Biblical Commission's document *The Jewish People and their Sacred Scriptures in the Christian Bible* in 2001 to get a detailed picture of how Catholic exegetes might read these texts within the Old Testament. At the time of *Notes* there was no consensus on how to read the Old Testament texts in terms of enduring promises to the Jewish people, or at least much less than then there is now. *Notes* continues that this reading of the Old Testament as containing promises regarding the land need not be owned by Catholics. It does not rule this out in the future, nor does it endorse it. In *Jewish People* (2001) the argument will change; see below, showing that Catholics can have confidence in biblically owning and affirming this teaching.

By referring to the 1975 US Catholic bishops' *Statement on Catholic-Jewish Relations* immediately after these two points, *Notes* indicates the political context that makes theological support of the land difficult. This is not stated explicitly in *Notes*.[24] The US bishops' statement comes as close to affirming the land as possible, given the unresolved Palestinian dispossession and the unresolved biblical issues. The US bishops say this about the Land of Israel:

> In dialogue with Christians, Jews have explained that they do not consider themselves as a church, a sect, or a denomination, as is the case among Christian communities, but rather as a peoplehood that is not solely racial, ethnic or religious, but in a sense a composite of all these. It is for such

---

23 Irving Greenberg, *For the Sake of Heaven and Earth: The New Encounter between Judaism and Christianity* (Philadelphia: Jewish Publication Society, 2004), 129.

24 See US Conference of Catholic Bishops, *Statement on Catholic-Jewish Relations*, (November 20, 1975).

reasons that an overwhelming majority of Jews see themselves bound in one way or another to the Land of Israel. Most Jews see this tie to the land as essential to their Jewishness. Whatever difficulties Christians may experience in sharing this view they should strive to understand this link between land and people which Jews have expressed in their writings and worship throughout two millennia as a longing for the homeland, Israel. Appreciation of this link is not to give assent to any particular religious interpretation of this bond. Nor is this affirmation meant to deny the legitimate rights of other parties in the region, or to adopt any political stance in the controversies over the Middle East, which lie beyond the purview of this statement.

These qualifications are all important, for they represent the Palestinian cause—the "legitimate rights of other parties in the region." Given this document's date before the Fundamental Agreement, it would hardly have been appropriate to theologically affirm the land when the Vatican had not even formally recognized, *de jure*, Israel as a state, which it would do eight years later.

The third paragraph affirms the State of Israel's "existence" based on international law. Here it establishes a clear distinction between people, people in the land (the first two paragraphs), and the state. In 1985, there was no Fundamental Agreement, but clearly the Catholic Church accepts Israel's legal right to exist. But it distances itself from affirming any political actions of that state or underwriting the state in theological terms. Given the above paragraph that implicitly gestures to the Palestinian people, the reason for this distancing is clear. However, its distancing also has theological reasons. We will return to this below.

The fourth paragraph breaks further ground. It contains two arguments. The first is radical. It unambiguously imputes God's actions in maintaining the "permanence" of the Jewish people. This is important in showing that Catholic theology is able to make decisions about specific concrete actions, "signs" in the world, signs of our times, related to the Jewish people. It can attribute such actions positively to "God's design." God's design would normally mean the actions are willed by God to reveal something about God's purpose. The US bishops *Statement* (1975), referred to earlier in the document, already acknowledges that the Jewish *people* see their covenant as intrinsically related to the *land*. While the priority is the people, and their continued existence and endurance is interpreted theologically, the land cannot be divorced from the people. The land is not the primary focus of God's gift. The people are the primary focus. It is to them that the covenant is promised; it is to them that the land is promised. To affirm that God is behind the Jewish people's survival and protection already gestures toward the embodied conditions that make this possible—the land promised by God.

The document treads a delicate line in holding together the primacy of the people, respecting and understanding their religious beliefs about the land, being open about how Catholics might interpret this, and giving the State of Israel a purely legal status and not viewing it theologically. This allows a pathway to explore the people and the land promise (our question 1), but signals a caution that that pathway does not entail a theological significance to the state as such (question 3).

In the terms set out at the beginning of this paper, *Notes* indicates that yes is possible to question 1 (regarding the Jewish people in the land called Israel), but that would not logically entail answering question 3 affirmatively (the State of Israel has theological meaning). However, the state is recognized under international law and has a right to exist.

Six years later, in 1991, John Paul II, when addressing a Jewish audience in Brazil, used Ezekiel 34:13 (a proof text regarding the ingathering of the peoples) to interpret the emergence of the land:

> May our Jewish brother and sisters, who have been led 'out from among the peoples and gathered from the foreign lands' and brought back 'to their own country' [Ezek 34.13], to the land of their ancestors, be able to live there in peace and security on the 'mountains of Israel', guarded by the protection of God, their true shepherd.[25]

This is being done without any reference to the state and prior to the Agreement, but it entails a theological significance to the Jewish people living in the land. An opening that appeared in *Notes* is stepped through by the pope in public. Although this text is very significant in providing a biblical underpinning to modern Israel, one should not overstate its eschatological significance as this kind of biblical reference is not used again by the pope in public.

We move now to the Fundamental Agreement of 1993. This was conducted by the secretary of state's office, but note the discreet theological underpinnings. The preamble affirms both communities' religious dimensions:

> The Holy See and the State of Israel, Mindful of the singular character and universal significance of the Holy Land; Aware of the unique nature of the relationship between the Catholic Church and the Jewish people, and of the historic process of reconciliation and growth in mutual understanding

---

[25] *The Saint for Shalom: How Pope John Paul II Transformed Catholic-Jewish Relations*, ed. Eugene J. Fisher (New York: Crossroads, 2011), 225.

and friendship between Catholics and Jews ... Agree upon the following articles.²⁶

It then proceeds with the legal Agreement. The "unique nature" can only refer to the *sui generis* theological relationship that the church has with the Jewish people, established clearly at Vatican II and endorsed and developed by Pope John Paul II, the presiding pope at the time of the Agreement. The "reconciliation and growth" could refer to the many religious steps taken by the Commission for Religious Relations with the Jews. Reconciliation is a theological term, although it does not exclude other usage, such as the diplomatic steps leading to this Agreement.

Supporting this tentative reading, a clearer theological note is found in the public signatory speech delivered by Msgr. Claudio Maria Celli, undersecretary for foreign affairs. He said the Agreement must be "acknowledged to have a fundamental religious and spiritual significance—not only for the Holy See and the State of Israel, but for millions of people throughout the world."²⁷ The latter reference relates to a worldwide Jewish diaspora and a transnational Catholic population, both of whom cherish the Holy land for religious and spiritual reasons. Richard Lux sees in this the Vatican's recognition that the Land of Israel cannot be divorced from Jews, from their covenantal aspirations, and from Christian sentiments toward the Jews and the Holy Land.²⁸ One must also recall that this Agreement was being signed with the understanding that peace was underway between Israel and the Palestinians, and a similar Agreement would be forthcoming between the Palestinians and the Holy See.

The final document in this section that I want to draw on is the Pontifical Biblical Commission report, *The Jewish People and their Sacred Scriptures*

---

26 See *Fundamental Agreement between the Holy See and the State of Israel* (December 30, 1993). This reading of the document is in contrast to Raymond Cohen, "Israel and the Holy See Negotiate," *The Hague Journal of Diplomacy* 5, no. 3 (2010), 213–34, 222, which says that "reconciliation and diplomacy were kept strictly separate." John Pawlikowski, "Land as an Issue in Christian-Jewish Dialogue," *Cross Currents* 59, no. 2 (2009): 197–209, at 199, 203 presents a reading that supports my own.

27 Statement by Claudio Maria Celli after the signing of the Fundamental Agreement, Jerusalem, December 30, 1993, available at https://unispal.un.org/DPA/DPR/unispal.nsf/0/24D3B040A6 F6404A85256052005A17B7, accessed August 10, 2021.

28 Richard C. Lux, *The Jewish People, the Holy Land, and the State of Israel. A Catholic View* (Mahwah, NJ: Paulist Press, 2010), 77. Raniero Cantalamessa, preacher to the papal household over two papacies and biblical scholar, writes: "We share with the Jews the biblical certainty that God gave them the country of Canaan forever (Genesis 17:8, Isaiah 43:5, Jeremiah 32:22, Ezekiel 36:24, Amos 9:14). We know that the gifts and the call of God are irrevocable." Raniero Cantalamessa, *The Mystery of Christmas: A Comment on the Magnificat, Gloria, Nunc Dimittis* (Collegeville, MN: Liturgical Press, 1989), 38.

in the Christian Bible (JPSSCB).[29] This is important as it explicitly addresses the question regarding the land promise in the Old Testament. I have discussed this document in some detail elsewhere.[30] Here I can only cite the main passages and summarize their teachings. Three points are important within this document.

First, it tackles the question of whether Jewish exegesis of the Old Testament is legitimate. It carefully answers: yes; and no. "Yes," insomuch as both Jewish and Catholic paradigms of reading the scriptural text are informed by differing presuppositions and beliefs, such that both communities have a hermeneutical right to read the texts as they do from their differing methodological and traditioned forms of reading. This does not mean that Jewish readings have any authority over Catholics, but Catholics might well learn from them. They both have legitimate reasons for reading the texts as they do: "As regards the first question, the situation is different, for Christians can and ought to admit that the Jewish reading of the Bible is a possible one, in continuity with the Jewish Sacred Scriptures from the Second Temple period, a reading analogous to the Christian reading which developed in parallel fashion. Both readings are bound up with the vision of their respective faiths, of which the readings are the result and expression. Consequently, both are irreducible."[31] "No," insomuch as Christian readings are developments out of the Old and New Testaments together, and thus materially will sometimes differ and even conflict with Rabbinic readings, not least in identifying that Jesus is the messiah. "Yes," insomuch as on historical critical grounds both communities might actually agree on material points. And most importantly, in relation to our question regarding the Jewish people in the land: "Yes," insomuch as biblical texts related to the land, while differently interpreted in the light of the New Testament, do not cancel out the promises found in the Old to the Jewish people. Please note, this is not applied to contemporary Jews or their relation to the land in Israel today—that was beyond the remit of the Pontifical Biblical Commission. However, it offers us biblical grounds to seriously consider the Jewish people in the land in the light of the biblical promises. In this section, all I wish to establish is that there are biblical grounds for the above pathway I have been exploring.

---

[29] Pontifical Biblical Commission, *The Jewish People and their Sacred Scriptures in the Christian Bible*, 2001.

[30] I refer readers to D'Costa, *Catholic Doctrines on the Jewish People*, 64–103.

[31] Pontifical Biblical Commission, *JPSSCB*, 22.

Second, the material texts of the Old Testament, as just indicated, do indicate a land promise to the Jewish people. Paragraph 56 is crucial and I cite it in full:

b) *The Promised Land*

56.(1) Every human group wishes to inhabit territory in a permanent manner. Otherwise, reduced to the status of stranger or refugee, it finds itself, at best, tolerated, or at worst, exploited and continually oppressed. Israel was freed from slavery in Egypt and received from God the promise of land. Its realization required time and gave rise to many problems throughout the course of its history. For the people of the Bible, even after the return from the Babylonian Exile, the land remained an object of hope: "Those blessed by the lord" will possess the land (Ps 37:22).

In the Old Testament

56.(2) The term "promised land" is not found in the Hebrew Bible, which has no word for "promise". The idea is expressed by the future tense of the verb "to give", or by using the verb "to swear": "the land which he swore to give to you" (Ex 13:5; 33:1, etc.).

56.(3) In the Abraham traditions, the promise of land will be fulfilled through descendants. It concerns the "land of Canaan" (Gn 17:8). God raises up a leader, Moses, to liberate Israel and lead it into the promised land. But the people as a whole lose faith: of those faithful from the beginning, only a few survive the long journey through the desert; it is the younger generation that will enter the land (Nu 14:26–38). Moses himself dies without being able to enter (Dt 34:1–5). Under the leadership of Joshua, the tribes of Israel are settled in the promised territory.

56.(4) For the Priestly tradition, the land must as far as possible be without blemish, for God himself dwells there (Nu 35:34). The gift is therefore conditioned by moral purity and by service to the Lord alone, to the exclusion of foreign gods (Jo 24:14–24). On the other hand, God himself is the owner of the land. If the Israelites dwell there, it is as "strangers and sojourners", like the patriarchs in former times (Gn 23:4; Ex 6:4).

56.(5) After the reign of Solomon, the heritage land was split into two rival kingdoms. The prophets condemn idolatry and social injustice; they threaten punishment: the loss of the land, conquered by foreigners, and the exile of its population. But they always leave open a way to return to a new occupation of the promised land, while emphasising also the central role of Jerusalem and its Temple. Later the perspective opens out to an eschatological future. Although occupying a limited geographical space, the promised land will become the focus of attraction for the nations.

56.(6) The theme of the land should not be allowed to overshadow the manner in which the book of Joshua recounts the entry to the promised land. Many texts speak of consecrating to God the fruits of victory, called the ban (*chérèm*). To prevent all foreign religious contamination, the ban imposed the obligation of destroying all places and objects of pagan cults (Dt 7:5), as well as all living beings (20:15-18). The same applies when an Israelite town succumbs to idolatry, [sic] Dt 13:16-18 prescribes that all its inhabitants be put to death and that the town itself be burned down.

56.(7) At the time when Deuteronomy was written—as well as the book of Joshua—the ban was a theoretical postulate, since non-Israelite populations no longer existed in Judah. The ban then could be the result of a projection into the past of later preoccupations. Indeed, Deuteronomy is anxious to reinforce the religious identity of a people exposed to the danger of foreign cults and mixed marriages.

56.(8) Therefore, to appreciate the ban, three factors must be taken into account in interpretation; theological, moral, and one mainly sociological: the recognition of the land as the inalienable domain of the lord; the necessity of guarding the people from all temptation which would compromise their fidelity to God; finally, the all too human temptation of mingling with religion the worst forms of resorting to violence.

The following summary would require more exegetical support, which is provided elsewhere, but it allows us to move the argument on in this context. The promise of the land is part of God's covenant with the Jewish people. This is the clear and unambiguous teaching of the Old Testament. That promise is unconditional but makes a demand upon the people that they give glory to God, live virtuously, and abstain from idolatry. God's people are to see the land as a way of giving praise to God, recognizing the realization of the land promise may take time and give rise to many problems in the process. The ingathering of the Jewish people is required for this process to begin. This ingathering can have eschatological significance, but one that does not denote a clear chronology, and a long process may lie ahead. Finally, the realization of the promise cannot involve non-defensive violence.

Applying these findings to 1948 and following regarding the Jewish people and the land is complicated. It is possible that each of these signs is present only inchoately and in part. There are certainly events that obscure these signs, most clearly the injustice to the Palestinian people. However, it is also the case that biblically there is recognition that the process is fraught and not always clear, as in biblical history. This means that there is room for a tentative yes to our first question. The gathering of Jewish people in the land called Israel does have theological significance, minimally: that God desires to preserve his people, Israel.

Third, the authors of *JPSSCB* argue that the New Testament provides overlapping as well as different trajectories, but do not negate the Old Testament promises. The two paragraphs on the land in the New Testament are as follows:

> 57.(1) The New Testament does not develop much further the theme of the promised land. The flight of Jesus and his parents to Egypt and their return to the "land of promise" (Mt 2:20–21) clearly retraces the journey of the ancestors; a theological typology undergirds this narrative. In Stephen's discourse which recalls their history, the word "promise" or "promised" is found side by side with "land" and "heritage" (Acts 7:2–7). Although not found in the Old Testament, the expression "land of promise" is found in the New (Heb 11:9), in a passage which, undoubtedly, recalls the historical experience of Abraham to better underline its provisional and incomplete character, and its orientation towards the absolute future of the world and history. For the author, the "land" of Israel is only a symbolic pointer towards a very different land, a "heavenly homeland". One of the beatitudes transforms the geographical and historical meaning into a more open-ended one, "the meek shall possess the land" (Mt 5:5); "the land" is equivalent here to "the kingdom of heaven" (5:3,10) in an eschatological horizon that is both present and future.

> 57.(2) The authors of the New Testament are only deepening a symbolic process already at work in the Old Testament and in intertestamental

Judaism. It should not be forgotten, however, that a specific land was promised by God to Israel and received as a heritage; this gift of the land was on condition of fidelity to the covenant (Lv 26; Dt 28).

The concluding sentence is remarkable, both in the way it concludes the New Testament treatment in a rather disjointed fashion and in that it affirms the findings established in the Old Testament section. It is a breakthrough in Catholic biblical exegesis, but perhaps lacking in developed justification. Whatever the New Testament hope regarding the land, the authors unequivocally endorse the promise of the land made to the Jewish people. No longer are the Jewish people an eternally wandering and landless people. The biblical building block for a Catholic affirmation of the people in the land is in place.

What then are the conclusions regarding my first question: Can there be a theological underpinning to Jewish people in the land after 1948? The answer I have been seeking to excavate, tentative though it is, is, yes, there are resources within the Catholic tradition that would support an affirmative answer. Any answer would entail recognizing the disparity between what is happening on the ground and what the biblical vision demands for it to be theologically affirmed. Equally, any answer must allow for an unresolved tension: the process of the return of the Jewish people to the land may be long and complicated and may not conform to what one might expect and hope to see. And any positive affirmation could not include violence, other than defensive. Drawing on our earlier findings regarding the Palestinian question, this could not involve the exclusion of the Palestinian people from the land, based on social justice and international law.[32] There are many further questions arising from this conclusion, but I have achieved my goal for now in answering question 1.

Let me now move to the final question: what of the state? If one says yes to the Jewish people settling in the land called Israel, does this logically entail a yes to the modern Jewish nation-state?

Catholics and the State of Israel (Question 3)

Catholic theology at present, and for most of its history since Augustine, has often held a principled dividing line between the powers of the state

---

[32] I realize more argument is required at this critical point to block a claim to a biblically founded "Greater Israel" that would then use the Bible to eject Palestinians and justify settlements to reclaim the land. David Novak, *Zionism and Judaism: A New Theory* (New York: Cambridge University Press, 2015) is helpful in presenting an intra-Jewish religious Zionist argument that justifies a full political settlement with the Palestinians.

and the power of the Church, without neglecting the different forms of due respect that each owes the other.[33] Since Vatican II, the Catholic Church has been developing a position to accommodate for the near virtual collapse of nation-states that identify themselves as Catholic. One might say the modern Catholic Church after Vatican II is suspicious of endorsing any state theologically, other than in terms of international law. To do so would compromise its political neutrality enshrined in the Lateran Treaty of 1929.

One can see an interesting set of positions in Catholic theology regarding the State of Israel, which has been associated with the Zionist project. The first, a position arising from traditional supersessionism, rejects it outright because it is unacceptable on either secular or religious grounds because both forms of Zionism are seen as contrary to the truth of Catholicism. The second position rejects supersessionism and cannot use the grounds employed in the first position, but it also rejects Zionism, as it equates it with a form of political-religious messianism that is contrary to Catholic claims regarding the messiah who is Jesus. Let me briefly look at these two instances. Then, one might tentatively ask: Are there other conceptual understandings of the State of Israel that should be considered?

Model one: supersessionist anti-Zionism. Theodor Herzl met Pope Pius X with Secretary of State Cardinal Merry del Val on January 26, 1904. We are reliant on Herzl's account.[34] Pius's theology of supersessionism was central to the pope's socio-political response to Zionism. Herzl recounts: "I briefly placed my request [for support of Jewish Zionist aspirations] before him." The pope replied:

> We cannot prevent the Jews from going to Jerusalem—but we could never sanction it. The soil of Jerusalem, if it was not always sacred, has been sanctified by the life of Jesus Christ. As the head of the Church I cannot tell you anything different. The Jews have not recognized our Lord, therefore we cannot recognize the Jewish people.

---

33 See the challenging work (although uneven and overstated in places) of Carys Moseley, *Nationhood, Providence, and Witness: Israel in Protestant Theology and Social Theory* (Eugene, OR: Cascade Books, 2013). For the official Catholic position, see the Pontifical Council for Justice and Peace, *Compendium of the Social Doctrine of the Catholic Church* (2005) 377–83; which underwrites the need for nations that are committed to the common good and seek to serve God.

34 Theodor Herzl, *The Complete Diaries of Theodor Herzl*, ed. Raphael Patai, vol. 4, *1602–04* (New York: Herzl P., 1960) for all quotes given. I omit the Italian that is given in part of Herzl's text. See also Shlomo Avineri, *Theodor Herzl and the Foundation of the Jewish State* (London: Weidenfeld and Nicolson, 2014), 249–56; which corroborates Herzl's account from other sources.

Herzl insisted that the Zionists wished "to avoid the religious issues"; their sole motivation being "the distress of the Jews" due to antisemitism. Pius responded:

> Yes, but we, and I as the head of the Church, cannot [support Zionism]. There are two possibilities. Either the Jews will cling to their faith and continue to await the Messiah who, for us, has already appeared. In that case they will be denying the divinity of Jesus and we cannot help them. Or else they will go there without any religion, and then we can be even less favorable to them.... The Jewish religion was the foundation of our own; but it was superseded by the teachings of Christ, and we cannot concede it any further validity. The Jews, who ought to have been the first to acknowledge Jesus Christ, have not done so to this day.

Herzl acknowledges Pius's friendship with Jews during his Mantua days, and the pope testifies to this: "I have always been on good terms with Jews.... After all, there are other bonds than those of religion: courtesy and philanthropy. These we do not deny to the Jews." Hence, the pope's objection was solely based on theological grounds.

Pius's response indicates the deep theological supersessionism within Catholic culture. Most Catholics held that since the Jews had rejected Jesus Christ, their religion was invalid. It had been superseded. For Pius to support Judaism would be, in his eyes, the equivalent to encouraging heretics to set up a heretical nation-state. The Vatican fiercely resisted Communism on different grounds, but equally strongly. If the Zionists were not religious, which was true of the majority, this only made matters worse: Catholics should not actively encourage secular states, for like the Communists, they may eventually curtail religious freedoms and form their nations with an attenuated sense of the common good. Clearly, the theological grounds undergirding this position have collapsed.

Model two: post-supersessionism anti-messianic Zionism. Now that supersessionism has been superseded and Catholics do business with many non-religious states and even those openly hostile to religion, we find an interesting alternative assessment of the Jewish State by Pope Emeritus Benedict XVI. He writes:

> The question of what to make of the Zionist project was also controversial for the Catholic Church. From the beginning, however, the dominant position was that a theologically-understood acquisition of land (in the sense of a new political messianism) was unacceptable. After the establishment of Israel as a country in 1948, a theological doctrine emerged that eventually enabled the political recognition of the State of Israel by the Vatican. At

its core is the conviction that a strictly theologically-understood state—a Jewish faith-state [*Glaubenstaat*] that would view itself as the theological and political fulfillment of the promises—is unthinkable within history according to Christian faith and contrary to the Christian understanding of the promises.[35]

Some have criticized Benedict for lapsing into supersessionism. However, his statement is ambiguous, as the terms "political messianism" and "Jewish faith-state" together dictate a rejection of a precise concept of the Jewish Zionist state as a political messianic faith state. Benedict is arguing that this understanding of the state is contrary to the Catholic faith because the messiah has come in Jesus Christ. There can be no contrary fulfillment of the messianic promise if it excludes and is indifferent to the truth of Jesus Christ.

However, this immediately raises the question: is this the only way the State of Israel can be understood? Could it be understood as other than a political messianic faith state? Could it be a contingent political formation that is corrupt and given to the misuse of power as are all states, while also a necessary historically contingent arrangement that has ensured the continuity of the Jewish people and thus God's fidelity to his people Israel? This latter view is signaled by Benedict when he writes a few sentences later:

> The Vatican has recognized the State of Israel as a modern constitutional state, and sees it as a legitimate home of the Jewish people, the rationale of which cannot be derived directly from Holy Scripture. Yet, in another sense, it expresses God's faithfulness to the people of Israel.

In one sense the rationale for the modern-day State of Israel cannot be derived "directly" from Scripture. It is, as we have seen above, a matter of applying scripture to modern history to discern the design of God. Benedict's last sentence echoes the link of God's fidelity with the Jewish people and the land made in *Notes* (as we saw above), the recognition that the people of Israel's existence on the land is part of God's fidelity. This requires us to think beyond the two models briefly outlined above, for Benedict's analysis opens up a vista that requires further exploration.

Other models of Catholic relationship to the State of Israel: There are many avenues to be explored. I will only briefly examine two. First, one might understand the State of Israel to be the beginning of the messianic times heralding the return of Jesus by virtue of it serving the reality of the

---

35 Pope Benedict XVI, "Grace and Vocation without Remorse: Comments on the Treatise 'De Iudaeis,'" trans. Nicholas J. Healy, *Communio: International Catholic Review* 45 (Spring 2018): 163–84.

return of the Jewish people to the land, which is a precursor to the return of Jesus. The focus on Jesus means that there is no contradiction between a messianic element to the state's foundation and its Christological dimensions. Clearly, this is not how Jews view the matter, but for the moment we are not focusing on Jewish self-understanding but Catholic self-understanding in the light of biblical teachings. This position need not entail underwriting the state's political form (currently a Jewish democracy) or prudential judgements, especially when the latter contradict principles of justice. This is the kind of critique that is carried out against many nation-states by Catholic social doctrine without calling the legitimacy of the state into question. This position would also allow for a healthy discussion related to borders and the legitimacy of a Palestinian state, such as the Catholic Church upholds.

One might argue that the necessary preconditions of the Jewish people living in the land (question 1) which is part of God's will has required a Jewish nation-state in 1948 (question 3), but with the qualifications regarding the extent to which the Jewish nation-state is being underwritten in such a claim. The Jewish nation-state is not an end in itself but serves two other purposes: making possible Jewish living on the land, and being a sign of the messianic end times.

Going down this road is fraught because Catholic thinking on this position has resisted attributing any messianic significance to the Jewish State or the return of the Jewish people to the land. Instead, as we have seen above it has arrived at a position whereby it is able to see in the Jewish people settling in the land an act of God's will, a part of God's design, and an expression of God's enduring love for his people. Catholic statements have not gone on to attribute any messianic significance other than in the one citation of Ezekiel by Pope John Paul II discussed above. This suggests that such a door is not closed, but that path requires a lot of careful exploration before opening the door more fully. There is also another possible model regarding the Jewish State.

In this alternative model, the messianic significance of the state is rejected. Instead, God's love of his people is central to the support of the Jewish people on the land. In this scenario, the state is instrumental in bringing about God's plan, but is not itself to be understood as intrinsic to that plan. We might envisage very different forms of governance preserving the Jewish people flourishing in the land. We could, for example, envisage a theocratic democratic state (as advanced by David Novak).[36] We might envisage a secular binational state or a religious binational state or

---

36 Novak, *Zionism*, 86–118.

a theocratic non-democratic state. The base line in these differing models would require that both Jews and Palestinians could live in safety and flourish within secure boundaries and have legitimate autonomy. This is in fact close to the Catholic Church's actual position as I have tried to show above.

Is this second model a coherent position? I think it is, even if it is not without problems. I'm not arguing it is the position taken by any formal Catholic teaching. I want to argue that there is a trajectory that might lead in this direction. The argument that this position is coherent could easily be developed by inspecting a range of what I term "Jewish minimalist Zionisms." By this I mean, Jews who support the Jewish people living on the land according to the 1947 UN Agreement, in accordance with justice to the Palestinians and their right to a state, and only under these conditions, affirming that the State of Israel contingently has a role in God's plan for his people. It would be unthinkable for Catholics to suggest that God's plan in any way underwrites the State of Israel in the manner that some American pastors have claimed: to support the State of Israel is to support the will of God. That kind of Zionism is not possible or desirable within Catholic thought. This minimalist Zionism can be found in my view in different and contrasting forms in the works of Hannah Arendt, Emmanuel Levinas, and more recently Judith Butler. Admittedly, they are also read as anti-Zionists, although this revolves around very fluid definitions of "Zionism."[37] Minimalist Zionism is also found in some Orthodox Jewish religious thinkers such as Michael Wyschogrod and David Novak. All are very reticent to theologically underwrite the State of Israel, but all affirm the link between the people and the land called Israel. All recognize that the state, guilty of many crimes and persecution against the Palestinian people and overreaching its legitimate boundaries, is also a contingent process that secured the safety of the Jewish people. All, contrary to more "maximalist" forms of Zionism, require that there be a healthy critique against the state and refuse in any way to give it *carte blanche* by granting it some high theological status. Clearly, to apply all this to Catholic qualified affirmation of the state such as I argue for here, as a contingent form of governance, requires considerable further research and debate.

I conclude this section with a modest and underdeveloped proposal. If the state is seen as a contingent arrangement that provides for the just safety of the Jewish people, without neglect for a just solution to attain a Palestinian homeland, would it then be possible for Catholics to affirm a minimalist theological affirmation of the state? This would not require it to endorse the

---

37 This is a complex and fraught claim. See Adam Shatz, ed. *Prophets Outcast: A Century of Dissident Jewish Writing About Zionism and Israel* (New York: Nation Books, 2004).

state's many prudential decisions or its different forms of government or particular political parties, but it could at least allow that the Jewish people's existence on the land does require some form of political and state apparatus to order such an existence. It would not underwrite that state as such, but only insomuch as it seeks to find justice for all parties in the region, and within God's design preserves his people so that they may give him glory. This would be my reading of the Catholic materials on our third question.

CONCLUSION

I began with three questions. In this paper I have argued that two of the questions can be answered positively: the Palestinian right to a state/homeland is unambiguously lodged in continuous Catholic legal and social justice concerns; there is a theological significance of the Jewish people in the land called Israel. This latter position has an increasingly strong trajectory within Catholic theology, especially given the growing appreciation of the continuing validity of the Jewish covenant which is never revoked by God. Regarding the third question concerning the theological status attributed to the State of Israel, there is considerable reticence on the part of Catholic theologians, partly because there is already a legal recognition of the State of Israel, partly because affirming any state theologically is not normally part of the Catholic tradition, and partly because any theological move here would seem to undermine the concern for Palestinian rights in the region. However, despite these problems, there are grounds for acknowledging that the state may be used instrumentally to achieve God's will regarding the settling of the Jewish people in the land called Israel.

8

DOES A CHRISTIAN THEOLOGY OF SACRAMENTS HELP TO ACHIEVE AN AFFIRMATIVE APPROACH TO THE STATE OF ISRAEL?

Dirk Ansorge

In the past, the Catholic Church carefully avoided any theological qualification of its relationship to the State of Israel. No theological argument, for instance, was introduced in the Fundamental Agreement between the Holy See and the State of Israel signed in 1993. Even in its preface, this agreement is confined to historical, political, and economic issues.[1]

On the other hand, the qualification of history as "salvation history" (*Heilsgeschichte*) is familiar to Christian faith and theology. Christianity conceives its origin and history as an integral dimension of a global salvation history that embraces humanity as a whole. The vocation of Abraham, the liberation of the people of Israel from Egypt, and the settlement in Canaan are pivotal steps in this salvation history that begins with creation.

I dedicate this essay to my dear friend Ulrich Winkler (1961–2021). We first met forty years ago while studying in Jerusalem. Three months after the congress "Catholic Thinking on the Land and State of Israel," which we both attended, Ulrich learned of his fatal disease. He bravely fought a battle he could not win. We will meet again in the heavenly Jerusalem.

[1] Exclusive of any theological allusion, the Fundamental Agreement is perfectly in line with a document of the Vatican Commission for Religious Relations with the Jews published on June 24, 1985: "The existence of the State of Israel and its political options should be envisaged not in a perspective which is in itself religious, but in their reference to the common principles of international law." Commission for Religious Relations with the Jews, *Notes on the Correct Way to Present the Jews and Judaism in the Preaching and Catechesis of the Catholic Church* (1985), no. 9. A summary of Catholic positions respecting the state of Israel until the signing of the Fundamental Agreement: Anthony Kenny, *Catholics, Jews, and the State of Israel* (Mahwah, NJ: Paulist Press, 1993).

Consequently, one may ask: Is the concept of "salvation history" void of consequences for the relationship between the Christian Church and the State of Israel founded in 1948?

The question is even more compelling once we recognize the singular and ongoing relationship between Christianity and Judaism. In the declaration *Nostra Aetate*, the Second Vatican Council (1962–1965) affirms that God's covenant with the people of Israel was not abandoned when the Church was established after the resurrection of Christ and the outpouring of the Holy Spirit. Recently, the Holy See affirmed that Christian belief in the universal salvific significance of Jesus Christ does by no means contradict God's never-revoked covenant with Israel.[2]

The Catholic Church understands itself as being essentially related to the people Israel. Paragraph four of *Nostra Aetate* opens with the programmatic statement: "As the sacred synod searches into the mystery of the Church, it remembers the bond that spiritually ties the people of the New Covenant to Abraham's stock." Consequently, the fate of the Jewish people is not simply a matter of historical interest for Catholics. Rather, Catholics are obliged to clarify their own faith in continuous dialogue with their Jewish brothers and sisters.[3] Judaism is a religion that Christians can neglect only at the cost of severe damage to their own faith. This impels the question: what is the impact of Jewish understanding of the State of Israel for Catholic faith?

Since the middle of the twentieth century, theologians of all Christian churches and denominations have published numerous articles and books respecting the relationship between Christianity and Judaism. Synods, Church leaderships, and mixed commissions of Jewish and Christian scholars have also published articles and declarations on this issue. Many of these texts deal with the relationship between Judaism and the Land of Israel. For the most part the authors appreciate the internal relationship between Judaism and the land. They declare that Christians—based on their own faith—can acknowledge this relationship without reservation.[4] By doing so, they renounce the

---

2 Commission for Religious Relations with the Jews, *"The Gifts and the Calling of God Are Irrevocable" (Rom 11:29): A Reflection on Theological Questions Pertaining to Catholic–Jewish Relations on the Occasion of the 50th Anniversary of "Nostra Aetate,"* (2015): "That the Jews are participants in God's salvation is theologically unquestionable, but how that can be possible without confessing Christ explicitly, is and remains an unfathomable divine mystery" (no. 36). "There cannot be two ways of salvation, therefore, since Christ is also the Redeemer of the Jews in addition to the Gentiles. Here we confront the mystery of God's work" (no. 37).

3 Cf. the documents of the Pontifical Biblical Commission: *The Interpretation of the Bible in the Church* (1993), and *The Jewish People and their Sacred Scriptures in the Christian Bible* (2001), esp. no. 23.

4 Cf., among many other texts: Hermann Peter Schneider, *The Christian Debate on Israel* (Birmingham: Centre for the Study of Judaism and Jewish-Christian Relations, 1985); Johannes

traditional supersessionist view in Christianity that the biblical promise of the land to Israel is universalized by the preaching of the Gospel and the worldwide spread of Christianity, and in that sense has become meaningless in relation to its territorial dimension for the Jewish people.[5]

What is still lacking is adequate theological reflection about whether Catholics may develop a positive approach to the spiritual relationship, not only between the people of Israel and the land, but also between Jews and the State of Israel. For Christians it is not insignificant that many Jews interpret the founding of the State of Israel and its ongoing existence as an outcome of God's salvific intervention in history. Consequently, Catholics must carefully consider if a theological approach to the State of Israel is required in order to achieve a more comprehensive approach to its relationship with Judaism. Such an approach by no means delegitimizes a secular view. Instead, it introduces an additional perspective that is justified by a religious interpretation of history.

This paper evaluates whether the concept of sacramentality could provide Catholics with a sustainable theological approach to the promise of the land and, moreover, to the political entity of the State of Israel. For the term "sacramentality" in Catholic understanding refers to the idea that God efficiently intervenes in space and time. This applies in particular by ritual

---

Ehmann, "Solidarität mit dem Staat Israel?: Der Staat Israel in evangelischen und ökumenischen Dokumenten und Verlautbarungen," *Kirche und Israel* 7, no. 2 (1992):149–60; Wilhelm Breder, *Der Staat Israel in der christlichen Theologie* (Trier: AphorismA, 1994); Eugene Fisher, "Reflections on Relations between the Holy See and the State of Israel," *Israel and the Holy See: A Catholic View of the State of Israel*, The First and Fifth Monsignor John M. Oesterreicher Memorial Lectures (South Orange, NJ: Seton Hall University, 2000), 4–19; Rolf Rendtorff, "Der Zionismus und der Staat Israel in offiziellen Erklärungen christlicher Kirchen," in *100 Jahre Zionismus: Von der Verwirklichung einer Vision: Judentum und Christentum*, ed. Ekkehard Stegemann (Stuttgart: Kohlhammer, 2000), 144–51; Michael Volkmann, *Zionismus und Staat Israel im christlich-jüdischen Dialog*, Evangelical Academy Bad Boll, 2006, accessed October 10, 2019, www.ev-akademie-boll.de; Daniel R. Langton, *Children of Zion: Jewish and Christian Perspectives on the Holy Land* (Cambridge: The Woolf Institute of Abrahamic Faith, 2008); Katja Kriener, "60 Jahre Staat Israel—ein Zeichen der Treue Gottes!? Die Evangelische Kirche im Rheinland im Ringen um ihre Aussagen zum Staat Israel," *Kirchliche Zeitgeschichte. Internationale Zeitschrift für Theologie und Geschichtswissenschaft* 21, no. 1 (2008): 22–38; John T. Pawlikowski, "Land as an Issue in Christian-Jewish Dialogue," *CrossCurrents* 59, no. 2 (2009), 197–209; Richard C. Lux, *The Jewish People, the Holy Land, and the State of Israel: A Catholic View* (Mahwah, NJ: Paulist Press, 2010); Philip A. Cunningham, "A Catholic Theology of the Land?: The State of Question," *Studies in Christian-Jewish Relations* 8, no. 1 (2013): 1–15.

5 Frequently in the Christian tradition it was argued that after Christ's resurrection and the coming of the Gospel to the pagans, any particular relationship of Israel to the land was invalidated. According to this view, Christian universality has replaced Jewish particularity—including the biblical promises of the land. In contrast, and particularly after Vatican II, many Christians make major efforts to achieve an affirmative attitude to the Jewish relationship to the land. Some go even further by searching for a theological approach to the State of Israel as it has existed since 1948.

celebration, but in an analogous way the Church as a whole can be understood as sacrament. Why not apply this concept to the State of Israel?

In order to examine the usefulness of the concept of sacramentality as a way to develop a theological approach to the State of Israel, I will first outline the theological challenge to identifying God's intervention in history. After that I will introduce two Christian approaches to the concept of sacramentality: that of the Austrian theologian Franz Schupp and that of the French theologian Louis-Marie Chauvet. I then discuss Michael Wyschogrod's concept of God's "incarnation" in the people of Israel. Finally, I sketch some of the benefits and limits of the Catholic concept of sacramentality when it is applied to the State of Israel.

My thesis is that the Christian concept of sacramentality bears some potential for understanding the particular relationship of Jews with the land and the State of Israel. However, it does not simply affirm the political reality of the state. Instead, the concept of sacramentality provides some criteria that allow us to criticize its politics from a Christian point of view.[6]

SACRAMENTS AND POLITICS: GOD'S INTERVENTION IN HISTORY AND ITS AMBIGUITIES

The question of whether the Catholic Church may achieve an affirmative theological attitude toward the State of Israel raises fundamental questions in Christian theology. How do Christians understand the concept of "revelation" in reference to God's will? How can Christians identify God's intervention in space and time? In what sense do Christians interpret specific events in history as effects of God's will and activity? What do Christians mean when they talk about the efficaciousness of God's grace and about divine providence? These questions are central to understanding the relationship between God and history.

Sacramentality and Politics

Many Evangelical Christians, especially in the United States, seem eager to affirm that God's biblical promises to Israel refer to a certain land and to a

---

6 I would emphasize that to distinguish legitimate criticism of Israel from antisemitism, any criticism of Israel must fulfill the three criteria put forth by Israeli politician Sharansky: under any circumstances, criticism of Israel must not include delegitimization of Israel, demonization of Israel, and subjecting Israel to double standards. See Natan Sharansky, "3D Test of Anti-Semitism: Demonization, Double Standards, Delegitimization," *Jewish Political Studies Review* 16, no. 3–4 (2004), https://www.jcpa.org/phas/phas-sharansky-f04.htm (accessed October 31, 2019).

specific state.⁷ In contrast, and with a view to multiple abuses in the past, many Christians in Europe have strong reservations about identifying God's will in particular political affairs.⁸ Following Saint Augustine's distinction between the "City of God" and the "City of the Earth," Protestant theology in general distinguishes between a spiritual and a secular "kingdom" (or "regiment").⁹

In contemporary Catholic theology, a separation between religion and politics is not only accepted on a practical level but is theologically grounded, using the concept of the "autonomy of earthly affairs." This concept was strengthened by the Second Vatican Council: "If by the autonomy of earthly affairs we mean that created things and societies themselves enjoy their own laws and values which must be gradually deciphered, put to use, and regulated by people, then it is entirely right to demand that autonomy." Autonomy of the creature, and particularly of human affairs, is theologically justified by the Christian belief that "the same God is Saviour and Creator, Lord of human history as well as of salvation history." The Council clearly affirms a separation between religion and politics: "The Church and the political community in their own fields are autonomous and independent from each other."¹⁰ We might then ask: how can we correctly interpret a specific event in history as an effect not only of God's will but of his intervention in human history—particularly if it is the founding of a state?

One approach might interpret particular events in history vis-à-vis their accordance or contradiction to God's will as it is revealed in the Holy Scriptures. In this view, biblical revelation seemingly provides criteria to identify God's intervention in history.¹¹ Irrespective of its historicity, for instance, neither Jews nor Christians will hesitate to interpret the narrative

---

7 Cf. Caitlin Carenen, *The Fervent Embrace: Liberal Protestants, Evangelicals, and Israel* (New York: New York University Press, 2012). See also Paul Merkley, *Christian Attitudes Towards the State of Israel* (Montreal: McGill-Queens University Press, 2001).

8 In Germany, this applies in particular with regard to the Theological Declaration of Barmen (1934). The rejection of the theology of the "German Christians" became the blueprint for later determinations of the relationship between God, politics, and history. Cf. Eberhard Busch, *The Barmen Theses Then and Now: The 2004 Warfield Lectures at Princeton Theological Seminary* (Grand Rapids, MI: Eerdmans, 2010); Fred Dallmayr, *The Legacy of the Barmen Declaration: Politics and the Kingdom,* Faith and Politics: Political Theology in a New Key (Lanham, MD: Lexington Books, 2019).

9 Cf. David Vandrunen, "The Two Kingdoms Doctrine and the Relationship of Church and State in the Early Reformed Tradition," *Journal of Church and State* 49, no. 4 (2007): 743–63.

10 Vatican Council II, *Gaudium et Spes*, no. 36, 41, 76 (December 7, 1965).

11 Admittedly, such an argument cannot escape the "hermeneutical circle." Scripture provides criteria that allow us to identify a particular event in history as an effect of God's acting in the world. In other words, revelation provides criteria that allow us to identify revelation.

of the exodus of the people of Israel from Egypt as reflecting God's will and activity in the world as liberating and biased in favor of the oppressed. Yet when it comes to the destruction of the Temple in the year 70 CE, Jews and Christians fundamentally disagreed on its interpretation in history. And what about the founding of a Jewish state in Palestine? It is well known that religious Zionists interpret the founding of the State of Israel in 1948 as a messianic event, while some ultra-Orthodox Jews condemn it as a blasphemous anticipation of the Messiah's mission.

The last example shows the ambivalence of any hermeneutical approach to history. The same event can usually be interpreted in a number of ways. There is a famous example in the Gospel of John, when Jesus prayed to his father: "Then came there a voice from heaven, saying, 'I have both glorified it, and will glorify it again.' The people therefore, that stood by, and heard it, said that it thundered: others said, 'An angel spoke to him'" (Jn 12:28–29). One could wonder if the bystanders were referring to the same event.

Even if one admits that there are events in history that reflect God's will, it is not always easy to discern clearly what God's will consists of. Like any other text, the texts of the Holy Bible are not accessible devoid of interpretation. When looking back in history, one perceives that such interpretations can be very diverse, not only between Judaism and Christianity, but also within each of those religious communities.[12]

This is not the space to address such questions in an exhaustive way. It suffices to say that both Jews and Christians believe that there *are* specific acts of divine revelation and activity in space and time. This allows us to ask: in what sense can Christians relate the biblical promises of the Land and the founding of the State of Israel to their own understanding of divine revelation and God's intervention in history?

Christian Ambiguity toward Political Affairs

Based on biblical revelation, Jews and Christians agree that God's will for human beings is not indifferent to the conditions under which they live. This includes economic, political, ecological, and other conditions of human life. However, neither Christian nor Jewish approaches to such issues are homogeneous. They range from different forms of political theology on the one hand to religious distance from politics on the other.[13]

---

[12] Negative theology frequently argues that respecting God's infiniteness implies that the meaning of his revelation in space and time is categorically inexhaustible.

[13] With regard to political theology, one might refer to certain branches of Christian theology of liberation but also to movements of Christian Zionism, as seen in organizations like the

Unlike Jews, Christians in Europe mostly benefitted from the dominant political order. In their liturgies, Christians frequently affirmed the existing political and social order through prayers and intercessions. In the fourth century, Bishop Eusebius of Cesarea welcomed the reign of Emperor Constantine as a manifestation of God's providence. Until modernity, emperors and kings in Europe claimed God's assistance in order to justify their legality and their respective policies.

However, with the distinction between *sacerdotium* and *regnum* in the Middle Ages, a development took place that in the long term led to the separation of religion and politics in Europe. In the twentieth century, following a long period of resistance, the Catholic Church recognized the autonomy of the political sphere. Subsequently, the Church refrained from promoting a specific political or societal order. Nevertheless, Christians continued advocating in the public sphere for social justice, human rights, or the right to life, in order to advance their understanding of the Gospel's ethics. After Vatican II, the popes increasingly promoted human rights throughout the world. The status of the Holy See as an international diplomatic entity facilitates this role.

While recognizing the "autonomy of earthly affairs," the Catholic Church does not cease expecting God's intervention in history. Were the Church to abandon this expectation, intercessions would be useless. Particularly in the form of the sacraments, the Catholic faithful rely on God's effective grace in their daily lives.[14]

Obviously on the level of natural science there is a tension between believing in God's salvific activity in space and time and recognizing the autonomy of creation.[15] Does this tension restrict our ability to speak of God's intervention in history? In fact, theological argumentation primarily refers to a certain interpretation of historical events. It respects the fact that we have no access to the past void of interpretation.[16] Consequently, and with

---

International Christian Embassy of Jerusalem. Theological distancing from politics is represented by some Evangelical and Pentecostal churches. On the Jewish side, one could name modern activists of religious Zionism like Gush Emunim. In contrast, some ultra-Orthodox communities like Neturei Karta reject any legitimacy of political Zionism and the State of Israel.

14 Cf. Stephan van Erp, "Living with the Hidden God: Sacramental Theology as Public Theology," *Encounter: A Journal of Interdisciplinary Reflections of Faith and Life* 9, no. 1 (2018): 20–39; and van Erp, "World and Sacrament: Foundations of the Political Theology of the Church," *Louvain Studies* 39, no. 2 (2016): 102–20.

15 This applies particularly to the concept of "miracle," conceived as an event that is caused by a particular divine action that does not follow natural laws.

16 Cf. Arthur C. Danto, *Analytical Philosophy of History* (London: Cambridge University Press, 1965); *Narration and Knowledge* (London: Columbia University Press, 1985).

respect to our guiding question, we may ask whether Catholic theology is capable or willing to interpret the founding of the State of Israel as a result of God's salvific intervention in history.

In order to answer this question, Christians are referred to the biblical promises of the land. These well-known texts encourage Jews to perceive the founding of the State of Israel as a fulfillment of divine promises. Doubtless, these texts are religious authorities for Jews as well as for Christians. Both understand these texts as testimonies of a comprehensive salvation history that encompasses social and political affairs. What are the implications of such a view for Christian thinking about the founding of the State of Israel? Does the Christian concept of "sacramentality" help to achieve an affirmative theological approach to the State of Israel?

"Sacramentality" as a Theological Concept in Christian Theology

The reason why "sacramentality" might provide a helpful concept thinking about God's intervention in history is that the concept, according to Christian doctrine, implies that God does not operate exclusively in the heart or in the soul of human beings. Rather, God's intervention in history is mediated by material means in space and time. According to Christian doctrine, sacraments are "outward (visible) signs of inward (invisible) grace."[17] Catholics believe that God's salvific intervention in history is mediated to the Christian faithful by material elements: by water in Baptism or by bread and wine in the Eucharist.[18]

Celebrating a sacrament means a ritual performance that communicates effectively God's grace to the world.[19] According to Christian faith, the ritual performance of sacraments effects a spiritual transformation of the person who receives a sacrament: Through baptism, an individual becomes a member of the Church, and through Eucharistic communion, a baptized person shares in the Body of Christ. Although not dependent on human merit, a sacrament is not magic, but dependent on God's promise to act in

---

17 Cf. Augustine, *Epist.* 105, 3,12; Hugo of St. Victor, *De sacr. christ. fidei* I 9, 2; Peter Lombard, IV *Sent.*, dist. 1, cap. 4.

18 According to Thomas Aquinas, in addition to the institution of a sacrament by Christ and its sanctification, it needs a "natural resemblance" (*naturalis similitudo*) of corporeal reality and spiritual reality that the sacraments perform: cf. Thomas Aquinas, *In IV Sent.*, dist. 25, q. 2, art. 2, qc. 1, ad 4.

19 Cf. Peter Lombard, IV *Sent.* dist. 1, cap. 2. I do not deal here with the pivotal question of what "grace" means in Christian understanding. For the moment, it suffices to understand the term as an indicator of the eternal God's acting in space and time.

this way. However, its spiritual effectiveness requires faith both on the side of the minister and on the side of the person who receives the sacrament.[20]

The encompassing spiritual and social context for celebrating the sacraments is the Church. Catholic faith conceives the Church as a visible and palpable entity. Starting with the letters of Saint Paul, the Church is understood as the "body of Christ" (1 Cor 12:27; Rom 12:5; cf. Eph 4:12). In this sense, one can conceive of the Church in terms of sacramentality. Consequently, Vatican II states: "The Church is in Christ like a sacrament or as a sign and instrument both of a very closely knit union with God and of the unity of the whole human race." Through the Holy Spirit, God "has established His Body which is the Church as the universal sacrament of salvation."[21]

More than in Protestant theology, Catholic doctrine stresses the fact that God's intervention in history is bound to special performances, ritual practices, and institutional patterns in space and time. God's grace does not only internally affect the human soul. Rather, it is bound to the Church, its ministry, and the rituals of sacramental performance.[22] Catholic theologians justify this view by referring to the incarnational dimension of revelation. Christ's hypostatic union of human and divine nature is the prototype of the Church and its sacramental practice. As the "Mystical Body of Christ," the Church forms "one complex reality which coalesces from a divine and a human element."[23]

Thus, referring to the Church and the sacraments performed by its members and ministers, Catholic theology has a basic concept of the unity of divine reality and physical elements. The question, then, is whether and how this concept might illuminate a theological approach to the State of Israel.

SACRAMENTALITY AND INCARNATION: CHRISTIAN AND JEWISH CONCEPTS

In order to answer this question, in this section, two Christian concepts of sacramentality are evaluated for their potential usefulness concerning a theological approach to the State of Israel. I explore the work of the Austrian theologian Franz Schupp (1936–2016) and the French theologian Louis-Marie Chauvet (born 1942). After this, I will assess the reflections of

---

20 Cf. International Theological Commission, *The Reciprocity between Faith and Sacraments in the Sacramental Economy*, no. 57–59 (March 2020).

21 Vatican Council II, *Lumen Gentium*, no. 1, 48.

22 Cf. Karl-Heinz Menke, *Sakramentalität: Wesen und Wunde des Katholizismus* (Regensburg: Pustet, 2012).

23 Vatican Council II, *Lumen Gentium*, no. 8.

the Orthodox Jewish scholar Michael Wyschogrod (1928–2015) on God's dwelling in Israel.

Franz Schupp: Political Dimensions of Sacramentality

In his pioneering book *Faith—Culture—Symbol: Essay of a Critical Theory of Sacramental Practice* (1974),[24] the Austrian theologian Franz Schupp seeks to regain the *material* dimension of sacramentality. Schupp elaborates his concept of sacramentality as opposed to concepts that emphasize the *spiritual* dimension of God's grace. According to this traditional perspective, the essence of sacramental practice is the ritually performed mediation of grace to the Christian faithful's heart. Consequently, matter is only a visible symbol of internal grace.[25] According to Schupp however, matter is not irrelevant when it comes to sacramental practice.

While emphasizing the impact of matter in sacramental practice, Schupp is inspired by the critical theory of the Frankfurt School of philosophy (Horkheimer, Adorno, Habermas). Against this background, Schupp not only reminds us of the constitutive role of matter in sacramental practice, but also refers to the impact of matter on human behavior and agency in general: "One cannot discuss the issue of matter without reflecting on the use made of it in history and society."[26] Consequently, sacramental practice is not primarily a symbolic practice or a ritual performance. It is also an approach to matter in an ethical, social, and political context.

Schupp justifies his concept of sacramentality by referring to the preaching and practice of Jesus. According to Schupp, Jesus did not introduce a new religious ritual. Instead, his behavior toward invalids, outcasts, and marginalized people, as it is reported in the Gospels, introduces non-exclusive language and inclusive social commitment. Jesus did not condemn prostitutes, tax collectors, and sinners but invited them to his meals and discipleship.

Consequently, and according to Schupp, the language of faith is primarily directed to social and even political issues. Its primacy in Christian faith means that social and political practice that is inspired and directed by the Gospels provide the criteria of sacramental practice in the Church. It respects the fact that in secular societies, the truth of Christian faith is not primarily communicated by ritual practice but by social and political agency.

24 Cf. Franz Schupp, *Glaube—Kultur—Symbol: Versuch einer kritischen Theorie sakramentaler Praxis* (Düsseldorf: Patmos, 1974).

25 Cf. Augustine, *Ennar. in Psalmos* XCVIII 9: "Sacramentum aliquod vobis commendavi; spiritualiter intellectum vivificabit vos. Etsi necesse est illud visibiliter celebrari, oportet tamen invisibiliter intellegi" (Corpus Christianorum Latinorum, vol. 39, Turnhout: Brepols, 1956), 1386.

26 Schupp, *Glaube—Kultur—Symbol*, 205.

The ultimate goal of social and political activity performed by Christians is reconciliation and justice: reconciliation between human beings and justice in society. Sacramental practice is only justified insofar as it encourages social activity and criticizes the abuse of political power. It receives its potency from biblical narratives that both retell God's salvific intervention in history and prefigure a reconciled society in the future.

In his book, Schupp reminds us of the fact that in the Middle Ages, Christian theologians progressively refrained from the simple affirmation of the existing political order that had prevailed since Constantine. With regard to the ordination of the Franks' King Pippin in 751, Christians were of the opinion that the anointed king is a "vicarius Christi" or "Christus Domini"—"vicar of Christ" or the "Lord's anointed."[27] Still in the eleventh century, Petrus Damiani (d. 1072) counted the royal ordination as a sacrament of the Church.[28] At the dawn of the twelfth century however, Ivo of Chartres (d. 1116) excluded the investiture of the king from ecclesiastical sacraments. Some years later, the Concordat of Worms (1122) established the basis of a progressive separation between secular and religious order in Europe. Despite persisting coalitions between throne and altar, the parting of *regnum et sacerdotium* opened the opportunity for the Church to criticize political order and social agency.

Taken as a whole, Schupp presents a theology of sacraments that aims at integrating the material, ethical, social, and political aspects of human being and behavior as well as its religious and spiritual dimensions. Introducing a strong need for justice in political affairs, he identifies criteria of a social and political practice that may reasonably claim to be in accordance with Jesus' preaching of the Kingdom of God.

Schupp's insistence on the material dimension of God's intervention in history, as it is performed by celebrating the sacraments, thereby suggests the possibility of conceiving the political reality of the State of Israel as an effect of God's activity in space and time. His concept of sacramentality firmly emphasizes the social and political implications of God's activity in history. On the other hand, Schupp's claim for justice provides quite clear criteria for judging politics. Even if Schupp himself does not explicitly refer his work to any particular state, his concept of sacramentality and the sacraments provides a useful tool that enables us to evaluate secular politics in the light of justice and righteousness.

---

[27] Cf. Schupp, *Glaube—Kultur—Symbol*, 123–31. It was only after 1200 that the popes of the Roman Catholic Church consistently used the title "vicarius Christi."

[28] According to Damiani, the royal unction was the fifth sacrament of twelve in total. The Catholic Church counts seven sacraments from the twelfth century on only.

Louis-Marie Chauvet: The Sacramental Body of Faith

As with Schupp, the French theologian Louis-Marie Chauvet is committed to the ethical dimension of sacramental practice in the Church. Christian faith expresses itself by specific patterns of behavior and conduct—including the practice of sacraments. Consequently, Chauvet stresses the symbolic dimension of the sacraments. Sacraments do not form a metaphysical reality independent of the human mind, its worldview, and its belief. Instead, sacraments receive their meaning only in the framework of a Christian community that practices sacraments as a certain ritual in order to affirm its identity in relation to God and his revelation in the Holy Scriptures.

In his groundbreaking book *Symbol and Sacraments* (1987),[29] Chauvet presents a theology of sacraments with particular respect to the liturgical rituals and the communities celebrating them. In this context, Chauvet considers sacraments as "symbolic figures." Such figures, according to Chauvet, express the sacramental structure of Christian existence and the corporeal condition of Christian faith. Faith is by no means a purely individual and intellectual matter. Instead, faith is inscribed in a human community, a particular assembly of faithful, a body of believers. Chauvet views everything in the human condition as mediated through the human body. Thus, the term "body" does not primarily refer to the physical human body but to the wholeness of things that comprise human existence in time and space. According to Chauvet, "faith cannot be lived in any other way, including what is most spiritual in it, than in the mediation of the body, the body of a society, of a desire, of a tradition, of a history, of an institution and so on. What is most spiritual always takes place in the most corporeal."[30]

Accordingly, Christian theology must always have as its point of departure a spirituality of the body on which God "inscribes" Christ's Spirit (in Jacques Derrida's sense of "arch-writing"[31]). The Holy Spirit is inscribed on the "body" of Scripture, and on the "body" of the Church's cultures, traditions, and institutions.[32] In this sense, corporeality—or embodiment—is the medium through which Christian faith becomes real and concrete.

---

29 Engl. trans.: Louis-Marie Chauvet, *Symbol and Sacrament: Sacramental Reinterpretation of Christian Existence*, trans. Patrick Madigan, SJ, and Madeleine Beaumont (Collegeville, MN: Liturgical Press, 2018).
30 Louis-Marie Chauvet, *The Sacraments: The Word of God at the Mercy of the Body* (Collegeville, MN: Liturgical Press, 2001), xii.
31 Cf. Jacques Derrida, *De la grammatologie* (Paris: Éditions de Minuit, 1967), cap. 1–2.
32 Cf. Chauvet, *Symbol and Sacrament*, 141–55, 213–27, 355–76.

Chauvet's concept of corporeality—or rather, embodiment—influences his notion of sacrament: "The element 'Sacrament' is thus the symbolic place of the on-going transition between Scripture and Ethics, from the letter to the body."[33] Consequently, "sacramentality" is not conceived as a metaphysical entity that is outside of corporeal and historical mediation, but as a symbolic mediation within the community of faithful human beings. Chauvet stresses the internal relationship that exists between Scripture, ethics, and sacraments: the Christian concept of sacramentality always refers to a social, political, and ecclesiastical dimension of interpretation and understanding. The only way human beings can live their Christian faith is by being radically invested in the symbolic life and world of the Christian narrative. In sacramentality, "we are simply trying to understand what we already believe, immersed as we are, through baptism and Eucharist."[34] Thus, Chauvet's concept of sacramentality stresses the mutual relationship between faith and the social reality of the Church. Faith not only *expresses* itself in the social body of the Church but also is *nourished* by it. The practice of sacraments realizes the reciprocal dynamics of Christian life.

Applying Chauvet's concept to the political entity of the State of Israel might help us to more deeply understand the interrelationship between the people of Israel and the State of Israel in the light of its religious traditions. Irrespective of frequent pragmatic arrangements, we might read the history of this state after 1948 as a continued "inscription" of Jewish traditions into the "body" of a state. And vice-versa: we can understand the existence and the policy of the state as symbolic representations of Jewish self-understanding and religious practice.

Thus, Chauvet's concept of sacramentality seems promising when and insofar as religious dimensions in the understanding of political affairs come into play. In this respect, however, and compared with other states, the State of Israel cannot claim a unique position. I only refer to the religiously based self-understandings of the Islamic Republic of Iran and the Kingdom of Saudi Arabia. Both states claim religious legitimacy for their political structures and their respective policies. For Christians, however, it is only Israel that shares a common history of salvation with the Church. It is precisely for this reason that Chauvet's concept of sacramentality may provide a helpful tool in order to achieve an affirmative approach to the Jewish attitude toward the State of Israel.

---

33 Chauvet, *Symbol and Sacrament*, 265.
34 Chauvet, *Symbol and Sacrament*, 2.

Michael Wyschogrod: The National Body of Faith

In search of a concept that corresponds to "sacramentality" in Jewish tradition, Christians frequently refer to the reflections of American Orthodox Rabbi Michael Wyschogrod (1928–2015). Many Christian theologians were fascinated by Wyschogrod's proposal to conceive the reality of the Jewish people as analogous to the Christian concept of incarnation.[35] Wyschogrod himself states that he wrote his magisterial book *The Body of Faith* (1989) in ongoing dialogue with Christianity.[36]

The starting point of Wyschogrod's argument is God's election of the Jewish people. By electing a particular people, God initiates a particular history of salvation in space and time: the story of Israel as it is reported in the Holy Scriptures and beyond. Throughout the centuries, revelation, teaching, and ethics progressively shaped Jewish identity. Wyschogrod places revelation, teaching, and ethics into close relationship to the people and the land. He conceives revelation as a way in which "teaching is fused with the existence of a people that becomes a physical embodiment of the teaching and whose land becomes a geographic epiphany and therefore the event that makes the ethical possible."[37]

Wyschogrod resolutely rejects the normative impact of any sort of universal ethics or philosophy on Jewish thinking and self-understanding. He argues, relying on biblical revelation and Jewish Orthodox tradition, that such a rejection is a necessary corrective to the secularization of Judaism.

Why did God elect Israel? The only reason for the election is God's unique and preferential love for the flesh-and-blood descendants of Abraham: "God chose the route of election, and of the election of a biological instead of an ideological people, because this was his free choice. He could have acted otherwise."[38] Human beings are not capable of identifying a sufficient reason for God's will and activity. There is no rationality that applies univocally to God

---

35 Cf. Elliot Wolfson, "Judaism and Incarnation: The Imaginal Body of God," in *Christianity in Jewish Terms*, ed. Tikva Frymer-Kensky et al. (Oxford: Westview, 2000), 239–53; Jean Bertrand Madragule Badi, *Inkarnation in der Perspektive des jüdisch-christlichen Dialogs*, Studien zu Judentum und Christentum (Paderborn: Schoeningh, 2006); Hans Hermann Henrix and Edward Kessler, "Gottes Gegenwart in Israel und die Inkarnation: Ein jüdisch-christlicher Dialog," *Freiburger Rundbrief: Neue Folge* 15 (2008): 6–25.

36 Michael Wyschogrod, *The Body of Faith: God and the People of Israel*, 2nd ed. (Lanham, MD: Rowman and Littlefield, 1996), p. xxxiv; cf. Wyschogrod, "A Jewish Perspective on Incarnation," *Modern Theology* 12, no. 2 (1996): 195–209.

37 Wyschogrod, *The Body of Faith*, 223.

38 Wyschogrod, *The Body of Faith*, 58. Consequently, conversion to Judaism is not a matter of free choice. Instead, it is only possible when God performs a miracle by which a human being is incorporated into the Jewish people.

and creation: "God must not be subject to necessity or to a good not of his own making. He is sovereign and his own master, and must not be judged by standards external to him."[39] Due to their limited insight into God's nature, mind, and will, human beings have to accept God's choice. Wyschogrod parallels this view with the Christian belief in the incarnation of the eternal Word of God—an event which was also God's free choice.

However, Wyschogrod strives to give some reason for God's election of a particular people. He refers to the Hegelian argument that freedom remains on an abstract level if it is not performed in a concrete manner. A general and unspecific love is no love at all, he argues.[40] Consequently, God decided to love humanity not in general and impartially, but in a human way. Any human way of loving inevitably implies exclusivity: "Any real love encounter ... is exclusive because it is genuinely directed to the uniqueness of the other."[41] Accordingly, God did not elect humanity as a whole but as a single people among the nations.

Affirmed by the philosophical argument that freedom must be performed in a concrete manner in order to become "real," Wyschogrod continues, it is in the offspring of Abraham that God's election comes to concreteness in history. God, beginning with the calling of Abraham (Gn 12:1), dwells in the living Jewish people.[42] Accordingly, the biblical insistence on God's indwelling in the people of Israel requires believing that God is present in the physical people to this day.

Does such an argument have any implications for how we think not only about the people of Israel but about the present State of Israel? Wyschogrod himself does not explicitly tackle this issue. However, his insistence on the corporeity of Judaism implies that one day the Temple in Jerusalem will be rebuilt and the practice of sacrifice will resume. Such a perspective directly follows from Wyschogrod's conviction that God's dwelling in history has concrete implications for Israel's religious and political practice. Against this background, the State of Israel appears as the historically necessary

---

39 Wyschogrod, *The Body of Faith*, 58.

40 Wyschogrod's argument is reminiscent of Hegel's insistence on the individual as a necessary reification of the general. Cf. G. W. F. Hegel, *The Encyclopaedia of the Philosophical Sciences* (1830), § 482: „If the will, therefore, in which the Idea thus appears is only finite, that will is also the act of developing the Idea, and of investing its self-unfolding content with an existence which, as realizing the idea, is actuality. It is thus 'Objective' Mind." (trans.: William Wallace).

41 Wyschogrod, *The Body of Faith*, 61.

42 Cf. Michael Wyschogrod, "Incarnation and God's Indwelling in Israel," *Abraham's Promise: Judaism and Jewish-Christian Relations,* ed. R. Kendall Soulen (Grand Rapids, MI: Eerdmans, 2004), 165–78.

consequence of the biblical faith that "God chose this people and loves it as no other, unto the end of time."[43]

However—can one accept such a position irrespective of its political consequences? In liberal societies, the problem arises at the moment when an individual's belief affects his neighbor or any other person in the community. Wyschogrod is aware of this. However, he decides to rely on a literal interpretation of the Holy Scriptures. Pointing to God's sovereignty and to the indisputable authority of God's revelation in human history, he regrets the unpleasant consequences of God's election of the Jewish people and the promise of the Land for the parties involved. Wyschogrod admits that the competing claims for the land put forth by Jews and Arabs originate from the same source: the person of Abraham. However, he argues, "the land belongs to the Jewish people because it was given by Hashem [God] to Abraham and his descendants."[44]

It is difficult to counter a literalist reading of the Bible among those who do reject a historical and critical hermeneutic approach to the Holy Scriptures. The only way to question this kind of reading consists in referring to the ethical and political consequences of the reading.

Wyschogrod is aware of the political dimension that is produced by particular religious concepts. In the preface of the second edition of his *The Body of Faith*, he outlines a conflict in summarizing the position of Messianic Zionism: "In the soul of Messianic Zionism, the holiness of the Land of Israel clashes with the divine image imprinted on the face of Palestinian Arabs."[45] Respecting the authority of the Holy Bible as God's revelation to Israel, there is no doubt that the people possess a right to the land. But whether that right is rightly exercised is far more difficult to say, Wyschogrod argues. Facing the opposing political claims of Jews and Arabs, he favors compromises. He agrees with Messianic Zionism when he states that the Jewish people, wherever it is found, is the dwelling place of God in the world. He differs with Messianic Zionism when he admits that for the long-term safety of the State of Israel, political compromises are necessary. While some judge Wyschogrod's theological reasoning dangerous with respect to the political implications, others judge differently.[46]

---

43 Michael Wyschogrod, "Divine Election and Commandments," *Abraham's Promise*, 25–28; 28.

44 Wyschogrod, *The Body of Faith*, 223.

45 Wyschogrod, *The Body of Faith*, xxviii. Respecting Messianic Zionism as a form of religious Zionism, see Dov Schwartz, *Faith at the Crossroads: A Theological Profile of Religious Zionism* (Leiden: Brill, 2002), esp. 131–210.

46 Cf. Alex S. Ozar, "Michael Wyschogrod's Messianic Zionism: A Non-Fanatical Interpretation," *Journal of Religious Ethics* 43, no. 4 (2015): 606–28; Leora Faya Batnitzky, *Idolatry and*

BENEFITS AND LIMITS TO A SACRAMENTAL CONCEPT OF GOD'S INTERVENTION IN HISTORY

In what sense do the reflections of Schupp, Chauvet, and Wyschogrod deepen our understanding of the connection of the Jewish people to the Land of Israel? Does the Christian concept of sacramentality really provide a helpful tool to achieve a theological approach to the State of Israel?

Schupp's insistence on the material and political dimension of sacramentality, and Chauvet's concept of "embodiment" of the Christian faith in religious practice, seem to encourage the implementation of the Christian concept of sacramentality with respect to the State of Israel. This is all the more compelling as Wyschogrod's concept of incarnation invites us from the Jewish side to verify whether we can apply the Christian concept of sacramentality to the State of Israel.

Chauvet's concept of sacramentality enables us to recognize God's intervention in history as it is mediated by ritual practice in religious communities. Encouraged by his reflections on sacramentality, Christians might understand the Jewish people as a corporeal entity in which God's promises are "inscribed." Evidently, this concept is very close to Wyschogrod when the Jewish scholar conceives the people of Israel as the "body of faith." The identity of this body is constituted by religious practice and learning.

Based on such a concept, Christians will not find it difficult to accept the idea that God elects a particular people in order to realize his presence in space and time. "Election" is first and foremost a theological category. It is challenging only insofar as it affects political behavior. By contrast, the founding of the State of Israel is an event in space and time with wide-ranging political, social, and economic consequences. Thus, the question remains if Christians might interpret the founding of the State of Israel as an effect of divine providence and a sign of God's salvific plan in history. It appears that the answer is not independent from the ethical qualification of the respective event.

This is where the reasoning of Schupp comes into play. The Austrian theologian directs us to the material dimension and to the political impact of sacramentality. Sacraments, he argues, are not only a means of transmission of internal grace but also effective signs of a renewed world. Such a

---

Representation: The Philosophy of Franz Rosenzweig Reconsidered (Princeton, NJ: Princeton University Press, 2000). Batnitzky argued that Wyschogrod's Zionism "suggests an absolute knowledge of God's will and an ability to manipulate that will," and as a result "tends toward a fanatical politics" (203). Against Batnizky, Ozar endeavors to prove that Wyschogrod's Zionism, while definitively messianic, is decidedly not fanatical or fundamentalist.

comprehensive renewal embraces social, political, and economic dimensions of human being. Jesus of Nazareth, by his words and deeds, transformed reality and—in a certain sense—anticipated the Kingdom of God. Celebrating sacraments reminds us of the salvific practice of Jesus and actualizes it efficiently. Thus, remembering Christ's advocacy of the Kingdom of God encourages Christian faithful to criticize any religious, social, or political practice when they have come to the conclusion that it contradicts the ethical values of Jesus' preaching.[47]

Although Schupp does not deal with the issue explicitly, we can easily refer his reasoning to the State of Israel. Respecting his insistence on justice in sacramental practice, one might even argue that had the founding of the state in 1948 been one of peace and harmony, and had Israel become a beacon of political integrity and righteousness, Christians might more easily identify in the state a manifestation of God's providence and a "sign of God's faithfulness."[48] Evidently, a number of Christians take this view. Others will hesitate because they cannot see a renewed and peaceful world in the Middle East, but rather the opposite.[49] In 1985, the Vatican Commission for Religious Relations with the Jews admitted reservedly, "The permanence of Israel (while so many ancient peoples have disappeared without trace) is a historic fact and a sign to be interpreted within God's design."[50]

Although he is fundamentally inspired by the Gospels, Schupp would never refrain from measuring secular ethics by the criteria of justice and righteousness that derive from universal human reasoning. In contrast,

---

[47] Admittedly, ethical questions frequently are a matter of fierce theological dispute in Christian communities. I only refer to issues of self-defense, homosexuality, premarital sex, gender equality, and same-sex marriage.

[48] Quotation from the 1980 Synod resolution of the Evangelical Church in the Rhineland (Germany). In the resolution, the Synod most clearly expressed the "insight that the continuing existence of the Jewish people, its return home to the land of the Promise and also the establishment of the State of Israel are a sign of God's faithfulness to his people." Protestant theologians have expressed similar views on the State of Israel. They range from understanding it as a "sign of election and God's providential mercy and faithfulness to the seed of Abraham" and an "eschatological sign" to the view of the Jews returning to the Land of Israel and the existence of the State of Israel as a "sign of pending equivalences to the Covenant fulfilled in Israel's Messiah." Cf. Evangelical Church in Germany, ed., *Promised Land? A new publication on the topic of Israel*, October 2012, accessed October 31, 2019, https://archiv.ekd.de/4250-edi_2012_10_10_promised_land_pubication_of_israel.html.

[49] Ironically, by doing so these Christians convert in a way a Jewish argument against the Christian faith: Jesus cannot be the expected Messiah because he has not significantly changed things for the better. Conversely, Christians refuse recognizing the State of Israel as an outcome of divine providence because the political situation in the Middle East since 1948 has not improved.

[50] Commission for Religious Relations with the Jews, *Notes on the Correct Way to Present the Jews and Judaism in Preaching and Catechesis in the Roman Catholic Church* (1985) no. VI 25.

Wyschogrod stresses the particularity of an ethics that originates from God's revelation in the history of Israel. Based on his Orthodox Jewish argument, he explicitly rejects any normative reference to universally binding ethics. Instead, he refers to God's will as Jews learn it from the Torah and from the Jewish tradition. Inevitably, this starting point leads to tensions with different forms of ethics, be they secular or religious.

On the basis of his concept of revelation and supported by the theory of historical concreteness, it is only logical for Wyschogrod to theologically affirm the existence of a Jewish state. This applies even in the case of detrimental results for its neighbors, as Wyschogrod's statements about Arabs indicate. Christian theology, in contrast, stresses the universal impact of God's salvific will. Even if Christians recognize a particular salvation history that was initiated by the election of Abraham and which culminated in the incarnation of the eternal Word of God, they insist, following Pentecost, on the universal mission of the Church. Hence, while fully recognizing the legitimacy of the State of Israel, the idea of universality encourages Christians to criticize the State of Israel concerning its politics on the basis of international law and human rights whenever they feel it is necessary.[51]

It is from the core of their faith that Christians hold the view that there is no fundamental difference between Christian ethics and secular ethics.[52] Christians base their opinion on the doctrine of the "hypostatic union" of divinity and humanity in Christ: both are intimately unified in the person of Christ but "without confusion or change." On the basis of this Christological doctrine, Vatican II not only affirmed the "autonomy of earthly affairs" but also the legitimacy of a secular state.[53] The autonomy of politics and ethics is not without implications in terms of a Christian approach to the State of Israel. It legitimizes an approach to the policy of the state based on the principles of universal ethics.

In Christian understanding, the theological terms "incarnation" and "sacraments" are closely interrelated but different concepts of God's presence in space and time. For Christians, the term "sacrament" essentially refers to the Christian faith in the incarnation of the Son of God. Based on this faith, sacraments are ritual practices that actualize God's salvific intervention in

---

[51] Respecting the close relationship between Israel and the Church however, any criticism must be offered in a constructive and benevolent manner. It must be like a criticism within the same family.

[52] Cf. Martin Rhonheimer, *Natural Law and Practical Reason: A Thomist View of Moral Autonomy* (New York: Fordham University Press, 2000).

[53] This was not always the case. Particularly in nineteenth century, the Catholic Church strongly rejected the idea of a secular state as it was established by the French revolution, for example.

history related to the incarnation of Christ. While Wyschogrod compares God's presence in Israel with the Christian concept of incarnation, Christians are more likely to think of the sacramental character of the Church upheld and performed by the Holy Spirit. They do not refer the term "incarnation" to the Church but to Jesus Christ. Accordingly, God's presence in history is a matter of sacramentality.

While God's salvific presence in the Church is mediated by the Holy Spirit, Jews might think of the *Shekinah* as an intermediation of God's presence in the world.[54] However, Christians restrict God's *immediate* presence in history to a single human being, the enfleshed eternal Word of God.[55] At the same time, they conceive God's ongoing presence in history as being mediated by the Holy Spirit in the Church. This applies particularly with regard to the sacraments. Consequently, God's presence in Jesus Christ and his presence in the Church are not identical. To conceive the Church as the mystical "Body of Christ" upholds the difference between the incarnated Son of God and the Church. The Church is in no way the "extended Christ" (*Christus prolongatus*).

Taken as a whole, and referring to its Christological foundation, the Christian concept of sacramentality would seem difficult to transfer to the State of Israel without reservation. Schupp as well as Chauvet present a concept of sacramentality that is explicitly based on Christology. Thus the concept cannot be transferred to any reality outside the Christian Church without undergoing substantial amendment. Even if the Jewish scholar Wyschogrod refers to "incarnation," his understanding of the term is quite different from the Christian understanding, which is ultimately based on the belief that God became man in a single human being. Wyschogrod, by contrast, conceives "incarnation" as exclusively referring to the "body" of the people of Israel.

Like every other event in history, Christians can interpret the founding of the State of Israel in 1948 as a manifestation of God's presence in space and time. Even if they consider the history of the people of Israel as an essential part of salvation history, this does not push them to abandon the prevailing reservations about secular power they assert with regard to any political entity. They will refer to the ethical criteria they derive both from the preaching of Christ and the universal norms of ethics.[56] Consequently

---

54 Cf. Joseph Dan, *Kabbalah: A Very Short Introduction* (Oxford: Oxford University Press, 2006), 46.

55 This by no means excludes different ways of understanding God's presence in history. However, the incarnation of God's only begotten son is a singular mode of divine presence in history.

56 Cf. Martin Buber, "We Need the Arabs, They Need Us!" [Jan. 1954], *A Land of Two Peoples*, ed. Paul Mendes-Flohr (Chicago: University of Chicago Press, 2005), 263–68.

many Christians hesitate to consider the foundation of the State of Israel as a "sign of God's faithfulness"[57] without introducing further explanation.

Due to the Christological foundation of the term "sacrament," Christians should be very careful when they attempt to understand the ties of Jews to the State of Israel in terms of sacramentality—even if at first glance such a concept sounds promising. However, the term runs the risk of sacralizing the State of Israel in a manner that is neither theologically nor politically acceptable. It is no coincidence that since the twelfth century, royal ordination has no longer been counted among the sacraments.

If a theological approach to the State of Israel is desirable at all, it needs a different concept of understanding. But perhaps the intellectual challenge points to the lasting difference between Judaism and Christianity—a difference that will be overcome only at the very end of history.[58] If that is the case, the gap between Jews and Christians in their respective understanding of the State of Israel cannot be bridged by any theological concepts.

---

57 View note 48.

58 Cf. Commission for Religious Relations with the Jews, *"The Gifts and the Calling of God are Irrevocable,"* no. 36.

Part III

SEEKING JUSTICE AND PEACE

A CATHOLIC PERSPECTIVE ON THE PEOPLE, LAND, AND STATE OF ISRAEL

David Mark Neuhaus, SJ

THEOLOGY AND BIOGRAPHY: A SITUATED PERSPECTIVE

One of the many revolutions associated with the Second Vatican Council is the anthropological revolution. The Council recognized the necessity of taking history and present reality seriously. Whereas speculation had played an important role in the writing of theology over the centuries, the Council promoted a theological reflection that began with the human person and the real context in which he or she lives. This places as the starting point of theological reflection the human experience. In writing theology, the human experience makes itself evident first in the experience of the theologian writing theology, and it is here that theology and biography begin to intertwine.

Theology is a discipline profoundly marked by the situation of the theologian. A study of the discipline reveals how much the sociopolitical context, intellectual formation, and personal commitments of the theologian influence his or her perspectives. Prefacing the word "perspective" with the word "Catholic" implies that the Church can achieve a perspective that strives for universality, beyond the individual situation of any one theologian or even that of a whole generation of theologians. However, it should not obscure the very partial perspective that emerges from any single situation. In doing Catholic theology, the individual theologian conforms to the teaching of Scripture, Tradition, and the Magisterium of the Church. Those elements of Catholic teaching must not be compromised and moreover are identified and respected. This entire operation is a delicate tightrope walk among tradition, innovation, and personal decisions and choices in each generation.

I will begin my reflection on the people, the land, and the state of Israel, themes that are controversial and even divisive in the life of the Church today, with a reflection on the situation of the one reflecting on these themes. My assumption is that this conscious identification of situation will ultimately frame my perspective, which will eventually confront other perspectives formulated in situations different from my own. It is in this confrontation that we might aspire to reach a perspective, ever broader and eventually Catholic.

I am a Jesuit religious and a Catholic priest who is a member of the Jewish people and an Israeli citizen. I am part of a Hebrew-speaking Church situated amidst an Arabic speaking diocese, and I feel at home in both milieus. I am embedded in the Jewish society of my birth through family and friends, history and education, but have also been adopted into a Muslim Palestinian family, where I have experienced warmth and care, giving rise to a sharp awareness of the Palestinian people and a desire to know the Arabic language and Arab civilization. My biological family was rooted in the world of German Jewry, a world it fled because of Nazi terror, and my adopted family was rooted in the world of pre-1948 Palestine, a world destroyed by the establishment of the state of Israel. To these data, I add the fact that I am a teacher of the Bible and Jewish studies to Christians, Jews, and Muslims in seminaries and academic institutions in Israel and Palestine, and a pastor preaching God's Word in the Holy Land in Hebrew and Arabic.

The divisiveness aroused in the Church today by the topic of the Jews and their relationship to the Land of Israel/Palestine and the state of Israel is at least partly due to two particular and yet seemingly contradictory turning points in Church teaching, both rooted in the Second Vatican Council.

One turning point is the beginning of a new relationship between Jews and Catholics in the modern world, rooted in paragraph 4 of the conciliar document *Nostra Aetate*. This has resulted in a 180-degree turnaround in teaching about the Jews, from a teaching of contempt to one of respect. The commitment that devolves from this turning point is a commitment to the dynamic path of reconciliation that many Catholics have embarked on in relationship to the Jewish people. These Catholics are committed to listening closely to how Jews define themselves and respect this self-definition. Many Jews today insist on closely binding together the people of Israel with the Land of Israel and the state of Israel, and, therefore, these Catholics, particularly in Europe and North America, are particularly sensitive to this specific formulation.

The other turning point is in the social doctrine of the Church. After the Council, the Church promoted the role of Catholics in society, particularly in the struggle for justice and peace in a world torn by conflict and violence. The commitment that devolves from this is to promote ardently justice and peace throughout the world and in the Middle East too. These Catholics listen closely to the cry of the Palestinian people, dispossessed since 1948, refusing to allow Christian theology and Holy Scripture to become a tool in perpetuating the exile and exclusion of Palestinians.

Are these two turning points, each giving rise to choices and commitments, each establishing its specific situation for theological reflection, mutually exclusive? This collection of articles by distinguished theologians might indeed help discern this matter. I seek to reflect here on the people, the land, and the state of Israel from within my own specific situation. In the light of this experiential starting point, I would like to enunciate six main points that will serve in the attempt to formulate my contribution to Catholic theological reflection:

- Reality of sin in doing theology
- Reflection in a land shared with others
- Diversity of the Jewish people
- Experience of the Palestinian people
- Groundedness in equality
- Catholicity of the Good News

REALITY OF SIN IN DOING THEOLOGY

I am a child of Jewish Europeans who lived in Germany for many centuries, until they were forced into exile in 1936. The Church invites all Catholics never to forget the centuries of Catholic "teaching of contempt" for Jews and Judaism, and I, as a member of the Jewish people doing theology as a Catholic, sense a particular obligation to remember. Since the Second Vatican Council, the Church has promoted a "teaching of respect," founded on dialogue with the Jews and a collaborative understanding of the relationship between Jews and Church, in which there is a deep process of reconciliation at work. This relationship, enriched by all Jews and Christians have in common, progressively makes place for difference between Jews and Christians, which can be recognized and affirmed without threatening partnership and shared vision. Among the most volatile differences in Jewish and Christian understandings of vocation, identity, and mission are the issue of Christ's universal role in salvation and the relationship between Jews and the land and state of Israel.

This is not the place to detail what others have documented elsewhere: the use of the Word of God to legitimate ideologies of marginalization of the Jews, often leading to reprehensible acts of exclusion and persecution. Only too sadly, it seems to have taken an event like the *Shoah* to provoke theologians in the Church to re-examine Catholic discourse and transform it, replacing a teaching of contempt with a teaching of respect. The Second Vatican Council's document *Nostra Aetate* marks a *prise de conscience* and the determination to forge a new beginning for the relationship between Jews and Christians. In its paragraph 4 on the Jewish people, the document admits to past failings and calls on all to "see to it, then, that in catechetical work or in the preaching of the word of God they do not teach anything that does not conform to the truth of the Gospel and the spirit of Christ."[1]

I dare say that *Nostra Aetate* was instrumental in my choosing the Catholic Church as my spiritual home once I had come to faith in Jesus within a Russian Orthodox community. Indeed, my parents' resounding interrogation, "How can you join them after what they did to us?" pushed me toward a Christian community that was committed to rethinking its theology, guarding against transforming theology into a justification for marginalization and exclusion. I had the distinct sentiment that my parents' searing question was shared by St. John XXIII, who initiated the Second Vatican Council, and by the Church at large. In the 1998 document *We Remember*, a quotation from St. John Paul II is striking in this regard: "The Church should become more fully conscious of the sinfulness of her children, recalling all those times in history when they departed from the spirit of Christ and his Gospel and, instead of offering to the world the witness of a life inspired by the values of faith, indulged in ways of thinking and acting which were truly forms of counter-witness and scandal."[2]

It should come as no surprise therefore that I would encourage suspicion with regard to all attempts to mobilize the Bible, Christian tradition, and theological language to legitimate ideologies of any coloration. Bible, tradition, and theology were mobilized with great aptitude in order to legitimate the teaching of contempt for Jews for centuries. The concrete and horrifying encounter with Jewish suffering during the *Shoah* obligated Christians to awaken to their own blindness in propagating ideologies of anti-Judaism and their remaining indifferent to antisemitism. Analogously, I hold a deep

---

[1] Vatican Council II, *Nostra Aetate*, no. 4 (1965).

[2] Commission for Religious Relations with the Jews, *We Remember: A Reflection on the Shoah* (1998).

hermeneutic of suspicion when, today, the Bible is mobilized to affirm ideologies of Zionism, attributing to God the establishment of the state of Israel, and thus, by direct implication, the dispossession of the Palestinian people, who have had to make way for the state defined as Jewish. The experiences of Palestinians, refugees, those who have lost loved ones and possessions, and those who live under the rule of discrimination in Israel and under continuing Israeli military occupation in Palestine, are also narratives of revelation that call us all to awaken to a dark side of Zionism that cannot be whitewashed with Biblical citations or theological speculation.

REFLECTING IN A LAND SHARED WITH OTHERS

I arrived in Jerusalem at the age of fifteen, formed as a modern Jew to believe that I was returning "home" to *Eretz Yisrael*. I was the product of years of Jewish Zionist education in a Jewish day school, where we had not only learnt the language of the Jewish Scriptures and Rabbinic tradition but also the modern discourse of Jewish nationalism, Zionism. It was, in fact, sometimes difficult to distinguish between the language of Scripture and the discourse of Zionism, itself so carefully crafted in Biblical idiom. The words "land," "covenant," "promise," "Israel," "people," "freedom," and "exile" all evoked realities that were at one and the same time Biblical and contemporary.

However, as a child raised in South Africa's dark days of *apartheid*, it did not take me long to realize that the land I had just settled in was a deeply divided place, where language, especially the formulation of terms and names, communicated much more than the sum-total of the words used. My encounter with Oussama, a Muslim Palestinian, who introduced me into his family circle, obliged me, a Jewish Israeli, to listen closely to the experience of Christian and Muslim Palestinians in the land I had been taught was my own. Challenged by Oussama, his family, and his friends, I made the resolute decision that ethically I could not opt to live in a uniquely Jewish or Hebrew-speaking world called Israel, marked by the borders of the Hebrew language and of Jewish experience and discourse. As I ventured beyond these borders, I encountered both Christian and Muslim Palestinians, entering a transformative dialogue with the Palestinian people, and came to know the reality of the land called Palestine. Rooted in the reality of the Jewish people, the encounter with the Palestinian people was foundational for the development of my reflections on land and state.

The Catholic Church, over the past century, has formulated a language about the land often termed "Holy Land," its peoples, and the structures of government. This language brings together Scripture, Christian tradition, concern for the living Christian communities, a commitment to dialogue with Jews but also with Muslims, and a particular insistence on promoting justice and peace for Israelis and Palestinians. Some portray this complex discourse as an exercise in consummate diplomacy, but I hold that it is a genuine and dynamic project to strive to speak the truth in a situation of division, conflict and violence. The Christian term "Holy Land" should not become an escape from saying "Israel" or "Palestine" but rather constitute a recalling of the vocation of this land to be a true home to many. That truth, a land called to be holy, cannot betray any one of the elements that make the land what it is today.

In his letter about Jerusalem, published in 1984, Saint John Paul II focused on those diverse characteristics of the land and the city that make it a theologically significant place.

> It is a land which we call holy, indeed the land which was the earthly homeland of Christ who walked about it "preaching the gospel of the kingdom and "healing every disease and every infirmity." ... Jerusalem was the historic site of the biblical revelation of God, the meeting place, as it were, of heaven and earth, in which more than in any other place the word of God was brought to men. Christians honor her with a religious and intent concern because there the words of Christ so often resounded; there the great events of the Redemption were accomplished. ... In the city of Jerusalem, the first Christian community sprang up and remained throughout the centuries a continual ecclesial presence despite difficulties. Jews ardently love her and, in every age, venerate her memory, abundant as she is in many remains and monuments. ... Therefore, they turn their minds to her daily, one may say, and point to her as the sign of their nation. Muslims also call Jerusalem "holy", with a profound attachment that goes back to the origins of Islam and springs from the fact that they have there, many special places of pilgrimage and for more than a thousand years have dwelt there. ...[3]

Catholic reflection is not uniquely on Holy Land, but also on *Eretz Yisrael* and on Palestine too. The attempt to grasp theologically the fullness of a worldly reality must ground even the most speculative of theological reflections, because God is always at work within the contingencies of human history. The Catholic tendency to expand the perspective beyond a singular situation or reality was already clear in the very dynamic of the production of *Nostra Aetate* at the Second Vatican Council. The blessed initiative that pushed the Council Fathers to debate the Jewish question, taking on the

---

[3] John Paul II, Apostolic Letter *Redemptionis Anno* (April 20, 1984).

challenge of reformulating Catholic discourse with regard to the Jews, ultimately led to the realization that the desire for change aroused the necessity to reformulate Church teaching with regard to other non-Christian communities too. This meant that the Church's teaching with regard to Muslims also had to move from contempt to respect. Thus, Catholic teaching on the land and on the state, based upon reflection on Sacred Scripture and Tradition and upholding a Christian attachment to the Holy Land, cannot ignore relationships with both Jews and Muslims. Nor could it avoid striving to promote justice and peace for both Israelis and Palestinians.

DIVERSITY OF THE JEWISH PEOPLE

Coming to faith in Christ at a young age, I realized that I lived in privileged times. I, unlike past generations of baptized Jews, was not obligated to sacrifice my cherished relations with family, friends, tradition, and history on receiving baptism. Unlike past generations of baptized Jews, I did not have to abjure "Jewish superstition." I could be a Christian Jew in a world already profoundly fragmented by the challenges of modernity and thus more comfortable with fragmented identities. However, in Israel I fast became aware that the Jewish world in which I had been born and raised, a Jewish world defined by a European milieu (specifically German), traumatized by the *Shoah* and supposedly reinvigorated by Zionism, was only one part of a diverse Jewish world in Israel.

Most Jews in Israel did not seek a theological affirmation for Jewish life in the Land of Israel or for the establishment of the state of Israel. In fact, in my experience, most Jews leave God out of their sociopolitical discourse if they relate to God at all. In the contemporary Jewish world, there is indeed a plethora of Zionist groups, some of which promote a messianic fervor about the land and the state, sometimes echoing Christian Biblical literalists, but as vocal as they are, they represent a margin. Rather, many Zionists do not seek a theological affirmation of their ideology, attributing the development of Zionism, its successes in the past, its troubled present, and its uncertain future, to the contingencies of history and politics. Furthermore, in Israel, I discovered the experiences of Jews who related differently to the reality of the state of Israel. Among these were Zionists critical of the policies of the state of Israel; ultra-Orthodox Jews, deeply suspicious of Jewish modernity and thus diametrically opposed to Zionism, perceived as a form of mass assimilation; and Jewish Arabs (Jews who had migrated from Arab countries), who rejected the abyss that Zionism had instituted between Jew and Arab.

Living in Israel allowed me to encounter a margin of the Zionist movement, led by intellectuals like Martin Buber, Judah Magnes, and Ernst Akiva Simon among others, who had recognized early on the importance of engaging the indigenous inhabitants of Palestine so that Zionism would not take on the traits of simply another, indistinguishable form of European colonialism. They were clairvoyantly aware of the danger of Zionism becoming a movement that displaced the indigenous inhabitants of Palestine. Martin Buber, Jewish German philosopher and refugee from the Nazi regime, wrote in May of 1948:

> Fifty years ago. When I joined the Zionist movement for the rebirth of Israel, my heart was whole. Today it is torn. The war being waged for a political structure risks becoming a war of national survival at any moment. ... I cannot even be joyful in anticipating victory, for I fear lest the significance of Jewish victory be the downfall of Zionism.[4]

His was a voice of anguish, raised as he saw the genesis of Israeli militarism, leading to the dearth of Zionist humanism. His anguish deepened as the Israeli authorities refused to take seriously the Palestinian refugees and instituted military rule over the Arabs who did not flee from the territory that became the state of Israel, facilitating the massive expropriation of Arab property after 1948. Thankfully, Buber died before witnessing the consequences of the 1967 War, and yet already in 1954, he was able to lucidly state,

> I believe our principal error was that when we first came here we did not endeavor to gain the Arabs' trust in political and economic matters. Thus, we gave cause to be regarded as aliens, as outsiders, who were not interested in befriending the Arabs. To a large measure, our subsequent difficulties are a consequence of this initial failure.[5]

In fact, with hindsight, by the 1930s, it was already clear that David Ben Gurion's "nationalist" Zionism, counting on the support of the colonial powers and mustering military strength, had prevailed over other forms of so-called "humanist" or "cultural" Zionism.

Particularly prophetic in her incisive analysis of the darker side of Zionism was the Jewish philosopher Hannah Arendt. Steeped in the study of totalitarianism in its modern forms, Arendt warned of the perils of Zionism

---

[4] Martin Buber, "Zionism and 'Zionism,'" in *Martin Buber on Jews and Arabs*, ed. P. Mendes-Flohr (Oxford, Oxford University Press, 1983), 198.

[5] Martin Buber, "We need the Arabs. They need us!" in *Martin Buber on Jews and Arabs*, ed. P. Mendes-Flohr (Oxford, Oxford University Press, 1983), 264–65.

for the Jewish people. Her writings, long rejected by many Jews, are inspiring a new generation of Jewish and Israeli scholars, who understand today that her clairvoyance was chillingly precise. In a 1945 article, Arendt wrote,

> The Zionists, if they continue to ignore the Mediterranean peoples and watch out only for the big faraway powers will appear only as their tools, the agents of foreign and hostile interests. Jews who know their own history should be aware that such a state of affairs will inevitably lead to a new wave of Jew-hatred.[6]

Other contemporary Israeli intellectuals like Orthodox philosopher Yeshayahu Leibowitz (d. 1994), academics Oren Yiftachel and Zeev Sternhell, author David Grossman, publicist Avraham Burg, cinematographers Amos Gitai and Eyal Sivan, and human rights activists and organizations have brought these reflections on the dark side of Jewish nationalism up to date, following the 1967 War and the ongoing occupation of the West Bank and Gaza Strip.

Whereas I had been educated in a system that took for granted the continuity between Judaism and modern Zionism, in the ultra-Orthodox Jewish world, I discovered the spiritual and intellectual critique of Zionism that raised a prophetic voice about the dangers of Zionism for the Jewish people. Whereas Jews were undoubtedly rooted in the Land of Israel, ultra-Orthodox thinkers had understood the pseudo-messianic attempts to take control of this land as a rebellion against God, the Lord of history. Furthermore, the adoption of a form of European-style nationalism, Zionism, would, according to the ultra-Orthodox critics of Zionism, lead to dangerous forms of collective assimilation and loss of Jewish identity. The Jewish people, seeking normalcy among the nations, would indeed become one of them, with all their moral failings, including the imposition of marginalization, discrimination, and military occupation on others when Jews became the empowered majority. This prophetic voice of dissent, almost extinguished in the Nazi gas chambers, is preserved and even being revived in pockets of Jewish ultra-Orthodox, Orthodox, and more progressive religious and secular thinking. The Jewish Voice for Peace, an organization based in the US, recently explained in a position paper on Zionism, "Through study and action, through deep relationship with Palestinians fighting for their own liberation, and through our own understanding of Jewish safety and self-determination, we have come to see that Zionism was a false and failed

---

6 Hannah Arendt, "Zionism Reconsidered," in *Zionism Reconsidered: The Rejection of Jewish Normalcy*, ed. M. Selzer (New York: Macmillan, 1970), 216.

answer to the desperately real question many of our ancestors faced of how to protect Jewish lives from murderous antisemitism in Europe."[7]

Likewise, the discovery of a Jewish rootedness in the world defined by Muslim Arab civilization also opened perspectives on Jewish identity in the Middle East that underlined the tragic failure of Zionism to open up to the Arabs in Palestine and beyond. I discovered some Jews who were unashamed to be Arabs and took pride in centuries of a Jewish civilization at home in Arabic.[8] The establishment of the state of Israel, created as a homeland for Jews marginalized, expelled, persecuted, and finally massmurdered in Europe, was an important factor in the uprooting and disappearance of almost one million Jews in the Arab world. Reactionary Arab regimes, explicitly or implicitly acting in concert with the state of Israel, brought to an end much of Jewish life in the Arab world as almost one million Jewish Arabs became exiles between 1948 and 1968, abandoning their homelands in Morocco, Iraq, Algeria, Yemen, Libya, Syria, Tunisia, Lebanon, and the Arab Gulf. Having lived through good times and bad in Muslim Arab lands for over one thousand years, these Jewish Arabs were forced to give up a civilization that had produced a Jewish way of being in the world marked by both dialogue and competition with Islam. This way of being in the world, at home in Arabic and among Arabs, almost totally disappeared within a state of Israel that opted for European hegemony. Aside from cuisine and pop music, Arabic language and culture have become foreign to most Jews, thus not only cutting them off from their neighbors in Palestine and throughout the Middle East but also from their own cultural and historical heritage.[9] This heritage is represented by the medieval religious genius of figures like Saadya Gaon (Sa'd bin Yusuf al-Fayyumi), not only renowned philosopher and Talmudist, but also translator of the Old Testament into Arabic, and Maimonides (Musa bin Maimun), whose *Guide for the Perplexed* was composed in Arabic. However, it includes also contemporary cultural icons like actress and singer Laila Murad from Egypt, singer Fairuz al-Halabiyya from Syria, master musicians and initiators of the Iraqi orchestra for radio Da'ud and Salih al-Kuwaiti from Iraq, and court singer Zohra al-Fassiyah from Morocco.

Whereas today a major part of the Jewish population lives in the state of Israel, Zionism does not reflect unanimity in the Jewish world as

---

[7] "Our Approach to Zionism," Jewish Voice for Peace, https://jewishvoiceforpeace.org/zionism/.

[8] Cf. David Neuhaus, "Shimon Balas: A Jewish Arab at 80," *Proche Orient chrétien* 59, no. 3/4 (2009): 352–61.

[9] Cf. Ammiel Alcalay, *After Jews and Arabs: Remaking Levantine Culture* (Minneapolis: University of Minnesota Press, 1993).

more and more Jews question its spiritual, ethical, and political character. Furthermore, there are those in the Jewish world today who question the very continuity between traditional Judaism and modern Zionism. US Talmud scholar Daniel Boyarin has been particularly eloquent in challenging Zionism from a religious Jewish perspective, arguing for "Diasporism" as an authentic Jewish response to the world.[10] Rabbinic Judaism paved the way for a Judaism that was at home in a world far beyond the borders of the Land of Israel, a Judaism that could celebrate the Jerusalems created in Cordoba, Vilna, Fes, Brooklyn, and many other Jewish skylines until a final eschatological ingathering that would bring all of humanity together. Some Jews have persistently pointed out that Zionism has all the trappings of other failed messianic movements (like those of Bar Kokhba in the second century and Shabbetai Zvi and Jacob Frank in the seventeenth and eighteenth centuries), movements that had inevitably led the people astray. From a more secular point of view, Jewish Italian historian Enzo Traverso has traced how Zionism brought to an end the Jewish modernity born in the *Haskalah* (Jewish Enlightenment), which had proclaimed a typically Jewish yet universal vision of humanity that had much in common with the vision of the prophets of ancient Israel.[11] Today, Catholics cannot afford to ignore the increasingly important pockets of Jewish dissent from Zionism when they try to understand how Jews understand themselves.

EXPERIENCE OF THE PALESTINIAN PEOPLE

In the light of my biography, the experience of the Palestinian people and particularly their dispossession in 1948 have played a central role in my reflections. In the light of the past seventy-one years of the Palestinian experience, it is particularly distressing when various and sundry Christian or Jewish theologies of land and state make no reference at all to the Palestinians, as ultimately it is they who have paid the heavy price of the establishment of the state in the land. During the 1948 War, hundreds of thousands of people became refugees overnight and still are forbidden to return home. In their stead, millions of Jews from all over the world have migrated to the state of Israel. This reality is foundational to any consideration of theologies affirming the Jewish connection to the land and state today.

---

10 Cf. Daniel Boyarin, "Answering the Mail: Toward a Radical Jewishness," *A Radical Jew: Paul and the Politics of Identity* (Berkeley: University of California Press, 1994), 228–60. See also by the same author *Unheroic Conduct: The Rise of Heterosexuality and the Invention of the Jewish Man* (Berkeley: University of California Press, 1997).

11 Cf. Enzo Traverso, *The End of Jewish Modernity* (London: Pluto Press, 2016).

Unfortunately, ethnic cleansing and mass dispossession are indeed the order of the day in the creation of modern nation-states. In a fascinating article in a new collection entitled *The Holocaust and the Nakba: A New Grammar of Trauma and History*, M. Levene documents "the repeated sequence of genocides or genocidal ethnic cleansings" in Europe between 1912 and 1948 that effaced "a multilayered, multiethnic coexistence [that] had been the prior norm."[12] This perspective places the *Shoah* and the *Nakba* within a common historical and ideological context, however different these two traumatic events might be.[13]

Pope Paul VI was the first pope to recognize the Palestinians as a people. In 1975, he declared:

> Although we are conscious of the still very recent tragedies which led the Jewish people to search for safe protection in a state of its own, sovereign and independent, and in fact precisely because we are aware of this, we would like to ask the sons of this people to recognize the rights and legitimate aspirations of another people, which have also suffered for a long time, the Palestinian people.[14]

His appeal has not fallen on deaf ears, and many, at least in the margins, have begun to question the way in which Palestinians have too often been seen as collateral damage in the establishment of the state of Israel.

Many Christians evoke both Scripture and the history of the Jews to justify the transformation of Palestine into Israel. Lord Arthur Balfour, avid Christian reader of the Bible, sympathizer with Jewish suffering in Eastern Europe, was the signatory of the famous British declaration of 1917 that recognized the legitimacy of establishing "a national home for the Jewish people in Palestine." In 1922, he tellingly commented,

> For in Palestine we do not propose even to go through the form of consulting the wishes of the present inhabitants of the country.... The Four Great Powers are committed to Zionism. And Zionism, be it right or wrong, good or bad, is rooted in age-long traditions, in present needs, in future hopes, of

---

12 M. Levene, "Harbingers of Jewish and Palestinian Disasters: European Nation-State Building and its Toxic Legacies, 1912–1948," in *The Holocaust and the Nakba: A New Grammar of Trauma and History*, ed. B. Bashir and A. Goldberg (New York: Columbia University Press, 2019), 46.

13 A remarkable literary treatment of the intertwining of *Shoah* and *Nakba* can be found in the 2016 novel of Lebanese writer Elias Khoury, *Children of the Ghetto: My Name is Adam* (Beirut: Dar al-Adab, 2016).

14 Paul VI, *Christmas Message*, 1975.

far profounder import than the desires or prejudices of the 700,000 Arabs who now inhabit that ancient land."[15]

Christian forms of support for Zionism often either ignore Palestinians or blame the victims of injustice for their situation, accusing the Palestinians of having refused the decision that handed their homeland to Jewish migrants who had just arrived from Europe. Far worse, some Jewish and Christian Biblical literalists even consider the Palestinian inhabitants of the land as "resident aliens" or, more dramatically, assimilate them to the ancient Canaanites who had to be driven out of the land according to the supposed Word of God in Biblical books like Deuteronomy (cf. 7:1–6 and 20:16–18) and Joshua (cf. 11:16–23 and 21:43–45). Whereas the Balfour Declaration's paragraph calling for the establishment of a Jewish homeland in Palestine was fully realized, the second paragraph calling for care to be taken that "nothing shall be done which may prejudice the civil and religious rights of existing non-Jewish communities in Palestine" has been blatantly ignored. Christian legitimation of Zionism by appeal to both Biblical authority and Jewish suffering in history must be challenged in the light of the ongoing consequences of Zionism, the exile of the Palestinian people from their homeland, and their experience of discrimination and occupation in the lands Israel rules. However, these are not only challenges for international lawyers and human rights advocates but rather challenges too for those who read the Bible, formulate theology, and teach catechism. Can these disciplines serenely legitimate or at least ignore injustice?

Patriarch Michel Sabbah, head of the Roman Catholic Church in the Holy Land for more than twenty years, during which the land witnessed two major uprisings against Israeli occupation, posed this burning theological question in his 1993 pastoral letter: "Could we be victims of our own salvation history, which seems to favor the Jewish people and condemn us? Is that truly the Will of God to which we must inexorably bow down, demanding that we deprive ourselves in favor of another people, with no possibility of appeal or discussion?"[16]

Among contemporary Catholic theologians who are sensitive to the Jewish claims to the land and the existence of a Jewish State, there are those who do try to take into account the call to respect the Palestinians and their right to justice and dignity. Among them are some who have contributed

---

15 Lord Balfour, quoted in D. Ingrams, *Palestine Papers 1917–1922: Seeds of Conflict* (London: John Murray, 1972), 73.

16 Michel Sabbah, Pastoral Letter *Reading the Bible in the Land of the Bible Today*, 7 (November 1993).

to this collection of articles, in particular Gavin D'Costa and Etienne Vetö. They do attempt to incorporate a serious reflection on the experience of Palestinians and their legitimate demand for justice within their arguments in support of a theological affirmation of Zionism.

D'Costa underlines how the changes in discourse about the Jews after the Second Vatican Council have enabled the Church to speak positively, not only about the Jews in general, but also about their continuing engagement with history, both in the Diaspora and in the land of their ancestors. No doubt, God also works within the contingencies of history, but this does not mean that God's express will is manifest in all events. The events of 1948, the establishment of a Jewish state, seen by some Zionists as a quasi-messianic event and the genesis of the Palestinian tragedy, cannot be neatly folded into an understanding of God's will without further discernment about the Church's understanding of God's will, her vision of human society, and the Kingdom that she is called to preach.

This Kingdom might indeed be dimly perceived in Vetö's interesting argument for the "purification and transfiguration" of the relationship to the land that would allow for the recognition "of the theological meaning to the presence of the Palestinian people on the land." Vetö goes on to promote a sharing of the land, understood as a divine call. Warning against the use of Biblical terminology like "stranger" or "resident alien," the author proposes that the mutual relationship of the Jewish and the Palestinian peoples is not that of peoples welcoming the other as aliens, but rather as coheirs. The land is promised, but it needs not be promised to one people in an exclusive manner. Transcending exclusivity is undoubtedly a Catholic intuition. However, Jewish exclusivity is the very fabric of Zionism as is manifest in the state established to be "a Jewish State."

Catholic unease with Zionism is not restricted to the ethical dimension concerning how the Palestinians have been victims of Zionism. Rather Catholic thinking manifests a much profounder theological discomfort with an ideology that promotes modern nationalism and the establishment of a nation-state. Zionism is more than just the attempt to rescue Jews from antisemitism, more than just the attempt to renew Jewish culture in a land reclaimed as "homeland"; Zionism is fundamentally an ideology that has fought to establish a "Jewish" state in Palestine and now strives to defend it as a nation-state.

BASIC EQUALITY FOR ALL PEOPLE

The Jewish people, like all peoples, has a right to express itself in its own terms as a people. Marginalized for centuries, Zionism expressed a rejection of that marginalization and a demand for empowerment. Zionists conceived *Eretz Yisrael* as a reestablished center of Jewish life, spiritual, social, and political, that would help Jews everywhere renew their sense of identity and vocation. When it comes to the intimate link between the people of Israel and the Land of Israel, the Church affirms this link in the face of centuries of traditional teaching that condemned the Jews to a perpetual state of exile as punishment for their refusal to accept Christ. The founder of modern political Zionism, Theodor Herzl, was reportedly told by Pope Pius X:

> We cannot give approval to this movement. We cannot prevent the Jews from going to Jerusalem—but we could never sanction it. The soil of Jerusalem, if it was not always sacred, has been sanctified by the life of Jesus Christ. As the head of the Church I cannot tell you anything different. The Jews have not recognized our Lord therefore we cannot recognize the Jewish people. ... And so, if you come to Palestine and settle your people there, we shall have churches and priests ready to baptize all of you.[17]

On the one hand, the Church today can and does recognize the ongoing specificity of the Jewish people and the Jewish attachment to the Land of Israel, striving to put aside all vestiges of supercessionism. However, on the other hand, the Church cannot theologically or religiously affirm the political and ideological program to control the land called *Eretz Yisrael* by Jews and Palestine by Palestinians, and promote a dominion in the name of exclusive rights that supplant the rights of others. Already in his letter to the secretary general of the League of Nations in 1922, the Holy See's Secretary of State Cardinal Pietro Gasparri wrote that although the Holy See had no objection to the British receiving the mandate for Palestine, it had great reservations about the implied change in the status of the Jews in Palestine. Article 4 of the Mandate foresaw the involvement of an "appropriate Jewish agency" in "the establishment of the Jewish national home"[18] and the evolution of the country. Gasparri, while stressing that "the Holy See does not oppose that the Jews have equal civil rights in Palestine," stressed that it could

---

17 Raphael Patai, ed., *The Complete Diaries of Theodor Herzl*, trans. Harry Zohn (New York: Herzl Press, 1960), 1601–5.

18 League of Nations, *Mandate for Palestine and Memorandum by the British Government Relating to Its Application to Transjordan,* approved by the Council of the League of Nations September 16, 1922, published in Geneva, Switzerland September 2, 1926, art. 4.

not accept that the Jews be granted a privileged position in comparison with the other inhabitants of the land.

Twenty-five years later, and after much bloodshed, the United Nations partition plan of 1947 provided for the division of Palestine into two separate nation-states, one for the Jews and one for the Palestinians (with an internationally administered zone that included Jerusalem and Bethlehem, not ceded to either of the two parties). The establishment of the state of Israel in the Land of Israel, accomplished in May of 1948, was supposed to go hand in hand with the creation of the state of Palestine in the land of Palestine, still unaccomplished despite decades of support for the establishment of a Palestinian state by the United Nations and the international community.

A particular Christian understanding, very widespread among Christian evangelicals but not foreign to some Catholic theologians too, sees the establishment of the state of Israel as a fulfillment of Biblical prophecy. I would insist here that even if the establishment of the state of Israel as a Jewish State had been a peaceful one, without the injustice perpetrated against the Palestinians and allowing for the establishment of a Palestinian state alongside it, this insistence on theologically affirming the state would be erroneous. The theological affirmation of the state of Israel is not primarily problematic because of the suffering of the Jews or the suffering of the Palestinians, but rather it is diametrically opposed to the vision that the Church promotes with regard to the future of humanity as a whole. The Church is not diametrically opposed to states but does not theologically affirm them. States come and go, playing benign or malevolent roles in the history of humanity, serving or obstructing the common good. In the light of history, the Church should have learnt that the theological affirmation of empires, kingdoms, and other earthly powers is a treacherous enterprise. The Church today seeks forgiveness for her members who have bought into ideologies of domination, enslavement, and discrimination. Modern nationalism, Zionism included, does not conform to the vision of the Church. The vision the Church promotes is one of a kingdom in which "there is no longer Jew or Greek, there is no longer slave or free, there is no longer male and female; for all of you are one in Christ Jesus" (Gal 3:28).

In dealing with the contemporary state of Israel, the Church must deal with the sociopolitical realities determined by history rather than with Biblical or theological categories. The state of Israel has established by force of law the reality of a state that is "Jewish." In very real ways, this means that state is not the state of all its citizens. Israel has no constitution, but in lieu thereof the Declaration of Independence insisted that the state would guarantee "complete equality of social and political rights to all its inhabitants irrespective of religion, race or sex; it will guarantee freedom of religion, conscience, language, education and culture." However, the same Declaration defined the state as a "Jewish State, to be called "Israel" . . . open for Jewish immigration and for the Ingathering of the Exiles."[19] In July 2018, the Israeli parliament passed the Nation-State Law, which served to emphasize even more categorically the Jewish character of the state. Israeli Prime Minister Benjamin Netanyahu proclaimed this "a defining moment in the history of Zionism and in the history of the state of Israel. One hundred twenty-two years after Herzl shared his vision, we have established into law the fundamental tenet of our existence. 'Israel' is the nation-state of the Jewish people."[20] The Catholic bishops of the Holy Land responded to this legislation:

> By promulgating "the development of Jewish settlement as a national value and will act to encourage and promote its establishment and consolidation", the law promotes an inherent discriminatory vision. In fact, other than seriously downgrading the standing of the Arab language in relationship to the Hebrew language, the law totally ignores the fact that there is another people, the Palestinian Arabs, and other major religious communities, Christians and Muslims as well as Druze and Baha'i, that are profoundly rooted in this land.[21]

For centuries, the Jews suffered from forms of religious exclusivism and ethnocentricity. Relegated to the margins almost everywhere, Jews in the modern world often became the critical voice that called for a sociopolitical system that guaranteed equality on the basis of citizenship rather than religious or ethnic belonging. The delicate question of how Jewish Zionists balance the desire for national sovereignty defined as Jewish and the rights of all citizens in the state of Israel is an issue that Zionists must tackle. However, the reality of more than seventy years of statehood is the grounded experience of those citizens who encounter manifold forms of discrimination, marginalization and exclusion. Too often defined as "non-Jews," they too must have a voice not only in the political arena but in our theological discussions about the land and the state of Israel. Theological speculation about the state of Israel and the Zionist ideology that made it the reality it is must be confronted with the mechanisms of discrimination and occupation that have characterized the state for all the years of its existence. With regard to

---

[19] Provisional Government of Israel, Declaration of Independence, *Official Gazette* no. 1 (May 14, 1948).
[20] Benjamin Netanyahu, quoted in Jonathan Lis and Noa Landau, "Israel Passes Controversial Jewish Nation-state Bill After Stormy Debate," *HaAretz*, July 19, 2018.
[21] Assembly of Catholic Ordinaries of the Holy Land, *On the Nation-State Law Passed by the Knesset*, October 31, 2018.

the future, whatever states will take form in the land, whether one binational state (for Israelis and Palestinians) or two national states (one Israeli and one Palestinian), the state must be a framework in which all citizens are treated equitably and able to participate fully in the life of the state and the distribution of its resources. Israeli and Palestinian, whether Jew, Christian, or Muslim, are part of a reality that cannot be ignored by referring to Biblical texts or theological concepts.

In reflecting on the contingencies of political events, the Church recognizes the authority of "international law," which attempts to establish criteria for promoting justice, equality, and peace on a universal scale. According to Catholic social doctrine, "International law becomes the guarantor of the international order that is of coexistence among political communities that seek individually to promote the common good of their citizens and strive collectively to guarantee that of all peoples, aware that the common good of a nation cannot be separated from the good of the entire human family."[22] The Church, in speaking about the land and the state of Israel, is committed to the language of international law. This language is not completely divorced from the language of revelation, for revelation too relies on categories of human rationality, universality, and humanism, even if it transcends these categories when it comes to the relationship between God and the human person. As the Church succinctly has been teaching since 1975:

> Christians are invited to understand this [Jewish] religious attachment which finds its roots in Biblical tradition, without however making their own any particular religious interpretation of this relationship (cf. Declaration of the US Conference of Catholic Bishops, November 20, 1975). The existence of the state of Israel and its political options should be envisaged not in a perspective which is in itself religious, but in their reference to the common principles of international law.[23]

This statement does not derive from "skillful Vatican juggling"[24] as supposed by Gavin D'Costa, but rather from a prudent reticence to theologize political realities without first discerning those realities in the light of values like justice, equality, and peace.

---

[22] Pontifical Council for Justice and Peace, *Compendium of the Social Doctrine of the Church* (2005), 434.

[23] Commission for Religious Relations with the Jews, *Notes on the Correct Way to Present the Jews and Judaism in Preaching and Catechesis in the Roman Catholic Church* 6.1 (June 24, 1985).

[24] Gavin D'Costa, "Search for the Promised Land," *The Tablet* (March 1, 2018): 9.

As a contemporary citizen of the state of Israel, I place myself on the side of the struggle for equality. However, I do so, believing that this is a value that cannot be laid aside in interpreting the Bible and doing theology. I echo here what was earlier cited from paragraph 4 of *Nostra Aetate*: Catholics should take care not to "teach anything that does not conform to the truth of the Gospel and the spirit of Christ." This cannot be understood to refer only to Jews and Judaism. Rather, the Catholic awareness of mechanisms that lead to marginalization and exclusion must be countered regarding all who are marginalized and excluded, and that includes Palestinians too.

In the ongoing events that provide the very ground for theological reflection, some in Israel/Palestine today, and I among them, believe that the truth of the Gospel and the Spirit of Christ would be best served by upholding the image and likeness of God in every Jew, in every Palestinian, in every human person. Whatever the framework set for a solution to the Israeli-Palestinian conflict, whether two states living side by side or one unique state for all, the ultimate principle that must be guaranteed on all sides is the equality of the human person, equal in rights and duties. A recent statement of the Catholic Bishops in the Holy Land underlined this struggle:

> We promote a vision according to which everyone in this Holy Land has full equality, the equality befitting all men and women created equal in God's own image and likeness. We believe that equality, whatever political solutions might be adopted, is a fundamental condition for a just and lasting peace. We have lived together in this land in the past, why should we not live together in the future too? This is our vision for Jerusalem and the whole land, called Israel and Palestine, between the Jordan River and the Mediterranean Sea.[25]

Believers and nonbelievers, Jews, Christians, and Muslims, are all represented among the two peoples laying claim to the land called Israel by some and Palestine by others. Whatever the lacunae of international law, there seems to be no viable alternative in the current situation of conflict to regulate claims and protect the individual and the group from violations of justice.

---

25 Assembly of Catholic Ordinaries of the Holy Land, *Righteousness and Peace Will Kiss Each Other*, May 20, 2019.

CATHOLICITY OF THE GOOD NEWS

The Catholic Church, by virtue of her catholicity, cannot but raise questions about all ideologies, including nineteenth-century ideologies of nation, land, and state that so emphasize borders that they become semi-sacralized. The history of the twentieth century sadly illustrates nationalism's exploitation of religion and religious language, too often replacing God with people, land, and state, justifying violence in religious language. Dominant forms of Zionism have not proved much different from other forms of nationalism, exuding an odor of modern idolatry. The Church does not undermine the right of peoples to self-determination, but her mission is to promote the Kingdom of God, which excludes discrimination and enmity. She is bound by a vision that brings humanity together, founded on the communion of Jew and Gentile, Israeli and Palestinian.

Christians are committed to preaching "good news," the same that Jesus came to proclaim, the Good News that death is vanquished and with it the elements of death that thrive in a world of conflict, violence, and hatred. Ultimately, this Good News is essentially about the stretching of borders to include more and more rather than the sanctification of borders that exclude others. There are natural circles of belonging that ground the human person in his or her identity: family, city, nation, country, and ultimately humanity. We each belong to a variety of cohesive social structures that extend beyond our individuality. Belonging to the Jewish people and being a citizen in the state of Israel are identities that the Church affirms along with belonging to the Palestinian people and being a citizen in the state of Palestine.

However, part and parcel of the Good News that Christ proclaims is that the human person is liberated from borders that close him or her in and restrict his or her going out toward the other. Liberation from those borders does not mean these borders simply evaporate as they continue to define the specificity of humanity in its specific incarnation. I remain a Jew, an Israeli, a Catholic, a Jesuit, and yet these characteristics, which allow me to feel at home in one place and celebrate what brings me together with those like me, are not turned into arguments for the exclusion of others. Borders that remain impenetrable and unchallenged create fortresses, not homes. In the Biblical narrative, the borders of Israel are constantly challenged by surprising encounters with enterprising non-Israelite individuals. Among them are Jethro the Midianite sage (Exodus), Rahab the Canaanite prostitute (Joshua), Ruth the Moabite widow (Ruth), Cyrus the Persian messiah (2 Chronicles and Ezra), Akhior the Ammonite chieftain (Judith), Job the sage from Oz, and many others (cf. Ex 18:1–27, Jo 2:1–21, Ru 1:1–4:22, 2 Chr 36:22–Ezr 1:11, Jdt 5:5–21, Jb 1:1ff). These remarkable figures remind us that

Israel's vocation is to be a source of blessing for all nations, who are called in turn to bless Israel, the people of God willing to go out and welcome others in. This language of mutual recognition and blessing is the language the Church is called to promote.

As we build the Kingdom of God together, man and woman, Jew and Gentile, free person and slave, each contributes from his or her own uniqueness so that the body will lack nothing of the gifts that God has bestowed on each one individually and on peoples corporately. Nationalism tends to narrow the focus to one particular aspect of identity, blurring other aspects. Internationalism might do the same, as was tragically obvious in most forms of communism and socialism. Both nationalist and internationalist ideologies have unleashed horrific waves of violence on humanity. The challenge is not to exclude any aspect of the particularities that define each human person, as each one opens the individual to an array of diverse ways to interconnect and build community, ultimately transforming the aggressive instinct to defend borders into reasons for reaching out and working together. In a remarkable eschatological vision, the prophet Isaiah writes: "On that day there will be a highway from Egypt to Assyria, and the Assyrian will come into Egypt, and the Egyptian into Assyria, and the Egyptians will worship with the Assyrians. On that day Israel will be the third with Egypt and Assyria, a blessing in the midst of the earth, whom the Lord of hosts has blessed, saying, 'Blessed be Egypt my people, and Assyria the work of my hands, and Israel my heritage'" (Is 19:23–25). Israel, in the midst of a world of hostile empires, portrayed here by Egypt and Assyria, was repeatedly crushed by one empire or another. However, Israel's vocation in the midst of these empires is to transform both empires into parts of God's Kingdom, where together Egyptians, Assyrians, and Israelites sing God's name in a symphony of praise.

Indeed, rather than sacralizing boundaries, Jesus came to go beyond them:

> For he is our peace; in his flesh he has made both groups into one and has broken down the dividing wall, that is, the hostility between us. He has abolished the law with its commandments and ordinances, that he might create in himself one new humanity in place of the two, thus making peace, and might reconcile both groups to God in one body through the cross, thus putting to death that hostility through it. So he came and proclaimed peace to you who were far off and peace to those who were near; for through him both of us have access in one Spirit to the Father. So then, you are no longer strangers and aliens, but you are citizens with the saints and also members of the household of God." (Eph 2:14–19)

The dividing wall is the one that separates us from them and prevents us from seeing not only their humanity but how, without them, we are less than fully who we are called to become.

The Catholic Church recognizes and respects the deep millennial spiritual, historical, national, and cultural links that Jews have with the Land of Israel. The Church also maintains her own spiritual and historical rootedness in this land, in which Christ lived, died, and rose from the dead, and where the Church was born. Furthermore, the Church never forgets that Muslims too look with veneration toward this land, visited by Islam's messenger, Muhammad. The Church distinguishes between various forms and degrees of attachment to the land, on the one hand, and formulations of rights to the land, rights of sovereignty and realities of borders, on the other hand. However, ultimately the Church must promote a vision of the land in which all people, Israelis and Palestinians, Jews, Christians, and Muslims, can be at home and enjoy citizenship in a political entity that guarantees the common good.

The two turning points of the Second Vatican Council, the insistence on the ongoing relationship between Jews and Christians including their shared responsibility for *tikkun olam* (repairing a broken world), and the growing awareness that Catholics must contribute to a world that is more just and in which there is an equitable distribution of resources, can come together. Catholics engaged in the dialogue with Jews must insist that they cannot justify the Palestinians' experience of discrimination and occupation in Israel/Palestine today, an experience rooted in how Zionism has been translated into harsh political realities in the state of Israel today. At the same time, Catholics engaged in profound solidarity with the Palestinians, founded on a commitment to the social doctrine of the Church, cannot adopt a teaching of contempt with regard to Jews even while opposing decisions, policies, and practices of the Israeli authorities. These two revolutions converge when Catholics promote justice and peace for all inhabitants of the Holy Land.

TRACTATIO THEOLOGICO-POLITICA
PALESTINIAN SUFFERING AND THE OFFICIAL CATHOLIC TEACHING ON THE STATE OF ISRAEL
Antoine Lévy, OP

THE CATHOLIC APPROACH TO THE LAND: COMPLEXITY OF THE THEOLOGICAL ISSUE

The Land—with a capital L; that is, the territory on which the State of Israel is currently established—is a problem for the world. But while the world wrestles with one problem, it is fair to claim that Catholic theologians wrestle with two. Just as any other foreign political entity, especially one that happens to have human and material interests in the country, the Vatican State is repeatedly asked to take a stand in the conflict that has been crippling the State of Israel since the first hours of its foundation in 1948. But unlike all the other states, the Vatican, being merely the political *persona* of the Holy See, anchors its political reasonings in a realm that it calls theology; that is, in a teaching that allegedly exceeds the capacity of the natural human intellect since it is supposed to draw its principles from God's revelation. Logically, discerning what is right or where justice lies in the conflict that pits Jews against Palestinians on the territory of Israel is a first-order problem. Discerning how Catholic theology should relate to this specific problem, being itself a theological endeavor, is a second-order problem or a metaproblem. Governments do not tamper with the constitution and laws of their state when they formulate a political stance regarding Israel; they act upon them. But on the same issue, the Church—from which the Vatican is the political emanation—must engage with the theological tenets that should determine her attitude. Catholic theologians are to define in what manner the knowledge they assume to be divinely revealed should interact with the concrete political dilemma brought about by the creation and ongoing existence of the State of Israel.

One could argue that this second-order problem is not much of a real one. After all, the Catholic Church, through the mouths of her leaders, is accustomed to formulating political stances every time a problem involving social justice becomes acute in a particular country. She does it on the basis of the body of theological teaching that she calls social doctrine. In the case of Israel, however, the Church is obliged to consider yet another aspect of her Magisterium or official theological teaching, namely, that which deals with the destiny of the Jewish people in relation to God's design as it unfolds in Sacred Scriptures. The articulation of these two theological registers, one as universal as possible, since social justice should apply equally to all the nations of the earth, and the other utterly specific, as it deals with the unique status of Israel as God's "chosen people," gives to this second-order problem a dimension of first-order complexity. To what extent and in what manner should the Church's "theology of Israel" affect her assessment of the Israeli conflict in terms of social justice? To formulate the same question in even more precise terms: what is there in a Catholic theology of Israel that qualifies it to determine an issue essentially dealing with social and political justice?

One cannot hope to provide an answer to this arduous question without clarifying what this social and political issue is in the concrete situation at stake. This is the first point that I will tackle. I will then proceed to examine the manner in which Church authorities have drawn—or not drawn—on a theology of Israel to solve this issue. Finally, I will challenge these authorities to revise their current position in regard to a core aspect of the articulation between a Catholic theology of Israel and a political stance on the State of Israel.

THE SOCIAL-POLITICAL APPROACH TO THE CONFLICT: LINGERING AMBIGUITIES IN THE OFFICIAL CATHOLIC TEACHING

If the bare mention of the State of Israel evokes a problem of social justice, it is because the existence of a Jewish State is a cause of suffering for the members of the entity that identifies with the Palestinian people. From whatever angle one sees it, this suffering is real, and no one is entitled to deny it. But a fact is not yet a problem. The moment when real suffering becomes a problem, that is, a point of contention between people with different opinions, is when it is associated with the term "unjust." Of course, suffering in itself is not necessarily unjust. Leaving aside natural sickness and death, in regard to which it is always possible to blame the Creator of the universe if he exists, the type of suffering that comes from a guilty conscience or from a punishment for some objectively evil deed are not unjust by definition. But suffering can also be morally neutral, as when I suffer because I need to leave a home that has been purchased by someone else. I can grieve because of the good memories associated with this house even as I find comfort in the thought of having sold it for a good price.

Speaking of the Palestinian suffering because of the Jewish State, there are objectively different opinions as to whether and to what extent this suffering is unjust—more or differently unjust than the suffering of the Jewish population caused by Palestinian so-called "acts of terror" for instance. If the issue is so controversial, it is because at no point of Israel's history has there been a legal norm of justice that would have been simultaneously acknowledged by both parties. In order for an action to be qualified as a crime, and therefore the punishment of a crime to be considered legitimate, the state and its laws must be, at least on paper, deemed to be approved by the citizens gathered as a political body. If such is not the case, an action that goes against the laws of a particular state could, under certain conditions (see the tradition on the "right of resistance" since Grotius and Pufendorf), be considered to be an act of resistance to oppression. In this configuration, punishment administered by the state would be liable to the same moral scrutiny as the action that provoked it. Even if the State of Israel was established in 1948 on the basis of a consensus of foreign nations, it never had a chance to be acknowledged by the whole population gathered as a body politic.[1] Indeed, little less than half of the total population fled in the wake of the war of independence (about 700,000 Palestinians from a territory that counted about 872,000 Jews), and there is not much evidence to back the claim that most of those who remained willfully embraced the decision made by the League of Nations. In the absence of any legal norm acknowledged by both parties, one is confronted with the logic of two self-consistent narratives: the first refers to the right of a population to resettle a territory they used to inhabit little less than two thousand years ago; the second to the right

---

1 "The Arabs immediately rejected the Partition Plan, arguing that the General Assembly was not authorized to make such a recommendation and that it was in breach of the Arab residents of Palestine to determinate their own political future," Matthijs de Blois and Andrew Tucker, *Israel on Trial: How International Law is Being Misused to Delegitimize the State of Israel* (Soest, Netherlands: The Hague Initiative for International Cooperation, 2018), 133.

of a population that was established on this territory until very recently to continue inhabiting it. As soon as one envisages the establishment of a legitimate Jewish State, the two narratives seem to collide: either the rights of the non-Jewish inhabitants are respected and it becomes difficult for the state to preserve its claim to be Jewish, or their rights are not respected and the state can no longer pretend to be legitimate. In a situation where there is no commonly acknowledged political norm and where there is no obvious way through which the respective narratives of the two parties in conflict could be reconciled, the criterion of what is just and what is not will very much depend on the narrative one adopts at the expense of the other. Seen from a unilaterally Zionist perspective, the undeniable suffering entailed by the death, or life-sentence, of a Palestinian "terrorist" is not unjust, while a unilaterally anti-Zionist perspective will consider it as utterly so; that is, as another instance in the spiral of repression of the legitimate aspirations of the Palestinian people.

Naturally, third parties are not obliged to endorse either of these unilateral perspectives. Seeing the conflict from a distance, they can claim that they are able to identify what is morally right in each of the two positions. With the goal of creating the conditions for a peaceful and legitimate solution to the conflict, they can strive to develop a view that singles out what is truly just in this concrete situation, a point of balance to which each party should eventually come, leaving some of their claims behind in order to preserve the chances of others. This is the current position of the Holy See, as typically expressed in the first document to officially mention the State of Israel, the Apostolic Letter of John Paul II *Redemptionis Anno* from 1984:

> For the Jewish people who live in the State of Israel and who preserve in that land such precious testimonies to their history and their faith, we must ask for the desired security and the due tranquility that is the prerogative of every nation and condition of life and of progress for every society. The Palestinian people who find their historical roots in that land and who for decades have been dispersed, have the natural right in justice to find a homeland and to be able to live in peace and tranquility with the other peoples of the area."[2]

Article 11 of the 1993 Fundamental Agreement between the Holy See and the State of Israel emphasizes that the first, being the legal *persona* of the Catholic Church's supreme authority "is solemnly committed to remaining a stranger to all merely temporal conflicts, which principle applies specifically

---

2 John Paul II, Apostolic Letter *Redemptionis Anno*," trans. *L'Osservatore Romano* (April 20, 1984).

to disputed territories and unsettled borders."³ But this political neutrality is precisely the guarantee of a fair judgment on these matters, as the Holy See shows itself equally eager to maintain "the right to exercise its moral and spiritual teaching-office."⁴

Most recently, the conclusive message of the Middle East Synod presided over by Pope Benedict (2010) preserves the skeleton, as it were, of an impartial view of the situation, giving its due to each party involved in the conflict:

> We have taken account of the impact of the Israeli-Palestinian conflict on the whole region, especially on the Palestinians who are suffering the consequences of the Israeli occupation: the lack of freedom of movement, the wall of separation and the military checkpoints, the political prisoners, the demolition of homes, the disturbance of socio-economic life and the thousands of refugees. We have reflected on the suffering and insecurity in which Israelis live.... With all this in mind, we see that a just and lasting peace is the only salvation for everyone and for the good of the region and its peoples."⁵

Developing an impartial view of the conflict implies that one is able to distinguish the just from the unjust or, equivalently, that one is able to refer to some norm of justice that would be acceptable to both parties as not being tied to a particular political, ideological, or religious agenda. The question reads: what is or what are this/these norm/s in a situation where the two parties derive entirely different and mutually exclusive conclusions from what they deem to be their respective rights to be on the Land? The easy answer is to point to existing international laws, such as the Geneva Convention, in the case of demolition of homes. But is referring to these laws and agreements morally right because they signal that the State of Israel has transgressed the boundaries within which it may legitimately operate or because they serve as an additional confirmation that the State of Israel has no legitimacy whatsoever? When the suffering of Palestinians is denounced as unjust, is the just measure a State of Israel that would be recognized as such and welcomed in the international community or a situation where Israel would not be allowed to function as a legitimate state under any circumstance? That I take someone to court for a punishable offence does not mean that, in my view,

---

3 *Fundamental Agreement between the Holy See and the State of Israel*, December 30, 1993, https://mfa.gov.il/mfa/mfa-archive/1993/pages/fundamental%20agreement%20-%20israel-holy%20see.aspx.

4 *Fundamental Agreement between the Holy See and the State of Israel*.

5 Pope Benedict XVI, *Synod for the Middle East: a Message to the People of God*, October 23, 2010.

this person is merely guilty of this particular offence. It can simply mean that I am unable to find any other way of bringing this person to court. In this configuration, the trial is not a way of ensuring that the notion of justice as embodied in the laws of the state and implemented by tribunals will be effectively respected. It rather becomes an additional tactic in a fight for an idea of justice that cannot be—or can only be very partially—applied by the existing legislation because it is foreign to it.[6] Accordingly, when Church authorities claim that, as representatives of a third and independent party, their one and only goal is to formulate where true justice lies, they will not be able to satisfy themselves by pointing at some existent piece of international legislation. The fact is that this very same argument can be inspired by notions of justice that are very much at odds with one another.

The reason for this ambiguity is that no international agreement stating the right of a Jewish State to exist and function within definite borders has ever been acknowledged on the Palestinian side. While the PLO endorsed UN Resolution 242, which speaks about the right of both parties to "live in peace within secure and recognized boundaries," the same 1993 resolution also mentions the necessity for Israel to withdraw from the territories conquered during the Six-Day War, thus leaving aside—or for the future—the issue of defining what these legitimate borders are. Even the geographical boundaries of the State of Israel as it emerged from the War of Independence in 1949 were never recognized as legitimate borders. The Israel-Jordan Armistice Agreement considered them as purely military lines that should not "in any way prejudice future arrangements or agreements under international law."[7] But if there is no agreed-upon understanding about what the legitimate State of Israel is and how it should function, how could there be some objective agreement about what it is not and why it does not function the way it should?

True, the League of Nations voted for the creation of the State of Israel in 1948. The right of Israel to exist was the object of an international consensus.

---

[6] Brooke Goldstein, a human rights lawyer, defines what she calls "the use of the law as a weapon of war or, more specifically, the abuse of Western laws and judicial systems to achieve strategic military or political ends" as follows: "It consists of the negative manipulation of international and national human rights laws to accomplish purposes other than, or contrary to those for which they were originally enacted. Lawfare is also evident in the manipulation of domestic legal systems (by state and non-state parties) to implement laws inconsistent with general principles of liberal democracy. The principles underlying lawfare are also present in glaring failures to apply human rights law and in the disproportionate and biased application of the law." See the Lawfare Project, "What is Lawfare," http://www.thelawfareproject.org/what-is-lawfare.html, quoted in de Blois and Tucker, *Israel on Trial*, 62.

[7] Quoted in Cynthia D. Wallace, "Secure and Recognized Borders: UN Resolution 242 and the '67 Lines," thinc., March 31, 2018, http://www.thinc.info/secure-and-recognized-borders-un-resolution-242-and-the-67-lines.

It is in reference to this decision of the international community that John Paul II could declare in an interview published in 1993: "It must be understood that Jews who for 2,000 years were dispersed among the nations of the world had decided to return to the land of their ancestors. This is their right and this right is recognized even by those who look upon the nation of Israel with an unsympathetic eye. This right was recognized from the outset by the Holy See and the act of establishing diplomatic relationship with Israel is simply an international affirmation of this relationship."[8]

No doubt the state of mind of a world that had gone through a war with Hitler's Germany and just discovered the full extent of the Holocaust had much to do with the decision that was made in 1948. Seventy years after, as the horror inspired by the *Shoah* is definitely subsiding, this right is also becoming much less obvious. The January 2011 issue of *Civiltà Cattolica*, the Jesuit publication submitted to the approval of the Vatican Secretariat of State, included an article by the priest Giovanni Sale in which the beginnings of the State of Israel are unilaterally designated under the term *Nakba*, the Arabic term for "disaster," in reference to the exodus mentioned above. In the article Sale declares: "the Zionists were cleverly able to exploit the Western sense of guilt for the *Shoah* to lay the foundations of their own state."[9]

Indeed, what if a confederation of Iroquois tribes reclaimed the State of New York and managed to take over Manhattan by force? Could Iroquois's suffering, tragic as it might have been, justify their claim to establish a state of their own in the eastern part of the present United States of America? The expulsion-dispersion of the Iroquois tribes happened little more than three centuries ago. What then about a people deciding to resettle on a land that they had relinquished two thousand years earlier?[10]

The fact that the local inhabitants of Palestine did not enjoy political independence at the time does not alter the fact that they suddenly found themselves compelled either to leave or to suffer the establishment of a state ruled by a conglomerate of more or less newcomers from Europe. One is obliged to concede that the claim of a nation that managed to survive an

---

8 Interview in the magazine *Parade*, 1993, quoted in Richard C. Lux, *The Jewish People, the Holy Land, and the State of Israel: A Catholic View* (New York: Paulist Press, 2010), 70.

9 "La fondazione dello Stato di Israele e il problema dei profughi palestinesi," *La Civiltà Cattolica* (January 2011), 107–20, 111. For a convincing refutation of this myth, see Alan Dershowitz, *The Case for Israel* (Hoboken, NJ: John Wiley and Sons, 2003), 53–62.

10 I agree with David Novak, who points out the weakness of a justification of Zionism on purely historical ground, apart from a theological perspective: "the 'historic connection' of the Jewish people seems rather tenuous in the face of the Palestinian Arabs who make the same historical claim on their side. So, if the Jewish people have a more cogent claim on the Land of Israel alone, that is, it is because God chose this and for the Jewish people to settle there as permanently as possible." *Zionism and Judaism: A New Theory* (New York: Cambridge University Press, 2015), 141.

exile of two thousand years to come back on the land they came from has no legal precedent. Accordingly, there is no international norm of law that could cogently justify their return to the Land. To contest the argument that their return is thoroughly unjust due to its dire consequences on the local Arab population, those who advocate the right for the State of Israel to exist and live within secure borders can only appeal to the immaterial force of a decision made by a foreign body of representatives and deprived of strong legal foundations. In this context, one does not see why the Palestinian fight against injustice should stop short of the liquidation of the State of Israel. After all, surely this international decision was inspired by the colonialist mentality that still prevailed in the immediate aftermath of World War II?[11] The case for the existence of this state is so weak from a philosophical and legal point of view, especially in the light of a counter-narrative pushing forward the theme of brutal dispossession and ongoing state violence, that one can hardly see how it could manage to secure one square meter of the Land for the Jewish population to enjoy without considerable pangs of moral conscience.[12]

How could a simple reference to the 1948 vote provide a sustainable framework for a state to "live in peace within secure and recognized boundaries"? If the fundamental injustice is the "occupation" of Palestine, to quote the term used by the Middle East Synod in its conclusive message, the existence of the State of Israel, even on such a small territory as the one originally defined by the 1948 vote, cannot but constitute an infringement of justice.[13] In this framework, nothing can prevent a decision destined to guarantee the security of the state from being denounced as unjust. The erection of a wall and the establishment of military checkpoints will not be seen as responding to the need to prevent terrorist attacks. To quote the conclusive message of the Middle East Synod again, they will rather be blamed as offenses against the "freedom of movement." In the same declaration, we read that those who have been put in prison because they perpetrated attacks or have been

---

11 Edward Said has famously theorized this approach to Zionism: "For although it coincided with an era of the most virulent Western antisemitism, Zionism also coincided with the period of unparalleled European territorial acquisition in Africa and Asia, and it was as part of this general movement of acquisition that Zionism was launched initially by Theodor Herzl." *The Question of Palestine* (New York: Random Books, 1980), 69.

12 In *The Case for Israel*, A. Dershowitz provided a substantial rationale for the legitimacy of the State of Israel in its current form from a strictly legal point of view. I personally subscribe to almost all the points he makes.

13 As a journalist and pro-Palestine activist wrote: "Even it were the size of a postal stamp... Israel has no right to exist," "Israel surely has no right to exist." Faisal Bodi, *The Guardian* (January 3, 2001), quoted in Dershowitz, *The Case for Israel*, 65.

planning to do the same are called "political prisoners" and not terrorists. The "demolition of homes," far from implementing a strategy of deterrence, is implicitly presented as a policy of gratuitous cruelty. Finally, there is no mention that the "disturbance of socio-economic life" has something to do with a concerted effort to rein in the smuggling of weapons into Gaza. One easily imagines the anguish of Israeli political leaders, witnessing the growing erosion of the State of Israel's legitimacy in the world's public opinion. Because they can no longer rely on a flow of external sympathy streaming to support their conviction that the Israeli state has a right to exist and a duty to protect itself, they naturally feel inclined to view the critical attitude of third parties as partaking of a biased and systematic attempt to undercut the very possibility of Israel's existence.

The State of Israel is often blamed for its reluctance to improve the material and legal status of the Palestinian population. It is repeatedly said that its refusal to give up territories and settlements is responsible for the conflict. What is implied is that Palestinians would come to recognize the legitimacy of a Jewish State living within secure borders should the State of Israel make more generous overtures to them. In this volume, E. Vetö argues that "sharing the Land" with the resident alien, *ger toshav*, is not only a means to alleviate the suffering that is at the core of the conflict, but that it is requisite for the recognition of the State of Israel's legitimacy both from the point of view of the Torah and that of Catholic theology. However, one might remember that the State of Israel has not shown itself as closed to the prospect of sharing land. Who refused to hear about the "sharing" that was key to the partition plan of 1948? Was it the Jewish political establishment or the Arab one? Negotiations about Israel's withdrawal from the territories gained during the Six-Day War started in the days that followed Israel's victory. After the Camp David agreements (1978), Israel gave up the large swathes of the Sinai Peninsula that it had conquered during the Yom Kippur War (1973). The Oslo process initiated in 1993 led to the Interim Agreement of 1995; that is, to the transfer of control over the Gaza Strip and 88 percent of the West Bank from the State of Israel to the Palestinian Authority. In 2008, PLO Chairman M. Abbas turned down Israel's Prime Minister E. Olmert's peace offer. Olmert declared himself ready to evacuate a great number of settlements, suggested land swaps that would have placed 100 percent of the West Bank Area under the authority of the PLO, and proposed a new partition of Jerusalem. None of these unilateral steps translated into a Palestinian recognition of a State of Israel living within definite borders. The crushing of these hopes currently sets the search for a two-state solution in jeopardy. Thus, historical facts offer the proof *a contrario* that the idea lying behind the lofty ideal of "sharing the Land" is simply wrong. As ethically and religiously inspired as this attitude might prove to be from a Jewish (and Catholic) point of view, giving up territories fails to trigger a reciprocal willingness to recognize the legitimacy of the State of Israel. I believe the reasons for this counter-intuitive truth to be simple: if making concessions does not lead to the recognition of Israel's borders, it is because the absence of such recognition is what leads Israel to making concessions. Of course, "sharing the Land" does not necessarily need to be taken in a geographical sense. The same notion can be understood as a challenge to foster political equality and social justice within the Israeli society. But one encounters the same type of issues in the absence of a common criterion of legitimacy: where does such a sharing start and where does it stop? Clearly, for Hajj Amin al-Husseini, the grand mufti of Jerusalem who lobbied against the idea of "sharing the Land" with Jews in 1948, the "sharing" of social privileges with them would not end before sending back recent Jewish immigrants to the countries they came from and having the remaining part of the Jewish population recover their traditional status as *dhimmis* in a Muslim-run state.

It is here that theology—namely, the type of theology that I described above as an effort to substantiate some definite political stand of the Catholic Church—becomes relevant and even crucial. What does an argumentation anchored in supernatural revelation have to say regarding a situation where discourses based on shared natural reason, whether philosophical or juridical, are no longer able to secure a notion of justice that would make room for Israel's sustainable existence as a state? Let us first examine the way in which the official teaching of the Catholic Church views the articulation between the theological sphere and the current conflict.

OFFICIAL DICASTERY TEACHINGS AND THE TEACHINGS OF THE FORMAL MAGISTERIUM: OPEN QUESTIONS

Among the fairly large number of Catholic official declarations regarding Jews and Judaism since and including *Nostra Aetate* (1965), only a few directly address the right of Israel to exist and the issue of justice associated with its realization. The use of silence is especially striking in documents such as the lengthy 2001 document entitled "The Jewish People and Their Sacred Scriptures in the Christian Bible" emanating from the Pontifical Biblical Commission, as it extensively evokes the Promise of the Land made to Abraham and his descendants. Let me quote a couple of lines from number 56: "Every human group wishes to inhabit territory in a permanent manner. Otherwise, reduced to the status of stranger or refugee, it finds itself, at best, tolerated, or at worst, exploited and continually oppressed. Israel was freed from slavery in Egypt and received from God the promise of land. ... The term 'promised land' is not found in the Hebrew Bible, which has no word for 'promise.' The idea is expressed by the future tense of the verb 'to give,' or by using the verb 'to swear': 'the land which he swore to give to you' (Ex 13:5; 33:1, etc.). In the Abraham traditions, the promise of land will be fulfilled through descendants."

Nevertheless, in the few official documents where the issue of the State of Israel is explicitly addressed, Church authorities appear eager to limit the theological validity of this specific aspect of God's Promise to a sphere of belief and identity—that associated with the Jewish tradition—presented as lying outside the teaching and tradition of the Church. Catholic faithful are invited to understand the essence of the Zionist position, controversial though it is, but they are firmly deterred from endorsing it. This stance is already expressed in the 1975 *Statement of the Conference of the United States Bishops on Catholic-Jewish Relations*, a declaration on the occasion of *Nostra Aetate*'s ten-year anniversary: "Whatever difficulties Christians may experience in sharing this view they should strive to understand this link between land and people which Jews have expressed in their writings and worship throughout two millennia as a longing for the homeland, holy Zion. Appreciation of this link is not to give assent to any particular religious interpretation of this bond."[14] The declaration does not dismiss outright the possibility of Zionism drawing some legal justification from these Biblical roots—it is not because this religious argumentation is foreign to Catholic theology that it has no validity whatsoever—but it states that this virtual validity cannot be the one and exclusive criterion of justice regarding the conflict: "this affirmation [of the link between the Land and the Jewish people] is not meant to deny the legitimate rights of other parties in the region, or to adopt any political stance in the controversies over the Middle East." Paragraph 6 of the 2001 *Notes on the Correct Way to Present the Jews and Judaism in Preaching and Catechesis in the Roman Catholic Church*, a document emanating from the Commission for Religious Relations with the Jews, follows the same pattern: "Christians are invited to understand this religious attachment which finds its roots in Biblical tradition, without however making their own any particular religious interpretation of this relationship." At the same time, it includes a consideration that adds a new level of both dogmatic radicality and philosophical ambiguity: "The existence of the State of Israel and its political options should be envisaged not in a perspective which is in itself religious, but in their reference to the

---

14 United States Conference of Catholic Bishops, *Statement on Catholic-Jewish Relations*, 1975.

common principles of international law."¹⁵ One finds no further elaboration of this remarkable statement, although the authors emphasize that it does not take away the religious element that Catholic faithful should discern in the bimillennial survival of the Jewish people: "The permanence of Israel (while so many ancient peoples have disappeared without trace) is a historic fact and a sign to be interpreted within God's design." What seems to be implied is that Catholics should limit this religious aspect to the sheer preservation of the Jewish people, so as not to associate a definite geographical place with their survival. This adds to the abrupt character of the preceding statement: for some reason, the Land is the only aspect of God's Promise that should not retain a perennial value in the case of Jews. The last document published by the same Commission, "The Gifts and the Calling of God are Irrevocable" (2015), goes back to this passage, quoting but also somehow softening it as the two statements are contrasted with the word "however": "The permanence of Israel is *however* to be perceived as an 'historic fact and a sign to be interpreted within God's design.'"¹⁶ However, this emphasis on the providential character unconditionally attached to Jewish ongoing existence renders the initial absence of explanation even more problematic: if Catholic faithful are so insistently asked to acknowledge God's providence at work in the ongoing existence of the Jewish nation—and this even when they look at the current situation from a purely social and political point of view as they are invited to do—for what reason are they prevented from also envisaging the "existence of the State of Israel," that is, the return of this Jewish nation to the Land of the Promise, from a "religious perspective"?

Obviously when it comes to the theme of the Land, that is, to aspects related to the existence and the political configuration of the State of Israel, the official teaching of the Catholic Church seems to dismiss any articulation between issues of social justice and a theology centered on the mystery of Israel. Through the voices of those who oversee representing her, the Church confesses that she is unable to supplement in any way with her own wisdom, derived from revelation, the secular wisdom of nations as it is expressed by international laws.

In a contribution included in this volume, Neuhaus writes: "The Church, in speaking about the land and the state of Israel, is committed to

---

15 Commission for Religious Relations with the Jews, *Notes on the Correct Way to Present the Jews and Judaism in Preaching and Catechesis in the Roman Catholic Church*, 6.1 (June 24, 1985). The document is quoting the 1975 *Statement of the Conference of the United States Bishops on Catholic-Jewish Relations*.

16 Commission for Religious Relations with the Jews, *"The Gifts and the Calling of God Are Irrevocable" (Rom 11:29): A Reflection on Theological Questions Pertaining to Catholic–Jewish Relations on the Occasion of the 50th Anniversary of "Nostra Aetate,"* 2015.

the language of international law. This language is not completely divorced from the language of revelation, for revelation too relies on categories of human rationality, universality and humanism, even if it transcends these categories when it comes to the relationship between God and the human person." But what about documents from the Magisterium stating that, in the case of Israel, considerations regarding the content of revelation should be kept separate from reasoning based on international law? I take Neuhaus to mean that revelation cannot but concur with such reasoning because it is the transcendent source of the moral principles to which international law refers. While this is hardly deniable from a theological standpoint, I claim that the revelation is not confined to providing moral and political laws with their ultimate source of intelligibility. Revelation is also about the destiny of a concrete and very unique nation from the time of Abraham to that of Jesus. *Per se*, the theological status that revelation grants to this nation has nothing to do with universal moral principles—and if it is true that this nation has *volens nolens* been the channel through with these principles were communicated to humankind, God could have communicated the same principles to humankind without granting the status of chosen people to Israel. Accordingly, one may well claim that, in the current treatment of the State of Israel by the Holy See, the language of revelation concurs with that of international law as long as one disregards revelation's core component, its being the story of Israel up to the manifestation of Israel's light to all the nations in Jesus Christ.

Certainly, a solution based on true justice, if it ever sees the light of day, will need to be formulated in the terms of international law. But the whole problem is that, as we saw earlier, one cannot solely rely on existing international law to find this solution. Claiming that international law is the only possible source of justice in situations where it cannot apply implies that one is left with nothing else than the violence and injustice of a rogue state. In order to ascribe some degree of legitimacy to this state, a state that owes its existence to the fact that it is geographically sustainable, one needs to draw on principles that are more fundamental than the available set of international laws, and this is the reason why the theological disengagement of the Church carries such heavy responsibility. It irresistibly calls to mind the behavior depicted in Matthew 27:24: "When Pilate saw that he was getting nowhere, but that instead an uproar was starting, he took water and washed his hands in front of the crowd."

Neuhaus in this volume writes: "Believers and nonbelievers, Jews, Christians, and Muslims, are represented among the two peoples laying claim to the land called Israel by some and Palestine by others. Whatever the lacunae of international law, there seems to be no viable alternative in the current situation of conflict to regulate claims and protect the individual and the group from violations of justice." He also says, "The Church recognizes the authority of 'international law,' which attempts to establish criteria for promoting justice, equality, and peace on a universal scale," and he quotes the *Compendium of the Social Doctrine of the Church*, paragraph 434: "International law becomes the guarantor of the international order: that is, of coexistence among political communities that seek individually to promote the common good of their citizens and strive collectively to guarantee that of all peoples, aware that the common good of a nation cannot be separated from the good of the entire human family." But when does international law *become* such a guarantor in the eyes of the Church? Neuhaus could have quoted the previous paragraph (433) of the same document since it specifies the conditions for international law to be considered such a guarantor: "The Church's teaching, with regard to the constitutive principles of the international community, requires that relations among peoples and political communities be justly regulated according to the principles of reason, equity, law and negotiation excluding recourse to violence and war, as well as to forms of discrimination, intimidation and deceit."[17]

Should the Church consider UN Resolution 3379 (1975), which equates Zionism with racism, to be a "guarantor of the international order"? The United Nations Human Rights Council (UNHRC) has issued more than one hundred resolutions regarding human rights violations in the world; half of them incriminate the State of Israel. Should these resolutions be deemed to be based on "principles of reason, equity, etc." as well as to be foreign to "forms of discrimination, intimidation, etc." because they emanate from the one and unique instance—the UN—whose role is to acknowledge what has legitimacy and what is deprived of it from the point of view of the international community? What if the only international arbitrator of such legitimacy fails to live up to the standards of equity that, according to the Magisterium, make of international law the "guarantor of the international order"? I agree with Neuhaus that "whatever the lacunae of international law, there seems to be no viable alternative in the current situation of conflict to regulate claims and protect the individual and the group from violations of justice." But what if instances that should be the voice of international law fail to regulate these "competing claims" in fairness because the decisions they make are biased? If a tin-opener cannot open tins because it is damaged, should I use it all the same because the function of a tin-opener is to open tins and because I can indeed *try* to open tins with it? It is not difficult

---

17 Pontifical Council for Justice and Peace, *Compendium of the Social Doctrine of the Church* (2005).

to understand why Israeli authorities resist the injunctions of such international bodies as well as their interpretation of existing laws and treaties when unilateral support for those committed to fight against the State of Israel is part of the alleged "lacunae" of these decisions.

The question that I want to raise is the following: Is the dismissal of any consideration regarding the mystery of Israel when discussing the issue of the Land—a dismissal that emanates from the current authorities of the Church—logically and theologically consistent? Can it be considered to be Catholic in the most fundamental sense of the word?

When a statement is given without explanation, what is implied most of the time is that it is self-evident, especially so in contexts that have explanation as a goal, such as in philosophy and theology. The statement that we are discussing gives this impression at first reading. How could a belief referring to events that might have occurred four thousand or three thousand years ago come to be considered as a serious source of juridical legitimacy when dealing with situations that are occurring and developing in our time? How could an ancient faith tradition justify the existence and commonweal of a modern state? But nothing is closer to self-evidence than fake evidence. With a slightly higher degree of self-awareness, the authors of this statement could have avoided this type of ambiguity. Indeed, what is the Holy See that they represent, if not a legal entity, encompassing an internationally recognized state called the Vatican, that draws its most fundamental and enduring justification from some ancient faith tradition? That the permanence of the Vatican as a state is no longer the source of a military conflict does not change the fact that this state sees the reason for its existence, and ultimately for its resistance to annihilation, in a religious belief going back to two-thousand-year-old events.

There are other ways of explaining this statement, but I remain unconvinced by every single one of them.

Besides issues of juridical method, one might point to religious interpretations that are incompatible with the respect due to international laws (second hypothesis after the alleged "obsolescence" of Israel's right to exist). On this matter, I can only agree—who would not?—with the principles voiced at the Middle East Synod: "Recourse to theological and biblical positions which use the Word of God to wrongly justify injustices is not acceptable. On the contrary recourse to religion must lead every person to see the face of God in others and to treat them according to the attributes of God and his commandments, namely, according to God's bountiful goodness, mercy, justice and love for us." Commenting on this passage in the concluding message of the Synod, at a press conference, Archbishop Cyril S. Bustros, the president of the commission that drafted it, mentioned the most controversial issue of settlements: "I was thinking in particular of Jewish settlers who claim their right to build on Palestinian territory by saying it forms part of biblical Israel, the land promised by God to the Jews according to the Old Testament."[18]

The ultra-controversial issue of settlements is a good example of the problematic implications derived from emphatic statements regarding justice in the region. There is no denying that a majority of West-Bank settlers are driven by religious beliefs. But when it is said that these religious beliefs "wrongly justify injustices"—as if one could rightly do so—one must ask again: how do we measure injustice in the absence of mutually recognized agreements regarding borders? In the case of settlements, should we measure it in reference to an interpretation of the fourth article from the Geneva convention prohibiting transfer of populations, the 1922 mandate for Palestine adopted by the League of Nation that authorizes Jewish settlements on these territories, or the decisions of Israel's High Court of Justice regarding which settlement is legal and which is not?

I am convinced that, ultimately, believers from the different religious traditions in the region want peace. The problem is that, drawing from their respective religious traditions, they usually support mutually exclusive ideas about what this peace should be like in order to be just. Even Daesh warriors would contend that they see the face of God in others and treat them according to his commandments. The question is therefore not whether religious ideologies can lead to justifying injustices. It is rather whether appealing to religious beliefs inevitably does so, a principle that could account for Catholic faithful being officially discouraged from using religious criteria in order to determine where justice lies in the region. Clearly, if one holds that religious beliefs intrinsically distort political judgment—actually a fairly paradoxical argument coming from Catholic theologians—then the State of Israel, fruit of the work of generations of settlers, has no right to exist.

All the documents emanating from the Holy See mentioned above acknowledge that the longing of Jews for the Land stems from their religious identity. True, a Jew does not need to believe and practice his own religious tradition in order to be a Zionist. Zionism itself was born out of the secular dream of providing a state for all the Jews of the world, scattered as they were, often living in dire conditions, and regardless of their degree of religious observance. But this does not alter the fact that this secular movement

---

18 Cyril S. Bustros, "Peace for the Holy Land: The Promised Land and the Chosen People—The Two-State Solution," *Israel, Palestine & Mid-East,* Council for Centers on Jewish-Christian Relations, November 11, 2010, https://www.ccjr.us/dialogika-resources/themes-in-today-s-dialogue/isrpal/bustros2010nov11.

found its way and its legitimacy by identifying itself with a longing that was consubstantial with the Jewish religious tradition.

In order to have a state of their own, Jews did not, at least deliberately, head for Uganda or Birobidjan. They went back to the Land that God had promised them in the person of Abraham, the Land to which Moses had led them from the slavery of Egypt, the Land that, since the time of David, had had Jerusalem-Zion for a capital and center of worship—hence the very concept of Zionism.[19] In the eyes of the international community, it is precisely this religious narrative that gave a legitimate content to the idea of establishing an independent Jewish State in the Palestine of the British Mandate. Official Catholic documents recommend that Catholic faithful, discarding religious interpretations of the Bible, rely on international agreements such as the 1948 decision to form their judgment regarding the conflict. But the 1948 international agreement, just as other similar decisions, is incomprehensible without the specific religious interpretation of the Bible associated with Zionism.[20] Religion lurks behind about every aspect of the conflict. How could considerations regarding justice not take the religious perspective into account?

Third hypothesis: the reason behind the position that we are discussing might be too problematic to be explicitly formulated. I am referring to the

---

[19] Reflecting on the origins of the Zionist movement, Emanuele Ottolenghi points out that the reference to Biblical Israel was a fundamental component of its success: "While elites selectively tapped into Jewish tradition, attempts to re-elaborate a collective identity in national terms would fail in the absence of a pre-existing strong, collective ethnic allegiance. Jews eventually embraced Zionism because it reflected elements of identity pre-dating the reformulation of Jewishness in modern nationalist terms." "A National Home," in *Modern Judaism*, ed. N. de Lange and M. Freud-Kandel (Oxford: Oxford University Press, 2005), 55–56.

[20] The Preamble to the Mandate given to Britain by the League of Nations in 1923 states that "recognition has thereby been given to the historical connection of the Jewish people with Palestine." Quoted in de Blois and Tucker, *Israel on Trial*, 121. Commenting on the notion of "natural and historic right" of the Jewish people to settle on the territory called Israel as expressed in its Declaration of Independence (1948), D. Novak observes: "how does an 'historic connection' to a land give a particular people the right to establish themselves there politically? Does 'history' grant or endow rights? In fact, natural rights are cogent only when the 'nature' upon which they are based is considered to be the freely chosen creation of God. . . . Likewise, historic rights are cogent only when the 'history' upon which they are based is considered to be the freely chosen creation of God." Novak, *Zionism and Judaism*, 168. True, natural and historic rights do not necessarily have to be derived from religion to have legitimacy and cogency (think of the natural right of human beings to reject slavery, of the historic claims of France—or Germany for that matter—over Alsace, etc.). But in the case in question, namely, the creation of a State that establishes the authority of a more or less "new" population at the expense of its more or less "traditional" ones, to what purely immanent natural or historic rights could one refer? Is the first category of human beings more "naturally" entitled to rule over the second than the converse? What are the immanent "historic rights" of a specific people over a territory out of which they were cast out about two thousand years ago?

concern about the effect that an official endorsement of basic Zionism would produce on the Catholic faithful established in the region, faithful who in their majority are Arab-speaking and tend to identify with the Palestinian people. If this statement proceeds from such a rationale, it is easy to understand why the latter remains implicit: theological affirmations are not exactly supposed to derive from the desire to make a part of the faithful feel morally or politically comfortable. The divine revelation that fully unfolded in Christ and in which theology claims to be anchored did disturb several people at the time, especially important ones, starting with King Herod. If the authorities of the Church believe that the truth of God's commandments regarding life and its preservation should prevail over the common sexual practices of modern couples—I am thinking of contraception and abortion of course—why should the truth of God's promise to Israel not be reckoned with, if abiding by God's understanding of justice is at stake, even if this might hurt the spontaneous political sensitivity of the faithful? Besides, if being careful not to upset Arab-speaking Catholics is the reason behind the official Catholic position, this would actually turn the formulation of the Catholic criteria of justice in the region into a typical illustration of deceitful bias: the political understanding that is peculiar to one of the two parties in the conflict would henceforth dictate the principles according to which "objective" justice should be served.

Finally, I can think of a fourth bad reason that might justify the position formulated by the Vatican commission. It is the fear that opening the door to religious interpretations of Israel's political existence and development would give way to wild eschatological expectations and speculations among Catholic faithful. Due to a number of factors that have to do as much with the traditional Catholic approach to theological wisdom as with political considerations, Catholic theologians are wary of Protestant dispensationalism in all its different forms. But none of these factors justifies throwing the baby out with the bathwater. In the bitter conflict that pits one notion of justice against another, the last things that Israeli political leaders are eager to hear from Catholic theologians and faithful are theocratic speculations and eschatological visions about what the state they serve is, should be, or is called by God to become.

They do not, because an overwhelming majority of them reject the notion of theocratic state. This is a consensus shared both by secular politicians (*hilonim*) and ultra-orthodox parties *(haredim)* for whom no attempt to foster theocracy should be made before the coming of Israel's Messiah. Even *Otzmat-le-Yisrael*, the small ultranationalist party, partially heir to Meir Kahane's *Kach*, is not officially supporting the idea of a state run according to the principles of Jewish *halakha*, orthodox Judaism's traditional code of conduct. The recent declaration of Itamar Ben Gvir, *Otzma*'s leader, that if appointed justice minister he would "restore the justice system according to the principles of Torah," perfectly vague in itself, immediately resulted in Israel's Prime Minister Benyamin Netanyahu appointing the first openly gay *Likud* politician to the position coveted by Smotrich. While David Novak is a self-declared proponent of the adoption of a theocratic regime by the citizens of Israel, he is the first to see why such theocracy cannot be identified with halachic rule: "the question arises of whether such a legal system could be operative in a state in which the majority of its citizens do not recognize its full authority."[21] Israel cannot be both a democratic and a halachic state because most Israeli citizens do not follow *halakha*, at least according to the standards of Orthodox Judaism.

The least one can say is that Novak's attempts to conceive a democratic form of Jewish theocracy are not convincing. It is not that a state where citizens would be free to consult rabbinical courts to solve their disputes and where all justice decisions would be pervaded with principles derived from the Torah is impossible to imagine;[22] it is that such a state already exists and that it is this very state of Israel that Novak blames for its myopic submission to secularist ideologies. What determines the fundamental character of the state is much less what its citizens can choose to do than what they are compelled to do. If (a) some citizens *may* decide to go before a rabbinical court but if they are all ultimately *obliged* to comply with the non-halachic, "Noahide" principles (minimal standards as to their moral content, but universal according to their extension) on which the laws of the state rely, and if (b) some judges *may* bolster their sentencing with principles borrowed from rabbinical tradition, but all judges *must* comply with a set of legal principles that are common to most democratic regimes, then (c) the state to which these citizens belong and that these judges serve is a secular democracy and not a theocracy. True, there are cases such as conversions and marriages/divorces where rabbinical courts legislate in the name of the State of Israel, but this goes to show that the secular character of this state is *already* mitigated by religious elements, so that one is at pains to conceive what Novak's mitigated concept of theocratic democracy would change to the current configuration. Adding explicit references regarding the God of Israel to a still virtual fundamental constitution or expanding the religious awareness of the Zionist movement are unlikely to trigger the radical shift of political paradigm Novak is advocating.

---

21 Novak, *Zionism and Judaism*, 157.
22 Novak, *Zionism and Judaism*, 159–77.

What is at stake is the determination of justice here and now, a judgment of Solomon deciding between the conflicting claims of the Palestinian people as they are and the Israeli state as it is—a democracy that, very much like any other democratic regime, is far from being morally flawless. It is not a justification for a political state in a moral state of perfect Levitical purity with a king-Messiah at its head that Israelis are hoping to hear from the mouth of the representatives of the Catholic Church. They are asking this determination for themselves: human beings, sinners, that nonetheless feel that they have a right to be where they are, a nation that, in spite of all its mistakes, is deeply, deeply proud of what has been accomplished during the last seventy years.

In short, I cannot see why Catholic theologians should discard Biblical revelation whenever they reflect on the type of issues of social and political justice raised by the conflict in the region. Manifestly, there is a logical gap between the Church's theology of Israel and the way it is currently applied to the analysis of the conflict. I would argue that it betrays a theoretical difficulty that is intrinsic to Catholic theology. It is this core theological problem that I would like to tackle in my last point.

SUPERSEDING SUPERCESSSIONISM

Discussing the Biblical foundations of the right of Israel to exist, official Catholic teaching is actually asking the faithful to master one of the most sophisticated thought-experiments of Husserlan phenomenology: they are supposed to develop a perfect state of empathy, *Einfühlung*, with the Jewish perspective on Zionism while suspending their personal judgment as to whether this perspective is right or not. I quoted above the statement from the Conference of the United States bishops: "Christians ... should strive to understand this link between land and people which Jews have expressed in their writings and worship throughout two millennia as a longing for the homeland, holy Zion. Appreciation of this link is not to give assent to any particular religious interpretation of this bond." We saw that this idea is reasserted in the *Notes on the Correct Way to Present the Jews and Judaism*: "Christians are invited to understand this religious attachment which finds its roots in Biblical tradition, without however making their own any particular religious interpretation of this relationship."

This strange phenomenological *epoché*, or suspension of truth-judgment, mirrors a lingering difference between the Jewish and the Catholic approaches to the Biblical roots that both traditions acknowledge as their own. When it comes to the topic of the Land, there is indeed a contrast between a reading based solely on the *Tanakh* and a reading that includes the writings of the New Testament. Among other considerations regarding the Land, the *Notes* provides the following comments in section 56: "For the author [of the Epistle to the Hebrews], the 'land' of Israel is only a symbolic pointer towards a very different land, a 'heavenly homeland.' One of the beatitudes transforms the geographical and historical meaning into a more open-ended one, 'the meek shall possess the land' (Mt 5:5); 'the land' is equivalent here to 'the kingdom of heaven' (5:3,10) in an eschatological horizon that is both present and future."

If there is no longer room for a concrete, geographical understanding of the Land given by God in a reinterpretation of the *Tanakh* in the light of the New Testament, how could the Church substantiate the right of Jews to settle on the territory where a local Palestinian population used to live, establishing thereon an independent Jewish State, on the basis of her own beliefs? As Archbishop Bustros explained in the press conference mentioned earlier, the sinister and barbaric picture of a warrior God is the immediate consequence of this outdated and superseded understanding of the Land:

> Some of the Israelis based their return on the Old Testament theme of the Promised Land. But this does not mean that God is behind their return and their victory against the Arabs. The idea of a "Warrior God" which we find in the Old Testament, a God who fights with his chosen people and condemns to death all his enemies cannot be accepted in Christianity. We have to read the Old Testament in the Spirit of Jesus Christ and in the light of His teachings. Jesus did not allow Peter to draw even a sword to fight for Him. According to Jesus' teachings, God is a God of love, peace, justice and mercy. How can we figure Him at the head of an army fighting with a particular people against other peoples?

With Bustros in the same interview, it is worth noting that the Church has not always stuck to the unilaterally metaphorized notion of the Land as well as supremely irenic picture of God that, according to Bustros, Jesus Christ came to reveal to mankind. Indeed, are medieval crusades not a proof that the Church's universalistic understanding of the kingdom of God has traditionally been perfectly compatible with the acknowledgement of ancient Canaan's special significance for the faithful, a significance so special, in actual fact, that her leaders had no qualms beseeching their warrior God to help the same Catholic faithful reconquer it by force? The call of Urban II at the cathedral of Clermont still loudly resounds in the historical memory of the Church:

> That land which as the Scripture says "floweth with milk and honey" was given by God into the possession of the children of Israel. Jerusalem is the

navel of the world; the land is fruitful above others, like another paradise of delights. This the Redeemer of the human race has made illustrious by His advent, has beautified by residence, has consecrated by suffering, has redeemed by death, has glorified by burial. This royal city, therefore, situated at the center of the world, is now held captive by His enemies, and is in subjection to those who do not know God, to the worship of the heathens. She seeks therefore and desires to be liberated and does not cease to implore you to come to her aid. From you especially she asks succor, because, as we have already said, God has conferred upon you above all nations great glory in arms."[23]

It is difficult to follow Bustros when he describes this remarkable relation of the Church to the territory of Biblical Israel as the transient "infiltration" of ideas foreign to authentic Christian faith. At least, these ideas were still very much present in the 1948 article of the *Osservatore Romano* that unofficially voiced the reaction of the Holy See to the birth of the State of Israel: "Modern Zionism is not the authentic heir of Biblical Israel but constitutes a lay-State.... This is why the Holy Land and its sacred places belong to Christianity, the true Israel."[24] Accordingly, if the authorities of the Catholic Church have shown reluctance to acknowledge the Zionist reference to Biblical Israel, it is not because they dismissed the perennial value of this territory from a religious perspective but because their religious perspective regarding this value found itself in competition with that of the Zionists. What is outdated from the point of view of modern Catholic theology is not the perennial religious significance of Biblical Canaan, but the use of the term "true Israel" to designate the advent of a Church that would simply replace the "old Israel," the Jewish nation reduced to obsolescence, cast out of God's providential design since its members refused to welcome Jesus as their Messiah and Savior.

In my opinion, what lies behind the enduring dilemma of Catholic theologians confronted with the reference of Zionism to Biblical Israel proceeds more or less consciously from a remnant of this same outdated or superseded

---

[23] Robert the Monk, *Historia Hierosolymitana*, in *Recueil des historiens des croisades*, "Historiens Occidentaux," vol. 3 (Paris: Imprimerie Royale, 1866).

[24] Quoted in Lux, *The Jewish People, the Holy Land, and the State of Israel*, 70–71. See also the answer from Pius X to Theodor Herzl seeking the support of the Vatican for the Zionist idea and movement (1904): "We cannot give approval to this movement. We cannot prevent the Jews from going to Jerusalem, but we could never sanction it. *The soil of Jerusalem, if it was not always sacred, has been sanctified by the life of Jesus Christ.* As the Head of the Church I cannot tell you anything different. The Jews have not recognized our Lord, therefore we cannot recognize the Jewish people." Quoted in Shlomo Avineri, *Herzl's Vision: Theodor Herzl and the Foundation of the Jewish State* (New York: Bluebridge, 2014), 204.

supersessionism, namely, how could the Jewish nation continue to be the object of God's providence, once again honoring his more than three-thousand-year-old promise, in spite of the Jewish rejection of Jesus, the one and only mediator of his salvation? Still proclaiming God's ongoing faithfulness to the people of the First Covenant along the lines of Paul's Romans 11 does not exclude confessing Jesus as universal mediator of God's grace. After all, why should God's faithfulness to the people of the First Covenant be conditioned by their acceptance of their true Savior? The authors of the "The Gifts and the Calling of God," the 2015 document mentioned earlier, explain that Catholic theology is not only capable of claiming that God's providence is still at work with the Jewish nation, but also that Jews who do not believe in Christ are not foreign to his grace, although non-partakers of its fullness, since the source of salvific grace is not subjective faith in Christ, but the very being of Christ. At section 26, one reads: "Christians affirm that Jesus Christ can be considered as 'the living Torah of God'. Torah and Christ are the Word of God, his revelation for us human beings as testimony of his boundless love. For Christians, the pre-existence of Christ as the Word and Son of the Father is a fundamental doctrine, and according to rabbinical tradition the Torah and the name of the Messiah exist already before creation (cf. *Genesis Rabbah* 1,1) ... Torah and Christ are the locus of the presence of God in the world as this presence is experienced in the respective worship communities."

The reassessment of the place of the Jewish nation in God's providential economy as it is presented in the most recent official documents of the Catholic Church cannot leave aside the issue of the Land. The authors of *The Jewish People and their Sacred Scriptures in the Christian Bible* already showed themselves eager to emphasize that the universalization of the concept of the Land in the New Testament does not cancel God's decision to give the Land to the Jewish nation: "It should not be forgotten, however, that a specific land was promised by God to Israel and received as a heritage; this gift of the land was on condition of fidelity to the Covenant (Lv 26; Dt 28)." One should not infer from the last sentence that, according to these theologians, the Land would be given to Israel on the condition that it becomes pure. As can be gathered from the references to Leviticus 16 and Deuteronomy 28, it is on the Land, once given, that Israel is called to offer the proof of its fidelity, lest the Land should be taken away from them. Supposing therefore, according to this modern Catholic theology of Israel, that the Jewish nation did not cease to be the object of God's providence, even after—and regardless of—its rejection of Jesus' messiahship, how could the return of Jews to the Land that God promised to give them once and for all not be interpreted as a sign of this ongoing providence? What is providence if it does not translate into concrete deeds—and what more spectacular materialization of this providence to the Jewish nation could one think of than the creation and development of the State of Israel after two thousand years of exile culminating in an attempt at global extermination? The truth is that the acknowledgement of the religious dimension of the State of Israel, a dimension that derives from its Biblical roots, is perfectly in line with the recent striving of official Catholic teaching to conceive the destiny of the Jewish nation in non-supersessionist terms. Meanwhile, the dismissal of this acknowledgement hides theological views that are downright opposed to the current tenets of this official teaching. In a word, the Magisterium is contradicting itself in the very texts that it issues.

Why not correct the problematic statements that we discussed? Why not declare, for instance, that the Church, while recognizing the religious foundations of the right of the State of Israel to exist, is committed to the implementation of existing international agreements and the search for political solutions acceptable to both parties? I already hear people arguing that a statement of this kind would achieve either too little or too much. Some will say that abstract and general concepts will hardly prevent the perpetuation of injustices on the ground, others that statements like the one just mentioned will end up justifying almost any crazy decisions made by the Israeli government. My answer to both lines of argumentation is that a stance of this kind, far from perpetuating injustices or endorsing new ones, cannot but contribute to formulating where objective justice lies in the current conflict. Indeed, objective justice proceeds from clearly defined principles of legitimacy.

Earlier, I argued that the legitimacy of international agreements, such as the never-implemented 1948 declaration that supports the creation of the State of Israel, is so much questioned that it can hardly contribute to determining political solutions along the lines of the 1993–1995 Oslo Accords; that is, a political solution that would be compatible with the existence of a viable Jewish State established within recognized and secure borders. Let me quote Archbishop Bustros once again: "The creation of the State of Israel in 1948—after the resolution of the UN in 1947 regarding the partition of Palestine which was under the British mandate between Arab and Jews—is a political issue, not a religious one. It is a fact of history like other facts: Jews who were persecuted in Europe and suffered the horrors of the *Shoah* decided to come to Palestine and build a country for their own."[25] Clearly, Bustros is arguing that what stands behind the decision by the League of Nations is the "historical fact" of Jews "wanting" to flee Europe because of the *Shoah* and "deciding" to submit by force the population living on the

---

25 Declaration of Principles on Interim Self-Government Arrangements, "Oslo Agreement," *supra* note 21 (September, 13 1993).

territory they covet in the name of their war-God. This hardly constitutes a legitimate basis for the State of Israel. In this configuration, how could measures destined to remedy unjust Palestinian suffering take into account the viability of a state established by violence? Achieving perfect justice in the case of Palestinians would necessarily imply the liquidation of this aggressive and illegitimate state. As Mahmud Abbas, the chairman of the Palestinian Authority recently wrote on his Facebook page: "Palestine means the entire national land, from the [Jordan] River to the [Mediterranean] Sea. The land is for us Palestine."[26] If Bustros shows himself so anxious to dismiss any religious aspect to the creation of the State of Israel, it is because he knows that the opposite stance would anchor the international decision in a sphere that is totally independent of modern political considerations and would therefore grant to the State of Israel the transcendent legitimacy that its leaders so desperately need in order to preserve the chances of negotiating what they see as a just and sustainable peace. Accordingly, far from being deprived of political impact, the religious dimension is key to finding a just political solution to the conflict.

The problem is that, while it can be driven by considerations related to religious factors, international law cannot itself affirm the truth of a definite religious tradition. Only a religious body can say something about the truth of another religious body. A number of Jewish politicians might be convinced of the Biblical truth of Zionism, but they will stand under the accusation of being biased as soon as they try to appeal to this truth in order to deal with the current conflict. Such is not the case of the Catholic Church, a Church that claims to be foreign to "temporal conflicts" and therefore able to deliver an impartial judgment on issues of social justice. One is left to imagine what the political impact would be of an acknowledgement of the religious truth associated with Zionism on the part of the Catholic Church.[27] What would happen if a major religious body that is not Judaism should recognize the religious foundations of the State of Israel on the basis of its common Biblical roots with a religious tradition that it has for centuries, if

---

[26] Itamar Marcus and Nan Jacques Zilberdik, "PA and Fatah present Israel 'as occupied Palestine,'" Palestinian Media Watch, May 13, 2015, http://palwatch.org/main.aspx?fi=157&doc_id=14801. It should be recalled that the charters of the PLO (1968) and Hamas (1988 and 2017) both view the State of Israel as entirely illegitimate and call for its destruction. The more lenient provisions of PLO's 1964 charter were deleted from the 1968 version that is still existent. In spite of PLO Chairman Yasser Arafat's promises to officially confirm the mutual recognition of his movement and Israeli authorities (letter of September 9, 1993 to Prime Minister Yitzhak Rabin), the 1968 PLO charter remains unchanged up to this day.

[27] Disagreeing with most commentators, I discern a skillful step in that direction in Pope Emeritus Benedict XVI, "Grace and Communion without Remorse: Comments on the Treatise *De Judaeis*," trans. Nicholas J. Healy, *Communio: International Catholic Review* 45 (Spring 2018): 163–84. True, Pope Benedict forcefully dismisses the notion of Israel as a theocratic state *de jure divino*.

not millennia, viewed as an obsolete and pernicious rival? In these circumstances, it would become much more difficult to discard the claims of Jewish politicians concerning the geographical viability and security of the Jewish State as devoid of legitimacy. The fact is that truly just political solutions on the ground must consider these vital tenets—viability and security—for the State of Israel. Catholic authorities, by radically modifying the current stance of the Magisterium regarding the conflict, could crucially contribute to the search for such a just solution.

Meanwhile, arguing that the impact of this contribution would necessarily exceed the intention of its authors by giving a free hand to the Israeli government is nothing short of nonsense in my humble opinion. Claiming that the State of Israel is heir to the Promise made to Abraham, the liberation initiated by Moses, and the kingdom ruled by David entails the exact opposite of a permission to ignore issues of social justice. If anything, it implies a duty to face them and deal with them according to the very principles that guided these Biblical forefathers. Let me ask: From where did the Church receive her understanding of justice if not from the Biblical tradition of Israel? Did the God and Messiah that she confesses not declare that he came to fulfil the Law and not to abolish it (Mt 5:17)? Torah is clearly not about sketching the outline of an ideal theocracy, not even of a perfect political state. If Torah teaches something in this respect, it is rather that all types of political states, even the most dedicated to true worship, are destined to fall apart at some point. What does not fall apart, though, is the notion of justice.

To conclude, rather than giving a free hand to the Israeli government of the moment, the acknowledgement of the religious dimension of the State of Israel would give to the Church the moral standing to single out the eventual injustices that such a government might be tempted to perpetrate. Sharing

---

He claims that, at the core of the theological doctrine that enabled the political recognition by the Vatican of the State of Israel, there "is the conviction that a strictly theologically-understood state—a Jewish faith-state [*Glaubenstaat*] that would view itself as the theological and political fulfilment of the promises—is unthinkable within history according to Christian faith and contrary to the Christian understanding of the promises," 178 (English version). I am not sure on what this "conviction" is based. There is little doubt that Benedict knows that the State of Israel in its current form is no perfect *Glaubenstaat*, neither in reality nor in the mind of its leaders. The reason for Benedict's negative emphasis might be to allow for a more subtle recognition of the providential dimension of the State of Israel *as it is*. Indeed, Benedict contrasts the "fulfilment of the promises" with their "growth and unfolding" that takes place "in the course of history." If, as Benedict shows, the Jewish exile has been an opportunity for such growth, especially when it comes to an authentic understanding of God, why should this growth and unfolding suddenly stop with the ingathering of Jews on the very Land from which they were originally scattered? The State of Israel is certainly bereft of a "theological character" according to its form and structure, but what about the very fact of its coming into existence and, last but far from least, that of its "perseverance in being"?

fundamental values regarding social justice with Jewish tradition, the leaders of the Church could denounce the objective failures of the Israeli government to comply with these values. Catholic authorities would exhort Israeli politicians to show themselves more faithful to the principles that she herself inherited from the tradition of ancient Israel. But they would do this in a spirit of humility and love, as a younger brother, mindful of his own flaws and failures, would entreat his elder brother. We are sadly far from contemplating such a disposition at this point in time.

Nothing is more trivial than claiming that religion stands in the way of a sound assessment of the rights and wrongs in a given political situation. What people usually mean by this is that one will never settle conflicts as long as one reasons in terms of the religious traditions that inspire them. Yet it is most surprising and troubling to see the official Catholic teaching embrace the same opinion and, as it were, apply it to itself: even as Church authorities claim to partake of an impartial approach to the issue, claiming to be "foreign to temporal conflicts," they shy away from a religious interpretation of it. What I have tried to show here is that this anti-theological attitude itself stems from a particular religious interpretation, albeit an outdated one, as this interpretation questions the very possibility of God's ongoing providence in favor of the Jewish nation. Even regarding such a concrete political issue as the Israeli conflict, Catholic official teaching cannot escape theology. It only needs to choose the right one—the one that is both consistent with the remaining part of the Magisterium and relevant to the search for a truly just solution to the conflict.

11

CHRISTIAN COMMUNITIES IN ISRAEL AND PALESTINE

H. B. Michel Sabbah, Patriarch Emeritus

THE LIVED EXPERIENCE OF CHRISTIAN PALESTINIANS IN ISRAEL AND PALESTINE

Who Are the Christian Palestinians?

Every believer from any religion also belongs to his/her people. Christians in France, Italy, or the United States belong to their peoples and countries. Christian French, Christian Americans, or Italians are French, Americans, or Italians. So too Palestinians are not merely Christians: they belong to a people, the Palestinian people. Palestinians are Christians, Muslims, Druze, Jews, Samaritans, or Bahais.

For the state of Israel, a Palestinian people does not exist; what exists are different ethnic or religious communities. Palestinian Arabs cannot register themselves as Palestinians in state ministries and are identified on their identity cards as Arabs, Druze, or even, most recently, Arameans. The Commission for Justice and Peace of the Assembly of the Catholic Ordinaries of the Holy Land said in one of its statements: "Israeli policy makers are increasingly insisting that Christian Palestinians are not Arabs and not part of the Palestinian people. This has been expressed in the campaign to draft Christian Palestinians into the Israeli military and most recently in a law proposed by Member of Knesset Yariv Levin, which introduces a distinction between Christian and Muslim Palestinians and states that Christian Palestinians are Christians and not Palestinians."[1]

The state divides the Palestinian population into religious communities: Muslim, Druze, Christian. The Bedouins are added to this religious division and are called by the same religious term *ta'ifa* (religious community), even though they are Muslims without distinction with regard to the rest of the Muslim community. The people, though, members of all these categories, know and are conscious that they constitute one national Palestinian community, which is characterized by different religions. Following this orientation, and due to the complex present political situation, some Christians are also confused. They sometimes insist on religion as the first and most important element of their identity. Their nation being in a situation of war, they do not know how to deal with this and thus do not see clearly who they are. Therefore, they cling to religion and the religious community, trying to find a point of stability. They take refuge in religion to survive, avoiding entering into the struggle, and allow themselves to be assimilated to this artificial political and social category, attempting to go with the flow.

A small minority has even inaugurated a new movement, holding an ideology that states that we are not Arabs but rather Arameans. It might be true that for centuries all Syria (Palestine included) spoke Aramaic. However, languages come and go following political and cultural conquests: Aramaic arrived with the Babylonians, Greek arrived with Alexander the Great and continued until the Byzantines, and then Arabic made its appearance in the seventh century with the Muslim Arab conquest and remains the language of the area. A dialect of Aramaic remains even today, in some parts of Iraq and Syria.[2] However, this overall linguistic evolution applies to Muslims and Christians alike. It applies to some Jewish communities as well, who spoke Aramaic before the revival of the modern Hebrew language (and it remains the vernacular of some Jews in places like Kurdistan even today). The people called the Arabs today assemble different ethnic populations—Copts in Egypt, Chaldeans or Assyrians in Iraq, Syrians in Syria—and all have the consciousness of sharing one history, one geographical region, belonging to the Arab people, with all its components and ethnic populations. The

---

[1] Justice and Peace Commission, March 19, 2014.

[2] The Greek language has been preserved in church liturgy in the Greek Orthodox and Catholic Churches; Syriac or Chaldean language in the Syriac, Chaldean, Maronite, and Assyrian liturgies (being also a mother tongue for some in Iraq and Syria); and Coptic in the Coptic Church in Egypt. However, today, Arabic is used everywhere as the national language, with only some expressions remaining in the ancient languages that are no longer widely spoken or understood.

Arabic language and civilization have provided an overarching identity, and Christians have contributed much to its formulation.

Christian Palestinians are certainly part of the Christian community, spread throughout the world, each local church being in communion with its mother church. According to the Middle East Council of Churches, the churches are divided into four families, the Greek Orthodox (Patriarchates of Jerusalem, Antioch, Alexandria, and the Archbishopric of Cyprus), the Eastern Oriental family (Assyrian, Chaldean, Syrian, Armenian, and Coptic), the Catholic family [seven patriarchates: the Copts, Syrians, Maronites, Greek Catholics, Chaldeans, Armenians, and the Latin (Roman Catholic) Patriarchate of Jerusalem], and finally, the extended Protestant family (the Anglicans, the Lutherans, the Presbyterians, and the Synod of the Nile). All these churches are in communion with their correspondent worldwide churches.

The Lived Experience of Christian Palestinians in Israel and Palestine

Since 1948, Christian Palestinians have lived in a situation of war that has not ended. In the state of Israel (created in 1948), this situation is expressed in the ongoing struggle for equality in a state that professes to be a democracy but institutes wide-ranging structures of discrimination because it insists that it is "a Jewish State." In Palestine (the West Bank, East Jerusalem, and Gaza) the situation is one of Israeli military occupation. Christian Palestinians live in this situation as Palestinians, hence as party to the conflict.

Inside the state of Israel, discrimination is part and parcel of the practical daily life of all Palestinian Arab citizens. There is inequality in opportunities for jobs, in access to education at every level, from kindergarten to university, in budgeting for Arab local government, in development and building, including demolition orders of so-called "illegal" houses and even entire villages, in confiscation of communal land, and in many other fields. After the promulgation of the Nation-State Law in July 2018, already-widespread discrimination became part of a basic law, affirming explicitly that the state is Jewish rather than being the state of all its citizens.

In 1948, villages which were completely or partially Christian, like hundreds of other Palestinian villages, were demolished. For example, the two completely Christian villages of Iqrit and Bir'im, on the northern border with Lebanon, were emptied of their inhabitants and then demolished. People of these two villages, living until today in Israel, are forbidden to go back home, despite a decision from the Israeli Supreme Court recognizing their right to return to their homes. There are a number of demolished or partially ruined churches as well in demolished villages and towns that were emptied of their original inhabitants inside Israel. The many Christians displaced from West Jerusalem, now living in East Jerusalem, as well as those from Haifa, Jaffa, Ramleh, and Lydda, are equally forbidden to go back home.

The attempts to wipe out the Palestinian presence, destroying the heritage of this people, including their churches and mosques, is not only a thing of the past. Continuing vandalism and attempts to burn churches and mosques and destroy cemeteries continues, promoted by extremists who are only rarely identified and sanctioned. Followers of Rabbi Meir Kahane, who formulated a particularly vicious hatred of all "non-Jews," were defended and promoted by Prime Minister Binyamin Netanyahu in the recent elections. The call too often heard, "Death to the Arabs," is directed to all members of the Palestinian people, whatever their religious belonging.

In Israel, there are also positive interactions between Palestinian citizens and the state. We have experienced a new type of social life, within the inclusive frame of civil life in Israel. Social security, particularly health care, is extended to all. However, even here discrimination is very clear, and one only needs to compare funding for institutions like schools, hospitals, and social welfare institutions in the Arab sector with those institutions in the Jewish sector to realize the extent of this discrimination.

Finally, it is noteworthy that Christian Palestinian citizens of Israel as well as their Muslim co-citizens live lives dominated by insecurity. Criminality is rife and often goes unpunished, without appropriate action by the police to maintain security. Each month, the lists of those who lose their lives in robberies, drug-related crimes, and violence against women grows. In the Occupied Territories, Palestinians, including Christian Palestinians, have almost no political rights. Often, they have no human rights either. They live under military rule. Their reality is defined by myriads of political prisoners, demolition of houses, reprisals and collective punishment, soldier, settler and police violence, and lack of freedom of movement. The siege of Gaza has been maintained for thirteen years now. All this imposed on Palestinians, Christians included. We are Palestinians. We are also human beings. All that defines the reality of others, Palestinians and Israelis too, defines our reality as Christians also.

One of the most important realities, harming the Christians beyond measure, is the confiscation of Christian-owned lands in the areas of Bethlehem (Beit-Jala, Beit Sahour) and around Ramallah.

Another tragic reality is the separation of family members, supposedly justified by security measures but implemented with no discrimination between Christian and Muslim. Palestinian, Christian, and Muslim families, wife, husband and children, are not allowed to live together because they hold different identity cards, one having an Israeli identity card, another a

Palestinian one or a foreign passport. Moreover, the threat of losing one's identity card and residency in Jerusalem because of travelling too often abroad or living in a nearby neighborhood because of the cost of living is a reality that hovers over the heads of many.

Another reality concerning all Palestinians in the West Bank and Gaza, including Christians too, is the closure of Jerusalem. Despite promises of freedom of access to the holy places, access is in fact difficult, conditioned by a system of military permits. Jerusalem is closed to many of this land's native people, those who have guarded their shrines for centuries. Jerusalem has been repeatedly declared the exclusive eternal capital of Israel and the Jewish people. However, in itself, Jerusalem is holy to three religions. So, to whom does it belong? Surely, to no one in exclusivity. It belongs to all. We must learn to adapt our national and religious rights and sentiments regarding the holiness of Jerusalem to this reality of three religions seeing in Jerusalem their holy city. God, the Lord of history, has allowed it to be for three religious communities. Jerusalem should be a place of prayer, not of war. It should be above and beyond our human violence. Presently, it is a city of war and mutual hatred, far from being holy.

These negative manifestations are fruits of the general ambiance of war and its impact on the souls of the people, generating hatred toward the other, whoever he or she is. This is also the fruit of certain theological claims and nationalist approaches formulated by some. It is the fruit of a concomitant education for war, a war that produces destruction and ruin, material and moral, also demolishing the human being. Christians are victims in this situation, like all others, victims also of theological perversion as well as of a deep human loss of perspective, expressed in the variety of destructive words and acts repeated again and again in time and place.

In fact, we are all victims, Palestinians and Israelis, of this loss of humanity, blindness in seeing the other, refusal to see the humanity of the other. This develops and spreads on both sides, whether strong or weak, oppressor or oppressed.

Jewish People and Palestinian People

Through war and daily existence, two peoples, Jewish Israelis and Palestinian Arabs, are linked. A human and Christian reflection must take into account the entire reality, seeing both Israeli and Palestinian sides. The Palestinians are a component of Israeli existence. The Israelis are a component of Palestinian existence in the concrete details of daily life in the land that is shared, in questions of war, security, justice, and peace, as well as in theological reflection.

Palestinians are at home here. For long centuries, they have been a part of the land's history. The product of this history is the reality of an indigenous people continuing its life despite the different conquerors of the country that have come and gone. They have their right to exist, to live, to develop their political and social structures and their state, a right no less significant than the right of the Jewish people. They constitute an ongoing existential question to the Jewish people and to the state of Israel. Are they allowed to exist in their land and homes not only as individuals but as an indigenous people according to Jewish Israeli and Zionist perspectives?

De facto, the relations between the two peoples are relations of a situation of war. However, on a deeper level, the relation is grounded in the fact that both peoples are made up of human beings. They live in the same land. In their search for peace and security, they confront a simple fact: one is oppressing the other. The Israeli side is the stronger, the oppressor, and the decision-maker. The Palestinians are those who react; they are in their land and homes and yet face those who have come to possess this same land. Israeli political leaders in power in recent times have repeatedly echoed an answer to the question about the right of the Palestinian people to exist in the land. They have said no to the existence of any Palestinian state, no to rights for the Palestinian people as a people. In this land there is room for a Jewish State, and there is no place for the Palestinians as a people. This means that the relationship between Jewish Israelis and Palestinian Arabs will remain defined by a situation of war.

The human being who is a believer, whether a Jew or a Christian or a Muslim, must seek for a different answer: the human being depends on God and not only on human decisions. A human and religious answer must be that both peoples are equal before God. Both are constituted of human beings. Furthermore, they can live together. God gave us both the capacity to love each other. Indeed, we can love each other, if we want to. Love makes space for the other. Political leaders should be helped to build their political vision on this reality of love and capacity of both peoples to live together and love each other. This is also a foundational aspect of interreligious dialogue here in Palestine-Israel. Any dialogue interested in the questions of God must be interested in the questions of humans, especially when humans are suffering and dying.

THEOLOGICAL REFLECTION: GOD, PEOPLE, AND WAR

I offer here some simple reflections on the biblical text, so often mobilized to justify the exclusive Jewish claim to the land. What kind of religious or theological reflection can be done in our present situation?

Theology means talking about God. It implies questions related not only to God, but also to the relationship of humanity with God, and to the call to reflect on the entirety of human reality in the light of God. All the present reality in Palestine-Israel described above is subject to religious reflection. What does God say? The Psalmist says: "I am listening. What is God's message? The Lord's message is peace for his people, for his faithful, if only they renounce their folly" (Ps 85:9). The prophet Jeremiah declares in a similar reflection: "I know what plans I have in mind for you, God declares, plans for peace, not for disaster, to give you a future and a hope" (Jer 29:11). God says peace: "justice and peace embrace" (Ps 85:11).

The basic relationship between Israelis and Palestinians today is a relationship of war, military occupation, and discrimination. A relationship of war is not a normal relationship between humans, though human history is full of wars. But if evil has dominated history, this does not make it good. Evil is evil. The same for war. War is war; it is evil, whenever it is present in human history.

What are peace and justice in this reality?

God called Abraham. He promised that he would become a great people. He promised to give him this land. With Moses, the Israelites walked toward the land and made war on the peoples they found on their way, before even reaching the Promised Land.

Under Joshua, they entered the land and were ordered to exterminate idolatry. The biblical historiographer wrote in the book of Deuteronomy, putting into the mouth of God: "As for the towns of these peoples that the Lord your God is giving you as an inheritance, you must not let anything that breathes remain alive. You shall annihilate them" (Dt 20:16–17). Extermination of humans and destruction of material objects is the literal meaning of the sacred text. But can it be understood simply literally? God is the Creator of all peoples. He is love and mercy for all. He is providence for all, today as in the past. Orders to kill and exterminate entire peoples are contradictory to the nature of God. God cannot be an exterminator of peoples. The biblical passages presenting God as a God of war have to be properly interpreted, according to the nature of God who is mercy and love.

We cannot reduce God to our own image. We are created in God's image; God is not formed in ours. God's word is life, but humans can make it a word of war or death. Likewise, the word of God in the Bible cannot be milked in order to support ideologies of death and destruction. This is a betrayal of God's word. The Bible is Good News for all, and when it is transformed into Bad News for some, it betrays what God wills for all.

Today, the land is inhabited by Palestinians, Muslims, and Christians, who cannot be assimilated to those accused of idolatry in the time of Moses and Joshua. War today is between modern Israelis and Palestinians, believers in one and the same God on both sides. As such, war is not against idolatry, it is rather against God, Creator of Israelis and Palestinians.

This land has been a Jewish land for millennia, but it has always had other populations too. Two thousand years ago, Christianity was born here, by the will of God. The Muslims arrived in the seventh century. Today, the land and those who live in it are the heirs of all three religions and of their common source in the lives of the ancient prophets of biblical Israel.

Human laws of war remain the same today as they have been for centuries, laws of man, not of God. Our times are no less cruel. We have intimate knowledge of war today like in the past. God does not take side in any of our wars, which mean destruction, demolition of the human person, and destruction of homes, simply killing others. In all wars, God says: do not kill, do not steal; all human beings, on both sides of the war, are my creatures and in my image.

Until this very day, humanity has not been able to free itself from war. Until this very day, the teaching about a just war remains unclear. If God indeed says anything within the context of our human wars, in this Palestinian-Israeli conflict too, it is the commandment: do not kill, but love one another.

The Bible is the word of God only when properly interpreted and understood. The only appropriate key of interpretation must be one that is compatible with the nature of God, our concept of God, the universal Creator of the human person, the one who comes to save that person from the consequences of bad choices. God is not the God of human armies furthering self-interest and seeking to dominate others, nor is God a God of cruel and bloody wars. In the Old Testament, when God is presented as a warrior, it is meant to underline that God cares deeply about his creatures, but as a whole, God is overwhelmingly presented as a God of mercy and compassion: "God is tenderness and pity, slow to anger and rich in faithful love" (Ps 102:10) or "I shall sing the faithful love of God forever" (Ps 89:1).

Whether in the Old Testament, or in light of Jesus Christ, or simply in the light of human wisdom and reason, God the Creator, source of all life and all goodness, is love for all creation. The vocation of the Jewish people was and still is to teach humanity who God is, a God of love and mercy, the God revealed in the pages of the Old Testament and in the teaching of Jesus.

The present situation in this land, however, is a situation of war. Yet, it should be stressed that believers in God and readers of God's word, whether Jews or Christians, whether in the land or in the rest of the world, have the same vocation: to restore the land, to make it again a land of God, who is love and mercy. A situation of war means people on each side are enemies of the other. This means, on both sides, the heart is at war; feelings are at war. It means death, the product of hardening of the heart and loss of humanity in oneself and in the other.

On the human level, one can speak about human rights versus military measures. In spiritual terms, the violation of human rights means that the other is suppressed in our heart, the other is humiliated, expelled from his home, killed, etc. The discourse of war determines who is right and who is wrong, who is oppressor and who is oppressed. However, before God, believers responsible for this cruel reality should attempt to enter into the vision of God, embodying God's love and mercy.

In this situation of war and hardening of hearts, we do fortunately find exceptions, times when the human heart triumphs, when voices and acts mobilize against war and for equality and justice. The strong of this world tend not to cede to their critics. However, those who speak out manifest hope: humanity is not lost in all hearts. Some keep it alive. They are voices of peace, of humanity on both sides, though they are not enough numerically to make a difference ... yet!

The political conflict can reach a solution. It is in the hands of the strong to restore hope and reorientation. The key is to see oneself and the other, whether Israeli or Palestinian, as a human being, and to deal with him or her as such, to make space for the other as for oneself. Equal in humanity, all creatures, created by the same God, have the same dignity, rights, and duties.

DIALOGUE WITH THE JEWISH PEOPLE WITHIN THE ISRAELI-PALESTINIAN CONTEXT

Relations between Jews and Christians for the Catholic Church is first and foremost a religious question. It is framed by the continuity between the Old Testament and the New, as stated by Our Lord Jesus Christ: "I did not come to abolish ... but to accomplish" (Mt 5:17). These relations were overshadowed for centuries from the perspective of Church discourse and teaching and the attitudes of many Christians, especially in the Christian West, where Christians held power for centuries. The "teaching of contempt" for Jews and Judaism in too many places and too often led to the marginalization and even persecution of Jews. Persecution reached its peak in the *Shoah* even though now it was the consequence of a secular ideology of extreme nationalism. Vatican II in 1965 forged a new beginning with paragraph 4 of the document *Nostra Aetate*. However, let us not forget that for Catholic Palestinians there is a second type of relation, that of daily life in this shared land, in a context of war.

The local Catholic Palestinians are, of course, party to all the decisions and positions of the Holy See on the religious level. However, to the universal Church's position, we, local Catholics and Christian Palestinians in general, add a particular light when it comes to these relations with the Jews: we add our daily life experience. Our specific input is that we are sharing daily life with Jews in Israel and Palestine, within the reality of a Jewish State and the reality of a military occupation. These relations are therefore complex. On the one hand, these are relations between two religious communities, Jews and Christians, but, on the other hand, these are also daily living relations between two peoples at war. Religion is not something abstract, removed from concrete life. It can be so for scholars in ivory towers, but not for believers sharing daily life in both good and bad contexts.

Dialogue between Jews and Catholics or Christians in general must also be a life dialogue between believers, dealing with both the vertical and horizontal dimensions of the life of the believer, that is, relationship with God and with humanity.

On the level of the vertical relationship with God, we are always faced with the same truth, the same commandment of love: love your neighbor as yourself. Jews are my neighbors; Palestinians are also my neighbors. Palestinians are also my own people. Before God, the same commandment of love rules in both cases, with the Jewish people and with my own people, the Palestinians. Love means to wish good for my neighbor, as God would want it, on all levels, religious, political, and in all other domains of life.

Biblical givens, like "chosen people," "covenant," and "promised land," when inserted into the political situation, pose challenges to Christian Palestinians and also to all Christians. What is the connection between these biblical givens and the ongoing violence in Palestine today? Religions, unfortunately, have been involved throughout the centuries in religious wars. The Bible has only too often been used as an instrument to justify these wars, mobilizing God on one side of the conflict. But let not human erring becoming a rule. It should be rather an experience by which we profit to correct our behavior today.

Our life as Palestinians, Christian Palestinians included, as has already been said, is subjected to Israeli violence, whether as reprisal for Palestinian violence or as a cause of it. What role does God play, in the Jewish faith and in the Catholic faith, in this violence when reflected on from a theological point of view? This is a question which must be answered.

Interreligious dialogue, especially Jewish-Christian dialogue, cannot ignore the whole reality of Palestine today, especially because that reality is seen, by Jews and Christians, through the lens of the Bible, too often positioning God on one side against the other. God cannot be taken as the justification for any act of human violence. Dialogue cannot be conducted at the expense of ignoring reality. Dialogue about God must bring to the fore what is most important for God: the human being and his or her relation with his or her neighbor, particularly when relations are difficult and provoke situations of hatred and death.

Our situation of war or non-war is an aspect of religious life. A double dialogue is needed: first, a political dialogue, to help all have a fair share in the land; second, a human and religious dialogue, to consider the human aspects of the conflict. Israelis and Palestinians being equal human beings, all created by God, all created to love as God Creator is love, must also have equal political rights and duties.

Today the two peoples are inextricably interlinked. They do not need more statements pro or contra; rather they need a vision of God, a God of all the universe and all humankind, of the Jewish people and the Palestinian people alike. They need a vision of the human person, based on a focus on the human being, Jews and Palestinians alike. They need people who work for reconciliation. The true friend of one and all, no matter what side he or she belongs to, is the one who helps bring peace and equality, and hence security. A friend that helps one side become stronger in war is not helping either side, as he abandons people to war.

When dialogue enables the word of God, common to both sides, to speak out loud and clear, the word of God speaks directly about past hostilities in the Holy Land, about the Jewish people, about the Palestinian people and their relationship to the land. The value of life is absolute. God cannot be considered as a destroyer of life or one who supports destruction. God does not even will the death of the sinner. God says through the Prophet Isaiah: "Let the wicked abandon his way and the evil one his thoughts. Let him turn back to God who will take pity on him, to our God, for he is rich in forgiveness" (Is 55:7; cf Ez 33:11).

God is love. He orders us to love one another, even the enemy. This means even if you are in a context of hostilities, you must seek ways out of this situation. Because war is not human, we cannot take refuge in God in order to kill or in order to make war.

ZIONISM AND ZIONIST APPROACHES OF SOME CHRISTIANS

Zionism is a political ideology that promoted the establishment of the state of Israel and continues to support it. This nineteenth-century European movement led to the foundation of the state of Israel in 1948. It has also led to concrete wars and the hostilities that still continue with the Palestinian people. Even today, much of Zionism is fully engaged in promoting a situation of war and taking concrete hostile actions against the Palestinian people.

It is true that there were Zionist thinkers like Martin Buber and Judah Magnes who were clairvoyant in perceiving the dark side of a Jewish nationalist movement that allied itself with colonial powers and ignored the existence of an indigenous population in Palestine. They issued warning after warning about the dire consequences of adopting a nationalism that obscured the humanity of the other, in particular the Palestinian other. Prophetic voices like theirs continue even today to warn about the choices of the Israeli political and military establishment, promoting occupation, discrimination, and ongoing violence and war. However, these voices have remained in the margins and have not succeeded in influencing the type of Zionism that has been adopted by the Israeli establishment from the time of David Ben Gurion in 1948 to Binyamin Netanyahu in the present. Humanist Zionism has remained only in words, but the actions of the state of Israel, driven by uncompromising nationalism, have created the cruel reality that Palestinians have to face.

A Christian Zionist vision supports the political facts that were determined by Jewish Zionists, creating the reality of war, justifying them with the Bible, and pretending that this is the word of God. Indeed, the word of God gives a special place to the Jewish people (using, in the Old Testament terms like "land," "covenant," and "election"), but the Word of God, in the unity of the Old Testament with the New, insists that the election of the Jews is for the benefit of all, a promise realized in the coming of Jesus Christ, the Jew from Nazareth. Jesus, in his flesh, brought down the walls of enmity between Jews and Gentiles and went beyond the borders between peoples, stretching them ever further until they are pushed to the ends of the earth. Dealing with God, we have already said, a Christian knows that God is for all. Saint John said, "God is love" (1 Jn 4:8.16), and his commandment for all is: love your neighbor, all neighbors, Israelis and Palestinians alike. To bring the Bible into a situation of war, a believer in God, whether Jew or Christian, needs to follow the logic of God, which is not a logic of human war. "My thoughts are not your thoughts and your ways are not my ways," God says (Is 55: 8).

Simple theology, based on the commandment of love, says: Love the Jewish people, let them have a state, but also love the Palestinian people and let them have a state, and let them live as equal citizens in any political solution, accepted by both, that guarantees absolute equality, regardless of ethnicity, religion, or origin. Christian Zionists, if they are Christian, need to take seriously this basic commandment of love. They love the Jewish people, and this is a Christian attitude. However, too many of them do not show any love for the Palestinian people, Muslims and Christians, and this is not a Christian attitude. If you are Christian, you love everybody, Israeli and Palestinian, and the true love of Israelis and Palestinians is to help them reach peace and reconciliation, guaranteeing justice, human dignity, and equality.

Zionism, whether Jewish or Christian, is a human ideology that too often promotes war. There are Zionists like Martin Buber and others that wanted to share the land. However, their voices are heard only in the margins. Too often, Zionism implies hostile actions in order to take all of Palestine and give it to the Jewish people alone. Zionism has too often promoted military modalities of action and encouraged warring with Palestinians, and the results are clear to those who look at history: massacres, expulsions, forced emigration, expropriation of land, confiscation of property, house demolition.... Human logic can see this, and theology should not be used to legitimate it. Sincere religion consists in adoring God and respecting all God's creatures. Christianity, and the Catholic Church as part of it, must recognize the Jewish people for what it is, but it cannot as Church support Zionism or any ideology of nationalism that promotes war against another people. The Church cannot support the oppression of one people by another people. Theology must not accept a doctrine that promotes harming the other. The Jewish people must be protected from all persecution and antisemitism, whether religious or racist. It might have a state, but not at the expense of another people.

Of course, this is a complex issue. The state of Israel was established at the expense of another people. In 1948, hundreds of thousands of Palestinians were expelled or fled from the territories that constituted the newly established state, which was recognized by the international community. Those who found themselves exiled from their homeland were not permitted to return even after the hostilities had ended. Instead, the state of Israel promoted the migration of hundreds of thousands of Jews to the new state, where they received immediate citizenship. Whereas the state of Israel legislated a "Law of Return" for Jews, allowing any Jew to come to Israel, the Palestinians' right of return to their homes was denied. The Palestinians have had to accept this reality, established in a grave injustice. However, what cannot continue is the ongoing trampling of the Palestinians' human rights. Those that remain in Israel must have full equality as equal citizens and participate in the governance of the state that has become theirs. Those Palestinians that live in the territories that were occupied by Israel after the 1967 War, when Israel conquered the rest of historical Palestine, must be liberated from the regime of military occupation and be empowered to have control over their lives, in their own independent state. And there remains the basic, yet always postponed, question of the refugees, promised, since the beginning, by an official international decision that they would be able to go back to their homes, and yet have always been forbidden to go home. It remains a capital pending problem.

Talk of even a minimal Zionism that can be recognized by the Catholic Church is to invite the Church to support an ideology that has led to war and racism and continues to block solutions to the problem it created. This is against the nature of the Church. This is against the nature of God. There cannot be a minimal or a maximal recognition of ideologies of exclusivist nationalism and war.

The concrete question, if we talk about Church recognition of Zionism, is: Are we, Christian Palestinians as well as our Muslim brothers and sisters, preordained by the word of God, to leave our land and our homes in favor of the Jews? What does the Catholic Church say? Does the Church have an answer to this question? Before thinking of any minimal recognition of Zionism, we need to think first about the people harmed by Zionist ideology since its inception.

The mission of Catholics, as Church, as theologians, and as individuals, toward the Jewish people and the state of Israel is to help both Israelis and Palestinians come to reconciliation on the basis of the same principles, as human beings, with the same God-given dignity, rights, and duties. The Church's mission is reconciliation, working for ever more justice and peace, first in the hearts of both parties, then on the ground. St. Paul says we are messengers of reconciliation: "He gave us the ministry of reconciliation" (2 Cor 5:18).

If you refer to God, this means that you make place for God and for all God's children, who are created in God's image. If you do not accept the logic of God, the love of God, do not ask God to support your wars. Make your wars alone, without God, without biblical references, and without the Church. When it comes to politics and war, we need even more a God of mercy and love, who commands all parties to practice mercy and love.

CONCLUSION

The Christian attitude to the Jewish people in Israel is to cultivate a relationship that is appropriate to the two religions, Christianity and Judaism. However, it is also a relationship to a living people, the Jews and Christians in the state of Israel. These two peoples are existentially linked, as Israelis and Palestinians, Jews as Israelis, Christians as Palestinians. Each one has become part of the existence of the other.

The state of Israel was created in 1948. In order to survive, and in order not to remain under permanent threat from its neighbors, someone must dare say to this state of Israel that the present situation of crushing the Palestinians is not the right way to security. Reconciliation is the right way, reconciliation on the basis of equality as citizens, as human beings, and as peoples. Once the Palestinians have the same rights as the Israelis, then Israel will be secure. It will win and survive.

Renowned Israeli writer David Grossman said in 2018 at a ceremony to commemorate the fallen of both sides:

> Home is a place whose walls—borders—are clear and accepted; whose existence is stable, solid, and relaxed; whose inhabitants know its intimate codes; whose relations with its neighbors have been settled. It projects a sense of the future. And we Israelis, even after 70 years ... we are not yet there. We are not yet home. Israel was established so that the Jewish people, who have nearly never felt at-home-in-the-world, would finally have a home. And now, 70 years later, strong Israel may be a fortress, but it is not yet a home. The solution to the great complexity of Israeli-Palestinian relations can be summed up in one short formula: if the Palestinians do not have a home, the Israelis won't have a home either. The opposite is also true: if Israel will not be a home, then neither will Palestine.

This country, with all of us in it, needs more spiritual purification, whatever religion we belong to, Jews, Christians, Muslims, Druze. There is too much hatred in the country, too much injustice, too much killing, too many political prisoners, and too little peace. We need more love; love will guide us toward justice. When each of us sees ourselves as human beings and sees the other as a human being, when we believe in ourselves and in the other, when we are able to love and to live together, when we exchange hatred with love, we will be able to live life to the full. This needs a new political vision and new political decisions. It needs, in particular, a new education of the people.

The Church, meanwhile, is not required to take partial steps in favor of this side or the other, such as the adoption of a "minimal Zionism," when in fact Zionist ideology has lit the fire of the refusal of the other, contributing to more hostility. Meanwhile, the Church and her theologians, who believe in God and human beings, must direct their reflection to help both peoples toward reconciliation.

The land of the Lord is today the Land of Israelis and Palestinians, Jews, Christians, Muslims and Druze. The holiness of the land also depends on peace in it, and that means equal dignity, rights, and duties for all. It requires that the Church's actions and the theologians' reflections have a common vision of all the inhabitants of the Holy Land, of all the religions there present, and constitute a help for them to come nearer to the holiness that the land is supposed to radiate. More love is required as well as mutual respect and equality. What is required from all is to be aware of the whole reality of the land, the Jewish reality, the Palestinian reality, the human reality, and the sad reality of war. We are still oppressor and oppressed, and the help needed for transformation is more love, more reconciliation. All those who love the Jewish people and want to help them should help them toward reconciliation. This is the true love for the land of God, for the Jewish people, and for the Palestinians, all of us creatures of God, all equal before him, created by him to live in peace, justice, equality, and security.

12

CHRISTIAN-JEWISH RELATIONS FROM A CHRISTIAN PALESTINIAN PERSPECTIVE
Jamal Khader

A Catholic engagement in relationship with the Jewish people is rooted in a context. For many in the Church today that context is forged in Europe in the mid-twentieth century. What do Christian-Jewish relations look like from the perspective of a Catholic theologian who is a Palestinian Arab? How does that perspective impact how Catholic theology might see the Land of Israel and the State of Israel?

In order to understand the Catholic teaching on the Land and the State of Israel, we need to go back to the Western context of the relations between Catholics and Jews. After centuries of negative attitude of the Church toward the Jews, World War II and the horrible events of the Holocaust represent a turning point in this attitude of the Catholic Church to begin a serious and beneficial dialogue with the Jews. The reply of Pope Pius X to Theodor Herzl in 1904 is known to everyone. The second half of the twentieth century represented a new context in the relations between the Catholic Church and the Jews, or the Jewish people, especially with the fourth paragraph of *Nostra Aetate* in the Second Vatican Council.

Is this the same context for the Christians of Palestine? Christian Palestinians did not see their relations with the Jews from a theological perspective, but from a political one. We reacted to the Jewish emigration to Palestine as Palestinians: we opposed the partition of Palestine in 1947 as an unjust plan; more than sixty thousand Christians were expelled from historic Palestine[1] (the two thirds of the Christians, the same percentage as

---

1 George Kossaibi, "Demographic Characteristics of the Arab Palestine People," in *The Sociology of the Palestinian*, ed. Khalil Nakhleh and Elia Zureik (London: Croom Helm, 1980), 18.

of all the Palestinians expelled from Palestine and becoming refugees); the Christian Palestinians joined the Palestinian National movement, like any other Palestinian. The Palestinian-Israeli conflict was seen as a political one.

When it comes to the land, the land for the Palestinian Christians is the space where we are called to worship God and build his Kingdom. We were born here. We lived here for the last two thousand years. This is our homeland, the only homeland that we have. Do we need a theology to justify belonging to this land? We were and still are blessed by being witnesses of our faith here, in the land sanctified by God's promises, and by the life, death, and resurrection of Jesus Christ.

A Palestinian theology of the land comes as a reaction to a Western theology that denies us the right of belonging to the land and justifies the dispossession of our homeland with supposedly biblical arguments. A Christian Palestinian perspective is not primarily "theological"—it is a reflection on the attachment to this land, an attachment required and inspired by our faith.

TRADITIONAL PALESTINIAN READINGS OF THE BIBLE

> Our connectedness to this land is a natural right. It is not an ideological or a theological question only. It is a matter of life and death.[2]

Allow me to tell you my story with the Bible, which is the story of all Christians in the Holy Land. I began reading the Bible at an early age, beginning with the New Testament. The Bible was always the Good News of our salvation. The story of the Bible was my story, the story of my land. God chose my land to reveal himself and to send the patriarchs, the prophets, and finally his son for all humanity. God sanctified our land with the events of salvation. Living around the holy places adds a spiritual value to our reading the Bible. The places it mentions are our towns and villages; the patriarchs and the prophets are our forefathers in faith. We are deeply acquainted with the geography of the land and the culture of the Bible, both in the Old and New Testaments. It is our culture.

Our religious life gravitates around the holy places. Christian feasts are celebrated in the holy places where they took place: Christmas in Bethlehem, the Annunciation in Nazareth, and Easter in Jerusalem. Pilgrimages are organized to Jerusalem to participate in the procession of Palm Sunday, to walk the Via Dolorosa on Good Friday, to visit in August (preferably on foot)

---

[2] *A moment of truth: A word of faith, hope and love from the heart of Palestinian suffering*, "Kairos Palestine Document," World Council of Churches, 2.3.4 (December 11, 2009).

the tomb of Mary at the Mount of Olives, and to participate in the holy fire ceremony on Holy Saturday. Besides the "history of salvation," there is also a "geography of salvation." The Holy Land becomes the fifth Gospel:

> This is a land where our Fathers in faith lived; a land where the voice of the prophets was heard speaking in the name of the God of Abraham, of Isaac and of Jacob; a land [where] the presence of Christ, most of all, blessed and sanctified all Christians and, we may say, all human kind. No one can forget that when God wanted to choose, as a human being, a home, a language, a family in this world, he took them from the East.... He became an infant in Bethlehem, a teenager and a worker in Nazareth, Master and Healer all over the region, Crucified and Risen from the tomb that still exists in the "Church of the Resurrection", as it is called by the Christians in that land.[3]

Our roots go back to the first apostolic community, and we continue the Christian presence in a long and sometimes difficult history, so that when pilgrims visit the holy places, they find a Christian community, the living stones of the local church. We witnessed to our faith in this land, we endured the vicissitudes of history, and we intend to continue this presence into the future. This is where God wants us to be and where we can fulfill our vocation as Christians.

The "fifth Gospel" is both the land and the people living in it. When we encourage Christian pilgrims from all over the world to come to the Holy Land, we ask them to "come and see," to meet the local community, the living witnesses of our faith, and then to return carrying a message of peace, love, and reconciliation.[4]

Spiritual Reading of the Bible

When we read the Bible we read it as one book, beginning with creation and ending with the Second Coming of Christ. God began his story with human beings at creation, and it culminates in Jesus Christ, until the Kingdom to come. The story told by the Bible is our story: we were in Egypt, we came to the Promised Land, and we were unfaithful to the law of God. Then the all-merciful God sent his Word, Jesus Christ, to fulfill the promises of the prophets. In that spiritual reading, we are the people of God. Abraham, Isaac, and Jacob are our forefathers, and the blessings of God continue in Jesus Christ. In that reading, we see the Almighty opening the borders of

---

3 Pope Paul VI, Apostolic Exhortation *Nobis in animo*, March 25, 1974.
4 See "Kairos Palestine Document," 6.2.

his chosen people to include all the nations. And when we read that Jesus "demolished the wall separating the Jews from the Gentiles" (Eph 2:14), we see ourselves as spiritual descendants of the first community of Jews who believed in Jesus, not from the Gentiles who joined the Church later. When I first read Acts 13, where Paul proclaimed in the synagogue of Antioch, "We now turn to the Gentiles. For so the Lord has commanded us, 'I have made you a light to the Gentiles, that you may be an instrument of salvation to the ends of the earth.' The Gentiles were delighted when they heard this and glorified the word of the Lord" (Acts 13:46–48), I felt the joy of the Gentiles joining the Church opening up to welcome all nations.

In that reading, we never gave political importance to the frontiers of the land, but we always recognized the land as holy because of its primordial place in God's history with humanity.

Palestinian Context

I was less than three years old in June 1967 when the Israeli army occupied the remaining Palestinian territories. My first memories in life were of sitting down on the ground in front of the parish church beside my mother and all the women and children in my native village, with my hands on my head, and soldiers pointing their guns against us. The men were gathered in a different place, but my father was not with them. He was on his way back from Germany, where he had been working since 1965. When he arrived, the war was over, with the occupation of my land, that occupation that is still there. He had to cross the Jordan River illegally, before the census began a month later. Like more than 90 percent of the Palestinians, we knew nothing in our lives but occupation.

In 1948, Palestinians lost 78 percent of the land, and more than 730,000 people became refugees. There are now more than 6 million still living in refugee camps. That was the *Nakba* (Catastrophe) of the Palestinians. In 1967, the remaining 22 percent of the land was occupied by the Israeli army, and the military occupation continues until today with no sense of an end in the near future. Palestinians were first denied their existence, with the slogan "a land without people for a people without land." We are denied our narrative, as the 1948 war is presented many times as "the aggression of the Arab countries against Israel" and the War of Independence, not the *Nakba*. We are denied not only our national and personal rights, but our suffering as well, as the dominant narrative suggests that only one people suffered: the Jewish people. And now the Bible is read in an anti-Palestinian way, turning it to be "bad news" for the Palestinians by justifying the dispossession of our land with the Bible. We've heard certain Catholic theologians affirm in various ways that the return of Jews to their land is a sign of hope, or a sign of God's faithfulness toward his people, or a sign of God's ongoing providence. These kinds of affirmations make the sufferings of the Palestinian people either irrelevant to God's plan or part of it. In both cases, God becomes a tribal God, not the Father and Creator of all human beings in his image and resemblance.

Any recognition of a religious nature of the right of the State of Israel to exist gives this same state a divine right which places it above international law. Is Israel a state like any other state, and therefore should it be treated according to international law and political principles? Or is it a divinely sanctioned state, different from any other state? Is the Catholic Church in favor of religious states, including Islamic states? Accepting that Israel is a Jewish State means that some of the citizens have more rights than others.

New Challenges Coming from the West

When we began to hear different readings of the Bible, mainly the Old Testament, linking the texts of the Old Testament with contemporary events, we were challenged by them, and many Christian Palestinians were shocked. In those new Jewish and Western readings, the Hebrews of the Bible become the Israelis, and Israel of the Bible is compared with the State of Israel. The promises of the Old Testament are applied to the new political realities.

The Bible is used to justify the occupation of my land and the oppression of my people. My land is presented as being the "Promised Land" that God gave to his "chosen people," the Jewish people. And many passages in the Bible affirm that this promise was eternal. I began to have problems reading the Bible, and I began struggling with the Bible, as Jacob did with the Angel of the Lord. I continue to struggle with it.

Many Jewish settlers come to take Palestinian land and build illegal settlements on it with the Bible in hand. If they are asked about the ownership of the land, they will use the Bible as their document of ownership. There are more than half a million religious and non-religious settlers in occupied Palestinian land.

Those readings represent an existential challenge, not an abstract or theological one. How can the God of Jesus Christ that I believe in take away my land to give it to another people?

Facing these new readings, some Palestinian Christians stopped reading the Old Testament, as they were confused by the political meaning given to the Word of God. In some liturgical texts, we even used to replace the word "Israel" with "Jacob," or "the people." The local Church kept the texts as they were, and tried to dissociate them from the political reality, and it always insisted on the unity of the Bible as the Word of God. One significant contribution of the Church was the pastoral letter of His Beatitude Michel Sabbah in 1993, "Reading the Bible Today in the Land of the Bible." In that letter, he wrote:

> For the Christian, the two Testaments form a single book, containing the whole of Revelation given by God for the salvation of humankind. No part of the Old or New Testament can be separated from it for any reason, whether political or otherwise. All of Sacred Scripture is the Word of God."[5]

The Second Vatican Council reiterated the unity of the two testaments as inspired by God:

> The Catholic Church, relying on the belief of the Apostles,[6] holds that the books of both the Old and New Testaments in their entirety, with all their parts, are sacred and canonical because written under the inspiration of the Holy Spirit, they have God as their author and have been handed on as such to the Church herself.[7]

Although we may still find some Christians who express confusion when some texts are read in churches, that tendency is very limited. The traditional teaching of the Church sees the realities and main figures of the Old Testament as prototypes of the New Testament. Isaac, Joseph, David, and Jonah are prototypes of Jesus. The law "was our guardian until Christ came that we might be justified by faith. Now that this faith has come, we are no longer under a guardian" (Gal 3:24–25). The Old Testament is the Word of God, and it helps us to understand the plan of God for human beings and the salvation of God in Jesus Christ.

In this reading of the texts of the Old Testament, the land is seen as a prototype of the Kingdom of God, the Church, or the Kingdom of Heaven: Jesus leads us to the Promised Land "flowing with milk and honey" (Jos 13:27); he guides us to the "new earth and new heavens" (Rv 21:1) where the "lamb" will be at the center of the heavenly Jerusalem (Rv 21:22). Several times, the "land" means simply the whole earth that God created and sanctified with his presence.

---

5 Fourth Pastoral Letter of Patriarch Michael Sabbah, *Reading the Bible Today in the Land of the Bible*, no. 9 (November 1993).

6 See Jn 20:31; 2 Tm 3:16; 2 Pt 1:19–20, 3:15–16.

7 Vatican Council II, *Dei Verbum*, no. 11 (November 18, 1965).

A Contextual Reading

Patriarch Emeritus Michael Sabbah summarizes the questions raised by those readings in his pastoral letter "Reading the Bible Today in the Land of the Bible":

> How is the Old Testament to be understood? What is the relationship between the Old and the New Testament? What is the relationship between ancient Biblical history and our contemporary history? Is Biblical Israel the same as the contemporary State of Israel? What is the meaning of the promises, the election, the Covenant and in particular the "promise and the gift of the land" to Abraham and his descendants? Does the Bible justify the present political claims? Could we be victims of our own salvation history, which seems to favor the Jewish people and condemn us? Is that truly the Will of God to which we must inexorably bow down, demanding that we deprive ourselves in favor of another people, with no possibility of appeal or discussion?[8]

Faced with those new challenges, local theologians began to reflect on the Bible and on our faith to find answers to them. The questions asked by Patriarch Sabbah in his pastoral letter are the same questions raised by the faithful to their pastors, and we need to address them. Let us have a quick look at those challenges, and then examine the response of Palestinian theology to them.

BIBLICAL ARGUMENTS CONCERNING THE LAND

After decades of national Zionism, a religious Zionism began to prevail, making the Palestinian-Israeli conflict a religious one. Biblical arguments are used by many religious Jews and politicians as well.

These religious Zionist arguments tend to go as follows: "God gave us this land; it is *Eretz Yisrael*; it is ours and only ours. If the State of Israel is part of the unfolding of a messianic scenario, then the miraculous victory of the 1967 War was an essential stage in that process. The territories belong to the Jewish people (i.e., the State of Israel) by divine decree, and they may not be handed over to foreign hands."[9]

---

8 Michael Sabbah, *Reading the Bible Today in the Land of the Bible*, n7c.

9 See Eliezer Siegel, *Zionism: Radical Messianic Zionism*, Jewish Virtual Library, http://www.jewishvirtuallibrary.org/radical-messianic-zionism.

The Israeli occupation of the West Bank in the 1967 War aroused the passionate determination in many Israelis to ensure that these territories should be permanently part of the State of Israel, mainly by establishing Jewish settlements in the occupied territories and by opposing any territorial concessions. Later the idea of promoting the extension of Israeli sovereignty over the occupied territories became a more acceptable idea for a few political parties.

Some rabbis, like Rabbi Zvi Yehuda Kook, believed that the era of redemption for the Jewish people had already begun with the rise of modern Zionism and the growing Zionist enterprise in Palestine, and that they were indeed living in the messianic age.[10] Rabbi Kook defined the State of Israel as the halakhic Kingdom of Israel, and the Kingdom of Israel as the Kingdom of Heaven on earth. Land acquired a sacred status as "the Land of Israel—every grain of its soil—is holy. Thus no individual can escape holiness and every place upon which a Jewish foot is set is holy."[11]

Few Jewish fundamentalists concentrated on the more aggressive biblical passages, in which God commanded the Israelites to drive out the indigenous people of the Promised Land, to make no treaty with them, to destroy their sacred symbols, and even to exterminate them.[12] Their reading of the Bible is selective.

The results of such beliefs are disastrous for Palestinians and for the possibilities of peace in Palestine/Israel. Palestinians are dispossessed of their land, they are not recognized as citizens with equal rights because the state is "Jewish" (that is, "not for all its citizens")[13], settlements are built on our land in the name of "returning to biblical sites," refugees are denied the right to return home to what has become Israel or even to the Occupied Territories. In our struggle to obtain our legitimate rights, we are faced with theological arguments to deny our national and personal rights.

After the Second World War, Western Christians have been progressively discovering the Jewish roots of their faith, increasing their sympathy for Jews and Jewish political claims. Zionism is interpreted in accordance with what the Bible says, particularly the Old Testament that posits the Jewish people in the land promised to them by God.

We can talk about two different Christian readings, one concerning the Christian Zionists and the second the European post-Holocaust reading.

10 See Zvi Yaron, *The Teaching of Rav Kook,* 3rd ed. (Jerusalem: Jewish Agency, 1979), 270–73.
11 Uriel Tal, "The Foundations of Political Messianism in Israel," *Ha'aretz,* September 26, 1984.
12 Ex 23:23–33; Jos 6:17–21, 8:20–29, 11:21- 25.
13 Israel Today, "Netanyahu: Israel is NOT a State of All Its Citizens. It's the JEWISH State," (March 10, 2019), https://www.israeltoday.co.il/read/netanyahu-israel-is-not-a-state-of-all-its-citizens-its-the-jewish-state/.

For Christian Zionists the biblical text is understood without any historical context or critical distance and the events described in the Bible are applied to present realities. An untroubled continuity is seen between the Jewish commonwealth in Palestine before 70 CE and the emergence of the State of Israel in 1948. The land has been promised to the Jews and this promise is as valid today as it was in the days of Abraham. God's plan for redemption works through Israel. It was only because Israel refused Jesus Christ that the Church was founded, this vision being founded on a reading of Romans 9–11. According to Christian Zionism, the time of the pagans (the time of the Church of the Gentiles) is coming to an end as predicted by Jesus in Luke 21:24. The events of 1948 (the establishment of the State of Israel) and 1967 (the extension of Jewish sovereignty over the Old City of Jerusalem) seem to point to the approaching end. In this war scenario, Islam and Muslims play the role of the powers of darkness.

Another Western theology comes from the European post-Holocaust context. After centuries of "the teaching of contempt" concerning the Jews, accusing them of refusing to believe in Jesus and asserting that they were replaced by the Christian Church as the people of God, a new approach to the Jews and the Old Testament emerged in Europe. These new theologies were mainly motivated by the horrors of the Holocaust and the need to build a positive relationship and dialogue with the Jewish people. In this context, a new dialogue was much-needed and it allowed Christians to discover the Jewish roots of our faith. In the meanwhile, some theologians translated this new approach into a political support for the State of Israel and its policies including the occupation of Palestinian lands. In those theologies, Palestinians are often absent.

Over the years, some of these Western theologians have realized that the Palestinian people exist. Among these theologians are those whose writings are present in this collection, like Gavin D'Costa and Etienne Vetö. Like their European colleagues, their basic theologies of reconciliation and solidarity with the Jewish people and support for a theological appreciation of the significance of the State of Israel have been formulated in the post-Holocaust European context. However, as they observe from afar the suffering of the Palestinian people resulting from the realities of Israeli occupation and discrimination, they have realized that completely ignoring the existence of the Palestinian people (or worse, justifying the Palestinian catastrophe in theological terms) is ethically unacceptable.

In their attempts to include a reflection on the Palestinians, they remain committed to their sympathy for Zionism and are unwilling or unable to make a separation (as have some anti-Zionist Jews) between a rereading of Jews and Judaism and the ideology of modern Zionism. Committed primarily to the reconciliation with the Jewish people, they place the Palestinian issue in the margins, first affirming Zionism and then struggling to minimize the injustices that are inherent to the Zionist ideology. They understand an acceptance of Zionism as essential to the noble project of reconstructing a healthy relationship with the Jewish people in a post-Holocaust world. Most of their Jewish partners in dialogue would insist on the essential inclusion of Zionism in an appreciation of who Jews are today and many of these partners squirm at the very mention of the Palestinian people.

However, it is not enough to attempt to mitigate the damage Zionism has caused. Instead, these theologians are invited to a radical reformulation of their theologies. Just as it was necessary to completely rethink Christian theology after Auschwitz, purging it of anti-Judaism, so it is necessary to put the reflection on the Palestinian *Nakba* at the center of a theology of the land and a theological reflection on the reality in Palestine/Israel today. It is not enough to adjust theologies that are basically sympathetic to Zionism in order to make them appear ethical. What is necessary is not just a theology that is sympathetic to Jewish sensibilities but a theology that is equally sympathetic to a Palestinian cry for justice in the land. Such a theology can only be enunciated when the theologian is willing to think from the Palestinian perspective. D'Costa and Vetö, along with others who see as they do that there is a troubling problem on the horizon, are invited into the Palestinian context. Perhaps they need to rethink their theologies from the other side of the Wall, in the heart of a Gaza under siege or a Palestinian refugee camp. From that perspective it becomes impossible to read the Bible in the same way.

A theology profoundly sensitive to Jews and Palestinians can embrace the revolution that has centralized the reflection on Jesus the Jew and the heritage that Jews and Christians hold in common. It would also embrace a Jesus who refuses occupation, discrimination, and the ideological manipulation of sacred text to justify them. Such a theology cannot make shortcuts to reconciliation that ignore the gaping wound that is Palestine and the Palestinians in today's world.

PALESTINIAN THEOLOGY OF THE LAND

In recent years, a few Palestinian theologians have published books and articles on the issue of the land, mainly in English. This effort was supported and motivated by the Kairos Palestine Document, with all the interest it sparked in many Christian environments. Within this work, Palestinian theology developed some interpretative keys. We cannot pretend that we have the answers to all the questions. We read the Bible to learn from it and find in it salvation and life, not to use and abuse it to make it support our positions.

A Christological Reading of the Old Testament

"Our Lord Jesus came, proclaiming that the Kingdom of God was near. He provoked a revolution in the life and faith of all humanity. He came with 'a new teaching' (Mk 1:27), casting a new light on the Old Testament, on the themes that relate to our Christian faith and our daily lives, themes such as the promises, the election, the people of God and the land."[14]

Jesus is the one who explains to us the Scriptures, including the meaning of "promised land," "chosen people," and "the promises." It is through the life, teaching, and mission of Jesus that we can understand the Old Testament. The Christological reading of the Old Testament is not the only reading of the Old Testament, but it is a legitimate and valid reading. The Old Testament and the New constitute one book. If we read the Old Testament as if the New does not exist, the message and life of Jesus is meaningless in its relation to the plan of God.

What about the promises of the Old Testament? The Old Testament is the first part of the Bible, and the meaning can be understood by the whole Bible. The New Testament testifies that those promises were fulfilled in Jesus Christ. "The promises were spoken to Abraham and to his seed. Scripture does not say 'and to seeds,' meaning many people, but 'and to your seed,' meaning one person, who is Christ. . . . If you belong to Christ, then you are Abraham's seed, and heirs according to the promise" (Gal 3:16, 29). "For all the promises of God are 'Yes' in Christ" (2 Cor 1:20).

In this vision of the unity of the Bible, we explore the teachings of Jesus about the land. Although we cannot find a "theology" of the land in the teachings of Jesus, we find clear indications of his vision. When asked about geography and a specific place to worship God, Jesus replied that "true worshippers will worship the Father in spirit and truth" (Jn 4:23). Jesus, who came from a specific people, the Jewish people, and lived in a specific land, the Holy Land, opens up his vision of the land to include the whole earth; he sends his disciples to preach the Good News to all nations: "Go and make disciples of all nations" (Mt 28:19; see Lk 24:47); according to Luke, Jesus sends his disciples to "be witnesses in Jerusalem, and in all Judea and Samaria, and to the end of the earth" (Acts 1:8). In Jesus Christ, the plan of salvation includes all humanity; now the whole earth is called to glorify and praise God (Ps 148).

---

14 "Kairos Palestine Document," 2.2.2.

Rejection of Ideological Readings of the Bible on the Land

Biblical texts cannot be used to justify political options and territorial ownership of the land. Whoever tries to use biblical sources for political argumentation will have to select certain passages and leave aside, ignore, or deny others. A clear view of the whole of biblical statements should lead to an abstention from political argumentation with biblical matters. To take isolated passages for the whole will lead from the use of scripture to its abuse and fundamentalism.

We need to distinguish four aspects in biblical texts on the land: first, there is the statement that the land will be given to the people of Israel as their property (Gn 12; Dt 4:1). Second, there is the contrary, that it will be taken away and the people will be expelled from their land (Dt 28:63; Is 5; Jer 24:10). The reason for this is as punishment for idolatry and the lack of social behavior. Third, there is the statement that the land is God's land (Lv 25:23) and that he alone decides what to do with it and to whom to give it. Fourth, there is the eschatological vision of the heavenly Jerusalem, the pilgrimage of the nations to Zion (Is 2; Ez 47:21–23). "The Land is mine" (Lv 25:23) is a theological, not a political, statement, as is the whole Bible. Making a selection from the texts of the Bible turns faith into an ideology and abuses the Word of God.

Some Western theologies on the land have negative consequences for Palestinians: theology is separated from the question of justice, as no theology can justify injustice and discrimination imposed on Palestinians or any other group of people.

We know that certain theologians in the West try to attach a biblical and theological legitimacy to the infringement of our rights. Thus, the promises, according to their interpretation, have become a menace to our very existence.[15]

We believe that the Bible is and should always be a source of life for all human beings, "good news" for all peoples as God is the Creator of all men and women in his image and likeness. The danger of using the Word of God to support our ideologies and to justify our actions and policies is always present in the history of theology.

Christian Palestinians do not see their connectedness to this land as theological or ideological; it is a natural right. We live on this land. Our ancestors lived, worked, died, and were buried in it. We are here, we will always continue to be here as this is the only land that we can call ours, and we want to live as free people in it.

---

15 "Kairos Palestine Document," 2.3.3.

And when we think theologically about this connectedness, we look for our mission and vocation on this land, not our right! When we are faced with "theologies" that deny us our rights, we try hard on the one hand to understand better those texts, and on the other to safeguard the Word of God as a source of life, not death and suffering, for us and for all.[16] It is in this land that we live and explore the will of God for us, here and now. Reading the Bible, we try to discover the will of God. One example is the fact that we are two peoples and three religions in this land. In this context, what can be the plan of God for us? In the Kairos Palestine Document, we read: "God has put us here as two peoples, and God gives us the capacity, if we have the will, to live together and establish in it justice and peace, making it in reality God's land."[17]

An Inclusive Reading of the Bible

In a context of exclusion coming from different fundamentalist theologies, Jewish and Christian, Christian Palestinians decided not to fall into the same trap. An inclusive theology is only capable of including the theology of justice with the theology of the land in ways that are often antithetical.

Theology of Creation

God created all men and women in his image and likeness. Since all men possess a rational soul and are created in God's likeness, since they have the same nature and origin, have been redeemed by Christ, and enjoy the same divine calling and destiny, the basic equality of all people must receive increasingly greater recognition.

Therefore, with respect to the fundamental rights of the person, every type of discrimination, whether social or cultural, whether based on sex, race, color, social condition, language, or religion, is to be overcome and eradicated as contrary to God's intent.[18]

At the same time, men and women are created to form a human family, called to live in peace, harmony, and equality. This means for us, here and now, in this land in particular, that God created us not so that "we might engage in strife and conflict but rather that we might come and know and love one another, and together build up the land in love and mutual respect."[19]

---

16 Cf. "Kairos Palestine Document," 2.3.4.
17 "Kairos Palestine Document," 2.3.1.
18 Vatican Council II, *Gaudium et Spes*, no. 29 (December 7, 1965).
19 "Kairos Palestine Document," 2.1.

This vision based on creation has the advantage of being inclusive. No just solution can be found at the expense of a people or any group of people, as all enjoy the same dignity and rights. The story of creation in the Bible precedes the story of the election, which is always a mystery, as we cannot find human reasons for the election of some people. Election is done by God, as he wishes and to whom he wishes, for a mission, not a privilege. He may choose someone or a group of people, but we always see a mission addressed to those chosen people. Many of them suffer and are persecuted because of that election.

God Is the Owner of the Land

God created the earth, and he is the owner of the land. He created human beings as stewards of this land, to live in it in peace and justice. *Ha'aretz* in the Bible may be this land (the Holy Land) or the whole earth, but in both cases, it is God's own. When we designate any land as "holy," that holiness comes from God, and it can be holy inasmuch as God is present in it. As for us, we are the stewards of creation and of the land, and we have the duty to respect the will of God for this land. "It is our duty to liberate it from the evil of injustice and war. It is God›s land and therefore it must be a land of reconciliation, peace and love. This is indeed possible: 'The earth is the Lord's and all that is in it, the world, and those who live in it' (Ps. 24:1)."[20]

In which way is our land "holy"? Is it holier than any other land? In the Christian tradition, this land was sanctified by the events of the life of Christ: he was born in Bethlehem, preached in Galilee, and died and rose from the dead in Jerusalem. God chose this land for the incarnation of Jesus and the events of our salvation. But the purpose of God's plan of salvation is the sanctification of human beings: "Be holy as your father is holy" (Mt 5:48; 1 Pt 1:16; Lv 19:2). We can make this land holy by cleansing it from evil, sin, injustice, and war. Christian Palestinians do not call this land "the Holy Land"—we just call it home. Its holiness is a mission, not a privilege. We worship God in the land. We do not worship the land in the name of God.

The Kingdom of God

The theology of the Kingdom of God is in continuation with the theology of creation: Our Lord Jesus Christ came, proclaiming that the Kingdom of God was near. He provoked a revolution in the life and faith of all humanity. The

---

20 "Kairos Palestine Document," 2.3.1.

Kingdom of God is addressed to all, as God is the Creator of all and Father of every human being.

The Kingdom of God is not a political program, nor is it tied to any earthly kingdom "but righteousness and peace and joy in the Holy Spirit" (Rom 14:17). Jesus came to establish a Kingdom that begins here on earth to be fulfilled in the eschatological times. The Kingdom is for all, as God "wants all people to be saved and to come to a knowledge of the truth" (1 Tim 2:4). And at the end of time, "God's dwelling will be here with humankind. He will dwell with them, and they will be his peoples. God himself will be with them as their God" (Rev 21:3). Here we see that "the Kingdom of God is among you" (Lk 17:21), and at the same time: "My Kingdom is not from this world" (Jn 18:36).

In the light of the teaching of the Bible, the promise of the land is the prelude to complete universal salvation. It was the initiation of the fulfillment of the Kingdom of God on earth.[21] The Kingdom of God is an ongoing endeavor; it cannot be identified with any political system, but it is present wherever justice and righteousness are practiced. And the mission of the Church is to proclaim the Kingdom of God, a kingdom of justice, truth, and human dignity.[22] In the Kairos document, we read: "The Kingdom of God on earth is not dependent on any political orientation, for it is greater and more inclusive than any particular political system."[23]

Universality versus Particularity

This land is particular to us as Palestinians, as this is the only land that we can call home. Many Jews consider this land particular to them too. What is the meaning of "particularity" and "universality" in this context? Are those two concepts mutually exclusive? I do believe that the opposite of universality is exclusivity, not particularity. This land may be particular to both Palestinians and Israelis; those two claims can be reconciled, unless one side wants to exclude the other. In other words, affirming that "this land is mine" is called particularity; but affirming that "this land is mine, and only mine" is an exclusive claim. We may begin talking about "multi-particularisms" of this land called holy.[24]

---

21 See "Kairos Palestine Document," 2.3.

22 See "Kairos Palestine Document," 3.4.2.

23 "Kairos Palestine Document," 3.4.3.

24 "Christians should affirm a multi-particularist vision of the co-humanity of many peoples and cultures. One should not use Jewish particularity to deny the rights of Palestinians nor the reverse." Rosemary Ruether, "Christian Zionism and Mainline Western Christian Churches," in *Challenging Christian Zionism: Theology, Politics and the Israel-Palestine Conflict,* ed. Ateek et al. (London: Melisende, 2005).

On the other hand, we believe that our land has a universal mission. The three monotheistic religions recognize a special connectedness to the land. All three religions consider Abraham as their father in faith. "In this universality, the meaning of the promises, of the land, of the election, of the people of God open up to include all of humanity, starting from all the peoples of this land."[25] Universality is a characteristic of the mission of Jesus Christ: "Go and preach to all nations" (Mt 28:19); and all promises find in him their fulfillment. If Christianity is universal, the Church is called to be incarnated in the human reality. We are the Church of the Holy Land; our mission should be incarnated in this land, without making it our final destination. Our connectedness with the land is not primarily theological, it is existential, and the milieu of our mission in this world. "Our presence in this land, as Christian and Muslim Palestinians, is not accidental but rather deeply rooted in the history and geography of this land."[26]

No Theology without Justice

Any theology based on the Bible, on faith, or on history, cannot result in an injustice. The plan of God is a plan of justice and salvation to all. When we link historical events with the fulfillment of the plan of God, or his faithfulness to his promises, we cannot justify any injustice done to anyone as part of that plan. Few theologians suggest that the creation of the State of Israel is the fulfillment of God's promises. The foundation of the State of Israel is a historical event that caused the *Nakba* (Catastrophe) of the Palestinian people when we lost most of our land and 75 percent of our people became refugees. How can a Christian Palestinian accept that what caused his suffering is part of "God's plan," or fulfillment of divine promises? Our God, the God of Jesus Christ that we believe in, is a Father to all his creatures, not a tribal god who fights with his own tribe against everyone else.

The Palestinian-Israeli conflict is a political, national, and territorial conflict, and it should be resolved as such. Theological claims that make the conflict a religious one also make it harder, if not impossible, to resolve. In our context, we face those claims coming from all three religions. Those fundamentalist exclusive claims do not do justice to the image of God. He becomes part of the conflict, fighting "on our side"!

In the Kairos Palestine Document, we read:

> Any theology ... that legitimizes the occupation, is far from Christian teachings, because it calls for violence and holy war in the name of God

---

[25] "Kairos Palestine Document," 2.3.
[26] "Kairos Palestine Document," 2.3.2.

Almighty, subordinating God to temporary human interests.... We call on these theologians to deepen their reflection on the Word of God and to rectify their interpretations so that they might see in the Word of God a source of life for all peoples.[27]

CONCLUSION

History teaches us that the Bible was used on many occasions to justify injustice: slavery was justified with the Bible, apartheid and racism were seen as compatible with the plan of God, the oppression of women in the Church was supported by biblical arguments, the war on Iraq was declared a just war by Catholic bishops, and the "teaching of contempt" toward Jews was part of the teaching of the Church. Accepting the dispossession of the Palestinians of their land in the name of the Bible and theology proves once again that we did not learn from our mistakes in the past, continuing the same logic of using and abusing the Bible.

Theology is not an abstract exercise to feel good about ourselves; it is not an easy way to manipulate the Word of God in order to reconcile with our past at the expense of others. For us, Christian Palestinians, it is an existential matter, a matter of life or death. If many said after World War II, "Never again," I say today, "Never again to anyone."

---

[27] "Kairos Palestine Document," 2.5.

Part IV

IN CONVERSATION

JEWISH RESPONSES

13

JEWISH-CHRISTIAN RELATIONS AND THE IRREVOCABLE PROBLEM OF POLITICAL THEOLOGY

Karma Ben Johanan

This anthology responds to a set of theological questions that have been occupying the Catholic intellectual world for many years, but that became especially urgent after the Commission for Religious Relations with the Jews (CRRJ) had promulgated *"The Gifts and the Calling of God Are Irrevocable"*[1] for the fiftieth anniversary of Vatican II's *Nostra Aetate*. With this document, the idea of the "irrevocability" of the Jews' covenant with God—which first entered the Catholic discourse through John Paul II's speech in 1980[2]—became a mantra for the new theological paradigm through which the Church perceives Jews and Judaism.

An essential part of this paradigm had been to reconnect the biblical promises given to the ancient Israelites with post-crucifixion Judaism, in a way that would not regard contemporary Jews' religious existence as obsolete, but would, instead, relate to it some sort of a continuous value. This also meant legitimizing the Jews' own hermeneutical approach to Scripture as the basis of their valid religious existence, that is, legitimizing how Jews interpret Judaism as their loyal response to God's continuous calling.

Legitimacy is, of course, a blurred concept. To what extent should the Church approve the Jewish interpretation of Scripture, i.e., the Jewish

---

1 Commission for Religious Relations with the Jews, *"The Gifts and the Calling of God Are Irrevocable"* (Rom 11:29): *A Reflection on Theological Questions Pertaining to Catholic–Jewish Relations on the Occasion of the 50th Anniversary of "Nostra Aetate,"* 2015.

2 John Paul II, *Address to Representatives of the West German Jewish Community*, Mainz, West Germany, November 17, 1980.

religion? What is the final aim of such legitimization? Is it simply to soften the gap between the two religions so that they won't be experienced as inimical to each other, or perhaps the magisterium has a more robust task in mind? Does it entail integrating the major Jewish hermeneutical principles into Catholic tradition, or only appreciating them from afar, like the Church can feel sympathy toward certain developments in general philosophy or in Islamic thought, for example?[3]

Even if the positive content of the "irrevocability" argument is yet to be clarified by theologians, we should at least be able to designate its negative content: irrevocability seeks to negate supersessionism. The claim according to which the Jewish covenant had never been revoked by God seems to point to the affirmation that the Christian reading of Scripture, i.e., Christianity, does not cancel out its Jewish reading, i.e., Judaism. Perhaps it even somehow contains it as part of its own reading.

Thus the paradigm of irrevocability was established as a replacement of the traditional paradigm of replacement, as a supersession of the trajectory which assigned the Church as superseding the ancient Israelites as the people of God. Yet like the concept of irrevocability, the concept of replacement is also far from being self-evident. The precise meaning of the irrevocability of God's covenant with the Jewish people and the positioning of this irrevocability in relation to the Catholic tradition (and whether the Church's traditional attitude to Judaism can be exhausted as supersessionism or not) thus became a central question for theologians who seek greater clarity.

The focal point in which the tension between irrevocability and replacement becomes the most prominent is where the question of the relationship between theology and politics is involved. The most famous text that exemplifies this fact is Pope Emeritus Benedict XVI's controversial "Grace and Vocation without Remorse," published in the summer of 2018 precisely to expel the theological fog that had accompanied, to a certain extent, both John Paul II's original "never revoked" statement and the more recent statement by the CRRJ. Interestingly enough, Benedict's analysis of both "substitution" and "irrevocability" lead directly to the political-theological question whether there is a theological meaning to the relationship between the Jews and the Land of Israel, and whether Catholics should regard the Jewish modern state of Israel as somehow mediating this meaning.

---

[3] One of the strongest examples for this equivocality regarding the "legitimacy" of Judaism, is the following paragraph from the Pontifical Biblical Commission's (PBC's) 2001 document "The Jewish People and Their Sacred Scriptures in the Christian Bible": "Christians can and ought to admit that the Jewish reading of the Bible is a *possible* one, in continuity with the Jewish Sacred Scriptures from the Second Temple period, a reading analogous to the Christian reading which developed in parallel fashion" (my emphasis). What does the word "possible" mean?

Benedict insists, regarding this question,

> the conviction that a strictly theologically-understood state—a Jewish faith-state [*Glaubenstaat*] that would view itself as the theological and political fulfillment of the promises—is unthinkable within history according to Christian faith and contrary to the Christian understanding of the promises.[4]

For Benedict, it is precisely at this point—when approaching the question of political messianism and of whether the promise of the Land should be theologically interpreted as referring to a specific polity related to a specific territory in the course of human history—that Christianity is offering a radically different interpretation of the Old Testament, one that does not coincide with the mainstream rabbinic interpretation (at least according to Benedict's understanding of it), or with its Zionist avatar (indeed, Benedict seems to regard Zionism as a continuation of the classical rabbinic interpretation of the Old Testament). In Benedict's eyes, the irrevocability of the Jews' covenant is not rooted in the rabbinic interpretation, but in the Christian one, which "fulfills" the promises precisely by transcending their pre-Christian interpretation. Though the Christian interpretation does not "substitute" the literal biblical sense of the promise, it certainly alters its center so that its "midpoint would be the gift of His body, by which the Sinai covenant would be brought to its definitive form, becoming the new covenant. At the same time, the covenant would be extended to all believers, thus giving the promise of land its definitive meaning."[5] Needless to say, not few Jews and Christians would have interpreted this sort of argument as at least slightly supersessionist, since it does reject the mainstream Jewish interpretation of the same biblical affirmations, which is confined to the more literal sense of a particular geographical area and of a particular ethnos, both designated by the name "Israel."

Leaving Benedict's answer to the questions of irrevocability and substitution aside for the moment, the authors of this volume seem to share the motivations of "Grace and Vocation without Remorse," even when they don't share Benedict's conviction. By exploring what is implied in the words "never revoked" and how they stand in relation to the Catholic tradition, the authors are also headed to this political-theological nerve center of the Jewish-Christian tension, namely, the attitude of Catholic theology to the existence or

---

4 Pope Emeritus Benedict XVI, "Grace and Vocation without Remorse: Comments on the Treatise 'De Iudaeis,'" trans. Nicholas J. Healy, *Communio: International Catholic Review* 45 (Spring 2018): 178.

5 Pope Emeritus Benedict XVI, "Grace and Vocation without Remorse," 166–67.

the absence of a theological meaning of the Jews' return, inhabitation, statehood, and political conflicts in the present and concrete Land of Israel.

In this volume, the tension is embodied in a complicated relationship between two theological trajectories. The first trajectory is focused on the singular role played by the history of the Jews in the history of salvation. This reasoning seeks to include the return of the Jews to the Land of Israel in the twentieth century, and to some extent also the establishment of the state of Israel and the moral challenge posed by the Israeli-Palestinian conflict, in the concept of the irrevocable covenant between God and the people of Israel. Theologians who follow this trajectory, as D'Costa argues in his article, relate "a theological significance [to] the Jewish people in the land called Israel," since the land is part of the biblical promise to the people of Israel and is therefore included in Paul's affirmation that "Theirs [are] the covenants . . . the temple worship and the promises" (Rom 9: 4–5), which are God's irrevocable gifts (according to Romans 11: 28, see also Garrigues and Kurylo). Moreover, as D'Costa affirms, if rabbinic Judaism is a legitimate and valid interpretation of the Old Testament, and the hope to return to the Land of Israel is an essential part of it, then the return of the Jews to the land of promise should carry with it a valid theological significance.[6] In other words, authors who follow this path integrate at least partially the mainstream Jewish (religious) political-theological interpretation of events into their own perception of the history of salvation, or in the authors' own words, as "signs of the times." The implications of this kind of interpretation are that the singular meaning of both the history of the Jewish people and the Land of Israel cannot be completely universalized (though they can carry universal implications), nor allegorized or spiritualized in a way that will overshadow their corporal particularity.

The other trajectory stands in tension with the application of the irrevocability of the covenant to the current Jewish people residing in Zion, seeing this kind of Jewish-Christian political theology as incommensurable with the Catholic profound suspicion toward the divinization of politics. This attitude—which is complex and internally diverse, contains a combination of two related traditions. The first is Vatican II's *Gaudium et Spes* formula, according to which the Church respects the independence of the political realm (see *GS* 76: "The Church and the political community in their own fields are autonomous and independent from each other"); i.e., theology and politics

---

[6] D'Costa argues that "those religious Jews who are invincibly ignorant of the truth of the gospel are in a valid covenant with the true and living God, who is faithful to his promises and gifts." In the category of invincible ignorance, it is implied that the validity of rabbinic Judaism is somehow *dependent on* Jewish ignorance, and therefore this validity will indeed be revoked or replaced as Jews come to Christ.

should be separated.⁷ The other is the Augustinian separation between the history of salvation and political, or "worldly," history (and I will return to this notion later), and the persistent refrainment from their confusion. This political-theological approach, which is at the same time deeply traditional and very much inclined to the modern liberal idea of separation between Church and state, is often defined in this volume as "indifference" to specific political arrangements, endowing the task of affirming or negating them to the realm of the "international law" (see Ansorge). I will call this Augustinian or liberal theological trajectory the "detheologization of politics," or concisely, "detheologization," even though it is a deeply theological argument.

I find two central variations of this argument in the collection, and it seems to me that the difference between them is worth mentioning, notwithstanding they are undifferentiated by the articles' authors. According to the first, a strict separation is needed between theology and politics, since this is the only way to protect religion (and politics, too) from the abuse of theology or of faith in the service of unjust regimes.⁸ In Khader's words, a separation should be made "between a rereading of Jews and Judaism and the ideology of modern Zionism," and he continues: "the biblical texts cannot be used to justify political options and territorial ownership of the land;" or, as Neuhaus puts it: "I would encourage suspicion with regard to all attempts to mobilize the Bible, Christian tradition, and theological language to legitimate ideologies of any coloration." Theology must come to a halt when it is facing politics. This means that the Jewish people's current presence in the Land of Israel has to be understood in purely secular terms.

The expropriation of the current situation of the Jewish people in Palestine from theology implies, of course, disregarding the issue's biblical roots, because taking these roots into account immediately makes the question of the Jews and their relation to the Land of Israel into a theological one. According to this logic, the relationship between the Jews and the land *cannot* have any *theological* significance. On the other hand, it also means that the Catholic theology of Judaism and the way it perceives the relationship between the Jewish people and God *cannot* have any *political* implications. There is no possible overlap between the theological and the political within the Catholic approach to Judaism.

This is certainly the reason why, as Neuhaus mentions, various local bishops' conferences who sought reconciliation with the Jews have repeatedly

---

7 See also her problematizing of this "secularized" reading of *GS* by Tracy Rowland, *Culture and the Thomist Tradition: After Vatican II* (London: Routledge, 2003), 36.

8 One may argue that the very aim of separating theology from politics is already the Church's acceptance of liberalism, that is, it is in itself an affirmation of a specific political form.

stated that they are willing to acknowledge the unique sentiments Jews have for the land and state of Israel, understanding that this is an essential part of Jewish self-understanding, but, on the other hand, warned against theologically adopting them, insisting on separating their spiritual love toward the Jews from supporting their political theology. This is also at the heart of Neuhaus's view of Zionism as a distortion of Judaism, since a political reading of the Bible is, according to this line, always a chauvinistic distortion of theology and not a viable theological horizon. This is in tension with Lévy, who identifies in Zionism an *aggiornamento* that faithfully responds to an established Jewish theological-political tradition, without which Zionism would have never been accepted so well into Judaism. I tend to agree with Lévy on that point. In this sense, there is a real difficulty in criticizing Zionism without also criticizing a major thread within the Jewish tradition.

The other variation of the detheologization trajectory is more permissive of the interference of theology in political matters, but only through a specific mode of interpretation, based on the Church's nonpartisan and encompassing abstinence from identification with any particular political institution or cause, as well as on emptying politics of eschatological content. According to this line of thought, there is, indeed, a certain separation between the Church and the political realm since the Church does not have a mandate to interfere in all aspects of political life, but there is always room for theology to evaluate and criticize specific contemporary political forms based on the Church's universal moral standards. This line leads to a universalization of the Catholic theology of politics, because the Church's mandate is based precisely on its inherent indifference toward particular existing power structures, which gives it a kind of a disengaged "objective" standpoint.[9] Therefore, even if the Bible is indeed the major source from which the Church retrieves its moral standards and ideas about fair politics, its interpretation of the Bible is guided by a universalizing principle, that is, it implies interpreting biblical Israel as a metonym for human behavior, for justice and injustice, and not as the unique historical or political case of the Jewish people according to the flesh (in Khader's words: "our God ... is a Father to all his creatures, not a tribal god who fights with his own tribe against everyone else"). Catholic social teaching is obliged to universal ethics that cannot contain any kind of double moral standards differently applicable

---

9 This argument is at the heart of Ratzinger's dialogue with Jürgen Habermas, "That which Holds the World Together: The Pre-Political Moral Foundations of a Free State," *The Dialectics of Secularization: On Reason and Religion*, ed. Jürgen Habermas and Joseph Ratzinger, trans. Brian McNeil, CRV (San Francisco: Ignatius Press, 2005), 52–80. See also Ben Johanan, "A Portrait of the Critique as a Churchman: Joseph Ratzinger and the Catholization of the Modern Project," *Theory and Criticism* 52 (Winter 2020): 89–114.

for different human groups in varying geographical settings. This perspective often necessitates a non-literal reading of the Old Testament that softens the "tribal" and the "brutal" stories whose literal meaning often point to what we perceive as injustice;[10] in other words, they require a Christological intervention that will take away the chauvinism embedded in their literal exclusivist interpretation. Joshua's ban reoccurs as the Old Testament's thirstiest text for such Christological mitigation, as Rutishauser writes: "for this new Joshua [i.e. Jesus Christ] the trademark for access to *Eretz Yisrael* is precisely non-violence: 'Blessed are the meek [those who do not use violence], for they will inherit the land' [Mt 5:5]."[11]

Both variations of the detheologization trajectory lead to the conclusion that with regards to politics, the paradigm of irrevocability—a paradigm that poses the uniqueness of the Jewish religious experience at its center and anchors this experience within the Old Testament—has to be suspended (and this is how I understand the core of Benedict's argument as well). In the specific context of the Israeli-Palestinian conflict, an interpretation that would emphasize the uniqueness of the Jewish covenant—i.e., Jewish difference—will contradict from the outset the universalist Catholic moral theology and as a result make the Church unable to fulfill its "objective" moral demands from both the Jewish and the Palestinian peoples. Mainstream (religious) Jewish subjectivity at this point is incommensurable with Catholic universality. The Church's theology, which seeks to detheologize politics and the Church's theology of Israel, are based on contradictory readings of the Old Testament.

As I will try to show now, this tension between a Catholic theology that interprets contemporary events—including events with political reverberations—as "signs of the times" pertaining to the history of salvation (and is therefore open to similar Jewish theologies), and a Catholic theology that warns against charging particular historical events (and especially politics) with a partisan theological meaning, did not start with the Second Vatican Council or with the establishment of the Jewish State, but indeed characterized the Jewish-Christian relationship from the outset, going back to the core polemic between Jews and Christians over the identity and the role of the messiah.

---

10 See Michael Wyschogrod's critique on Ratzinger's preface to the PBC's document, in which he regards the Old Testament stories when unmediated by Christology as "brutal," as containing anti-Jewish residues. "The Jewish People and Their Sacred Scriptures in the Christian Bible, by the Pontifical Commission Rome 2001," *New Perspectives on Jewish-Christian Relations in Honor of David Berger*, ed. Elisheva Carlebach and Jacob J. Schacter (Leiden and Boston: Brill, 2012), 522.

11 This, as D'Costa mentioned, is where the PBC insists on a non-literal reading of the Old Testament, since unlike in the literal narrative of the Bible, "the realization of the Promise cannot involve non-defensive violence."

A SHORT POLITICAL-THEOLOGICAL HISTORY OF THE JEWISH-CHRISTIAN POLEMIC

The authors of this volume have touched upon many of the critical historical and political intersections which shaped (and were shaped by) both Jewish and Christian theologies through the ages. In what follows I will try to connect these dots in order to provide a rough narrative. Since both Christianity and Judaism have always contained a plethora of messianic ideas, any attempt to juxtapose them as dichotomous to each other is clumsy and imprecise. My intention is not to present essentialist arguments about the central political theology of either Judaism or Christianity. Instead, I focus on the major generalizations which have characterized both traditions, as well as their reciprocal perceptions. The crucial task of recovering the nuanced historical variety of Jewish and Christian political theologies is done by many prominent scholars, and transcends this brief summary, which is mainly dedicated to the history of reception. As Israel Knohl argues, the controversy over the political or apolitical nature of the messiah and of the possibility of bringing forward the kingdom of God in the framework of historical time is already strongly present in the Old Testament, and it proceeds through the New Testament.[12] Nevertheless, in their reception history each of the faiths came to be identified with a specific view regarding the relation between redemption and politics.

A prevalent expectation among New Testament Jews, as vividly depicted by the callings of the people toward Jesus as he approaches the city (Mark 11: 9–10), or in the apostles' question in Acts 1:6 (as Feingold and Garrigues & Kurylo have indicated), was to wait for the Davidic king messiah that would renew their kingdom and political independence as an earthly king should do. As the encounter on the way to Emmaus exemplifies, the crucifixion sowed confusion among many Jews, who had a difficulty reconciling the scandal of the crucified Christ with their own political-theological messianic expectations. Thus the refusal of the vast majority of the Jews to accept Jesus as their Christ relates to his not rebuilding the kingdom or renewing the political independence of Israel in the earthly sense that they expected.

Rabbinic Judaism maintained and further cultivated this political-theological line as is famously depicted in Chazal's dictum, according to which "the only difference between this world and the days of the messiah is with regard to servitude to foreign kingdoms alone."[13] This principle is

---

12 Israel Knohl, *The Messianic Controversy* (Hevel Modiin: Kinneret Zmora-Bitan Dvir, 2019).
13 Berakhot 34b:20.

then repeated and systematized in Maimonides' *Mishneh Torah*, with the affirmation that a messiah can only be recognized by his worldly success in redeeming Israel, renewing the kingdom, rebuilding the Temple, and enforcing the *Halakha*.[14]

While Judaism came to be realized as focused on a messianic political figure (a Davidic king), so did Christianity come to separate itself from political messianic aspirations, as is sometimes described through Jesus' claim that "my kingdom is not of this world" (Jn 18: 36). Since Jesus did not renew the kingdom in the earthly sense during his lifetime in the Land of Israel, his disciples in generations to come have interpreted his messianic message as pointing to a different end (even if, as Feingold suggests, the possibility that he will also "restore the kingdom to Israel" in its earthly form upon his return had never been totally negated).

The New Testament was therefore largely interpreted as ambivalent toward the kind of political theology which aspires for an earthly political messianic revival. The New Testament was often read through the prism of a heavenly city replacing the earthly city, and of Christ's resurrected body replacing the Temple, that is, transforming the Jewish messianic hopes of the rebuilding of Jerusalem and the renewal of Jewish kingship into a non-political kind of messianism that carries an extra-historical eschatological meaning. This sometimes entails a transference or typological move that renders the actual land a "spiritual" one. This spiritualization was also connected with a universalization of the land, precisely as Israel of the spirit meant the opening of the borders of carnal Israel to include the entire human race.

Yet this approach is only one aspect of the Christian perception of history and politics. In fact, the Church maintained an internal controversy over the political nature of its messianism, and whether the kingdom of God—or at least its traces—could be identified within history or transcended it. In this sense, the attitude that became identified with Judaism remained, to a certain extent, also internal to Christianity.

This became especially prominent as the political conditions in which Christianity existed changed dramatically over the fourth century, with the Christian community transforming from a persecuted sect to a permitted religion and finally to the empire's official religion. Eusebius of Caesarea, friend and biographer of the Emperor Constantine, had seen the Christianization of the Roman Empire as a realization (even though only a partial one) of the prophecies of the Old Testament. The Christian Empire was for him an expression of the divine plan of redemption and a tool for its

---

14 Maimonides, *Mishnesh Torah*, Laws of Kings and Wars 10:1.

promotion. The historical process was a transparent mirror of God's will for humanity, facilitating the Church's ability to proclaim its message throughout the entire world. This Eusebian approach also became part and parcel of the Christian tradition, and it accompanied Christendom in different variations for generations to come, through both the middle ages and the modern period.[15]

But the euphoria of a Christianized Rome did not last for long. With the deterioration of the empire in the West, Augustine of Hippo developed a different conception, based on a clear distinction between historical success and the program of salvation. In response to the accusation directed by pagans at Christians that it was the Christianization of Rome that led to its political decline and to the defeats on the battleground, Augustine retorted in his *City of God*, that the plan of salvation is progressing regardless of the rise and fall of kingdoms. "Sacred history" is a process focused on safely bringing the community of the elect to its goal—the Kingdom of Heaven. The other process is that of human history, which is subject to the laws of this world and has no impact whatsoever on the final accounting. The rise and fall of empires, be they Christian or not, are expressions of the power systems operating in a world that God left to its own devices to act as it will, rather than as part of the program of salvation. In this world, it may happen that evil parties have the upper hand, while good parties have the lower hand—and none of this betrays God's will for his chosen.[16]

This Eusebian-Augustinian ambivalence, which continued to accompany the Catholic tradition throughout the centuries, was also closely related to the Church's ambivalence toward the Jews. The Church fathers viewed the exile of the Jews and the destruction of Jerusalem as evidence that the Jewish interpretation of Scripture was erroneous, for the prophecies of the Jewish prophets had not come true for the "Israel of the Flesh" in the earthly manner which the Jews aspired for. The historical achievements of Christianity, the

---

15 On the history of the theological-political controversy within the Christian tradition, see Eric Voegelin's seminal work *The New Science of Politics* (Brantford, ON: W. Ross MacDonald School, Resource Services Library, 2005). Voegelin identifies the recurrence of the "Eusebian" perception (which had pagan-Roman roots) with the immanentization of redemption in the works of Joachim of Fiore, later growing in power to forge the heart of modernity. Voegelin "outsources" this perception as an incarnation of Gnosticism, thus separating it from what he defines as the traditional political-theological perception of Christianity (which he terms "dedivinization").

16 This did not mean—as Augustine himself noted, that the Church should not aspire for the Christianization of its politics, and that such Christianization was not willed by God. It simply meant looking at historical processes with a grain of salt, as they can never bring nor represent salvation, which exists beyond history. See, for example Johannes van Oort, *Jerusalem and Babylon: A Study of Augustine's City of God and the Sources of his Doctrine of the Two Cities* (Leiden: Brill, 2013), 108–63.

"Israel of the Spirit," were perceived as evidence of God's Grace, and of the Christians being the Chosen People for which the prophecies came true.[17]

Thus in its theological disputations with the Jews, the Church attacked Judaism for its overly "earthly" messianic hope (and for rejecting Christ for not fulfilling their political aspirations). Yet in its historical disputation, the Church utilized the Biblical prophecies of success as clear evidence of Christian election and viewed the temporal success of the Church as an appropriate reflection of God's grace (as evidenced also in Augustine's *City of God* itself). God had become disaffected with the Jews and expressed His discontent by destroying the Temple in Jerusalem and scattering the Jews in their lands of exile, submitting them to the grace of Christians. It is worth noting the irony, that both types of views saw the history of the Jews as theologically narrated, even when history was seen as divested of God's dealings. Christianity thus criticized the "Eusebian" messianism of Judaism that identified actual historical success with spiritual triumph, while at the same time, it used the same Eusebian logic to validate Christianity itself. Thus the Jews, according to pre-*Nostra Aetate* Catholic tradition, were punished with political inferiority within the Christian kingdom for connecting too tightly politics and salvation. Their political losses—in particular their exile and the destruction of their theo-political center in Jerusalem were—to use *Gaudium et Spes* terminology—the signs of the times.

At the same time Jews continued to see their existence outside of the land as a devastating exile and to wait for the messiah who will indeed do all those things that Jesus was expected to do and failed (see Maimonides' reference to Jesus in the Laws of Kings and Wars 11:4). Their messianic hopes remained pregnant with political tension, as an integral part of it was their persistent longing for the time when they will no longer be ruled by the nations.

Yet even though exile was despised by the Jews who continued to wish for its termination, it also became the theological category through which they were able to survive and maintain and develop their tradition (as noted by D'Costa, Vetö and Rutishauser) without identifying with the existing political powers.[18] Ironically, through their exile the Jews became the living example of the Augustinian *civitas peregrina*, being in the (largely Christian) *civitas terrena* but not of it, crossing history patiently without calculating the end, separating their eschatological aspirations from worldly, earthly

---

[17] See for example Rosemary Radford Ruther, *Faith and Fratricide: The Theological Roots of Anti-Semitism* (New York: The Seabury Press, 1974), 217–26.

[18] See especially the works of Amnon Raz-Krakotzkin, "Exile, History, and the Nationalization of Jewish Memory: Some Reflections on the Zionist Notion of History and Return," *Journal of Levantine Studies 3*, no. 2 (Winter 2013): 37–70.

politics. Thus the non-messianic political theology of the Church and the overly messianic political theology of the Jews were reversely mirrored in the fact that the Church triumphed in worldly affairs while the Jews were destined to contempt barely tolerated within Christendom. The theological aspects of the Jewish-Christian tension were saturated in the actual power-structure of these communities—the politics of a small religious minority within another religion's kingdom.

TWENTIETH-CENTURY CATHOLIC POLITICAL AWARENESS AND THE CHURCH'S TURN TOWARD THE JEWS

The second half of the twentieth century has called the Church to develop a new political awareness. As theologians and Church officials became acquainted with the messianic fervor that accompanied both Nazism and Communism, they became doubly critical of political utopias, which invested their eschatological hopes in political revolutions. Moreover, coping with the critique that stressed the Church's ties with the colonial enterprise on the one hand, and with the vast process of secularization on the other, the Church no longer wished to, nor could it, identify itself with the hegemonic powers in the West.

Retrieving their response to the events of the present from the Catholic tradition, theologians and clergy have returned to Augustine, eager to revalidate the traditional distinction between the Church as a universal (and—for the present—supra-national) spiritual community and worldly political communities, and between the hope for salvation in the next world and any political type of aspiration for redemption. In Rutishauser's words: "The Church no longer defines itself so much as *societas perfecta*, but rather as the people of God on pilgrimage." Or, as Neuhaus writes,

> In the light of history, the Church should have learnt that the theological affirmation of empires, kingdoms and other earthly powers is a treacherous enterprise. The Church today seeks forgiveness for her members who have bought into ideologies of domination, enslavement and discrimination. Modern nationalism ... does not conform to the vision of the Church.

Learning to acknowledge its own limits of power in a rapidly secularizing world, accounting for its own colonial and imperial tendencies, and adapting itself to a new liberal political order, the Church began to draw inspiration precisely from those who were the victims of the twentieth century's political triumphalism, those exiled, dislocated, suffering, and powerless. All those stories that were once marginalized by the Church's own narrative were now looked at differently in an encompassing Catholic effort of self-accounting. The epitome of this kind of existence was concentrated in the fate of European Jews. The Holocaust was thus experienced by many Catholics as a sign of the times. The fact that this great tragedy of modernity happened precisely to the Jews, to the people from which Christ emerged, was interpreted as a witness to God's continuous love for his chosen people.[19] Jewish suffering was no longer a sign of God's wrath, but exactly the opposite—a sign of his love and loyalty.

In their aversion to political messianism, some Catholic thinkers even drew inspiration from the Jewish resistance to accepting the Christological conception according to which the world has already been redeemed with the coming of Christ, and preferred to emphasize, along with the Jews, that full redemption was yet to come. Ironically, this enthusiasm over the Jewish postponement of the messiah to the future took place at the very moment that Jewish denominations began to develop renewed enthusiasm for the possibility of political messianism here and now. The Jewish State came into being precisely when the Church was making tremendous efforts to disengage from its ties to worldly power. The state of Israel constituted a Jewish effort to be rid of the (alleged or real) historical-political disengagement of the Jews and replace it with earthly power. Not only did the Jews suddenly become a sovereign political entity, but, as was becoming increasingly evident, this was an entity that had inherited from European politics the volatile mix of secularism (or seeming secularism), the adoration of power, and eutopianism, a mix that gave rise, in the second half of the twentieth century, to acute allergic reactions on the part of the Church in particular and the West in general. At the very point in time that the Church learned to retreat from its political demands, to distance itself from the mundane and postpone salvation once more to the end of history, the Jews rediscovered the redemptive value of worldly power and identified the "surplus spirituality" that had characterized them in the past as a disease for which power was the cure.

In this respect, both Zionism and the post–Vatican II "aggiornamented" Church fulfilled (with some variations) their traditional roles in the ancient Jewish-Christian polemic: the former yearned for political redemption and celebrated its worldly power, while the latter demanded that a distinction be made between matters of redemption (unto God) and matters of politics

---

19 For a prominent example see Jacques Maritain, "Le mystère d'Israël," *Le mystère d'Israël et autres essais* (Paris: Desclée de Brouwer, 1965), 19–62. For further discussion see my own *A Pottage of Lentils: Mutual Perceptions of Christians and Jews in the Age of Reconciliation* (Tel Aviv: Tel Aviv University Press, 2020), 68–78.

(unto Caesar). Though unorthodox in many ways, while jumping over Judaism's rich diasporic legacy, Zionism had indeed smoothly anchored itself within that specific thread of both biblical and post-biblical Jewish political theology.

For Jews, therefore, it was largely the foundation of the state of Israel, not the Holocaust, which was a sign of the times—it was their miraculous release from exile and subversion (often symbolized by Christianity), which gave new life to their old political messianic expectations, mocked for centuries by Christians. This was why so many of them found it hard to understand how the Church related messianic significance to their victimization, while refusing to give such meaning to their victory, without interpreting this against the background of Christian supersessionsm, which again absorbed Jewish suffering in a triumphalist Christian narrative.

Vis-à-vis this self-perception of Jews, the Church found itself in a quandary. Any objection to the Jewish State on theological grounds was out of the question, since it recreated the logic of the rejected replacement theology; any support for the state of Israel for theological reasons would be a blatant breach of the distinction between religion and politics and the principle of political neutrality, but a non-theological position vis-à-vis Jewish politics conflicted with tradition, precisely because there was no area of the Jewish-Christian relationship that was free of political theology.

THE CURRENT VOLUME IN THIS NARRATIVE

I initially framed the discussion as trending between two trajectories: the first, which I termed "irrevocability," emphasizes the particularity of Jewish existence, and seeks to legitimize the Jewish claim for a biblically based unique connection between the Jews and the Land of Israel. This trajectory is also in line with what I described as the "Eusebian" perception of history, since it endows particular political events with theological, and even eschatological, meaning. The second trajectory, which I called "detheologization," wished to abstain from infusing political institutions and events with theological content other than evaluating them on a universal moral basis. In our specific context, this trajectory entails refraining from ascribing to the Jews a unique and unparalleled bond to the Land of Israel, and especially from extending the mediation of this bond to the state. However, it is worth remembering that this theological position regarding the Jewish people is linked to the Church's self-accounting for its own moments of theological-political triumphalism, or "Eusebianism," now rejected for the sake of an updated Augustinian approach.

The authors of this volume offer several solutions that soften this tension. First and foremost, they seek to bridge the gap between acknowledging the singular mission of the Jews and the universality of Catholic theology in interpreting the Old Testament. They subvert, for example, the commonplace idea that Catholic universality entails replacing the flesh with the spirit, that is, turning Israel of the flesh into merely a metaphor for Israel of the spirit, as well as turning the concrete piece of land promised to Israel into merely a metaphor for the kingdom of heaven. Instead of this dichotomous perception of Catholicism vis-à-vis Judaism, the authors show that Catholic theology is actually much more susceptible to corporality than usually assumed, and therefore also closer to Judaism. Ansorge works in that direction by presenting the land through the lens of sacramentality, anchoring sacramentality in both corporal and social structures. Feingold, Tapie, and Chenchiah all work on the controversial concept of typology, retrieving from a variety of traditional sources a richer concept than what is usually ascribed to it, at least in the realm of Jewish-Christian dialogue. As both Feingold and Chenchiah remind the readers, typology enforces the uniqueness of the types and does not negate them, while charging them with a significance that points beyond themselves. This way the eschatological importance of the return of the Jews to the land is not superseded by Christological eschatological interpretations, but on the contrary, it is precisely that Christological framework that reinforces it. Tapie's discussion of Thomas introduces the idea that the land does not lose its corporal meaning, but is rather transfigured, in the same way that Christ's own flesh remains circumcised after its resurrection. With this move Tapie softens the tension between the irrevocability of the Jewish covenant (*brit*, which is the same word for circumcision, *brit mila*) and the more suspicious attitude toward historical particularity.

Rutishauser offers to move Judaism closer to Catholicism rather than the opposite, using Augustinian ecclesiological concepts to somehow help save Judaism from itself. Just like the Church is perceived not as a perfect society upon earth, but as a duality of the earthly Church and the heavenly community of the saints, so should Israel's existence be perceived as composed of a visible and an invisible side—the "earthly" Israel is always exposed to sin, to injustice, and to change, while the "heavenly" Israel remains "a spiritual-metaphysical reality that connects all who were born of a Jewish mother or who through conversion profess Judaism." This, in a sense, exempts Judaism from the political-theological danger by introducing a duality that may help Jews separate their eschatological ideals from their actual capabilities within history, without attempting to judge their earthly behavior according to the impossible standards of Israel's metaphysical aspects.

In all these cases, there is an attempt to peel the supersessionist layer off from Catholic universality, and integrate the "irrevocability" trajectory into Catholic theology writ large. The two articles that go the greatest distance in that direction are Vetö's and Lévy's.

Vetö first solves the problem of the Church's neutrality toward politics by regarding not only the Jewish return to the land, but also the Israeli-Palestinian conflict as belonging to the realm of theology, and not of pure politics. In his affirmation that "true theology can neither be disconnected from historical, sociopolitical and existential situations," Vetö distances himself from the detheologization trajectory and its commonplace perception of "the relationship of *Am Yisrael* to *Eretz Yisrael* [as] strongly relativized and to a major extent replaced by the relationship of all peoples to the whole earth." Vetö even admits to not negating the famous (or infamous—depends whom one is asking) religious-Zionist dictum that the state of Israel is "the beginning of our salvation," stirring close to the messianic theological ideas of Rav Kook.

Yet after rehabilitating the stature of both corporality and politics within Catholic theology, I would argue that the tension between the two theological trajectories—one represented by an openness to Jewish singularity and the other represented by a universalistic refrain from affirming such singularity when it comes to actual politics—reappears in Vetö's discussion of the place of the Palestinian people in God's salvific plan for the Jewish people:

> There is a similar call for the Palestinian people: their presence is legitimate, they also have a God-given right to full protection, subsistence and development—and they are likewise called to share. The legitimate presence of two peoples on one land is a test for the people of God, as it is for the Palestinian people. No other people takes the place of Israel as people of God; no other people receive the land as their promised land, according to a divine word revealed in the Bible. However, there is a mysteriously unique place for the Palestinian people in the history of salvation: to be the people with whom Israel shares the land of the promise; to be the people who share the land with Israel; to be associated in a special way with the chosen people.

In this paragraph, Vetö seems to fluctuate between two different logics. On the one hand, he argues that the Palestinian presence in the Land of Israel exists as a moral test for the Jews, a test which is an inherent part of the gift, and in a certain sense conditions it: the return and the inhabitation of the land have a messianic potentiality whose fulfillment is dependent on the Jews' moral behavior toward their neighbors. This approach, as Vetö explains, is rooted in the Old Testament, in the moral attitude required by the Jews toward *resident aliens* ("resident strangers will not only be welcome but will even be given land in the same way as the tribes of Israel").

This part of Vetö's argument puts at its center Jewish subjectivity, the Jews' process of conversion and purification, without universalizing or abstracting either the land or the identity of Israel. According to this logic, the Palestinians have indeed a role in the history of salvation, yet this role is as the Other of Jewish consciousness, "associated in a special way with the chosen people," not as the Jews' equals.[20] This kind of a role brings to mind the traditional role which the Jews have played within medieval Christendom, when their unwilled testimony to the truthfulness of Christianity provided Christian society with the justification to tolerate them, while other minorities were not tolerated. This solution is indeed consistent with the irrevocability trajectory, to which it manages to integrate the Palestinians in a meaningful way—yet it is blatantly non-egalitarian—a fact that seems to be at odds with Vetö's own moral intuitions.

For this reason, Vetö quickly retreats from his suggestion to see the Palestinians as "resident aliens," since the land is also *theirs*, as much as it belongs to the people of Israel. Here, the universalizing logic comes back into play: "[T]here is a *similar* call for the Palestinian people ... they *also* have a God-given right to full protection, subsistence and development—and they are *likewise* called to share. The legitimate presence of two peoples on one land is a test for the people of God, *as it is* for the Palestinian people" (emphasis is mine). Reading these lines raises the question: Is there a difference between Jews and Palestinians in relation to the Land of Israel, or isn't there? Is Israel a light to the nations in the sense that all peoples can learn from the Old Testament that they are called to share their lands, that is, to identify themselves with *biblical* Israel, or rather all peoples (including the Palestinians) are called to learn something uniquely from the contemporary *Jewish behavior* in the Israeli-Palestinian conflict today?[21] In other words, do contemporary Jews represent biblical Israel in a way that is different from the way the Palestinians represent it? Can the Palestinians be included in God's promise of the land without either negating the uniqueness of God's relationship with Israel or, alternatively, negating their own self-perception?

Where Vetö's argument reflects the heart of the tension between these two deeply Catholic perceptions, Lévy's article seems to go even further

---

20 Interestingly, this role of the Palestinians, and especially the notion of "the mystery" of Palestinian suffering, brings to mind the pre-conciliar idea of "the mystery of Israel," discovered through Jewish suffering for reasons of antisemitism. See Maritain, "Le mystère d'Israël," 19–62.

21 An additional question would be: Why should Muslim Palestinians accept Jewish sovereignty if it is derived from a canon which they do not hold as sacred?

with the irrevocability trajectory, to the point of completely revoking the detheologization trajectory. Lévy points to the absurdity in the Church's call to avoid endowing political events with theological meaning, a call that embraces the secular standpoint according to which religion is incapable of helping us solve political conflicts (which, at least in our case, have started on religious grounds). Behind this allegedly "anti-theological" attitude to the renewed relationship between the Jews and the Holy Land, Lévy argues, lies nothing other than that persistent pre-conciliar obsolete devil called supersessionism. For the sake of consistency, Lévy suggests, the Church should not shy away from taking a theological stand regarding the land and state of Israel and include recent political events in its post–*Nostra Aetate* paradigm of "irrevocability" (while also applying a theological, biblically based justice to the Israeli-Palestinian conflict).

Yet as we have seen, the detheologization trajectory which Lévy rejects should not be reduced to an inconsistent adoption of secular reasoning nor to a remnant of classical supersessionism (though supersessionism is clearly essential to this theological position). It is embedded in the Catholic tradition beyond its attitude to Jews and Judaism, and it is revived and readjusted to the contemporary setting in *Gaudium et Spes*. This means that in order to consistently adhere to *Nostra Aetate*'s teaching regarding Judaism, Lévy must reject *Gaudium et Spes*'s teaching regarding the separation of politics from theology, and reject an ancient tradition that looks suspiciously on the theological value of politics. This choice may indeed bring the Church closer to the Jewish people and is more consistent in its theological attitude to the Jews, but it causes a lack of consistency in other areas.

In the context of the Israeli-Palestinian conflict, revoking the Catholic move of universalizing the Old Testament land promise to the point of secularizing politics leads to a reverse supersessionist attitude toward Catholic Palestinians. Suppressing Catholic universality under the principle of Jewish difference means that Catholic Palestinians' own Christological reading of the Old Testament is superseded by the Jewish or the pro-Jewish reading. In the compelling words of Michael Sabbah (also quoted by Neuhaus and Khader), "Could we be victims of our own salvation history, which seems to favor the Jewish people and condemn us? Is that truly the Will of God to which we must inexorably bow down, demanding that we deprive ourselves in favor of another people ... ?"[22] This sentence could be applied (one only has to switch "the Jewish people" with "Christians") to the way pre–*Nostra Aetate* Jews experienced the Catholic approach toward them, which deprives

---

22 Fourth Pastoral Letter of Patriarch Michael Sabbah, *Reading the Bible Today in the Land of the Bible*, no. 7 (November 1993).

them of their sense of meaning and treats them as satellites in someone else's galaxy. Catholic theology is therefore torn here between listening to Judaism as a living reality that is also part of the Church's own identity, and its universalistic heritage, which negates, to a certain extent, the Jewish difference and Judaism's vitality. It is impossible to choose one trajectory without suppressing the other.

To conclude, let us go back for a moment to the Eusebian-Augustinian distinction. The Church wanted to supersede its supersessionism against the Jews, because this approach was connected to its Eusebian, triumphalist self-perception, a paradigm it used in order to justify immoral behavior toward its traditional Others, and first and foremost the Jews themselves. In the second half of the twentieth century, the Church wished to release itself from the remnants of this Eusebianism and give more room to other voices that were previously marginalized by it, and first and foremost to Jewish voices. Yet not activating supersessionism toward Judaism turned out to entail embracing the Eusebianism of Judaism itself, in the figure of theological Zionism. On the other hand, a coherent Augustinian position on behalf of the Church—i.e., an inherent suspicion toward the divinization of political processes—leads directly (and in Augustine himself) to a supersessionist perception of Judaism. Paradoxically, an adoption of Augustinian political theology entails an Eusebian, triumphalist replacement of Jewish political messianism with the "right" and "just" anti-political messianism of the Church—which is once again, the exact opposite of what the Church sought to achieve.

14

JEWS, CATHOLICS, AND ISRAEL
CAN WE FIND A SHARED LANGUAGE?
Faydra L. Shapiro

I offer this response as a person rather invested in the topic—a religious Jew and an Israeli. I did not grow up as either, but the two are deeply connected in my own life. It was only on my first trip to Israel at the age of thirteen that it really occurred to me that there existed a world of rich Jewish faith and practice that could be gingerly approached, one that was quite unlike what I experienced as the sterile and class-ridden religious expressions of my Jewish upbringing in Canada. I came back to Israel again and again for stays short and long, increasingly unable to breathe outside this world of faith and meaning. I married an Israeli, in Israel. And ultimately we chose to make our home and raise our family here, many years ago. At the same time, I also write as a Jew who is somewhat immersed in Catholic things due to my own research projects and interests.[1]

Because this article concerns a political topic, a word about my connection to such things. My politics are uninteresting, and I have no political engagement outside of voting in national and municipal elections. But I am a Zionist, however ambivalent at times. I believe in the importance of the state of Israel and in a state of Israel that gives specific and limited extra protection to its Jewish character. I recognize that this unavoidably gives rise to situations of inequality, not unlike any social or political program that seeks to level

---

1 My sincere thanks go out to the colleagues and friends who graciously read and commented on earlier drafts of this paper, including Adam Gregerman, Murray Watson, and Judith Wolfe, as well as several of the contributors to this volume. Special appreciation to Yoel Katzenstein for his assistance with sources.

historical and structural injustices through unequal distribution of rights such as gender- or race-based affirmative action, indigenous tax exemptions on native lands, or veterans' rights. It is the undoubtedly challenging job of the state to strive for the best possible balance between Jewishness and democracy. Having grown up as a minority religion in Canada, where Catholic students receive public funding but Jewish (and other religious) schools do not, where Christmas and Good Friday are national days of rest but Jewish (and other religious) holidays are not, and where university exams were never on a Sunday but could be on a Saturday, I know Israel is not the only state to struggle with this issue. I also recognize that the choices we've made for our family—where we live in Israel, our children's education, their army service—are implicated in systems and structures. While we might not have actively or consciously chosen those systems and structures, it means our own choices cannot be entirely innocent either.

When it comes to issues of Israel-Palestine, I am stubbornly and unfashionably committed to a two-state solution, to the chagrin of my friends to the right and left who favor various kinds of one-state solutions. I believe in a democratic and sovereign Palestine both because I think it is morally correct and because it is good for Israel. I am against the Israeli occupation of the disputed territories, and I am eager for a time when Israel can feel secure enough to dismantle that apparatus. I am also not certain that this time has yet come. Responsibility for this seemingly intractable state of affairs is shared, I believe, between several groups and factors. But the question of blame also hardly matters for our reflection here.

I would insist that no thinking about the state of Israel—by Catholics, or anyone for that matter—can take place without keeping two very different, but both important, realities in full view: on the one side, the Holocaust and the Jewish struggle for national liberation and survival, and on the other, Palestinian suffering and the Palestinian struggle for national liberation. To lose sight of either one of these while thinking theologically about the state of Israel is not only to do bad theology, but also immoral and intellectually untenable. To make note of these two realities is not to compare them or draw false equivalencies them, but to simply speak the truth about our lives and senses of suffering and vulnerability here.

For those who like labels, my first instinct is to say that I'm a religious Zionist, because in its simplest and purest sense that is true. But the term has come to mean so many things that I reject, that I am forced to search out a new adjective, despite being both what we call in Israel "religious" and also "a Zionist." Perhaps "an-ambivalent-but-still-hopeful-religious Zionist" is as close as we can get at this stage.

One of the essential questions that hovers around this volume concerns the definition of Zionism. Surprisingly, and most encouraging, both Palestinian contributors to this volume appear to make room for a Jewish State alongside a Palestinian one. For most Jews, this "two-state" formulation would fall very much within the realm of what constitutes a "Zionist" approach. Sabbah even invokes the security and survival of the Jewish State, while Khader uses the language of "multiparticularity" to respect both Jewish and Palestinian claims to the land. Yet at the same time both contributors are unflinching in their assessments of the injustice and suffering perpetrated in the name of Zionism. That suffering and injustice prompt me to wonder if this aspect is a *necessary* aspect of Zionism, or if it is still possible to redeem the Zionist project in a transformed spiritual and moral articulation. Is there a way to think religiously about the state of Israel—for Jews or Catholics—*without* falling into the obvious traps—of justifying injustice, replacing faith with nationalism, and making an idol out of Land or state? I am one of the many Jewish Israelis who quite hope so. And it is my goal to try to think this through here.

In terms of the task at hand, trying to sort out what I am *not* doing here is perhaps easier than knowing what I *am* doing here, and might help to clarify the latter. I am most assuredly not trying to present any kind of classic or normative Jewish thinking on the Land and State of Israel. There are many people far more knowledgeable and more suited to do that than I. Aside from being not especially able at that task, that kind of response doesn't immediately strike me as what is appropriate to this volume in terms of a "response" to Catholic thinking on this topic. I understand my task in the response as one of translating at least a small part of Jewish experience/priorities/categories into something plausible for a thoughtful Catholic audience. At the same time I want to think as a Jew, alongside my Catholic friends and colleagues, in ways that are hopefully both critical and supportive at the same time. We reflect on these issues as Jews and Catholics, often in ways that are quite different. We need to learn to speak one another's languages a bit, and come to feel comfortable visiting—however briefly—one another's environment of concern, hope, and fear. At best that's a project that might result in something vaguely recognizable on either side of the conversation, but not fully at home anywhere. It's hardly going to result in orthodox Jewish thought, or normal Catholic ways of thinking. But it might perhaps offer some initial useful tools to help us all safely through some small corners of this complex conversation.

Allow me to begin, then, with the challenge set out by my coeditor in this volume. Gavin D'Costa outlines the issues for affirming the State of Israel for Catholic thought with consummate clarity. The options seem constrained, and so he searches outside the usual models to mobilize the possibility he sees opened by Benedict XVI's controversial "Grace and Vocation." D'Costa writes,

> Could it [the State of Israel] be understood as other than a political messianic faith state? Could it be a contingent political formation that is corrupt and given to the misuse of power as are all states, while also a necessary historically contingent arrangement that has ensured the continuity of the Jewish people and thus God's fidelity to his people Israel? ... If the State is seen as a contingent arrangement that provides for the just safety of the Jewish people, without neglect for a just solution to attain a Palestinian homeland, would it then be possible for Catholics to affirm a minimalist theological affirmation of the state?

Here D'Costa skillfully teases out a tentative path through the jungle of possibilities and constraints that Catholics who seek a "minimalist Zionism" might follow. My own efforts are focused differently, with perhaps the audacity sufferable only in a theological dilettante such as I am. What I wonder about in this paper is, beyond questions about the "legitimacy" of the State of Israel, whether and where we might be able to locate actual positive value in the State of Israel for Catholics.

And while the Catholic Church is of course under no expectation to think like Jews we might say that one of the fundamental tenets of interreligious dialogue is the effort to understand the other according to its own terms. Naturally that doesn't mean that one party ought to agree with the terms of another, a move that would render interfaith dialogue ultimately senseless. Dialogue is predicated on disagreement. But the effort to seek out some common language or at least principles for translation would go a long way in terms of Jewish-Catholic dialogue were we to feel that we are not *a priori* speaking in irreconcilable terms.

It is precisely the conviction that there is a connection that exists between us, beyond the level of basic neighborliness or historical encounter, that opens up the possibility of finding some shared domain of discourse, however particular the local dialect. I am inspired in this by the words of Jacques Maritain when he wrote of the connection between the Jewish people, the Church, and the world: "Israel is a mystery. Of the same order as the mystery of the world or the mystery of the Church. Like them, it lies at the heart of redemption."[2] Taking this cue from Maritain, I have divided my reflection into three sections: the Church, the Jewish people, and the world.

---

2 Jacques Maritain, "Anti-Semitism," in *The Social and Political Philosophy of Jacques Maritain: Selected Readings*, ed. Jacques Maritain, Joseph W. Evans, and Leo R. Ward (New York: Image Books, 1965), 199.

THE VOCATION OF THE CHURCH

There are a number of different ways that Christians tend to approach Israel: as a theological "problem" that needs to be explained, as a "sign" that tells us something about God's faithfulness, as a kind of "pointer" that directs attention to the End Times, as an "issue" that complicates Jewish-Christian dialogue. For Catholics probably the most common is through the lens of "the Holy Land"—a place of encounter with Christ through the events of his life, mission, death, and resurrection, and pilgrimage to those sites where the Church has expressed her faith in those events. It is important, I believe, for Christians to begin to get a sense of the ways that Israel matters in the real world, to real people.

One important but often overlooked role for the state of Israel is as a concrete environment, the location for a renewed possibility of encounter between Christians and Jews in a new key. An encounter not tied to the classic formulation of Christian power and Jewish victimhood, but one that can open up new ways of relation and reconciliation. Much as Jews might prefer not to think about it, the state of Israel has served as a concrete location for a new kind of Jewish encounter with Christianity. The situation of Jewish security can begin to allow for an authentic Jewish-Christian conversation in a slightly less defensive mode. I believe that the two Jewish respondents here—Karma ben Johanan and myself—might serve as examples of that.

Interestingly, Feingold's contribution hopes that the State of Israel might facilitate a quite different kind of Jewish encounter with Christianity. He connects the return of the Jews to the Land of Israel to a development that he, and presumably most Christians, would find very welcome: the growing number of Jews who assert their Jewishness together with faith in Christ. Feingold is excited by the return of Jews to the Land of Israel in sovereignty and suggests the importance of Israel as offering "a renewed possibility for a corporate encounter with Jesus in a way different than in the diaspora." This perspective is a rather delicate one in terms of Jewish-Christian relations, but I will say that my own fieldwork research bears this out. Without doubt, naming this as of specific importance or value to the state of Israel is, to normal Jewish ears, both incoherent and threatening. But for a Christian, and I would think particularly for those Jews whose very lives have been changed by the kind of "encounter with Jesus" that Feingold envisions, the state of Israel as a flourishing and full-bodied Jewish context for the gospel cannot be discounted as anything less than essential.

Jews have our own reasons for insisting that Israel matters in terms of concrete, lived experience that are utterly unrelated to Christianity. To Jewish listeners, Christian theologians might try too hard, we might say, to justify with fancy theology the social-historically obvious fact that the state of Israel is essential to Jewish survival. At a time when Jews are warned not to walk the streets looking "Jewish" for fear of (increasingly common) violent attack, when Jewish cemeteries are desecrated, neo-Nazi graffiti resurfaces, and anti-Jewish tropes are found in national newspapers, we are compelled to recall that this historical moment has arisen when Auschwitz is still within living memory, and when the world's cries of "never again" still echo. So while Jewish history was not the unrelenting and lachrymose series of tragedies and persecutions that is sometimes presented, history has also been a lesson to remind us of the continuing fragility and insecurity that the Jewish people face among the nations. It is not alarmist, hyperbolic, or paranoid to suggest that the state of Israel plays an essential role in the survival and flourishing of the Jewish people into the future.

Simply put, if we think the world is a better one with Jews in it, then the state of Israel is non-negotiable, as both a defense of the Jewish people in the present and a safe haven in the future. In all frankness, for the Jewish experience, the need for a Jewish State is really not at all about land promises, covenants (conditional or unconditional), or eschatology but "simply" about the survival of a people that on a good day numbers a scant fifteen million souls. It behooves Catholics to remember that there are more Seventh Day Adventists in the world today than there are Jews. This is so much the case that in 1980 one of the greatest halachic authorities of this era, who served as Chief Sefaradi Rabbi of the state of Israel for ten years, Rav Ovadiah Yosef, ruled that territorial compromise ("land for peace") is permissible were it to lead to Jewish lives saved.[3] An attachment to the Land is subordinate to the survival of the Jewish people.

While it goes without saying that Jews care about Jewish survival, for Christians the question of Jewish survival is also a pressing one, albeit differently so, because we are not speaking of the survival of just any people, or the survival of people generally. Jewish survival is not the same as the survival of disappearing Amazon tribes or any other salvage operation. As I have written elsewhere,

> While there's good reason to be cautious about anachronisms, and prudent about what this should mean for contemporary Christian practice, Christians I think can also understand something about God himself, through the exercise of consciously and attentively seeking to understand the people whom He loves. That in orthodox Christian understanding

[3] Ovadia Yosef, "Returning Territories from the Land of Israel in Order to Save Lives," *Torah Shebe'al Peh* 21 (1980): 12–21.

the physical locus of the incarnation is not Rome or Alexandria, but deep in the Jewish people, in the womb of a daughter of Israel in the Land of Israel, is neither a random nor a meaningless choice. This divine choice is one full of theological meaning and implications. But it's a choice that also has social-historical implications, ones that bind the body of Christ to the Jewish people in not only mystical but also very concrete ways. The Jewish people not only can nourish the Church in mystical/theological dimensions, but also through the fruit of its own providentially-guided experience.[4]

Or in other words, Christians can, perhaps even must, learn from Jews in order to enrich and fully flesh out their own faith.

Jews are special, both theologically and historically, for Christians, both because they are special to God and because they form the context and cradle for Christianity, helping to define its fundamental concepts, hopes, and anxieties. And while this might offend democratic sensibilities—not to mention anti-Semites—this fact is one that pursues the Church through her own history.

For Catholics this situation is even more acute. Beholden to a sense of obedience to authoritative tradition, magisterial documents emerging out of the Second Vatican Council have made the State of Israel issue an unavoidably relevant issue for every Catholic, as reflected by the essays in this collection. The Church's renewed relationship with the Jewish people, beginning with *Nostra Aetate* and continuing along that trajectory, is one characterized by a degree of intimacy, understanding, and support. Yet that trajectory is on an obvious and inevitable collision course with the reluctant, arm's-length attitude that the Vatican has taken toward the State of Israel. The fact that it took the Holy See until 1993 to enter into diplomatic relations with the State of Israel is an example of that reluctance.

It quickly becomes clear to any reader of *Nostra Aetate* that the Church understands its relationship with the Jewish people as unique among the non-Christian relations. *Nostra Aetate*, as we know, began in efforts to formulate a statement specifically on the Jewish people, and only secondarily developed into a statement concerning "non-Christian religions." The very structure of its paragraphs carries in it the realization that Jews possess a specific theological significance and historical burden, and thus require significantly more attention, and attention of a more complex degree, than that given to the other religions.

---

4 Faydra L. Shapiro, "Beyond Dialogue: Envisioning a Jewishly Enriched Body of Christ," *Pro Ecclesia* 28, no. 3 (2019): 3.

The Church today is able to assert that Israel is an essential, unique, significant, and ongoing part of God's plan for the world. As such the Church strives mightily to make theological sense of every part of Israel—her suffering, her "unbelief," her role, and her destiny. It cannot appear like anything other than a dereliction of duty for the Church to suggest—amidst all this profound theological significance—that Israel's return to the Land, in safety and in sovereignty, has no theological significance whatsoever.

Thus I find a bit puzzling Neuhaus's argument that the correct approach to Israel is to be found in a retreat to the artificial safety ground of secular international law. Certainly international law is an essential element for establishing universal norms of justice and equality in the political sphere. There is no doubt that Israel as a modern nation-state must operate as part of the international community, and it is bound as any state to standards of international law. But secular, political international law can hardly be sufficient to the task of interpreting Israel as either nation or state, and I find it mystifying why a religious faith ought to embrace such constructed standards as anything more than a minimal, if necessary, set of criteria for political entities. There is indeed something amiss with the "theological disengagement" that Lévy describes, and a fruitless circularity at work in asserting that Israel's return to the land is not theological and that therefore it can only be understood through a non-theological lens.

The Church is instructed to remember that these deep points of connection with the Jewish people are not solely historical, and that the relationship to the Jews and Judaism is not fully completed or fulfilled by noting the Jewish context for the emergence of Christianity. As Ansorge notes, "Catholics are obliged to clarify their own faith in continuous dialogue with their Jewish brothers and sisters." *Nostra Aetate* is at its most daring when it uses the present continuous in writing of the Church's relation to the Jewish people as one that is ongoing and eternal: "the bond that spiritually *ties* the people of the New Covenant to Abraham's stock" that the Church remembers as it strives to make sense of itself. Equally, the Church cannot "forget that she *draws* sustenance from the root of that well-cultivated olive tree" onto which the Gentiles have been grafted. Finally, the Church "*keeps ever in mind* the words of the Apostle about his kinsmen" (that to them belong the sonship and the glory and the covenant and the law, etc.) and also "*recalls* that the Apostles, the Church's main-stay and pillars, as well as most of the early disciples who proclaimed Christ's Gospel to the world, sprang from the Jewish people."

The Church is intimately bound up with the Jewish people for its own foundation and identity *in an ongoing sense*. Which means, simply put, that the Jewish people is essential for the Church to know who it is, not just in the past, but in this very moment as well.

And as such, we can imagine, the actual continued existence of the Jewish people is thus of special importance to the Church. The existence and survival of the Jewish people is qualitatively different for the Church than the existence and survival of other peoples, a fact that should in no way serve to diminish the importance of other nations, for two reasons. First, as above—because the Jewish people is an integral and inseparable part of the mystical essence of the Church. This realization is powerfully expressed in the surprising and poignant institutional fact that the Commission for Religious Relations with the Jews falls to the responsibility of the Pontifical Council for Promoting Christian Unity. In contrast, for example, the Commission for Religious Relations with Muslims is part of the Pontifical Council for Interreligious Dialogue. The Catholic Church understands that there is something qualitatively different about its relationship with the Jewish people.

Second, the existence and survival of the Jewish people into the future must be important to the faithful because God *himself* is committed to the survival of that very people. The notion of "*she'arit Yisrael*," the remnant of Israel, that appears in several of the prophetic books of the Hebrew Bible, is significant enough for Paul to refer to it in Romans 9:27, quoting Isaiah 10:22. It's worth noting that this passage is often misread as one presenting a message of judgment due to the common translation with the word "only," at least in English translations, i.e., that *only* a remnant will survive. But both the Hebrew in Isaiah and the Greek in Romans suggest no such "only." Thus we are encouraged to read this as a statement of promise and comfort—that notwithstanding the vicissitudes of history, a remnant will survive—rather than one of judgment and punishment. God promises that Jews will survive.

For the Church to rightly understand both herself and the God she serves is dependent on knowing, in a profound way, the Jewish people. And that requires, at a minimum, that there be Jews. It is in this space of peoplehood and survival, it would seem to me, that a productive and positive (perhaps D'Costa would say "minimalist") Catholic approach to the State of Israel, and one that is at the same time not at odds with Catholic social teaching, could be articulated, dependent solely on very clear magisterial teaching rather than anything especially debatable or buried deeply in tradition and history. It is also an understanding of the state and its importance that could be recognizable to the Jewish people ourselves.

THE VOCATION OF THE JEWISH PEOPLE

Neuhaus writes that "Israel's vocation is to be a source of blessing for all" and to, in an eschatological vision welcome "empires into God's Kingdom, where together Egyptians, Assyrians, and Israelites sing God's name in a symphony of praise." Isaiah reminds us in 49:6 that being God's servant and the raising up and restoration of the tribes of Jacob and the offspring of Israel are not the total of what is to come, but also we are called outward, to be a light to the nations. And assuming that this mission is not *completely* fulfilled when Simeon holds the baby Jesus in his arms and declares him a light for revelation to the Gentiles, Catholics can have confidence that Israel still has some role to play. If Israel still has such a mission and vocation given to her by God, then we must ask ourselves what are the ideal conditions for fulfilling that mission. Can the people of Israel truly be a source of blessing for all when she is weak, endangered, frightened, and insular? It is only with security and stability that Jews might have a possibility of developing a deeper engagement with the world.

In the previous section we considered the value of the state of Israel for the Church, in serving her ability to know herself and her true identity through the Jewish people. Indeed the Church's amnesia about its Jewishness is one kind of challenge. But it is also a challenge for the Jewish people to come to understand our own identity and calling. This challenge has been greatly exacerbated by the conditions under which we have lived, particularly under Christian history. Thus for the nation of Israel to similarly come to know more deeply and grow toward being able to fulfill its own identity and mission, the basic conditions necessary to discern that nature and calling are needed. The State of Israel—notwithstanding the many and obvious dangers, misdirections, and pitfalls—holds out the possibility of offering the Jewish people enough normalization to awaken the ability and desire to assess our uniqueness and our unique role in the world.

The greatest possibility of the modern state of Israel is precisely this: to present the conditions where Israel takes on the challenge of fully becoming who God has called her to be. A place where Israel might become transformed into the true Israel, where the people might be healed from her wounds, grow in moral virtue, and take up her vocation. An environment that can allow, inspire, and challenge Israel to rise up and take her real place in God's economy. In reality, this transformation of the people Israel in the state of Israel is a most perilous path, one fraught with pitfalls, temptation, and excess. It is a path that we modern Israelis have not navigated anywhere near as well as we might wish, thus far. And yet, this dangerous road is one that has the potential to transfigure us, as a people, with God's help.

Ezekiel's prophecy of the dry bones in chapter 37 can help us to see this. The fact that the dry bones are knitted together physically first before actually being infused with God's spirit and brought to life offers us a vivid metaphor to think with. Recalling that our sense of time and God's sense of time are distinct, one might fruitfully imagine this process as one taking place in immensely slow motion, perhaps over years and decades. We might try to consider what the whole thing might look like to a person who walked into the middle of the story, without the knowledge that we readers of the Bible have. It might present a telling combination of a situation that is both awesomely miraculous and embarrassingly incomplete. A moment where we are forced both to recognize what is and to yearn for what is not yet. In this scenario the physical resurrection plays a necessary but clearly not sufficient part in the final "making live" of these dry bones. It would suggest great blindness to not be able to envision the so much more that God plans for these bones in terms of spiritual regeneration and actually coming to life. But at the same time it would take immense blindness to be able to stand in that incomplete moment and not recognize the awesomeness of the divine move that has collected those bones together in physical regeneration. The State of Israel stands in that long moment between the physical rebirth and the spiritual animation to come. And we are compelled to remember that the basic safety and security it offers to Jews are an essential piece in the Jewish people's ability to turn toward our spiritual identity and mission to the world. It is only with security and stability that Jews might have a possibility of developing a deeper engagement with the world.

Thus I think the call that Rutishauser issues is an essential one for the development of an "Israelology" that would correspond to the way that ecclesiology serves for understanding the Church in a theological fashion. His discussion of Judaism as both a people, with its institutions, social structures, and obligation to holiness, and also a spiritual-metaphysical reality is an important one, and this is precisely the difference between *Am Yisrael* and *Knesset Yisrael*. Rutishauser notes that the Church "no longer defines itself so much as *societas perfecta*, but rather as the people of God on pilgrimage." Similarly, I would suggest that Israel might understand itself as God's people *en route* through the "worldly-material" to become more and more the people of God. The State of Israel—just as the Land of Israel—has an essential role to play in this process. And it is for this reason that I feel that Chenchiah's paper falls just one step short of the most important conclusion: when the Land of Israel reaches its true *telos*, there the *nation* of Israel (rather than the Land, as Chenchiah asserts) will be resurrected. It is then and there that the people constituted imperfectly in the Exodus will achieve its fullness of being in the "true and ideal" Exodus, as Chenchiah so beautifully describes. Thus I believe Garrigues and Kurylo's conclusion to be not only useful for understanding the essence of the Land but also helpful in that it is with an example that can speak to both Catholics and Jews when they note that

> the first piece of promised land, that of the cave at Machpelah, was not originally conquered, but purchased by Abraham as a "funeral concession" (Gn 23:9) and the burial place for Sarah, for himself (cf. Gn 25:9) and for their descendants (cf. Gn 49:29–32; 50:13). The land is given by God first of all as a place of burial, of a paschal journey through death, as a place of waiting and of welcome for the Resurrection.

This speaks to Tapie's examination of Aquinas's Christological interpretation of the Land as *terra viventium*, the "land of the living." And of course, returning to the example of Ezekiel 37 above, the Land is specifically the locus of that resurrected national life as in verses 12–14.

This transformation and resurrection of *Am Yisrael* will happen not simply through the experience of sovereignty and the existence of the state of Israel (as Zionist history would read), but through at least meeting the challenges of the state, as a both historical and theologically significant vehicle through which the Land can become holy and the people truly Israel.

Theologians and Bible scholars often formulate the issue in a bit of a simplistic fashion: Is the promise of Land to the Jewish people one that is "conditional" or "unconditional"? And as such, is the national expectation of Land something that can be lost due to the infidelity of the people, or is it eternal and in some sense independent of any such behavioral tests? Theologians and scholars mobilize arguments in favor of one of the other of these options as needed. But a third approach is also possible—the promise of land is both unconditional and conditional at the same time. The two ostensibly conflictual approaches can be squared with a confidence in the transformation of the people. That is, the confidence that while the people can indeed be in a state where they do not merit the land, the very eternality of that promise asserts that the people will ultimately *become* that people. Thus, I am reluctant to suggest, as does Vetö, that "the rightful presence of two people on one land is a test for the people of God, as it is for the Palestinian people." Tests can be failed. We know that despite the current state of things, despite our falling into many kinds of errors and temptations when it comes to the state of Israel and the possession of Land, the people will ultimately not fail this test. The promise of the Land is unconditional and eternal. Rather than a test, we might understand this situation best as an opportunity; an invitation to become transformed from the people of Israel that we are into the people of Israel that we are meant to be: a true blessing to the world.

Neuhaus rightly cautions that "the Christian term 'Holy Land' should not become an escape from saying 'Israel' or 'Palestine.'" This is important, as we live this reality in the concrete historical situatedness, and it is a violation of both peoples to evade this into some spiritual reality. However, Neuhaus continues, the Christian term "Holy Land" should at the same time not be entirely mired in this concrete reality, that it should also "constitute a recalling of the vocation of this land to be a true home to many . . . a land called to be holy." Indeed the Land has its own vocation. Feingold notes, "The relationship of Israel with the Land is a type of the relationship of Israel with the Lord." We are—Jews and Christians—called to be holy as God is holy. The vocation of the Land is, I believe, to challenge us, to inspire us, to tempt us, and to "nourish our yearning" (as Feingold writes) to be that kind of holy.

Thus the state of Israel seems to me not the *accomplishment* of the promises, but rather a *necessary step* toward their actual accomplishment. It is only a people with a transfigured sense: of identity, of possession, of vulnerability, of trust—that can ultimately merit to see those promises fulfilled. That transfiguration can only happen to the nation reborn on the land, healing from the past with a sense of national security, struggling through the temptations of national independence and power.

All of which reminds me of a most wonderful formulation I have heard in Catholic liturgical contexts, where the faithful pray "to become worthy of the promises of Christ." This is a prayer that we—Jews and Christians—can use to think with most fruitfully. It opens up the possibility that God will help make us all into the kinds of people we ought to be, people who cultivate the seed of holiness that God has placed in us, and people who can see and help to cultivate that same holiness in others. Would not that very striving for holiness help to make us at the same time both a blessing to the world and worthy of the promise of the Land?

THE VOCATION OF THE PALESTINIANS?

I find Vetö's argument that the Land is *a priori* one that must be shared, where the "problem" of otherness must be solved, to be a compelling one. This is part of how the Land can serve as a locus for blessing to the world, and the only path to achieving the promise of Isaiah 56:7 that God's house will be a house of prayer for all nations. However, I also believe that this argument can be achieved without invoking categories of salvation specially concerning the Palestinians in order to do so.

Vetö's proposition here is intriguing, arguing that the Palestinian people themselves have a vocation and that "there is a mysteriously unique place for the Palestinian people in the history of salvation: to be the people with whom Israel shares the land of the promise; to be the people who share the land with Israel; to be to associated in a special way with the chosen people." To my mind, in order to take seriously the dignity of the Palestinian people, Vetö has perhaps unnecessarily theologized them to a place that unwittingly compromises a Christian understanding of the uniqueness of the Jewish people. I would agree that the Palestinians have an essential role to play at this historical stage, in helping Israel to fulfill her vocation and become all that she can/could/should be. However, I might further suggest this is a role shared by all the "others" that challenge corporate Israel toward holiness in the Land, be they poor, dissenters, *Shoah* survivors, the disabled, or asylum seekers.

To argue as Vetö does that "Concretely speaking, the God-given relation of the *Am Ysrael* to *Eretz Yisrael* cannot be taken as an absolute if it is at the cost of the integrity and dignity of the Palestinian people—and reciprocally, the relation of the Palestinian people to their land is not an absolute if puts to risk the existence and dignity of the Jewish people," is to my mind a case of making questionable and unsupportable equivalencies, even if the motivation is a praiseworthy one.

We can understand the Palestinian people as presenting a God-willed and potentially fruitful moral challenge to Israel within the realm of contingent history without mobilizing any specifically theological arguments and categories of "mystery" or "salvation." We must avoid underestimating the historical and reading too much through the lens of revelation, just as much as we must avoid the temptation in the other direction, the opposite, as perhaps Neuhaus, Khader, and Sabbah are inclined to remind us.

Yet on this subject, I am concerned by the "third hypothesis" Lévy offers as he seeks a reason for this "theological disengagement" of the Catholic Church from the State of Israel. Lévy suggests that this might be because an "official endorsement of basic Zionism" could be a problem for Arabic-speaking Christians in the region. His argument, simply, is that sometimes the truth hurts. As he proclaims, "theological affirmations are not exactly supposed to derive from the desire to make a part of the faithful feel morally or politically comfortable." As true as this may be, theological affirmations also cannot exist entirely abstracted from the real-life situation of the people. When I mentally "translate" this idea into Jewish terms, I find no analogy— "the faithful" are not some afterthought that might find the truth difficult but somehow have to live with it. They are, in some way, constitutive of that truth. Jewish *halakha* not only ideally relates to the particular circumstances of the individuals and communities being addressed but even can arise from those very particular circumstances of the people themselves.[5]

If the Church truly understands herself as the body of Christ, its members joined together in something even stronger than the physical kinship ties of carnal Israel, then we might expect the sense of mutual responsibility and obligation to other Christians to be extraordinarily strong. One would think then that Catholic sensitivity to the lives, experiences, hopes, and fears of other Catholics ought to be more than just a pastoral question, but rather an essential component of Catholic reasoning. And thus just as no Jew could be able to think about the State of Israel without giving thought to the safety, survival, and flourishing of his kin, so too no Catholic should be able to think about the State of Israel without some thought to the safety, survival, and flourishing of his spiritual kin.

Thus while I am not sure I am ready to agree with Vetö's proposition that the Palestinian people hold a unique role in salvation history in the moral challenge they offer to Israel, I would at the same time question the direction that Lévy implies, wherein the role of the Palestinians is to serve in their suffering as a kind of "witness people" to the "theological truth" of Jewish chosenness.

THE VOCATION OF THE WORLD

To a Jewish way of thinking, it is not insignificant that Israel's independence day always falls during the counting of the *Omer*, the seven weeks between the Jewish holidays of Passover and *Shavuot* (Feast of Weeks), a time of journey from being a nation freed from physical slavery toward a nation that is spiritually free, one truly animated by and subject to God's word. The modern State of Israel we might imagine as standing somewhere in this uncomfortable yet fruitful in-between, in the very process of becoming truly and fully alive. The tension of this time is one that plagues the people of Israel (literally) and can help us to understand its presence in the modern State of Israel, enabling us to be both grateful for what is and enflamed with and straining toward a sense of what is to come.

For Jews, this period of "counting the *Omer*" between Passover and *Shavuot* is referred to as "Days of Judgment." They can productively be understood as offering a developmental process, from a passive reliance

---

[5] A good example of this is the well-known stringency of Rabbi Zeira (Babylonian Talmud Brachot 31a) where "the daughters of Israel were stringent with themselves," and this evolved into set practice for the future.

on God's *chesed* (I'll call it "grace" here) that we see God's taking us out of Egypt to an increasing level of responsibility, accountability, and human activity that is found in *Shavuot*. But this does not come all at once, or fall upon us without preparation. Rather there is a process of becoming, of slow transformation from what is to what will be. Concerning this forty-nine-day counting of the *Omer*, (*sefirat haOmer*), which begins on the second day of Passover and continues until *Shavuot*, the Torah commands us to "count for yourselves" (Lv 23:15, Dt 16:9).[6] Each night of this time, Jews specifically make a blessing and count "Today is the first day of the *Omer*," "Today is the second day of the *Omer*," all the way through. One famous teaching explains that by emphasizing that we do it for ourselves, the Torah is indicating that it's actually for our own good.[7] We benefit from this counting. We can also see this in terms of Temple offerings. As this period began on the second day of Passover, a special *Omer* offering was brought to the Temple in the waving of a barley sheaf. This is a very simple offering, the first harvesting of barley, food fit for animals. But seven weeks later, on *Shavuot*, the counting is complete. And the *Shavuot* offering is quite different: two loaves of leavened bread. From freshly cut barley fit only for animals to baked bread, the work of human hands and food fit for man. The nation born in the Exodus and the first *Pesach* gains its true meaning and identity from what it becomes at *Shavuot*—a nation covenanted to God. The people that emerges from Egypt is something important that is inextricably linked to what we will become.[8]

However, we must look elsewhere for equivalent images that can help Catholics specifically to think about that tension between the "now" and the "not yet," and that challenge of living in the present with an eye to the future. Perhaps this takes Ansorge's focus on sacramentality in a direction he might reject entirely. In an interesting essay on "Eucharistic Theology and the Rite of Mass," Aidan Nichols writes about the intense power of prolepsis—more pronounced, he notes, in some Eucharistic liturgies than others—wherein the dedicated gifts are seen to anticipate and thus in some way actually already be the body and blood of Christ that they will become with the act of Consecration.

> It's as though the Church can't wait to get to the Prayer of Oblation, and above all to the Consecration, the moment when her gifts, which represent herself, will be transformed into Christ's Gift which does not simply

---

6 Deuteronomy 16:9 is in the singular.

7 Shalom Noach Berezovsky, "Omer HaTenufa," *Netivot Shalom*, vol. 2 (Jerusalem: Yeshivat Bet Avraham Slonim, 1982).

8 See, for example, *Sefer HaChinukh*, "Commandment 306: The Commandment of Counting the Omer," paragraph 4.

represent him but embodies him in his Sacrifice for her. The Bride is impatient to get to the Nuptials on the Cross, to the Paschal mystery, the thought of which is so fascinating that it draws to itself by anticipation what is in a preliminary way being done. The loss of these prayers undermines the way we should habituate ourselves to inhabit Eucharistic time, and, as I say, it also weakens the sense of the Mass as Sacrifice."[9]

Perhaps we might cautiously consider this as a model in terms of how to read other things that are present before us in one form, yet on their way to something else at the hands of a radical transformation. The ability of Catholics to anticipate and to proleptically glimpse the body and blood of Christ they will become as in some way *already present* in the blessed bread and wine, is to be able to look with a Eucharistic sight. Christians, I think, are—or ought to be—so similarly impatient for the Second Coming and the "not yet" that we are promised, that even in the midst of the incomplete (dirty, noisy, divided) "now" of the earthly Jerusalem, they are able to see it shot through with the Heavenly Jerusalem it will become. This move is one that might help Christians to develop a Kingdom-focused sight.

It is also a powerful exercise that can both reflect and build confidence in precisely that impossible transformative power that only God wields, and which no amount or degree of human action can replace. We cannot build the New Jerusalem with our hands. We can only anticipate it with our hearts, but anticipate it we must. That anticipation forces us to look with great care on the current form of things. And that includes, in a most singular way, to be able to look with special vision on the current, messy and very much imperfect city that Jerusalem is. Jerusalem, like the dedicated gifts at the altar, not only might but *must* be recognized as something different than any other city.

Jerusalem, while a city like any other, can never be only that. Jerusalem does not point to itself in some tiresome play of self-referential signs. Jerusalem points to the people we could be, and the God that eternally is, who does not forget us and is faithful to us even in the state that we currently still are. Jean-Louis Chretien writes in a most powerful image connecting Christ's wounds in this world with Christ's eternal and glorified body that, while transformed, always and eternally bears memory:

> The exiled of Psalm 137 can and must say: "If I forget you, O Jerusalem, let my right hand wither! Let my tongue cleave to the roof of my mouth,

---

[9] Aidan Nichols, "Eucharistic Theology and the Rite of Mass," *Lost in Wonder: Essays on Liturgy and the Arts* (Surrey and Burlington: Ashgate Press, 2011), 41.

if I do not remember you." As pledge of their fidelity they offer their hand and their voice, those things that make one human. To forget Jerusalem would be to no longer be oneself.... Human faithfulness par excellence signals toward divine faithfulness. But it does not furnish the ultimate measure of divine faithfulness. Even if the improbable were to occur—if a mother were to forget her child—still, God would not forget it. And even if we forget Jerusalem, and our hand withers, the hands of God eternally bear the unforgettable. The following verse says: "Behold, I have graven you on the palm of my hands." Who could wipe away what God has graven on his hands? The hands of the glorious body of Christ bear forever their scars (stigmates) of the unforgettable, as an eternal memorial of time and history."[10]

Our task is to look at Jerusalem—and perhaps even the State of Israel—as it is, and to see curled tightly within it, God's own eternal vision for the world and the future.

CAN WE FIND A SHARED LANGUAGE?

This is one of the meta-questions that hovers over this topic, and is one that I've struggled with myself, both in the Jerusalem conference and this collection (Who should respond, and why? What are legitimate respondents?) and in this contribution of mine specifically. What is the role of a Jewish voice in this Catholic conversation?

I refused the obvious and easiest route, which would be to think Jewish Zionist thoughts and try to make them clearer or stronger for readers. I did spend a great deal of time worrying about what my role was in this volume. Can Catholics have this conversation without Jewish input? What is the role—and what are the limits—of that Jewish input? How can Jewish interlocutors be the most useful in providing a constructive voice in an internal Catholic conversation? As such, I would offer a few suggestions to Jews who are impatient to see developments in Catholic approaches to the State of Israel:

1. Recognize that the Catholic conversation is unique. It is entirely distinct from the Evangelical Christian conversation about Israel. It has its own possibilities and resources, challenges and limitations, that both inspire and restrict it by virtue of its specific Catholicness.

---

[10] Jean-Louis Chretien, *The Unforgettable and the Unhoped For* (New York: Fordham University Press, 2002), 97–98.

2. Be sensitive to how easily the broader Jewish-Evangelical Christian conversation about Israel and Zionism can play into an anti-Catholic agenda.

3. Jews and Christians read the Bible differently. Christians read the Hebrew Bible through the lens of the New Testament—what we can call a Christological reading—and Jews obviously do not. As Khader notes in this volume, "If we [Christians] read the Old Testament as if the New does not exist, the message and life of Jesus is meaningless in its relation to the plan of God." This means that the same scriptural texts can have quite different meanings and implications for Jews and Christians. We must take care that we do not to expect Christians to always understand the *Tanakh* in the same way as Jews do.

4. Jewish arguments in favor of Zionism are interesting and useful for Catholics to take note of. They cannot, however, replace Catholic arguments. They can only be data—relevant data, no doubt—that has a role to play in the Catholic process of theological reasoning. It is important for Catholics to be sensitive to and understand more about the importance and role of Israel for Jews. It does not imply that Catholics must share these. Refusing to "think Jewishly" does not make Catholics anti-Semitic.

5. We must remember that Jews do not have a monopoly on Israel. Recognizing that it is a Jewish State with a Jewish majority, we must still remember that our (Jewish) opinions about Israel are not worth more than others'. We Jews might have more to gain, or lose, in conversations about Israel than do other peoples. We might, if we are Israelis, have more invested as far as "skin in the game." Literally. But this does not mean that Jewish-Israeli opinions are to be privileged for Catholics. We have indeed privileged them in this volume with our choice of only Jewish-Israeli respondents. While that choice makes sense in terms of our decision to situate this conversation within the context of Jewish-Catholic dialogue, it is not the only context for discussion of a Catholic approach to Zionism. That the local church here is overwhelmingly Palestinian and the fact of minority Catholic populations in Arab countries throughout the Middle East must remind us that this is an issue with many stakeholders and sensitivities. Jews thus must remember that the Church has a responsibility both to its Jewish interlocutors and its own faithful in approaching this matter. The Jewish-Catholic aspect and the Church's extraordinary work to continue to progress in its relations with the Jewish people comprises one corner of this issue.

Equally, there are a few basic things that Catholics could do well to bear in mind as this conversation about the State of Israel develops between Jews and Catholics:

1. Jews understand ourselves as a vulnerable, at-risk people. It can be a challenge for the Christian to really comprehend and empathize with the deep, visceral sense of being threatened which pervades the Jewish community. This is part of the burden of our history, and it is the hermeneutical lens through which we read most issues. For the majority of Jews, Israel is not felt to be some optional part of Jewish identity or a political matter at all, but rather an essential component of Jewishness.

2. Jews are more interested in socio-historical issues than in theological matters. The State of Israel matters to us far more because of the former, than the latter. Don't expect Jews to talk about land promises or covenant or conditional or unconditional when we talk about Israel. Do expect us to talk about the Holocaust. About antisemitism. And about the existential threats we face.

3. You might disagree with the opinions of the Jews that you meet for various reasons. That's fine. But do remember that while being invested—even with your own life and those of your children—doesn't automatically make an opinion correct, it does demand a certain humility on the part of others in the face of those opinions. Because right or wrong in our (so diverse!) approaches and opinions, the outcomes matter to us more than they do to non-Jews, non-Israelis, and non-Palestinians. It's a lot easier to speak about "risks for peace" when you aren't the one taking the risks.

4. History, or more accurately, our understanding of history, has taught us to expect antisemitism from the Church. It will take much effort to convince Jews that anti-Zionism is not at some level antisemitism. It is useful for Catholics to know that to say "I am not a Zionist" is received by Jews like a slap in the face. It is taken to mean that you do not support the right of the Jewish State to exist. Perhaps that is indeed what you mean to say. Perhaps not. Because many Jews hear in statements like "I am not a Zionist" the message that our lives don't really matter all that much. Be thoughtful about language and how your intended meaning and received meaning may not match up. Be especially thoughtful about how that might sit within the context of historical Church teachings on the Jewish people and Jewish sensitivities around this.

SELECTED BIBLIOGRAPHY

Ateek, Naim Stifan. *A Palestinian Christian Cry for Reconciliation.* New York: Maryknoll, Orbis, 2008.

Ateek, Naim Stifan, Cedar Duaybis, and Maurine Tobin, eds. *Challenging Christian Zionism: Theology, Politics and the Israel-Palestine Conflict.* London: Melisende, 2005.

Bashir, Bashir and Amos Goldberg, eds. *The Holocaust and the Nakba: A New Grammar of Trauma and History.* New York: Columbia University Press, 2019.

Benedict XVI, Pope Emeritus. "Grace and Vocation without Remorse: Comments on the Treatise 'De Iudaeis.'" Translated by Nicholas J. Healy. *Communio : International Catholic Review* 45 (Spring 2018): 163–84.

Buber, Martin. *Israel und Palästina: Zur Geschichte einer Idee* [Israel and Palestine: The History of an Idea]. Edited by Ruth Langer and Jesper Svartvik. Zürich: Artemis, 1950.

Cunningham, Philip A., Ruth Langer, and Jesper Svartvik, eds. *Enabling Dialogue about the Land.* New York: Paulist Press, 2020.

D'Costa, Gavin. *Catholic Doctrines on the Jewish People after Vatican II.* Oxford: Oxford University Press, 2019.

Farkasfalvy, Denis. "The Pontifical Biblical Commission's Document on Jews and Christians and Their Scriptures: Attempt at an Evaluation." *Communio: International Catholic Review* 29 (Winter 2002): 715–37.

Fohrman, David. *The Exodus You Almost Passed Over.* New York: Aleph Beta Press, 2016.

Friedman, Elias. *Jewish Identity.* New York: Miriam Press, 1987.

Gregerman, Adam. "Is the Biblical Land Promise Irrevocable?: Post–*Nostra Aetate* Catholic Theologies of the Jewish Covenant and the Land of Israel." *Modern Theology* 34, no. 2 (2017): 137–58.

Hammer, Leonard. "Discerning Israel's Interpretation of the 1993 Holy See–Israel Fundamental Agreement." In *The Vatican-Israel Accords: Political, Legal, Theological Contexts*, edited by Marshall J. Breger, 67–96. Notre Dame, IN: University of Notre Dame Press, 2004.

———. "The Holy See–PLO Agreement and Its Significance for Israel." In *The Vatican-Israel Accords: Political, Legal, Theological Contexts*. Edited by Marshall J. Breger, 150–67. Notre Dame, IN: University of Notre Dame Press, 2004.

Heschel, Abraham Joshua. *Israel: An Echo of Eternity*. New York: Farrar, Straus and Giroux, 1969.

Inbari, Motti "Religious Zionism and the Temple Mount Dilemma—Key Trends," *Israel Studies* 12, no. 2 (2007): 29–47.

Irani, George Emile. *The Papacy and the Middle East: The Role of the Holy See in the Arab-Israeli Conflict, 1962–1984*. Notre Dame, IN: University of Notre Dame Press, 1986.

Isaac, Munther. *From Land to Lands, from Eden to the Renewed Earth: A Christ-Centered Biblical Theology of the Promised Land*. Milton Keynes, UK: Langham Monographs, 2016.

Katanacho, Yohanna. *The Land of Christ: A Palestinian Cry*. Bethlehem: Bethlehem Bible College, 2012.

Khoury, Rafiq. *Sudasiyyah li-Azmina Jadidah: Al-Rasa'il al-Ra'awiyyah al-Sit al-Ula li-Batarikat al-Sharq al-Kathuliki* [A Sextet for New Times: The First Six Pastoral Letters of the Catholic Patriarchs of the East]. Beirut: Matabi' al-Karim, 2008.

———. *Al-Lahut al-Mahali al-Falistini (1967–2019): Ru'iyah Shamilah* [Palestinian Local Theology (1967–2019): An Integral Vision]. Jerusalem: Liqa' Center, 2019.

Khoury, Rafiq and Rainer Zimmer-Winkel, eds. *Christian Theology in the Palestinian Context*. Berlin: AphorismaA, 2019.

Kinzer, Mark. *Jerusalem Crucified, Jerusalem Risen: The Resurrected Messiah, the Jewish People, and the Land of Promise*. Eugene, OR: Wipf and Stock, 2018.

Kopp, Matthias. *Franziskus im Heiligen Land: Päpste als Botschafter des Friedens: Paul VI.–Johannes Paul II.–Benedikt XVI.–Franziskus* [Francis in the Holy Land: Popes as Ambassadors of Peace: Paul VI.–John Paul II.–Benedict XVI.–Francis]. Kevelaer: Butzon und Bercker, 2014.

Kreutz, Andrej. *Vatican Policy on the Palestinian-Israeli Conflict: The Struggle for the Holy Land*. London: Greenwood, 1990.

Lapide, Pinchas E. *The Last Three Popes and the Jews*. London: Souvenir Press, 1967.

Lewis, Donald M. *The Origins of Christian Zionism: Lord Shaftesbury and Evangelical Support for a Jewish Homeland*. Cambridge: Cambridge University Press, 2010.

Lux, Richard C. *The Jewish People, the Holy Land, and the State of Israel: A Catholic View*. New York: Paulist Press, 2010.

Marchadour, Alain and David Neuhaus. *The Land, the Bible, and History*. New York: Fordham University Press, 2007.

Maritain, Jacques. "Le mystère d'Israël" [The Mystery of Israel]. In *Le mystère d'Israël et autres essais* [The Mystery of Israel and Other Essays], 19–62. Paris: Desclée de Brouwer, 1965.

———. *On the Church of Christ: The Person of the Church and Her Personnel*. London: Notre Dame University Press, 1973.

Masalha, Nur and Lisa Isherwood, eds. *Theologies of Liberation in Palestine-Israel: Indigenous, Contextual, and Postcolonial Perspectives*. Eugene, OR: Pickwick Publications, 2014.

Meyer, David and Philippe Bernard, eds. *Europe et Israël: deux destins inaccomplis : Regards croisés entre un diplomate et un rabbin* [Europe and Israel: Two Unfulfilled Destinies]. Paris: Lessius, 2017.

Meyer, David, and Michel Remaud, and Tareq Ou bro. *La Vocation de la Terre sainte: un juif, un chrétien, un musulman s'interrogent* [The Vocation of the Holy Land: Reflections by a Jew, a Christian, and a Muslim]. Bruxelles: Lessius, 2014.

Minerbi, Sergio I. *The Vatican and Zionism: Conflict in the Holy Land, 1895–1925*. Translated by Arnold Schwarz. New York: Oxford: Oxford University Press, 1990.

Neuhaus, David. *Writing from the Holy Land*. Jerusalem: Studium Theologicum Salesianum Publications, 2017.

Raheb, Mitri. *I Am a Palestinian Christian*. Minneapolis: Fortress, 1995.

Ratzinger, Joseph. "That Which Holds the World Together: The Pre-Political Moral Foundations of a Free State." In *The Dialectics of Secularization: On Reason and Religion*, edited by Jürgen Habermas and Joseph Ratzinger, translated by Brian McNeil, CRV, 52–80. San Francisco: Ignatius Press, 2005.

Raz-Krakotzkin, Amnon. "Exile, History, and the Nationalization of Jewish Memory: Some Reflections on the Zionist Notion of History and Return." *Journal of Levantine Studies* 3 (Winter 2013): 37–70.

Radford Reuther, Rosemary. *The Wrath of Jonah: The Crisis of Religious Nationalism in the Israeli-Palestinian Conflict*. San Francisco: Harper and Row, 1989.

Rutishauser, Christian M. "Versuche zu einer katholischen Theologie des Landes Israel" [An Attempt at a Catholic Theology of the Land of Israel]. *Theologische Quartalsschrift Tübingen* 201, no. 1 (2021): 72–89.

Sabbah, Michel. *Reading the Bible in the Land of the Bible Today*. Jerusalem: Latin Patriarchate Printing Press, 1993.

———. *Faithful Witness: On Reconciliation and Peace in the Holy Land*. New York: New City Press, 2009.

Selzer, Michael, ed. *Zionism Reconsidered: The Rejection of Jewish Normalcy*. New York: Macmillan Press, 1970.

Shapiro, Faydra. *Christian Zionism: Navigating the Jewish-Christian Border*. Eugene OR: Wipf and Stock, 2015.

Ska, Jean-Louis. "Israël et ses problèmes d'identité" [Israel and its Problems of Identity]. In *"Vous serez mon peuple et je serai votre Dieu" (Ez 36,28): réalisations et promesses* ["You will be my people and I will be your God" (Ez 36:28): Realizations and Promises], edited by F. Lestang, 21–51. Bruxelles: Lessius, 2016.

Trigano, Shmuel. *Un exil sans retour? Lettres à un Juif égaré* [An Exile without Return? Letters to a Lost Jew]. Paris: Stock, 1996.

Wolfson, Elliot. "Judaism and Incarnation: The Imaginal Body of God." In *Christianity in Jewish Terms*, edited by Tikva Frymer-Kensky, 239–253. Oxford: Westview, 2000.

Wyschogrod, Michael. *Abraham's Promise: Judaism and Jewish-Christian Relations*. Grand Rapids, MI: Eerdmans, 2004.

———. *The Body of Faith: God and the People of Israel*. 2nd ed. Lanham, MD: Rowman and Littlefield, 1996.

———. "A King in Israel." *First Things*, May 2010.

VATICAN II TEXTS

Vatican Council II. *Gaudium et Spes*. December 7, 1965.

———. *Lumen Gentium*. November 21, 1964.

———. *Nostra Aetate*. October 28, 1965.

OTHER VATICAN DOCUMENTS

Commission for Religious Relations with the Jews. *"The Gifts and the Calling of God are Irrevocable" (Rom 11:29): A Reflection on Theological Questions Pertaining to Catholic-Jewish Relations on the Occasion of the 50th Anniversary of "Nostra Aetate."* 2015.

———. *Guidelines and Suggestions for Implementing the Conciliar Declaration "Nostra Aetate" (n. 4)*. 1974.

———. *Notes on the Correct Way to Present the Jews and Judaism in Preaching and Catechesis in the Roman Catholic Church*. 1985.

———. "We Remember: A Reflection on the Shoah." 1998.

Pontifical Biblical Commission. *The Jewish People and Their Sacred Scriptures in the Christian Bible*. 2001.

CONTRIBUTOR BIOGRAPHIES

DIRK ANSORGE
Institution: **Philosophisch-Theologische Hochschule Sankt Georgen**

Since 2012, Dirk Ansorge has held the chair for dogmatic theology (with history of dogma and history of theology) at Sankt Georgen Graduate School of Philosophy and Theology, a Jesuit institution for higher education. He studied philosophy and Catholic theology in Bochum, Jerusalem, Strasbourg, Tuebingen, and Muenster. At present he is the head of Alois-Kardinal-Grillmeier Institute for History of Dogma, Ecumenism, and Interreligious Dialogue in Frankfurt. Moreover, he is a member of the advisory board of the Centre for Christian-Muslim Encounter and Documentation (Cibedo), the University Platform for Research on Islam in Europe and Lebanon (Pluriel), the advisory board of the Hamburg Institute for Theology and Peace (ITHF), and the task force for Christians in the Middle East established by the German Bishops' Conference. Dirk Ansorge has published a number of articles on Jewish-Christian-Muslim relations, the problem of conflicting truth claims in religion and society, the interrelation between religion and politics in the Middle East, and the contribution of religions to violence and conflict resolution.

KARMA BEN JOHANAN

Institution: **Humboldt University**

Karma Ben Johanan is a professor of Jewish-Christian relations at the Faculty of Theology at the Humboldt University of Berlin. An Israeli, she holds a PhD in historical studies from Tel Aviv University. She was a Fulbright postdoctoral scholar at the Department of History, the University of California, Berkeley; a fellow at the Polonsky Academy for Advanced Studies in the Humanities and Social Sciences at the Van Leer Jerusalem Institute; and a visiting lecturer at the Cardinal Bea Centre for Judaic Studies at the Pontifical Gregorian University in Rome. She is the author of *Jacob's Younger Brother: Christian-Jewish Relations after Vatican II*. Her scholarly interests are contemporary Jewish-Christian relations, political theology, and the history of modern religious thought.

ISAAC VIKRAM CHENCHIAH

Institution: **University of Bristol**

Isaac Chenchiah has an MA in systematic and philosophical theology from the University of Nottingham. His dissertation, "The Messiah, Torah and Israel," draws on Origen to outline one possible Christian response to Jacob Neusner's "A Rabbi Talks with Jesus" and also engages with Michael Wyschogrod's understanding of divine election. His other interests include patristic, scholastic, Byzantine, and modern Jewish theology.

GAVIN D'COSTA

Institution: **University of Bristol**

Gavin D'Costa is professor of Catholic theology at the University of Bristol. He was born in Kenya, and his parents are from India. He is the author of seven books, most recently *Vatican II: Catholic Doctrines on Jews and Muslims* (OUP, 2014) and *Catholic Doctrines on the Jewish People after Vatican II* (OUP, 2019). D'Costa has also published a book of poetry. His interests are in theology of religions, specifically the relation of Catholicism to Jews and Muslims. He is an advisor to the Vatican Pontifical Council for Interreligious Dialogue and the Roman Catholic Bishops in England and Wales on matters related to other religions.

LAWRENCE FEINGOLD

Institution: Kenrick Glennon Seminary, St. Louis

Dr. Lawrence Feingold converted to Catholicism in 1989 together with his wife. He is the author of *The Natural Desire to See God According to St. Thomas Aquinas and His Interpreters*, *The Mystery of Israel and the Church* (3 vols.), *Faith Comes from What Is Heard: An Introduction to Fundamental Theology*, and *The Eucharist: Mystery of Presence, Sacrifice, and Communion*.

FR. JEAN-MIGUEL GARRIGUES, OP

Institution: Institut Supérieur Saint Thomas d'Aquin, Toulouse

Fr. Garrigues was secretary of the drafting committee of the *Catechism of the Catholic Church*. He has participated as a speaker at the two symposia, one on anti-Judaism in the Christian world and the other on the Inquisition, convened by Pope John Paul II at the Vatican in 1997 and 1998 to prepare acts of repentance. He is currently a brother at the Saint-Thomas-d'Aquin convent in Toulouse, where he teaches theology at Studium, at the St. Thomas Aquinas Institute (ISTA). Recent publications include *The People of the First Covenant: Christian Approaches to the Mystery of Israel* (Deer, 2011) and *The Holy Spirit, Seal of the Trinity: The "Filioque" and Trinitarian Originality of the Spirit in His Person and His Mission* (Cerf, 2011).

FR. JAMAL KHADER

Institution: Latin Patriarchate of Jerusalem

Fr. Jamal Khader was born in the Christian Palestinian village of Zababdeh (Jenin). He earned a doctorate in dogmatic theology from the Pontifical Gregorian University in Rome, where he completed his thesis on the official dialogue between the Catholic Church and the Orthodox Church. He was a member of the Theological Reflection Committee of the Latin Patriarchate and of the Committee of Dialogue with Jews. Fr. Khader was the dean of the Faculty of Arts (2007–2013), professor of theology (2000–2014), and chair of the Department of Religious Studies (2003–2013) at Bethlehem University in Palestine, and the John A. Mackay Visiting Professor of World Christianity at Princeton Theological Seminary for Spring 2013. From 2013 to 2017, he served as rector of the Latin Patriarchate Seminary (Beit Jala) and then as parish priest of the Holy Family Church in Ramallah. He was appointed

Patriarchal Vicar for Jordan in 2021. Fr. Khader is one of the authors of "Kairos Palestine," a document written by Palestinian Christians as a "word to the world about what is happening in Palestine" (www.kairospalestine.ps).

SR. ELIANA KURYLO, CB

Institution: **Community of the Beatitudes**

Sr. Eliana Kurylo has been a member of the Community of the Beatitudes since 2002 and involved with Jewish-Christian dialogue for many years. She is a specialist in modern languages with a diploma in Biblical Hebrew. She is currently completing a graduate degree in theology at the Pontifical Faculty of Theology in Warsaw.

FR. ANTOINE LÉVY, OP

Institution: **University of Helsinki/University of Eastern Finland**

Fr. Antoine Lévy, OP, was born in Paris in 1962. He was raised in a non-religious Zionist home. He discovered Christian faith while studying philosophy at the Sorbonne and at the École Normale Supérieure (St. Cloud). After receiving baptism in the Catholic Church, he entered the Dominican Order in 1990. He completed a PhD in dogmatics at the University of Fribourg (Switzerland) in 2002. He was appointed director of the Helsinki Studium Catholicum in 2004. He became an adjunct professor at the University of Helsinki in 2009 and was appointed strategic professor at the University of Eastern Finland in 2013. Fr. Antoine is the author of a monograph on St. Maximus the Confessor and St. Thomas Aquinas, and has published journal articles in French, English, and Finnish on a variety of subjects, including patristics, medieval theology, Orthodox spirituality, Russian political philosophy, and Messianic Judaism. With Mark Kinzer, a distinguished Jewish Messianic theologian, he launched the Helsinki Consultation on Jewish Continuity in the Body of Messiah in 2009. He is also a member of the Roman Catholic–Messianic Jewish Dialogue Group.

FR. DAVID MARK NEUHAUS, SJ

Institution: **Pontifical Biblical Institute, Jerusalem**

Fr. David Mark Neuhaus teaches Scripture in Israel and Palestine, at Bethlehem University, the Latin Seminary in Beit Jala, and the Salesian Theological Institute in Jerusalem. He completed his PhD (political science) at Hebrew University, Jerusalem, and pontifical degrees in theology and Scripture in Paris (Centre Sevres) and Rome (Pontifical Biblical Institute). He has published extensively on interreligious dialogue, biblical theology, and the Church in Israel/Palestine.

H. B. PIERBATTISTA PIZZABALLA, OFM

Institution: **Latin Patriarchate of Jerusalem**

His Beatitude Archbishop Pierbattista Pizzaballa was appointed by His Holiness Pope Francis as apostolic administrator of the Latin Patriarchate of Jerusalem in 2016 and, in October 2020, Latin patriarch for the same diocese. Prior to this Fr. Pizzaballa was custos of the Holy Land for twelve years and Latin patriarchal vicar general for the pastoral care of Hebrew-speaking Catholics in Israel. He has been serving in the Holy Land since 1990.

DR. CHRISTIAN M. RUTISHAUSER, SJ

Institution: **Society of Jesus, Central European Province**

Dr. Christian M. Rutishauser is the former program director of the Lassalle-Haus Bad Schönbrunn, Centre for Spirituality, Interreligious Dialogue, and Social Responsibility in Switzerland. He has also been a lecturer for Jewish studies and Jewish-Christian relations at Philosophische Hochschule (Munich), Centre Cardinal Bea Gregoriana (Rome), and Deutsches Studienjahr Dormitio (Jerusalem), and is a current member of the Swiss and German Episcopal Conference Commissions for the Dialogue with Judaism. Additionally, he has been a permanent counselor of the Holy See for the religious relations with Judaism since 2014, and makes study trips to Israel/Palestine on a regular basis.

H. B. MICHEL SABBAH

Institution: **Latin Patriarchate of Jerusalem**

Born in Nazareth on March 19, 1933, Sabbah studied in the Latin Patriarchal Seminary in Beit-Jala. He was ordained a priest on June 29, 1955, after studying philosophy and theology. He completed a PhD in Arabic at the Sorbonne in Paris in 1973. He served in various positions in the Holy Land and abroad. From 1988 until 2008, he served as the patriarch of Jerusalem, the most senior Roman Catholic cleric in Jordan, Palestine, Israel, and Cyprus. He published a series of important pastoral letters. Having retired in 2008, Sabbah continues to be engaged in the life of the Church and society in the Holy Land and serves as president of the Commission for Justice and Peace of the Catholic Church in Jerusalem.

FAYDRA L. SHAPIRO

Institution: **Tel Hai College, Israel**

Dr. Faydra L. Shapiro is the founding director of the Israel Center for Jewish-Christian Relations, and holds a PhD in religious studies from McMaster University. She is also a member of the Center for the Study of Religion at Tel Hai College in Israel. Faydra began her career as a university professor in Canada in a department of religion and culture, where she worked for thirteen years. Her first book won a National Jewish Book Award in 2006. Faydra also writes regular academic articles and popular op-eds on Jewish-Christian relations, and is passionate about her mission of creating greater understanding between Jews and Christians. Her most recent book is *Christian Zionism: Navigating the Jewish-Christian Border*.

MATTHEW A. TAPIE

Institution: **Saint Leo University**

Dr. Tapie is an assistant professor of theology, and director of the Center for Catholic-Jewish Studies at Saint Leo University, Saint Leo, Florida. His teaching and research interests are in the thought of St. Thomas Aquinas, Judaism and Christian theology, and moral theology. From 2012 to 2014, Dr. Tapie was a visiting assistant professor of theology at the Catholic University of America, and was appointed a research fellow at CUA's Institute for Interreligious Study and Dialogue. Dr. Tapie is the author of *Aquinas on Israel and the Church: A Study of the Question of Supersessionism in the Theology of Thomas Aquinas* (Pickwick/Wipf and Stock, 2014), which was the focus of a special session at the fifty-first International Congress on Medieval Studies. He is also coeditor, with Daniel McClain, of *Reading Scripture as a Political Act: Essays on the Theopolitical Interpretation of the Bible* (Fortress Press, 2015). Dr. Tapie has published scholarly articles in the *European Journal for the Study of Thomas Aquinas*, *Studies in Christian-Jewish Relations*, the *Journal of Moral Theology*, and *The Bulletin of Medieval Canon Law*.

FR. ETIENNE VETÖ, CCN

Institution: **Pontifical Gregorian University**

Etienne Vetö is a Roman Catholic priest and a member of the Chemin Neuf Community. After teaching philosophy at the Centre Sèvres Jesuit university in Paris, he is now teaching theology at the Pontifical Gregorian University in Rome, specializing in the Trinity, theological anthropology, ecumenism, and theology of Jewish-Christian relations. Recent publications include *The Breath of God: An Essay on the Holy Spirit in the Trinity* (Cascade, 2019).

INDEX

A

Abraham: allegorical interpretation, 63, 67–68, 72–73, 112, 137; calling of, 163, 242; father of faith, 56, 61, 242, 249; God's fidelity to Abraham's descendants, 93, 145–46, 158–59, 162n48, 279; and God's promise of blessing for all families of the earth, 7–8, 18n46, 36; and God's promise of the land, 23–24, 29, 45, 52, 58, 105, 160, 200–1, 207, 216, 224, 240; and Jesus Christ, 89, 203, 236, 244; purchasing a portion of the promised land, 29, 57, 84, 283; sharing with Lot, 31, 34

Adversus Judaeos, xiii, xvi

Aliyah, 73n51, 86, 93–95

Am Yisrael. See *Eretz Yisrael*

Anti-Judaism, xiv–xv, 94, 172, 243, 299

Antisemitism, xiv–xv, 52, 55, 73n51, 140, 148n6, 172, 178, 182, 198n11, 230, 269n20, 291

Anti-Zionism, 139, 291. *See also* Zionism

Aquinas, Thomas, 4n5, 14n40, 16–17, 27, 102–9, 111, 116, 117n73, 118–20, 152n18

Arendt, Hannah, 143, 176–77

Augustine, 4n5, 8n19, 49–50, 111, 118, 138, 149, 262–63, 264, 271

B

Benedict XV, Pope, 127–28

Benedict XVI, Pope, xvi, 5n9, 19n49, 92, 82n2, 102n5, 127, 140–41, 195, 215n27, 254–55, 259, 275

Buber, Martin, 87, 176, 229, 230

C

Canaan, 28n13, 31, 53, 56, 70–71, 133n28, 135, 145, 181, 211, 212

Catechism of the Catholic Church, 5–6, 7, 9n23, 14n40, 16, 37n27, 49, 50n15, 52, 102, 126, 181

Catholic social teaching, xx, 19, 48, 82, 83, 98–99, 258, 280

Chauvet, Louis-Marie, xx, 148, 153–54, 156–57, 161, 164

Chrysostom, John, 58, 68, 106, 118

Commandments, 24, 25, 27, 48, 75, 84, 87, 96, 189, 205, 206, 208

Comprehensive Agreement between the State of Palestine and the Holy See, 124

Covenant, xi, 42, 173, 229, 287; with Abraham, 89, 146, 240; dual covenant theory, 4n3; fulfillment of Old in New, 102n5, 162n48, 255; God's fidelity to, 85, 93, 97, 141, 213, 275; irrevocability of covenant with Jewish people, xvi, 4–9, 37, 50n18, 82, 95, 100, 125–26, 144, 146, 253, 253–56, 259, 267; Israel's keeping of covenant as condition for promises, 8, 63, 112n52, 138, 213; and land, 8–9, 82, 111, 112n52, 131, 136; Mosaic, 4n4, 5; New (Christ's), 4, 43, 57, 82, 100, 113–14, 146; Old (first), x, 4, 50, 100; Rabbinic Judaism as inheritor of, xvi, 127; renewal after exile, 85; and state of Israel, 18, 19, 98, 133, 227; subordination to question of survival, 277, 291; and the Torah, 84; as "voluntary," 34n23. *See also* Gifts and Calling of God Are Irrevocable; Supersessionism

D

Deicide, xiii, xiv–xv, 126

Diaspora, 8, 9, 14n41, 18, 27–28, 44, 46, 53, 85, 86, 87, 89, 92, 95–96, 117, 121, 128, 133, 182, 276,

E

Eden, 60, 74

Election: of Abraham, 163, 249; of biblical Israel, 27, 89, 117, 159, 229, 244; Christians as elect, 120, 262–63; democratic, 221, 272; Jews as chosen people, 3–5, 6n10, 48, 119, 120, 158, 160, 229; Jews losing status as chosen, 4; link to Messiah, 7–8; purpose of, 59, 62, 158–61, 240, 247; state of Israel as sign of, 93, 162n48. *See also* Covenant; Supersessionism

Eretz Yisrael. Christian interpretation of, 18, 31, 58–59, 88, 91–92, 93, 95–100, 174; Jewish interpretation of, 86–87, 173, 183, 240; and nonviolence, 88, 259; relationship to *Am Yisrael*, 21–23, 26–30, 32–33, 35–41, 59–60, 74–77, 268, 285. *See also* Temple

Eschatology/eschatological: both present and future, 112, 116, 137, 211; Christian allegorical/typological/spiritual interpretation, 38, 112, 114, 115n68, 116, 119n81, 248, 261; and corporate salvation, 25–26; detheologization of Israel and politics, 132, 208, 258, 263–64, 266, 277; discourse of Jesus, 10, 14, 15n42, 43; divine intervention, 38; final judgment, 50; hope, 28, 40, 49, 56; Jewish believers in Jesus as sign, 18, 49, 95; peace with Egypt and Assyria, 189, 281; politics in relation to, 19; preaching to all nations as sign, 14; rabbinic, 119n81, 179, 267; realism, 52; rebuilding of Jerusalem Temple/heavenly Jerusalem, 51, 111, 245, 261; return to land of Israel as sign, xviii, 3n1, 4, 9–13, 20, 47, 49, 56, 85, 86, 136–37, 162n48, 266, 267; and sharing the land with Palestinians 32, 40; and Vladimir Solovyov, 52–53; and Zionism, 86

Eusebianism, 262, 266, 271

Eusebius, 151, 261

Evangelii Gaudium, 6

Exile: Babylonian, 27, 45, 84–86, 108, 135; and Benedict XVI, 216n27; Cain's, 61; Christian positive understanding of, 9, 264–65, 288–89; and Church Fathers, 262; connection to justice, 77; foretold by Jesus, 13, 43; of German Jews from Germany, 171; importance to Jewish identity, 10, 33n20, 263; of Jewish Arabs, 178; of Palestinians, 171, 181, 230; "partial voluntary exile of sovereignty," 34; as punishment, 12, 111, 136, 183, 263; return after two thousand years, x, 11, 48, 197–98, 214, 266; and Zionism, 173, 185

Exodus from Egypt, xix, 24, 58–59, 64, 65, 66, 69–73, 75–76, 83–84, 130, 150, 282–83, 287

F

Francis, Pope, 6, 98, 127, 129n21. *See also Evangelii Gaudium*

Fundamental Agreement between the Holy See and Israel, 124, 128, 131, 132–33, 145, 194

G

Gaudium et Spes, 30n16, 149n10, 246n18, 256, 263, 270

Gifts and Calling of God Are Irrevocable, xvn7, 5n8, 7n16, 7n17, 37n27, 82n2, 126, 127, 146n2, 165n58, 202, 213, 253

Gnosticism, 38, 51, 262n15

Grace and Vocation without Remorse, xvin8, 141n35, 254–55, 275

H

Halakha, 34, 98, 208–9, 261, 285–86

Herzl, Theodor, 46, 90, 139–40, 183, 185, 198n11, 212n24, 234

Heschel, Abraham Joshua, 8n18, 10n25, 11n30, 17n46, 19n49, 87, 110

Holocaust, 291; connection to Christian theology, xiv, 90, 129, 172, 226–27, 234, 265; European response to, xiv, xvii, 46, 175, 197, 214–15, 241–43; and God's plan, 87, 97, 100, 130, 265, 266; and the Jewish struggle for survival, 273, 291; relative to Palestinian experience, xvii, 180, 273; survivors of, 54n39, 55, 285. *See also* Nakba; Zionism

I

Idolatry, 26, 28n13, 39, 65, 136–37, 188, 224–25, 245

In Multiplicibus Curis, 90

Irenaeus of Lyon, 12n34, 50–51, 52, 66n22

Isaac, Jules, xiv–xv

Islam, 5, 28n13, 81, 82, 83, 157, 174, 178, 190, 238, 242, 254. *See also* Muslim/ Muslims

J

Jerusalem: city of God, 19, 26, 43, 74–75, 83, 109, 159, 207, 212, 288; conquering of, 76n61, 88; destruction of, 4n5, 9–10, 12n33, 13–14, 15n42, 43–45, 84, 85, 262, 263; heavenly, 9n33, 10, 51, 89, 90, 104, 107–8, 145, 239, 245, 288; as home of organizations and persons, 98, 173; host city of conference, xvii, xxi; international status proposed by Holy See, 90, 124, 184; Jewish return to, 45, 50, 55, 85, 87, 104n11, 139, 261; New, 25–26, 51, 103–4, 107–8, 114, 115, 116, 288; partition of, 199, 220; place in Jewish piety, ix, xi, 10–11, 27–28, 111, 129, 136; sharing with other peoples, 31, 34, 187, 200, 222, 242; significance for Christians, xi, xvi, 13, 16, 49–50, 77, 88–91, 103, 111, 220–21, 235, 244, 247, 263; "soil of Jerusalem" (Pope Pius X quote), 139, 183, 212n24. *See also* Temple

Jewish-Christian relationship, viii, 56, 90, 93, 101, 228, 255, 256, 259, 264, 265, 266, 267, 276

Jewish People and Their Sacred Scriptures in the Christian Bible, xix, 6n10, 92, 102, 103, 109–17, 130, 134, 137, 146n3, 200, 213, 254n3, 259n10

John XXIII, Pope, xiv, 172

John Paul II, Pope, xv, 5, 49n11, 56, 91, 101n1, 117, 118n74, 127, 128, 129n20, 132, 133, 142, 172, 174, 194, 197, 253, 254

K

Kairos Palestine, 94, 235n2, 236n4, 243, 244n14, 246, 247n20, 248, 249, 250n27

Kingdom of God, 25, 49, 94, 155, 162, 188, 189, 211, 239, 244, 247–48, 260, 261

Kinzer, Mark, 12n33, 15n42, 43n2

Knesset Yisrael, 282

Kook, Abraham Isaac, 26n7, 32, 38, 75, 86, 268

Kook, Zvi Yehuda, 32, 241

L

Law of Return, 93, 230

Liberation theology, Palestinian, 46, 82n5, 94, 150n13, 177, 273

Lumen Gentium, xv, 6n11, 7n16, 96, 100, 126, 153n21, 153n23

M

Maimonides, 28n13, 74–75, 77n67, 178, 260–61, 263

Maritain, Jacques, 53–54, 93, 265n19, 269n20, 275

Middle East Synod, 195, 198, 205

Millennialism, xviii, 10, 49–51, 104n11

Muslim/Muslims: Arab, 178, 219; claim to the land of Israel, xvii, 83, 91, 98, 174, 185, 186, 187, 190, 203, 225, 233, 249; *dhimmi* status of Jews in Muslim countries, 200; dialogue with Catholics, xvii, 83, 174–75, 280; equality of, 19n49, 28n13, 91, 170, 223, 231; Palestinian, viii, 87, 95, 170, 173, 190, 218, 219, 221, 230, 232, 269n21; seen as "powers of darkness," 242

N

Nakba, xvi, 180, 197, 237, 243, 249

Nationalism, 26, 28, 35, 94, 173, 177, 182

Nation-State Law, 185, 220

Nostra Aetate, xv, xix, 5, 82–83, 90, 93, 109, 110, 117, 126, 146, 170, 172, 174, 187, 200, 201, 227, 234, 253, 263, 270–71, 278, 279

Notes on the Correct way to Present the Jews and Judaism in the Preaching and Catechesis of the Catholic Church, 5n8, 7n15, 8n20, 12n35, 19, 91–92, 110, 117, 118, 128, 130, 132, 141, 201, 210–11

Novak, David, 138n32, 142, 143, 197n10, 209

O

Occupation, military, xvii, 173, 177, 181, 185, 190, 195, 220, 221, 224, 227, 229, 231, 237, 238, 241–43, 249, 273; entire state of Israel viewed as illegitimate, 198, 215n26

Occupied Territories. *See* Occupation, military

Origen, 50, 89, 103–5, 110n43, 111, 118

Oslo Accords, 199, 214

P

Paul VI, Pope, 180, 236n3

Palestine. *See* Exile; *Kairos Palestine*; Liberation theology, Palestinian; Muslim/Muslims; Occupation, military; Zionism

Pilgrimage, viii, x, 18, 19n49, 88, 89, 90, 96–97, 174, 235, 236, 245, 264, 276, 282

Pius X, Pope, 90, 139, 183, 212n24, 234

Pius XII, Pope, 90–91, 102n5

R

Rabbinic Judaism, xv, xvi, 127, 129, 179, 256, 260. *See also* Covenant

Reading the Bible Today in the Land of the Bible, 239, 240

Redemptionis Anno, 91, 174n3, 194

Rufeisen, Daniel, 93

S

Sacramentality, xx, 89, 96, 97, 147–65, 267, 287

Sacraments, xix, 63, 96, 98, 145, 148, 151–53, 155–57, 161–65

Schupp, Franz, xx, 148, 153, 154–55, 161–62, 164

Second Vatican Council, xiv, xv, 3, 5, 6n12, 22, 30, 56, 83, 90, 125, 126, 127, 133, 139, 146, 147n5, 149, 151, 153, 163, 169, 170, 171–72, 174, 182, 190, 227, 234, 239, 259, 265, 278. *See also Gaudium et Spes; Nostra Aetate*

Settlements, 138n32, 199, 206, 238, 241. *See also* Occupation, military

Shoah. *See* Holocaust; Zionism

Supersessionism, xviii, 3, 4, 6, 9, 27, 50, 119n81, 126, 139, 140–41, 147, 213, 254, 255, 268, 270, 271

T

Tanakh, 27, 37, 40, 60n5, 62, 65, 129, 211, 290

Temple: body of Jesus Christ as, 77, 108n31, 111, 114–16, 119n81, 261; destruction of Jerusalem Temple, xiii, 77, 130, 150, 263; God's dwelling place, 10, 13, 24, 28, 109; *hekdesh* objects, 34; Israel as temple-land, 58–60, 74–77; meaning of Jerusalem Temple, xvi; and medieval Christianity, 90; offerings/worship, 256, 287; profaning of Jerusalem Temple, 44; and prophets, 136; rebuilding of Jerusalem Temple, 50, 159, 261; Second, 18, 43, 46, 130, 134, 254n3. *See also Eretz Yisrael*

Theology of liberation. *See* Liberation theology, Palestinian

Typology, 3, 6n13, 7n15, 8–9, 59, 65–67, 68, 102n5, 112, 115n68, 137, 267. *See also* Eschatology/eschatological

U

United States Conference of Catholic Bishops *Statement on Catholic-Jewish Relations*, 130, 201n14

V

Vatican II. *See* Second Vatican Council

W

Wyschogrod, Michael, 10n26, 11n31, 13n38, 19n49, 27n11, 40, 58n1, 77n71, 74n55, 101, 143, 148, 154, 158–61, 163, 164, 259n10

Z

Zionism, 173, 175–82, 183–85, 265–66; Christian, 46–48, 54–55, 83, 94–95, 150n13, 181, 229–30, 241–42, 248n24, 258; and Christian evangelical/fundamentalist support of, 46, 94; Christian opposition to, 12, 139, 183–84, 212–13; cultural, 87, 176; dark side of, 173, 176, 229–31; dissent from, 179, 188, 243; and European colonialism, 94, 122, 176, 198n11; and European Protestant theology, 93; humanist, 176, 229; Messianic, 13, 160–61, 240n9; "minimalist," xix, 137, 143, 209, 231–32, 275, 280; and Palestinian displacement, xx, 33, 94, 176, 182, 190, 194, 223, 231, 243, 285; perspective of an ambivalent Zionist, 272–75, 289–91; political, 33, 55, 90, 127, 150n13, 183; religious, 76n63, 87, 151n13, 160, 209, 215, 240, 268, 271; *Shoah* as justification for, 46, 87, 97, 100, 129, 175, 197, 214–15, 243; socialist, 122; state of Israel as incomplete Promised Land, 32–33, 86–87, 138n32, 241; ultra-orthodox, 48, 150, 175, 177; and the United Nations, 204; and Vatican, 90–91, 123n3, 127–28, 139–41, 183, 201, 206–8, 210, 212, 215–16, 255; as violent nationalist ideology, 173, 175, 182–83, 185, 188, 229–31, 233, 242–43, 245, 257–58. *See also* Arendt, Hannah; Buber, Martin; Herzl, Theodor; Kook, Abraham Isaac; Maritain, Jacques; Wyschogrod, Michael

www.ingramcontent.com/pod-product-compliance
Lightning Source LLC
Chambersburg PA
CBHW020314010526
44107CB00054B/1841